# Myles Munroe Devotional & Journal

## 365 Days to Realize Your Potential

By Myles Munroe

Journal compiled by Jan Sherman

DESTINY IMAGE® PUBLISHERS, INC.
P.O. Box 310, Shippensburg, PA 17257-0310

*"Speaking to the Purposes of God for this Generation and for the Generations to Come."*

This book and all other Destiny Image, Revival Press, Mercy Place, Fresh Bread, Destiny Image Fiction, and Treasure House books are available at Christian bookstores and distributors worldwide.

For a U.S. bookstore nearest you, call 1-800-722-6774.
For more information on foreign distributors, call 717-532-3040.
Or reach us on the Internet: www.destinyimage.com

ISBN 13: 978-0-7684-2728-8
ISBN 10: 0-7684-2728-2
For Worldwide Distribution, Printed in the U.S.A.
1 2 3 4 5 6 7 8 9 10 11 / 09 08 07

## The Wealthiest Spot on Earth

*Now to Him who is able to do immeasurably more than all we ask or imagine, according to His power that is at work within us* (Ephesians 3:20 NIV).

BOOK QUOTE: *Understanding Your Potential* [Preface]

The wealthiest spot on this planet is not the oil fields of Kuwait, Iraq, or Saudi Arabia. Neither is it the gold and diamond mines of South Africa, the uranium mines of the Soviet Union, or the silver mines of Africa. Though it may surprise you, the richest deposits on our planet lie just a few blocks from your house. They rest in your local cemetery or graveyard. Buried beneath the soil within the walls of those sacred grounds are dreams that never came to pass, songs that were never sung, books that were never written, paintings that never filled a canvas, ideas that were never shared, visions that never became reality, inventions that were never designed, plans that never went beyond the drawing board of the mind, and purposes that were never fulfilled. Our graveyards are filled with potential that remained potential. *What a tragedy!*

Only a minute percentage of the five billion people on this planet will experience a significant portion of their true potential. Are you a candidate for contributing to the wealth of the cemetery? Ask yourself the following questions.

Who am I?
Why am I here?
How much potential do I have?
What am I capable of doing?
By what criteria should I measure my ability?
Who sets the standards?
By what process can I maximize my ability?
What are my limitations?

Within the answers to these questions lies the key to a fulfilled, effective life.

One of the greatest tragedies in life is to watch potential die untapped. Many potentially great men and women never realize their potential because they do not understand the nature and concept of the potential principle. As God has revealed to me the nature of potential, I have received a burden to teach others what I have learned.

> One of the greatest tragedies in life is to watch potential die untapped.

There's a wealth of potential in you. I know, because God has shown me the vast store He placed in me. My purpose is to help you understand that potential and get it out. You must decide if you are going to rob the world or bless it with the rich, valuable, potent, untapped resources locked away within you.

*You are more than what you have done.*

## Potential Defined

*Now it is God who has made us for this very purpose and has given us the Spirit as a deposit, guaranteeing what is to come* (2 Corinthians 5:5 NIV).

BOOK QUOTE: *Understanding Your Potential* [Chapter 1]

It is a tragedy to know that with over five billion people on this planet today, only a minute percentage will experience a significant fraction of their true potential. Perhaps you are a candidate for contributing to the wealth of the cemetery. Your potential was not given for you to deposit in the grave. You must understand the tremendous potential you possess and commit yourself to maximizing it in your short lifetime. What is potential, anyway?

*Potential is...dormant ability...reserved power...untapped strength...unused success...hidden talents...capped capability.*

*All you can be but have not yet become...all you can do but have not yet done...how far you can reach but have not yet reached...what you can accomplish but have not yet accomplished. Potential is unexposed ability and latent power.*

Potential is therefore not what you have done, but what you are yet able to do. In other words, what you have done is no longer your potential. What you have successfully accomplished is no longer potential. It is said that unless you do something beyond what you have done, you will never grow or experience your full potential. Potential demands that you never settle for what you have accomplished. One of the great enemies of your potential is success. In order to realize your full potential, you must never be satisfied with your last accomplishment. It is also important that you never let what you *cannot do* interfere with what you *can do*. The greatest tragedy in life is not death, but a life that never realized its full potential. You must decide today not to rob the world of the rich, valuable, potent, untapped resources locked away within you. *Potential never has a retirement plan.*

> The greatest tragedy in life is not death, but a life that never realized its full potential.

## The Potential Principle

*The field is the world, and the good seed stands for the sons of the Kingdom* (Matthew 13:38a).

BOOK QUOTE: *Understanding Your Potential* [Chapter 1]

To understand your potential, let us look at one of the most powerful elements in nature…the seed. If I held a seed in my hand and asked you, "What do I have in my hand?" what would you say? Perhaps you would answer what seems to be the obvious…a seed. However, if you understand the nature of a seed, your answer would be *fact* but not *truth*.

The truth is I hold a forest in my hand. Why? Because in every seed there is a tree, and in every tree there is fruit or flowers with seeds in them. And these seeds also have trees that have fruit that have seeds…that have trees that have fruit that have seeds, etc. In essence, *what you see is not all there is. That is potential. Not what is, but what could be.*

God created everything with potential, including you. He placed the seed of each thing within itself (see Genesis 1:12), and planted within each person or thing He created the ability to be much more than it is at any one moment. Thus, everything in life has potential.

Nothing in life is instant. People think miracles are instant, but they really are not. They are just a process that has been sped up. Nothing God created is instant, because God does not operate in the instant. He is a God of the potential principle. Everything begins as potential.

He did not create a ready-made human race—the earth was not given an instant population. God made one person—not a million people. He started with one seed. Then from that one He created another. Then He said to those seeds, "Bless you (that means, 'You have My permission'). Be fruitful and multiply and replenish the earth."

In Adam, God gave the earth a seed with the potential of one…one hundred…one thousand…one million…. The five billion people on the earth today were in that one man's loins. God knew that in Adam and Eve there were enough people to fill the earth. That's the way God works. He knows the potential principle because He introduced it. It is Him.

> God created everything with potential, including you.

## Don't Settle for What You Have

*So we fix our eyes not on what is seen, but on what is unseen. For what is seen is temporary, but what is unseen is eternal* (2 Corinthians 4:18 NIV).

BOOK QUOTE: *Understanding Your Potential* [Chapter 1]

Potential is always present, waiting to be exposed. It demands that you never settle for what you have accomplished. One of the greatest enemies of your potential is success. God wants you to maximize the potential He has given to you. You are not yet what you are supposed to be—though you may be pleased with what you now are. Don't accept your present state in life as final, because it is just that, a state. Don't be satisfied with your last accomplishment, because there are many accomplishments yet to be perfected. Since you are full of potential, you should not be the same person next year that you are this year.

Never accept success as a lifestyle—it is but a phase. Never accept an accomplishment as the end—it is but a mark in the process. Because you are God's offspring, there are many selves within you that lie dormant, untapped and unused. Your primary problem is that you do not think like God does.

There are many selves within you that lie dormant, untapped and unused.

God is always looking for what is not yet visible. He expects to find inside each person and thing He created more than is evident on the outside. On the other hand, man is often satisfied with what he has—or at least if not satisfied, he thinks there is nothing better. Thus he settles for what he has.

Therein lies the tragedy of life. The minute we begin to settle down and be satisfied with what we have, we lose the possibility of revealing what is really inside us. Too often we die without exploring the gifts, abilities, and successes that lay hidden within us. Our thoughts, ideas, and possibilities are not used. We fail to realize the vast potential that is stored within us. We are like batteries in a radio that is never played—our potential is wasted.

Since you are full of potential, you should not be the same person next year that you are this year.

## Don't Die With My Things

*Do not neglect your gift, which was given you through a prophetic message when the body of elders laid their hands on you* (1 Timothy 4:14).

BOOK QUOTE: *Understanding Your Potential* [Chapter 1]

Suppose...

Suppose Shakespeare had died before he wrote his poems and plays—the potential of *Macbeth* would have been buried. Suppose Michelangelo had died before he painted the Sistine Chapel or DaVinci the Mona Lisa—the beauty of their paintings would have been lost. Suppose Mozart had died with all that music in his bosom.

Suppose Moses had died before he saw the burning bush...Paul before he met Jesus on the Damascus Road...Abraham before Isaac was born. How different the pages of Scripture and history would be. Suppose Martin Luther had died without writing the thesis...Charles Wesley without penning the hymns...John Wycliffe without translating the Bible into English. How different the history of the Church might have been.

Can you imagine how many great works of art, music, and literature are buried in the graveyard near your house? Can you imagine how many solutions to the problems we face today are buried with someone you knew? People die without getting out their full potential. They fail to use all that was stored in them for the benefit of the world.

I wonder what would have happened if your father had died before you were conceived or your mother before you were born. What would the world have lost if you had not been born? What will the world lack because you fail to live out your potential? Will you carry songs, books, inventions, cures, or discoveries to your grave?

What would the world have lost if you had not been born?

Our teens are committing suicide. I wonder who they were supposed to be and what they were supposed to do that we will never know. Have we lost some great leaders? Was your grandchild's professor or another Martin Luther King among them?

> What will the world lack because you fail to live out your potential.

## Complete Your Race

*...and to know this love that surpasses knowledge—that you may be filled to the measure of all the fullness of God* (Ephesians 3:19).

BOOK QUOTE: *Understanding Your Potential* [Chapter 1]

As the time for His crucifixion drew near, Jesus spoke of the potential principle in terms of His life. He compared Himself to a kernel of wheat that falls into the ground and dies (see John 12:23-24). A kernel of wheat, when planted, yields many more kernels. Within Jesus was the potential to bring millions of people to God. Thank God Herod didn't succeed when he tried to wipe out Jesus. If he had, Jesus would have died before He could offer Himself as our atonement. His great purpose in life would have been wasted. The seed of His life was much more than His disciples could see. That one seed had the potential to give life to many.

There was a time early in his ministry when the apostle Paul said, "I'd like to leave." Though he preferred to die and be with Christ, he knew his purpose in life had not been completely fulfilled. There was yet much fruitful labor for him to do. It was necessary for the Church that he continue to live. Thank God Paul did not die. The benefit of his wisdom would have been lost to the early Church and to us. His potential to write Colossians and Ephesians may have been forfeited.

Later, near his death, Paul wrote: "Timothy, I've run the race. I've finished the course. I've kept the faith. I've done the work. My award awaits me. I'm ready to die. Keep working after I'm gone" (see 2 Timothy 4:5-7). Everything in life has the potential to fulfill its purpose. *People who die without achieving their full potential rob their generation of their latent ability.* Many have robbed me—they've also robbed you. *To die with ability is irresponsible.*

People who die without achieving their full potential rob their generation of their latent ability.

## What's in Your Package?

*We have different gifts, according to the grace given us* (Romans 12:6a).

BOOK QUOTE: *Understanding Your Potential* [Chapter 1]

Perhaps you are wasting your life doing nothing with all you have. God packaged some things in you for the good of the world—use them. We will never know the wealth God planted in you until you bring it up. There's always something in you that we haven't yet seen because that's the way God thinks. Release your ability before you die. Use the power and strength within you for the good of yourself and others. I believe there are books, songs, art works, businesses, poems, inventions, and investments in you that God intended for my children to enjoy. Don't give up until you have lived out the full extent of your potential, because *you have no right to die with my things*. Don't rob the next generation of the wealth, treasure, and tremendous gifts buried deep within you.

If you want to succeed, strike out on new paths. Don't travel the worn paths of accepted success.

No man can climb beyond the limitations of his own belief.

Every day sends to the grave obscure men and women whom fear prevented from realizing their true and full potential.

Failure is not the absence of success. Failure is the neglect of trying.

What you see is not all there is. There is something in everything.

What you have done is no longer your potential.

Potential is what you can do but have not yet done.

God packaged some things in you for the good of the world—use them.

## EVIEW the Principles From This Week:

- God created everything with potential.
- Nothing in life is instant.
- Everything in life has the potential to fulfill its purpose.
- Don't be satisfied with what you now are.
- Don't die without using your full potential.
- The greatest threat to progress is your last successful accomplishment.

## Junk or Jewel

*So God created man in his own image...God saw all that He had made, and it was very good* (Genesis 1:27a,31a).

BOOK QUOTE: *Understanding Your Potential* [Introduction]

The old sculptor made his way to his humble home outside the village center. On his way he passed by the great white mansion of the plantation owner who, with his field workers, was felling one of the age-old trees. The old sculptor suddenly stopped and called over the wall with a note of interest, "What will you do with those discarded stumps of wood?"

The owner replied, "These are good for nothing but firewood. I have no use for this junk."

The old sculptor begged for a piece of the "junk" wood and with care lifted the knotted tree trunk to his shoulders. With a smile of gratitude, he staggered into the distance carrying his burdensome treasure.

After entering his cottage, the old man placed the jagged piece of tree in the center of the floor. Then, in a seemingly mysterious and ceremonious manner, he walked around what the plantation owner had called "useless junk." As the old man picked up his hammer and chisel, a strange smile pierced his leathered face. Attacking the wood, he worked as though under a mandate to set something free from the gnarled, weathered trunk.

The following morning, the sun found the sculptor asleep on the floor of his cottage, clutching a beautifully sculptured bird. He had freed the bird from the bondage of the junk wood. Later he placed the bird on the railing of his front porch and forgot it.

Weeks later the plantation owner came by to visit. When he saw the bird, he asked to buy it—offering whatever price the sculptor might name. Satisfied that he had made an excellent bargain, the gentleman walked away, hugging the newly acquired treasure. The old sculptor, sitting on the steps of his simple cottage, counted his spoil and thought, "Junk is in the eyes of the beholder. Some look, but others see."

Today there are many individuals whose lives are like the old tree. Trapped within them is a beautiful bird of potential that may never fly. Society, like the plantation owner, sees nothing in them but a useless, worthless person on his way to the garbage heap of life. But we must remember that one man's junk is another man's jewel.

> . . . We must remember that one man's junk is another man's jewel.

# Everything Comes From God

*Through Him all things were made; without Him nothing was made that has been made* (John 1:3).

BOOK QUOTE: *Understanding Your Potential* [Chapter 2]

Everything in life was created with potential and possesses the potential principle. Creation abounds with potential because the Creator Himself is the potential principle.

When we describe God, we often say He is omnipotent. *Omnipotent* means that *God is always potent.* Made up of two words: *omni*, meaning "always," and *potent*, meaning "full of power," *omnipotent* means that God is potentially everything. He has within Him the potential for all that is, was, or ever will be. He is omni-potent or omnipotent.

*Everything that was, and everything that is, was in God.* That's a very important concept. Everything that was and is, was in God. We have to start with God. Before God made anything, before He created things, there was only God. So before anything was, God is. God is the root, or source, of all life.

Before anything was, God is.

Before there was time, time was—but it was in God. Before God created a galaxy or the Milky Way, they existed. Before there was a universe or a planetary system with the third planet called earth revolving around the sun—before any of that was—they were.

I wonder what it must have been like when God was just by Himself. Let's try to imagine that for a bit. Here's God. He steps out on nothing to view nothing, for there was nothing except God. And so God is standing on top of nothing, looking at nothing because everything was in Him.

The Bible tells us: "*In the beginning, God...*" That means before there was a beginning, there was God. Therefore, God began the beginning and verse 0 of the first chapter of Genesis might possibly read: In God was the beginning. Everything that is was in God. Everything that has ever been made was made by God.

When we connect Genesis 1:0—in God was the beginning—and John 1:1—in the beginning was the Word, and the Word was with God...He was with God in the beginning—we see that the Word was with God *in* the beginning, not *at* the beginning.

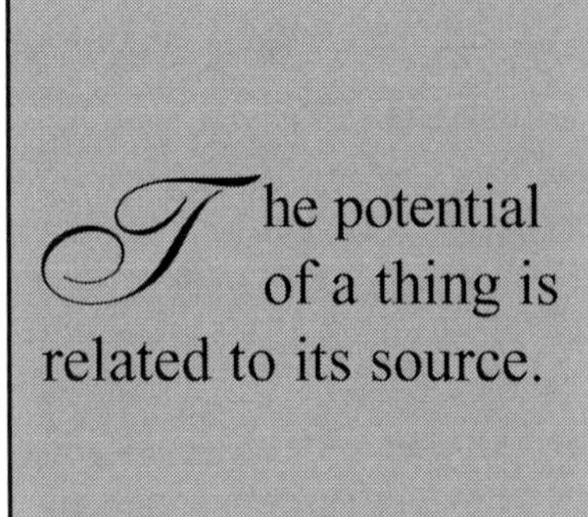

## In God Was the Beginning

*In the beginning was the Word, and the Word was with God, and the Word was God. He was with God in the beginning. Through Him all things were made; without Him nothing was made that has been made. In Him was life...*(John 1:1-4).

BOOK QUOTE: *Understanding Your Potential* [Chapter 2]

Before there was a beginning, there was God. Everything that is was in God.

The Gospel of John tells us that all things were made by the Word.

Nothing that was created was made without the Word. In *the Word* was life. *Life* came out of God. Therefore, before you knew life, life was. *All* things were made by God. Everything you see, hear, smell, taste, and touch was in God before they came to be. Even what you discern first existed in God.

Now let me be a little ridiculous to prove my point. God had roaches and mosquitoes and rats in Him. He had suns and clouds and planets in Him. The cows to make shoe leather...the oil to run our cars...the ore from the mountains to make steel—all these things were in God. Everything on this earth is God's property. If God would ever call in His property, we would be in big trouble. All things were in God and thus belong to Him. God, in the beginning when there was nothing, contained everything that man *has seen*. He also contained everything man *will ever see.*

Thus if you had talked to God on the highway of nothingness, you would have been talking to millions of cows and horses and mountains and trees and limousines and hotels and beaches. They all were in God. They were in Him, but no one saw them. That's why we call God omnipotent. He's always full of the potential to bring forth what you see. God is pregnant with the universe. In essence, if you met God on the highway of nothing, by the corner of nowhere, before there was anything, and you shook His hand, you would be shaking hands with *everything*, but would not know it. You would be with potential.

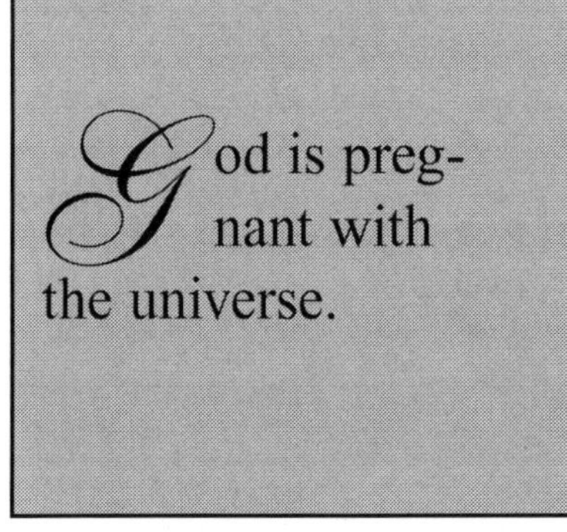

## The Invisible Became Visible

*By faith we understand that the universe was formed at God's command, so that what is seen was not made out of what was visible* (Hebrews 11:3).

BOOK QUOTE: *Understanding Your Potential* [Chapter 2]

In the beginning, God was pregnant with the universe and all things were made by Him. But how did these things come out of Him? How was the universe formed? All things were formed at God's command. He spat them out—poof! From the invisible came the visible. Things that are seen came from things that were unseen.

God always had everything in Him, but we couldn't see it. All we now see was once in an invisible state. Everything that man has ever seen first existed in an invisible state. (Please note that invisible does not mean nonexistent.)

All the buildings we see and the businesses we frequent—people making money and investing money—all that stuff began as ideas. We couldn't see them because they were in somebody's mind. The stores where we shop, also everything on the shelves and racks in those stores, began as ideas in someone's mind. They didn't exist before, yet they did. Although they weren't present in their current form, they existed as lumber and concrete and nails, cotton and wool and flax, steel and pulleys and motors.

Someone had an idea. Through work they put their idea into things that are visible. Today they take your money. Everything starts in the invisible state. Everything we now see used to be unseen.

In the beginning there was only God. At creation the entire unseen universe became visible. Everything that has been created was made by the word of God. Although it already existed, God spoke so that what was invisible could become visible. You would never have known it existed, except God spat it out in faith.

By faith God spat out what was in Him. Everything in Him started to come forth. What we now see was birthed by God from what was invisibly within Him. Whatever you see came from the unseen—nothing exists that was not at some time in God. Thus, *faith is not the evidence of things that do not exist. It is the evidence of things that are not yet seen.* Everything we see has always been. It became visible when God spoke it into being. God is the source of life.

> What we now see was birthed by God from what was invisibly within Him.

## *POKE* Was Hard Work

*My own hand laid the foundations of the earth, and My right hand spread out the heavens; when I summon them, they all stand up together* (Isaiah 48:13).

BOOK QUOTE: *Understanding Your Potential* [Chapter 2]

Everything we see has always been. It became visible when God spoke it into being. God is the source of life.

What happened when God spoke at creation? How did He get the invisible to become visible? First let me broaden your idea of the word spoke.

*Spoke* was a process. What God spoke into visibility began as an idea in His mind. God first conceived in His mind what He wanted to create. He didn't just say, "I want this." The prophet Isaiah tells us that God created the earth by first planning its foundations (See Isaiah 48:13). After the plans were in His mind, God spoke them into existence. When God was ready to speak, it was just a matter of taking what was in the plan and putting it on the site.

*Spoke* was a process.

God laid the groundwork for the earth and spread out the heavens. He created the sun to shine during the day and the moon and stars at night. He gave every star a name. He ordered clouds to fill the sky and breezes to blow. He made the waves to roar in the sea. He sent rain to water the earth and grass to cover the hillside. Thunder and lightning were created by His command; hail and sleet were formed by His word. A wool-like blanket of snow He produced for winter; frost and dew He designed.

After the plans were in His mind, God spoke them into existence.

## God's Imagination at Work

*By the seventh day God had finished the work He had been doing; so on the seventh day He rested from all His work. And God blessed the seventh day and made it holy, because on it He rested from all the work of creating that He had done* (Genesis 2:2-3).

BOOK QUOTE: *Understanding Your Potential* [Chapter 2]

God was full of imagination. He was pregnant with many thoughts. His thoughts became ideas, and the ideas became images. Everything that is came out of God as He *spoke* those images. The unseen became seen—the invisible became visible.

God's speaking was much like the contractions of a woman in labor. With effort He pushed out each detailed creation. Then God began organizing the things that appeared. He was busy as He set them up, organizing and organizing and reorganizing. Finally God said, "This is good."

God didn't create the world by just *thinking* the whole thing into being. He *worked* it into being. After creating a plan in His mind, God spoke to make visible the invisible. (Speaking was one of the ways He worked.) All that was made came from God. Through work He created the world.

For six days God created the heavens and the earth. On the seventh day He rested.

*Spoke* must be a fairly serious thing. If God, who is almighty and all powerful, had to rest after creation, *spoke it* must have been very hard work.

When creation was completed, God rested. God was the first one to *sabbat*—He intended the Sabbath to be a blessing. He knows that life produces work, and work creates the need to rest.

> All that was made came from God. Through work He created the world.

## The Work of Creation Is Not Yet Complete

*What has been will be again, what has been done will be done again; there is nothing new under the sun* (Ecclesiastes 1:9).

BOOK QUOTE: *Understanding Your Potential* [Chapter 2]

The work of God is not complete—He has not delivered all His babies. He will keep on delivering as long as you deliver, because you are the continuation of His deliveries. God can still create. When you ask for something in prayer, God doesn't have to shift things around because He is going broke. If it doesn't exist in a visible form, God will speak it. He'll make whatever is necessary. He continues to be pregnant with many things.

Because all things are in God, you can ask God for anything. An idea is around in God a long time before it comes out. Nothing we think or do is new (see Ecclesiastes 1:9). Everything that has been done will be done again—what we think is new has already been here for a long time.

There's a guy in China right now who is thinking about the idea you thought was yours. When the idea came out of God, many people got it. Because everything comes out of God, you all received the idea from the same Source. Until that idea is transformed by action, God will continue to leak that idea into men and women. Why? Because God is a God of potential. Although *He* is the source of all things, He shares His omnipotent powers with His creation. We, like God, are pregnant with many things. We are full of imagination, having the potential power to be more than we visibly are. There are dreams, visions, plans and ideas in us that need to be released. God wants us to tap His power and use it, because God made us with potential.

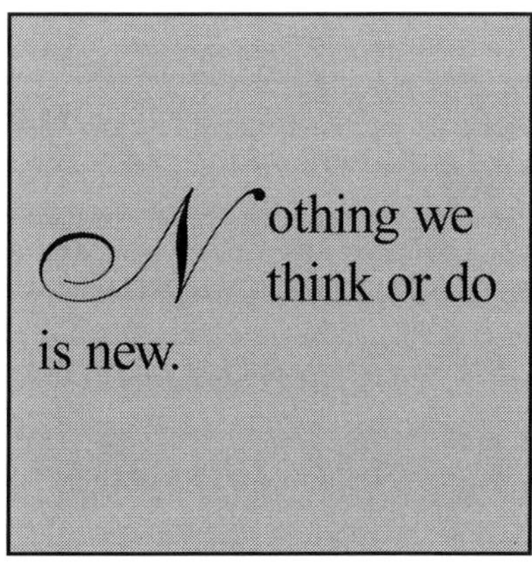

# EVIEW the Principles From This Week:

- Everything that was and is, was in God.
- God is the Source of all potential.
- All things were formed at God's command so the invisible became visible.
- God planned the world in His mind before speaking it into existence.

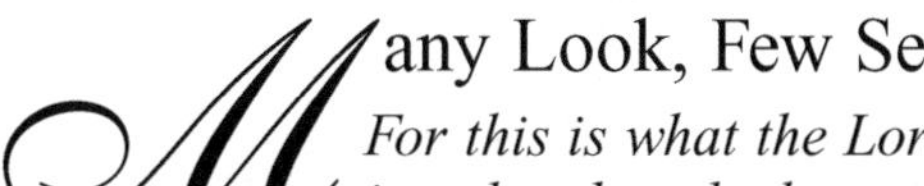

## Many Look, Few See

*For this is what the Lord says—He who created the heavens, He is God; He who fashioned and made the earth, He founded it; He did not create it to be empty, but formed it to be inhabited—He says: "I am the Lord, and there is no other"* (Isaiah 45:18).

BOOK QUOTE: *Understanding Your Potential* [Chapter 3]

A sculptor works in a very interesting way. I'm an artist of sorts, so I have a bit of an understanding how artists work. One thing I have learned is that you never argue with an artist until he is finished. Don't discuss anything with a painter or a sculptor until his work is completed. An artist can be very rude if you disturb him before he has accomplished what he intends to do, because he sees differently than those who are not artists.

An artist can walk by the stone in your front yard and see a figure in it. He may stop by your house and beg you for a stone you have walked past many times without noticing. The dogs may have been doing stuff on it. You may even have been planning to get rid of it because it's a nuisance. But the artist walks into your yard and sees something beautiful in that stone beyond what you can imagine.

Two months later when the artist invites you to his workshop he says, "Do you see that? Do you know where that came from?"

"England or France?" you ask.

"No," says the artist. "It came from your yard."

"Do you mean…?"

"Yes."

"Five hundred dollars, please."

You were sitting on $500. The dogs were doing stuff on $500. But you couldn't see the potential in the rock.

> Who you are is related to where you came from.

## ou Are Not Junk

*I praise You because I am fearfully and wonderfully made; Your works are wonderful, I know that full well* (Psalm 139:14).

BOOK QUOTE: *Understanding Your Potential* [Chapter 3]

There are many people who are being passed by because others don't see what is in them. But God has shown me what's in me, and I know it is in you too. My job is to stop you and say: "Can you see what's in you? Do you know your potential? Do you know that you are not just someone born in a ghetto over the hill? There's a wealth of potential in you."

A sculptor sees so differently. They say Michelangelo used to walk around a block of marble for days—just walking around it, talking to himself. First he would see things in the rock; then he would go and take them out.

Insight like that of a sculptor is seen in the Bible. When the world dumps and rejects you, and you land on the garbage heap of the world, God walks along and picks you up. He looks deep within you and sees a person of great worth.

Don't ever let anybody throw you away. You are not junk. When God looks at you, He sees things that everybody else ignores. You are worth so much that Jesus went to Calvary to salvage and reclaim you. The Spirit of God connected to your spirit is the only true judge of your worth. Don't accept the opinions of others because they do not see what God sees.

When God looks at you, He sees things that everybody else ignores.

## od Looked and Saw…

*All the days ordained for me were written in Your book before one of them came to be* (Psalm 139:16b).

BOOK QUOTE: *Understanding Your Potential* [Chapter 3]

God looked at Adam and saw a world. He looked at Abraham and saw nations. In Jacob, a deceiver, He saw a Messiah. In Moses the murderer, God saw a deliverer. Can you imagine looking at a stammering young man and seeing the greatest leader in history?

God saw a king in a shepherd boy. When the Israelites wanted a king, God sent Samuel to the home of Jesse. All the sons of Jesse twirled out before Samuel, from the greatest to the least. Finally, after Jesse had paraded all of his sons before him, Samuel said, "I'm sorry. None of these is God's choice for king. Do you have any other sons?"

Then Jesse said, "Yes…well no. I just remembered. I do have a little boy, my youngest son. He's just a little runt who's out taking care of the sheep.

"Bring him," Samuel replied. "Let me look at him."

So Jesse sent for his youngest son. When Samuel saw Jesse's youngest son walk into the house, a little boy, he began to unscrew the lid of his vase. "I think I have found the guy I'm looking for," Samuel said. (Notice that God chose the son who was out working. He was busy. God chooses busy people.)

Most of us are like Jesse. We look, but we don't see. Were you the black sheep in your family? (You know God likes sheep.) Has your family told you that you are a nobody? Have you been put off and put out and told so many times that you will amount to nothing that you have begun to believe it? Do you *feel* like the black sheep?

You are probably the one God is waiting for in the house. God sees things deep within you that others can't see. They look at you and see a nobody; God looks at you and sees a worthwhile somebody. You may spend your whole life competing with others—trying to prove that you are somebody—and still feel like nobody. Be free from that today! You do not have to live with that any longer. You don't have to *try* to be somebody, because you are somebody.

## he Source of Your Creation

*So God created man in His own image, in the image of God He created him; male and female He created them* (Genesis 1:27).

BOOK QUOTE: *Understanding Your Potential* [Chapter 3]

When God created the heavens and the earth, He first decided what He wanted to make something out of and then He spoke to that source. When God wanted plants He spoke to the dirt. When God wanted fish He spoke to the waters. When God wanted animals He spoke to the ground. *Whatever God spoke to became the source from which the created thing came.*

Plants thus came from the dirt, fish from the water and animals from the ground. Furthermore, plants return to the dirt, fish return to the sea and animals return to the ground when they die.

All things have the same components and essence as their source. What God created is, in essence, like the substance from which it came. That means plants are 100 percent dirt because they came from dirt. Animals are 100 percent dirt because they came from the ground. If we would take an animal apart, we would come up with genuine dirt. If we would put a plant under a microscope and decipher all the different components, we would find that everything in that plant is in dirt, because the plant is dirt. God called it from the dirt.

Whatever God spoke to became the source from which the created thing came.

## ou Came Out of God

*Then God said, "Let us make man in Our image, in Our likeness...*(Genesis 1:26a).

BOOK QUOTE: *Understanding Your Potential* [Chapter 3]

Not only are all things composed of that from which they came, they must also remain attached to that source in order to live. All things must be maintained and sustained by where they came from. The minute a plant decides it doesn't like the earth anymore, it dies. The minute the fish decide they are tired of water, they die. The minute animals decide, "We don't want to eat any more dirt," they begin to die.

Thus, whatever God created came from that to which He spoke. All things were created by God's word to a source. The source of the creation also becomes, then, the essence of that creation. All things are composed of whatever they came from and hence contain the potential of that source. That means plants only have the potential of the soil. Animals only have the potential of dirt.

All things are composed of whatever they came from and hence contain the potential of that source.

When God wanted fish, He spoke to the water. When He wanted animals, He spoke to the dirt. When God created human beings, He spoke to Himself.

> *Then God said, "Let Us make man in Our image, in Our likeness...." So God created man in His own image, in the image of God He created him; male and female He created them* (Genesis 1:26-27).

God created you by speaking to Himself. You came out of God and thus bear His image and likeness.

> You came out of God and thus bear His image and likeness.

## Look at the Inventor, Not the Invention

*For although they knew God, they neither glorified Him as God nor gave thanks to Him, but their thinking became futile and their foolish hearts were darkened* (Romans 1:21).

BOOK QUOTE: *Understanding Your Potential* [Chapter 3]

Never use the creation to find out who you are, because the purpose of something is only in the mind of the One who made it. That is one of the reasons why God has a tremendous problem with idol worship. How can you identify your ability by worshiping a snake? How can you find out your worth by believing that you will come back as a rat or a roach? How dare you believe that your purpose for existence can be discovered in a relationship with a wooden statue? You will never know yourself by relating to the creation, only to the Creator. *The key to understanding life is in the source of life, not in the life itself.*

Many of the inventions man has produced would be misunderstood if only the invention were considered and not the intention of the inventor. In other words, the man who created the refrigerator had in his mind what it was supposed to be used for. He did not intend that it should be used for a trap in the backyard for a kid to be locked in and die from suffocation. Even though thousands of children have died in refrigerators, that was not the inventor's intention.

The automobile is tearing out lampposts all over the world and destroying people's homes and lives. But Mr. Ford, who first developed the assembly line to mass produce the automobile, never thought about it that way. He was thinking about transporting people and helping the human race to become a mobile community. He started us to thinking about trolleys and trains and buses. The many people who died through accidents and derailments were not part of his intention. They were not in his mind when he designed his famous T. Ford automobile.

> You will never know yourself by relating to the creation, only to the Creator.

## ou Have Part of God

*And just as we have borne the likeness of the earthly man, so shall we bear the likeness of the Man from Heaven* (1 Corinthians 15:49).

BOOK QUOTE: *Understanding Your Potential* [Chapter 3]

You will never discover who you were meant to be if you use another person to find yourself. You will never know what you can do by using what I've done to measure your ability. You will never know why you exist if you use my existence to measure it. All you will see is what I've done or who I am. If you want to know who you are, look at God. The key to understanding life is in the source of life, not in the life itself. You are who you are because God took you out of Himself. If you want to know who you are, you must look at the Creator, not the creation.

There are three words we use to describe God. First, God is omniscient—which means He is all knowing. Second, God is omnipresent—which means God is present everywhere. Third, God is omnipotent—which means God is always potent. God is always full of power—He has in Him the potential for everything. From the beginning, God gave that same ability to be potent to all His creation. He planted within each person or thing He created—including you—the ability to be much more than it is at any one moment. Thus God created you to be omni-potent.

That is not to say we are equal to God. No. What I am saying is that the word *omnipotent* relates not only to God, but to us as well. We are always full of potential. Our potential is the dormant ability, reserved power, untapped strength and unused success God designed into each of us. What I see when I look at you is not all you are. It is only what you have become so far. Your potential is much greater than what you are right now. What you will become is much more than we could ever believe now. You are somebody because you came out of God, and He leaked some of Himself into you.

> You are who you are because God took you out of Himself.

## EVIEW the Principles From This Week:

- All things have the same components and essence as their source.
- When God created human beings, He spoke to Himself.
- You came out of God.
- You will never know yourself by relating to the creation, only to the Creator.

## od Pronounces What He Sees

*And I tell you that you are Peter, and on this rock I will build my Church, and the gates of Hades will not overcome it* (Matthew 16:18).

BOOK QUOTE: *Understanding Your Potential* [Chapter 3]

How you feel or what others say about you is not important. You are who God says you are; He sees in you more than you can possibly imagine. Your potential is limited only by God, not others.

Coward or Warrior?

God came to a frightened young man named Gideon. Gideon obviously thought God was talking to someone else when the angel of the Lord called him a mighty warrior (see Judges 6:12). The angel didn't say, "Oh, coward. Do you know you have strength?" Nor did the angel say, "Oh black man, do you know that you can be like the white man?" The angel just came in and announced what he saw: "Oh mighty man of war power." That means "Oh great warrior."

Think about it. Warrior? Gideon was hiding from the enemy trying to separate some wheat from the chaff so he wouldn't starve. He was doing it underground so no one could see him. When the angel said, "You are a brave man," Gideon started looking around to see whom the angel was talking to.

God never tells us what others see. He never calls us what others call us. Gideon thought he was a coward. God knew him to be a great warrior and pronounced what He saw.

Flaky, Flaky.

God also saw in Peter what others failed to see. His given name was Simon, which means *meek*. (Literally it means "unstable, flaky, leaf.") When Jesus met Simon, he was the flakiest, leafiest man you ever met. He was always going with the wind—changing his mind. But God saw a stone in the leaf. The first time Jesus met Peter, He changed Peter's name from Simon (leaf) to Peter (stone). Although Simon was an unstable guy, Jesus said, "I'm going to change your name. Your name is Peter." Peter acted like a leaf throughout Jesus' earthly ministry. Still Jesus called him *rock* every morning. Jesus saw in Peter something his mother had not seen. He kept chipping until finally, at Pentecost, Peter's true nature was revealed.

> You are who God says you are: He sees in you more than you can possibly imagine.

## Stop Believing What Others Say

*How can you believe if you accept praise from one another, yet make no effort to obtain the praise that comes from the only God?* (John 5:44).

BOOK QUOTE: *Understanding Your Potential* [Chapter 3]

Too often we believe the lies we are told. We believe that we are "no good" and worthless. Jesus says, "Not so. I came to show you that you are more than you think you are." You are the image of God.

God always *sees* what men and women only *look* at. In a manger, God saw a King…in a servant, a Savior…in a sacrifice, salvation… in a crucifixion, a resurrection. In death, God was working at life; in defeat, He was looking at victory. What you or I, or your country or my country, looks like is not what God sees. God looks beyond the surface to the potential deep within. That is God's way of thinking about everything. Beyond the immediate troubles God sees success, and He continues to call it forth until what He sees becomes reality.

Remember that the seed of every tree is in the fruit of the tree. That means the blessings of the Third World nations are in the Third World nations, and the prosperity of America is in America. When we become concerned about our individual lives or the corporate life of our countries, we come up with all kinds of schemes and plans to solve the problem. But the answer is not in a multitude of systems and programs. The answer is right inside of us. It's our attitudes that make the difference. No one can *make you* rowdy or careless or thoughtless. You *are* rowdy and careless and thoughtless because you *choose* to be. So stop it! Stop being rowdy…stop being careless…stop being thoughtless. Only you can control how you act. You've got the potential to be considerate and sensitive.

God looks beyond the surface to the potential deep within.

## hat Others Look At Is Not Important

*For I know the plans I have for you," declares the Lord, "plans to prosper you and not to harm you, plans to give you hope and a future"* (Jeremiah 29:11).

BOOK QUOTE: *Understanding Your Potential* [Chapter 3]

Too often we believe the lies we are told. We believe that we are "no good" and worthless. Jesus says, "Not so. I came to show you that you are more than you think you are." You are the image of God.

God saw in Peter something that Peter had never seen in himself. Peter was so busy agreeing with what others called him that he missed his true potential. When we start believing what others call us, we are in big trouble. Then we throw our hands up in despair and refuse to try. People call us lazy, so we become lazy. People call us careless or stupid or clumsy, so we become careless or stupid or clumsy. Watch it! What others look at is not important. Who we are depends on what we see.

Do you believe you could walk into a prison and meet some of the greatest men and women in the world? Can you think that way? They made a mistake. They made a misjudgment. They made poor decisions. But that doesn't invalidate their potential. It doesn't destroy who they can be. In that jail there may be a murderer on death row. But when God looks at that person, He doesn't see a murderer; He sees an author or a leader or a great world changer.

Many times God is in disagreement with the people closest to you. He may even be in disagreement with you, because the only person God agrees with is Himself—only He knows your true potential. Have you failed? Go to God. He'll call you "success" and keep calling you "success" until you feel it. That's what Jesus did for Peter.

> Go to God. He'll call you "success" and keep calling you "success" until you feel it.

## What Does God See in You?

*Since you are precious and honored in my sight, and because I love you, I will give men in exchange for you, and people in exchange for your life* (Isaiah 43:4).

BOOK QUOTE: *Understanding Your Potential* [Chapter 3]

I wonder what God sees as He walks around you. I'm sure He sees beautiful things in you, but you believe what other people are saying. People say: "You are no good. You'll never be somebody." But God is saying: "I see a jewel." We are diamonds in the rough. Just keep on believing that. Keep on moving forward to your goal. Remember that there is something in you more precious than what others have said about you. The sculptor never gives up until he gets out of the rock what he sees.

I have a piece of wooden sculpture in my home that I did about 15 years ago. The sculpture isn't what I intended it to be because as I was chiseling out the image that I had seen in the tree, part of it was knocked off by too much pressure. Because that part dropped off, I could no longer create the image that I had intended. So I looked at the piece of wood again. I walked around it thinking, "I've gotta change my concept a little." I had to rethink how to retain the beauty of the sculpture though I had lost an important part of the wood.

Eventually, I modified my design. The modification is not evident in the finished form. People have admired that piece of wood for many years. They look at it and say, "Wow! This is beautiful."

That piece of sculpture sitting in my home reminds me of your life and mine. Parts of our lives have been knocked off by our past. We've done some dumb things that have messed up the beauty God intended. But look what God has done. He's saved us. Instead of discarding us because we have not turned out like He intended us to be, He has taken us—including our marred and chipped and rusted and knocked off past—and formed us into something beautiful. When people see us now, they won't believe what we used to be. God can bring beauty out of your mistakes. He can take what you have messed up and bless it up. He can take the thing that seemed impossible to you and form it into something beautiful.

There is something in you more precious than what others have said about you.

## Christ Is In You

*To them God has chosen to make known among the Gentiles the glorious riches of this mystery, which is Christ in you, the hope of glory* (Colossians 1:27).

BOOK QUOTE: *Understanding Your Potential* [Chapter 3]

I wonder what God sees when He looks at you. I believe He sees Christ. When God looks at you, He does not see you. He sees Christ. Paul, when writing to the Colossian church, proclaimed that God had chosen to make known a mystery.

The mystery is *that Christ is in you*. That is your hope of glory. This suggests, then, that our task is not to get Christ *into* us, but *out* of us. Please get this into your minds. *What God sees when He looks at you is Christ.*

Most of us want to be like Jesus. That's not what God wants. God wants us to be like Christ. Jesus came to show us what Christ looks like when He takes on human form. But it is Christ that God's looking at. God sees Christ in you. That's the hope of glory—*Christ in you*. Let me explain.

Christ is the image of God. The word *image* does not mean "a statue of something." It means "the essence of the being." Christ is the image of God. That means when God created you, He created you in His image, and His image is Christ. That's why the Bible never calls us the Body of Jesus. Jesus was the human manifestation of the heavenly Christ. We humans on earth, with all our fallibilities and weaknesses—God pronounces on us: "You are the Body of Christ."

In other words, Christ is in us somewhere. Christ is in me. Christ is in you. God knows He is there. His image is there. So God called us Christ.

Our task is not to get Christ into us, but out of us.

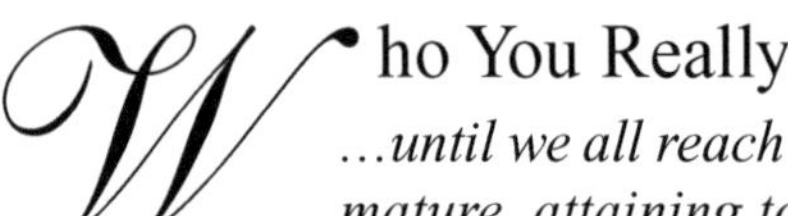

## Who You Really Are

*...until we all reach unity in the faith and in the knowledge of the Son of God and become mature, attaining to the whole measure of the fullness of Christ* (Ephesians 4:13).

BOOK QUOTE: *Understanding Your Potential* [Chapter 3]

We humans on earth, with all our fallibilities and weaknesses—God pronounces on us: "You are the Body of Christ."

In other words, Christ is in us somewhere. Christ is in me. Christ is in you. God knows He is there. His image is there. So God called us Christ.

If we go to God and say, "God, please introduce me to your people," God will say, "Sure. Here is Christ." But we'll say, "No. No. No. I want to meet Christ," to which God will reply, "Sure. Here's Christ" as He shows us the Church. When we want to meet Christ, God will show us the Church. But we can't accept this because we think Christ is in Heaven. No, He isn't. *Jesus* is in Heaven. *Christ* is sitting in your clothes, living in the body of the believer. Christ is the essence of God—He's God Himself.

God intended for you to be created in His image. Although you may say, "I want to be like Jesus," God says, "There's something deeper." You were lost and Jesus came to bring you back. God sent Jesus so you could see yourself.

God already knows who He is—He doesn't need your praise to make Him feel like God. God doesn't need you to tell Him how great He is—He knew it before you ever thought of praising Him. God wants you to know who you are—who you were supposed to look like. He's after the real person buried under the cap of your sin. Your IQ doesn't measure who you are, God does. Your true IQ is spelled *H-O-L-Y S-P-I-R-I-T*, because you have what God is. Christ is in you. That's who you are.

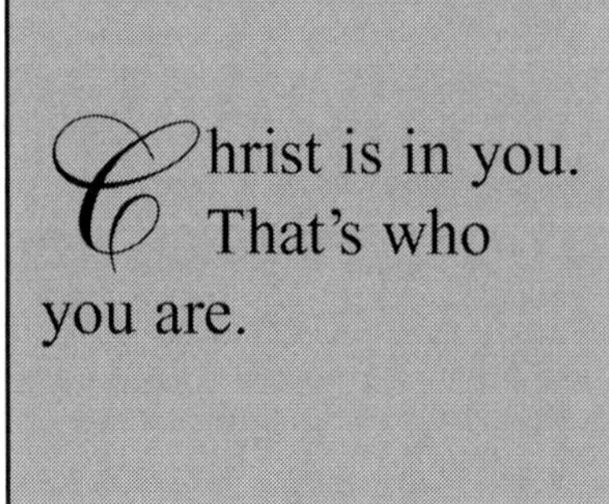

## on't Bury Your Talent

*But the man who had received the one talent went off, dug a hole in the ground and hid his master's money* (Matthew 25:18).

BOOK QUOTE: *Understanding Your Potential* [Introduction]

Scientists in the field of human potential have estimated that we use as little as ten percent of our abilities. Ninety percent of our capabilities lie dormant and wasted. It is sad that we use only a small part of our abilities and talents. Most of us have no idea how much talent and potential we possess.

Consider the life of Abraham Lincoln. His story is one of the most dramatic examples of a man struggling to release the wealth of potential locked up inside him:

He lost his job in 1832.
He was elected to the legislature in 1834.
He suffered the death of his sweetheart in 1834.
He suffered a nervous breakdown in 1836.
He was defeated for speaker of the State Legislature in 1838.
He was defeated for nomination for Congress in 1843.
He was elected to Congress in 1846.
He was rejected for the position of land officer in 1849.
He was defeated for the Senate in 1854.
He was defeated for the nomination for vice president of the United States in 1856.
He again was defeated for the Senate in 1858.
He was elected president of the United States in 1860.

*Everything in life was created with potential and possesses the potential principle.* In every seed there is a tree…in every bird a flock…in every fish a school…in every sheep a flock… in every cow a herd…in every boy a man…in every girl a woman…in every nation a generation. Tragedy strikes when a tree dies in a seed, a man in a boy, a woman in a girl, an idea in a mind. For untold millions, visions die unseen, songs die unsung, plans die unexecuted and futures die buried in the past. The problems of our world go unanswered because potential remains buried.

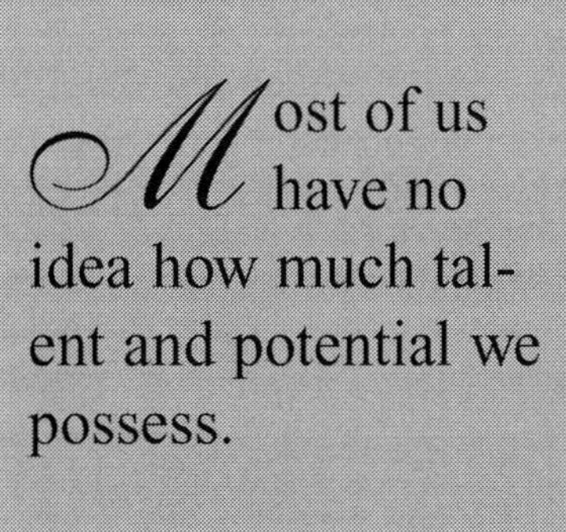

## EVIEW the Principles From This Week:

- Your potential is much greater than what you are right now.
- Your potential is limited only by God, not others.
- God sees Christ in you.

## No Limits

*...The reason the Son of God appeared was to destroy the devil's work* (1 John 3:8).

BOOK QUOTE: *Understanding Your Potential* [Chapter 4]

In the beginning, God created man by speaking to Himself. He took a little bit of Himself and put it into the first man so Adam would be like Him and could share in His life.

But the life God intended for His children was destroyed by their disobedience. Satan's deception and the sin of the man and the woman destroyed the relationship between God and the creatures He had taken out of Himself. The fellowship of like thoughts and purposes was broken, and man's relationship with God became distorted and skewed. Human beings lost their potential to be like the Creator—to know His thoughts and see through His eyes. Through sin, our access to God was cut off and the wealth of God's secret wisdom was buried. The deep things of God became more than we could know or comprehend.

Satan came into our lives to minimize, nullify, and destroy our potential. He has killed, stolen, and destroyed what God planted deep within each person. Through the years, the devil has succeeded in convincing men and women, each with a little part of God, that they are worthless, rotten, incapable people. But in the fullness of time Jesus came into the world to address this very problem.

Jesus came to wage "the battle of the caps"—*the battle of the destroyers.* There are two destroyers in the world. One is satan; the other is Jesus. Satan comes to destroy, and Jesus comes to destroy.

> When man puts a limit on what he can be, he has put a limit on what he will be.

## o You Want To Be Like God?

*For God knows that when you eat of it your eyes will be opened, and you will be like God, knowing good and evil* (Genesis 3:5).

BOOK QUOTE: *Understanding Your Potential* [Chapter 4]

> *Now the serpent was more crafty than any of the wild animals the Lord God had made. He said to the woman, "Did God really say, 'You must not eat from any tree in the garden'?" The woman said to the serpent, "We may eat fruit from the trees in the garden, but God did say, 'You must not eat fruit from the tree that is in the middle of the garden, and you must not touch it, or you will die.'"*
>
> *"You will not surely die," the serpent said to the woman. "For God knows that when you eat of it your eyes will be opened, and you will be like God, knowing good and evil." When the woman saw that the fruit of the tree was good for food and pleasing to the eye, and also desirable for gaining wisdom, she took some and ate it. She also gave some to her husband, who was with her, and he ate it. Then the eyes of both of them were opened, and they realized they were naked; so they sewed fig leaves together and made coverings for themselves* (Genesis 3:1-7).

Satan is God's enemy and ours. He is our adversary, out to blind us to the truth of God's love and the wisdom that offers us hope. Anything that is destructive—anything that steals something from you or destroys something that belongs to you—is from the enemy. He is a destruction mechanism that comes to destroy, kill and steal. But what is he destroying? First, satan destroyed man's potential to be like his Creator. Satan said to Adam, "Do you want to be like God? Pick that fruit." The man and woman already were like God; but by following the advice of satan they were destroyed. Their potential to be like God was clogged up right then when they failed—it was capped off.

> Satan destroyed man's potential to be like his Creator.

## God's Holding Back On You

*I know that everything God does will endure forever; nothing can be added to it and nothing taken from it. God does it so that men will revere Him* (Ecclesiastes 3:14).

BOOK QUOTE: *Understanding Your Potential* [Chapter 4]

> *"Father, I want those you have given Me to be with Me where I am, and to see My glory, the glory you have given Me because you loved Me before the creation of the world. Righteous Father, though the world does not know You, I know You, and they know that You have sent Me. I have made You known to them, and will continue to make You known in order that the love You have for Me may be in them and that I myself may be in them"* (John 17:24-26).

In the Garden of Eden, satan first deceived Eve by questioning whether God actually said that she could not eat from the forbidden tree. Next, the devil deceived her by telling her that she could be like God. Then, satan continued to work his art of deception when he said, "God is hiding something from you." He destroyed Adam and Eve's concept of God. To the man and the woman, God became someone who was holding back on them. Satan said, "God doesn't want you to know what He knows." What do you mean God didn't want Adam and Eve to know what He knew? Adam and Eve were *born* related in spirit with God. God *created* them to know Him. Thus, satan stole both man's potential to be like God and his understanding of God.

God created them [people] to know Him.

## ren't You Ugly!

*When he lies, he speaks his native language, for he is a liar and the father of lies* (John 8:44b).

BOOK QUOTE: *Understanding Your Potential* [Chapter 4]

The deceiver also distorted man's self-concept. He said to them: "Look at you. You are naked." So the man and woman felt bad about themselves and they put on clothes. They tried to cover up their bodies.

Ever since that day, we have become professional "*cover-ups*." We don't like ourselves. We don't like our physical bodies. Yuk! I don't like how skinny I am…how fat I am…how my hair grows…how my eyes are…how my lips are. I don't like my black, brown, red, yellow, or white skin. So we try to cover up what we don't like. It is strange how we work on things. If our hair is curly, we straighten it. If our skin is too pale, we get a tan. We don't like what we are. Nobody is satisfied with themselves. We all walk around saying, "Why do you want to be like me? I want to be like you."

This attitude is from the devil. We can't just be ourselves because satan has destroyed our appreciation of what God made. Our potential has been distorted so that we don't want to be black or tall or fat. We don't want to have curly hair or fat lips or small eyes. We have accepted satan's ploy to destroy our esteem for the beautiful creation God made us to be.

Satan, who comes to destroy everything God created, has destroyed our concepts of ourselves. Because we do not like ourselves, we do all kinds of dumb things. If you love yourself, you are not going to lower your standards. You will not sell yourself to anybody. You won't allow anybody to buy you—you are too expensive.

## Come On—Get Smart!

*Let us discern for ourselves what is right; let us learn together what is good* (Job 34:4).

BOOK QUOTE: *Understanding Your Potential* [Chapter 4]

Satan came to destroy our real intelligence. In the Garden, a strange word is used in the Hebrew to talk about knowing. The Bible says Adam and Eve *knew* that they were naked (see Genesis 3:7). *Knew* means they "became physically—or sensually—aware." Their senses suddenly took on leadership. Thus the soul became alive without the spirit directing it. Man began to live from the outside, instead of the inside. Adam and Eve became aware of their nakedness. They became aware of the leaves that could be used to cover themselves. They became conscious of shame and fear—the things that come from the outside, from the intellect.

Satan destroyed man's true intelligence, which is a spiritual relationship with God. When we are connected with God, our spirits can know anything. That's why the knowledge God communicates is not learned. It is discerned. The knowledge of God isn't found in any book; it's a deeper knowledge. Your real intelligence is not studied; it is discerned. Wow!

When man lost his relationship with God, he became a victim of education. He began to look to books and movies and the words of others—what he can see, hear, taste, feel, and touch—to gain knowledge. Those things became our sources of information. When satan destroyed our real intelligence, we looked outside ourselves to find knowledge.

> Your real intelligence is not studied, it is discerned.

## ou'll Never Be Anything

*Commit to the Lord whatever you do, and your plans will succeed* (Proverbs 16:3).

BOOK QUOTE: *Understanding Your Potential* [Chapter 4 and Introduction]

Everything in life was created with potential and possesses the potential principle. In every seed there is a tree…in every bird a flock…in every fish a school…in every sheep a flock…in every cow a herd…in every boy a man…in every girl a woman…in every nation a generation. Tragedy strikes when a tree dies in a seed, a man in a boy, a woman in a girl, an idea in a mind. For untold millions, visions die unseen, songs die unsung, plans die unexecuted and futures die buried in the past. The problems of our world go unanswered because potential remains buried.

By destroying our relationship with God, satan capped off our life potential. He continually destroys any possibility that we might become more than we already are: He puts teachers in our classrooms to call us stupid. He sends brothers and sisters to call us dumb and "no good." He gives us parents who tell us, "You'll never be anything."

Satan sets us up. He anoints your mother to call you a bastard. He sets her up to cap off what you are. Satan chops up your self-confidence and slams the door on your potential by convincing you that you are nothing: "You'll never rise above your family's status. You'll never go beyond where your neighborhood took you. You'll never be any more than your mom and your pa. You don't stand a chance." The devil has been teaching and preaching that to keep us down. He is very skilled at this deceptive art.

By destroying our relationship with God, satan capped off our life potential.

## What You Have Isn't Life

*...whoever drinks the water I give him will never thirst. Indeed, the water I give him will become in him a spring of water welling up to eternal life* (John 4:14).

BOOK QUOTE: *Understanding Your Potential* [Chapter 4]

But Jesus came to destroy satan's lies. He came to free us from those things that retard, distort, and short-circuit everything we are capable of being and doing. He said,

> *"I am come that they might have life, and might have it abundantly"* (John 10:10 KJV).

OK. That's fine. I have life now.

"But no, that's not enough. I came that you may have an abundance of life."

We think life is what we have now. No! In the Greek, the same word is used for abundance as is used for fountain. Jesus came to take the cap off your well…to unclog the true you…to open up the capacity of who you are and who you can be. We are going to have an oil spill. This thing is going to explode. Jesus didn't come just to take off your well cover. He came to start an explosion of water—a potential welling up and never stopping.

He said, "*Whoever believes in Me, as the Scripture has said, streams of living water will flow from within him*" (John 7:38).

> Jesus came to take the cap off your well…to unclog the true you.

## EVIEW the Principles From This Week:

- Satan destroyed man's potential to be like his Creator.
- Satan distorted man's self-concept—his esteem for the beautiful creation God made him to be.
- Satan destroyed man's true intelligence, which is a spiritual relationship with God.
- When satan crippled man's real intelligence, man looked outside himself to find knowledge.

## Fountains of Life

*I am come that they might have life, and might have it abundantly* (John 10:10 KJV).

BOOK QUOTE: *Understanding Your Potential* [Chapter 4]

Jesus came to start an explosion of water—a potential welling up and never stopping. He said,

> *"Whoever believes in Me, as the Scripture has said, streams of living water will flow from within him"* (John 7:38).
>
> *"...whoever drinks the water I give him will never thirst. Indeed, the water I give him will become in him a spring of water welling up to eternal life"* (John 4:14).

Jesus came so we can have fountains of life. Man, that's impressive to me!

That means until we get saved, we don't have any life. If you just became born again, you are finally getting back to your real self. All you have done for the last ten years that made you think you were somebody is but a trickle. You haven't changed the world, man. You haven't changed a man's life for eternity yet. You haven't touched a young boy for eternal life yet. You've put clothes on the boy's back, but you haven't put anything on his spirit. You haven't done anything yet! But there is a fountain, an abundance of life, welling up in you so you can do and be something. It begins when you return to your Source through Jesus Christ.

> There is an abundance of life, welling up in you so you can do and be something.

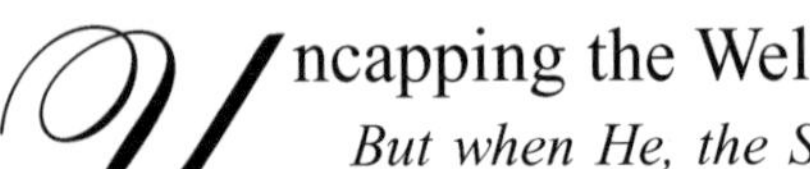

## Uncapping the Well

*But when He, the Spirit of truth, comes, He will guide you into all truth. He will not speak on His own; He will speak only what He hears, and He will tell you what is yet to come* (John 16:13).

BOOK QUOTE: *Understanding Your Potential* [Chapter 4]

Satan is the destroyer who comes to kill and steal and destroy. No one in the world stifles and clogs up and caps your potential like the devil does. He comes with a scheme to make you believe you can be nothing more than you have already seen. Jesus came to destroy this scheme. He came to unclog you and show you your true self. He's the best destroyer I know. I love this destroyer.

> *He who does what is sinful is of the devil, because the devil has been sinning from the beginning. The reason the Son of God appeared was to destroy the devil's work* (1 John 3:8).

First John 3:8 says that Jesus came into the world *to destroy* the works of the devil. The work of the devil is to kill and steal and destroy—he delights in capping off our potential. The work of Jesus is to tear off the cap—opening up what satan closed. Jesus came to do exactly the opposite of what satan has done. Jesus came, not to convince God of anything, but to convince us about who we really are. His job is to put us back in touch with what God put within us at birth.

Jesus came, not to convince God of anything, but to convince us about who we really are.

## Destruction Destroyed

[Christ] *who gave Himself for our sins to rescue us from the present evil age, according to the will of our God and Father* (Galatians 1:4).

BOOK QUOTE: *Understanding Your Potential* [Chapter 4]

Scientists in the field of human potential have estimated that we use as little as ten percent of our abilities. Ninety percent of our capacities lie dormant and wasted. It is sad that we use only a small part of our abilities and talents. Most of us have no idea how much talent and potential we possess.

The work of the devil is to kill and steal and destroy—he delights up capping off our potential. But 1 John 3:8b says,

> *The reason the Son of God appeared was to destroy the devil's work.*

What does it mean to destroy the works of the devil? How does Jesus do His job? Jesus reverses what satan has done. Whatever Jesus undoes, satan did. Whatever works Jesus does, satan undid it first.

For example, when Jesus took sickness from a person's body, He undid the works of the devil. Thus the work of the devil was to put the sickness into that body. When Jesus took away our sins, He destroyed the devil's work of convincing us to sin. If Jesus fed hungry people, then it must mean that satan brings poverty and hunger. If Jesus opened the eyes of the blind, then satan must close them. Jesus came to destroy the works of the devil. Whatever He did destroyed satan's previous works. Thus when Jesus says, "Everything is possible if you'll just believe" (see Mark 9:23), He is reversing the lies satan has fed us. Jesus came to destroy satan's destruction.

Jesus came to destroy satan's destruction.

## The Cap and the Crowbar

*Whoever believes in Me, as the Scripture has said, streams of living water will flow from within him* (John 7:38).

BOOK QUOTE: *Understanding Your Potential* [Chapter 4]

Satan tells you that you aren't going to amount to anything: "You aren't going to be anything...you can't do anything...you will always be what you now are." Jesus comes to undo that. He says, "You can be anything you think." Jesus rips the top right off your capped well. He says, "Go ahead, gush forth."

Thus, a tremendous struggle between two destroyers goes on within us—one destroyer uses a cap, the other a crowbar. Every time the one with the crowbar yanks the top off, the other guy runs around with the cap. The minute we give him a chance, he covers us up again. The struggle is continual. Each day we experience the tension.

Jesus says, "You are saved." Satan says, "You aren't saved." Jesus says, "You are healed." Satan says, "But you still feel the pain." Jesus says, "You are free from drugs." Satan says, "You are hooked for life."

Jesus came to reverse what the devil has done. The devil came to destroy our potential. He distorts, retards, short-circuits and caps off that which God has placed within us. He uses sin to clog up our potential capacity.

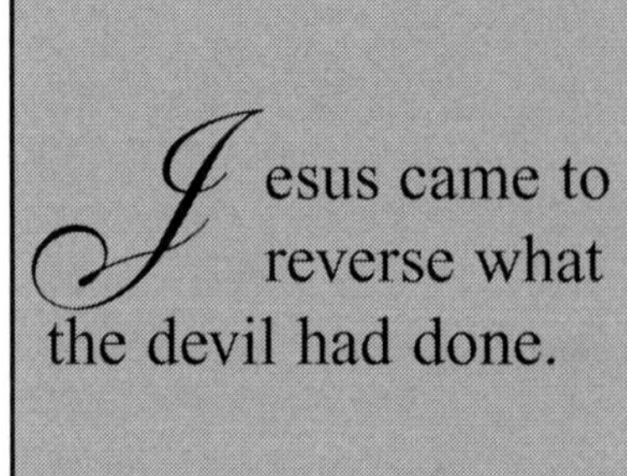

## All Clogged Up

*...made us alive with Christ even when we were dead in transgressions—it is by grace you have been saved* (Ephesians 2:5).

BOOK QUOTE: *Understanding Your Potential* [Chapter 4]

Are there things in your life that have been holding you back from the things you should be doing? Are you a potential leader in your community but you're full of alcohol and you're lying in the gutter? Has cocaine stolen your potential to be the top student in your class? Is your brain all messed up so you can't even think any more? Are you in danger of being kicked out of school though you were an A student before you took the stuff? Have you run off with a dumb guy and gotten pregnant? Do you have to drop out of school and give up your visions of becoming a doctor or a lawyer, a scientist or an agricultural expert? Has sin clogged up your potential?

Did you have a business that was going well, with limitless potential, until somebody said to you, "I want you to sell some drugs for me. You'll make a lot more than you do in this business"? So you became greedy. You went ahead and sold the drugs—only you were caught and now you have a record and your business is destroyed.

Sin clogs our potential. It messes up the plan God has for each of our lives.

Sin clogs our potential.

## The Clog In Our Potential

*For You know the grace of our Lord Jesus Christ, that though He was rich, yet for your sakes He became poor, so that you through His poverty might become rich* (2 Corinthians 8:9).

BOOK QUOTE: *Understanding Your Potential* [Chapter 4]

Sin clogs our potential. It messes up the plan God has for each of our lives. It takes away the "And they lived happily ever after" and replaces it with "And they struggled but didn't make it through the day."

Don't let that be the last chapter in the book God has written on you. God sent Jesus to die for you, not for Himself. Jesus knows *His* potential. He doesn't need to find out what it is. God doesn't have any problem with His potential. He is omnipotent. The problem is that *you* don't know *your* potential. You have been destroyed by the devil, and sin is stunting your growth.

Jesus came, not to die for Himself, but for you, so you could be reconnected with the Source of Life. For this reason Jesus came into the world—to destroy the works of the devil that are holding you down. Jesus came to uncap your well. He gave His life to restore your relationship with God—to give you abundant, flowing, gushing life.

Sin messes up the plan God has for each of our lives.

## Get Out the Clog

*His master replied, "Well done, good and faithful servant! You have been faithful with a few things; I will put you in charge of many things. Come and share your master's happiness!"* (Matthew 25:21).

BOOK QUOTE: *Understanding Your Potential* [Introduction]

The Bible tells a story about talents and potential. The talents in the story are symbols of the vast store of abilities our Creator has planted within us. In the story, the master of the estate entrusts some of his wealth to three of his servants. The first man invests his talent and doubles the wealth the master had entrusted to his care. The second servant also doubles what the master had given him. With them the master is very pleased. Finally the master turns to the third servant and asks, "What have you done with your talent?"

The servant answered, "I was afraid to misuse the talent, so I carefully hid it. Here it is. I am giving it back to you in the same condition that I received it."

In fury the master rebuked his servant, "You wicked and lazy servant. How dare you not use the gifts I gave to you?"

The master then said, "Take my money from him and throw this useless fellow into the street."

We are responsible for the potential stored within us. We must learn to understand it and effectively use it. Too often our successes prevent us from seeking that which yet lies within us. Success becomes our enemy as we settle for what we have. Refuse to be satisfied with your last accomplishment, because potential never has a retirement plan. Do not let what you *cannot* do interfere with what you *can* do. In essence, what you see is not all there is.

We are responsible for the potential stored within us.

## EVIEW the Principles From This Week:

- There is an abundance of life within us.
- Sin clogs our potential.
- Jesus came to bring us abundant, refreshing new life.
- We are responsible to the potential stored within us.

## he Potential to Understand

*Wisdom is supreme; therefore get wisdom...* (Proverbs 4:7).

BOOK QUOTE: *Understanding Your Potential* [Chapter 5]

Potential is dormant ability. (The word dormant literally means "that which is, but it is just lying there below its full strength, unused.") It is also reserved power, untapped strength, and unused success. Potential is everything that a thing is, that has not yet been seen or manifested. Everything in life begins as potential. All things have the potential to fulfill themselves, because God created everything with potential. There is no fulfillment in life without understanding the reason for being. If we want to know the real potential of something, we first have to know what that thing was created to do.

So if you have a seed in your hand, a kernel of corn or a pea, you will never get the seed's complete fulfillment until you know that there is a plant inside that seed. It is only as we look beyond the seed to the plant that we understand its true potential.

The same is true of our relationship with God. God created each man with a great wealth of potential. Too often, however, we look only at what we presently have. We look at our last dollar and say, "All I have is one dollar."

But God says, "No. That is not all you have. If you only knew the potential of that dollar."

And we reply, "But God you don't understand. There's a one next to that '$' thing."

Again God says, "No. If you could just take this dollar and put it into a certain condition, it would multiply."

Wisdom prtoects us from the dangers of knowledge.

## Our Main Goal

*Who endowed the heart with wisdom or gave understanding to the mind?* (Job 38:36).

BOOK QUOTE: *Understanding Your Potential* [Chapter 5]

The potential of everything is related to its purpose for being. Before we can understand the potential of a thing or person, we first must know the conditions under which it was meant to exist. Thus the most important thing for you and me, as human beings, is to try and find out for the rest of our lives what is the purpose for everything in life. That is our main goal. Unless we ask ourselves, "What is the purpose for everything in life?" we will die without having experienced the potential of everything. We will miss the wisdom of God in creation.

The apostle Paul, in the first chapter of First Corinthians, describes the wisdom of the world and the wisdom of God.

> *Where is the wise man? Where is the scholar? Where is the philosopher of this age? has not God made foolish the wisdom of the world? For since in the wisdom of God the world through its wisdom did not know Him, God was pleased through the foolishness of what was preached to save those who believe. Jews demand miraculous signs and Greeks look for wisdom, but we preach Christ crucified: a stumbling block to Jews and foolishness to Gentiles* (1 Corinthians 1:20-23).

When somebody tells you they are wise, don't get carried away. Although they may have wisdom, it might not be the right kind of wisdom.

> The most important thing is to try and find out what is the purpose for everything in life.

## The Wisdom of the World

*Your heart became proud on account of your beauty, and you corrupted your wisdom because of your splendor. So I threw you to the earth; I made a spectacle of you before kings* (Ezekiel 28:17).

BOOK QUOTE: *Understanding Your Potential* [Chapter 5]

Did you know that satan still has wisdom? Ezekiel 28:17 tells us that satan's wisdom became corrupted. God could not take back what He had given, so satan is still wise. But his wisdom is corrupt.

Before the fall, lucifer's responsibility in Heaven was to be the music and worship leader. He was designed with the potential not only to lead in music and worship, but also to produce it. Lucifer's body was made with pipes in it so that every time he lifted a wing, a sound came out—music. He never taught an orchestra because the orchestra arrived when he did. As soon as he started fanning his wings, the angels started singing. This guy was a beautiful angel. He had the potential to lead all Heaven, that other world out there, into worship and music. But that wisdom became corrupted. It was not taken from him, it just got corrupted. God is the Creator, but satan is the perverter. God creates everything; satan creates nothing. But everything God creates, satan perverts.

That's why music is such an important part of our world today. The guy who is running the spirit of the world is a cheap musician. The amounts of money the devil uses to support the music ministry of the world is amazing. Michael Jackson alone made $220 million in one year. Whitney Houston made $84 million—in just one year. And the Church can't raise even one million. Although that may sound strange, it is possible because the cheap musician who fell is the one who is backing the music industry. He is manipulating that stuff. He knows just what to do. But God still has the final word, and I like what He has done. God has put music into the Church and into us. He now calls for praise from man. But the point is, satan's potential is related to his purpose.

> God is the Creator, but satan is the perverter.

## What Is Wisdom?

*Hear this, you foolish and senseless people, who have eyes but do not see, who have ears but do not hear* (Jeremiah 5:21).

BOOK QUOTE: *Understanding Your Potential* [Chapter 5]

In First Corinthians, Paul scoffs: "Where are you, those who think you are wise? Is not your wisdom just so much foolishness?" Attacking the supposed wisdom of the world, the apostle declares that it is foolishness. God, in His wisdom, has made the wisdom of the world to be just so much folly (see 1 Corinthians 1:20).

God considers foolishness any wisdom that does not fulfill its original purpose. So if you are wise and you can really figure things out, but you use it to steal, God says, "You are foolish." If you are a very skillful musician, but you use it to create lewdness and sensuality, and to cause people to go into perversion, then God calls that foolishness. If you know that the power you have to believe was given to you by God, but you prefer to believe there is no God, God calls you a fool. For when you use the belief God has given to you to say you don't believe in Him, your wisdom becomes foolishness. The fool says in his heart, "There is no God." He takes the ability God gave him to believe and uses that belief power to not believe in God. God says, "That's foolishness!"

God considers foolishness any wisdom that does not fulfill its original purpose.

## The World's Wisdom Is Perverted

*For the wisdom of this world is foolishness in God's sight. As it is written: "He catches the wise in their craftiness"* (1 Corinthians 3:19).

BOOK QUOTE: *Understanding Your Potential* [Chapter 5]

Although God calls the wisdom of the world foolishness (see 1 Corinthians 1:20-22), it is still wisdom. It's a perverted wisdom used by the chief of perverters to blind us to its very foolishness. For who could believe God would use a crucifixion to bring salvation to the world. That is not the way we expect Him to work. We look for miraculous signs and unusual insights to indicate the presence and working of God. What wisdom would choose a poor carpenter to bring the greatest gift the world has ever known? Surely not the wisdom of the world, which looks to the wealthy and the well-educated.

But for those who believe in Jesus Christ, God's apparent foolishness is revealed as true wisdom. The wisest of human thoughts appear puny beside this foolishness of God, and the greatest of man's strengths pales beside Christ's weakness. What is a stumbling block or pure foolishness for those who don't believe in Christ, stands—for the Christian—as a towering source of truth, strength and hope. *That* is wisdom.

God considers foolishness any wisdom that does not fulfill its orignial purpose.

## our Secret Wisdom

*We do, however, speak a message of wisdom among the mature, but not the wisdom of this age or of the rulers of this age, who are coming to nothing. No, we speak of God's secret wisdom, a wisdom that has been hidden and that God destined for our glory before time began* (1 Corinthians 2:6-7).

BOOK QUOTE: *Understanding Your Potential* [Chapter 5]

God has given you a secret wisdom that He placed in you before you were born. He planted within you a potential something—a wisdom to know who you are and what you were created to be and do. That potential something was in God, but He allowed it to leak into you when He pulled you out of Himself. It's a hidden understanding that follows neither the wisdom of our society nor the insights of our leaders. Unlike the wisdom of the world, which is worthless, God's secret wisdom about you is a priceless jewel.

Many people die without unveiling their wealth of wisdom. They die in total foolishness, without experiencing the life that dwells within. What a pity! They have missed God's secret wisdom. (*Secret* here does not mean "to be withheld from." It rather has the meaning of "to have never known existed." There is a difference. God is not holding back from the world. He is not withholding from us our true potential. It's just that we have never known that it is within us.) They have missed the wisdom God designed before the beginning of time for the honor of man.

This wisdom is like a secret that was supposed to be known before we were created. It's a wisdom from God that He is keeping for us. It was in God and now it dwells in *us*. In other words, you were born with wisdom that literally came out of God. You have the ability to line up with God. You are in the God class.

> You have the ability to line up with God.

## Born With Wisdom

*"...No eye has seen, no ear has heard, no mind has conceived what God has prepared for those who love Him"—but God has revealed it to us by His Spirit* (1 Corinthians 2:9-10a).

BOOK QUOTE: *Understanding Your Potential* [Chapter 5]

You were born with wisdom that literally came out of God.

I know you may find that hard to accept—perhaps you think I am a mad man. But the truth is you'll be shocked when you understand who you really are. You don't know what you have inside that you are selling so cheaply. You have God's secret wisdom, a wisdom that you should be using to discover the earth.

None of the rulers of this world understand it, nor have they ever understood it. If only we could understand who we are (and I guess I include Christians, because we used to be there, and we need to find out where we used to be). We keep thinking that the life we left behind is better than the life toward which we are headed. We are constantly dipping into the ways and wisdom of the world to try and solve our present situations. But the world does not know the wisdom and potential God has already destined for us. They don't understand it, because if they had understood it they would not have crucified the Lord Jesus!

Your eyes can't see, your ears can't hear, neither can your mind imagine what God intends for His children. It's totally beyond what you can understand. If you could see through your eyes what you were created to be, you'd change your life. If you could hear through your ears or perceive through your mind—but the Scriptures say you can't. Your situation sounds hopeless: No eyes have seen it…no ears have heard it…no mind has conceived it. Your eyes and ears and mind cannot help you understand what God prepared for you before you were born. If they could, you'd shape up!

> You have God's secret wisdom, a wisdom that you should be using to discover the truth.

## EVIEW the Principles From This Week:

- The potential of everything is related to its purpose for being.
- The wisdom of the world is a foolish, corrupt wisdom.
- For those who believe, Jesus Christ is both the power and the wisdom of God.
- God has given you a wisdom that He placed in you before you were born.

## he Deep Things of God

*...but God has revealed it to us by His Spirit. The Spirit searches all things, even the deep things of God* (1 Corinthians 2:10).

BOOK QUOTE: *Understanding Your Potential* [Chapter 5]

> *No eye has seen, no ear has heard; no mind has conceived what God has prepared for those who love Him—**but** God has revealed it to us by His Spirit* (1 Corinthians 2:9-10).

But indicates a change. But inserts hope in the midst of hopelessness. Most people do not know what God intends for their lives. They have not seen their secret wisdom, nor have they heard about it. They have never even thought about the stuff because there are certain things we cannot understand unless the Holy Spirit reveals them to us. They are so deep within our potential that we need help to drag them out.

God had those deep things within Him before He made us; He put them into us at birth. But we don't know they exist because sin has clogged up the entry way. It is as if God struck a well and put wealth in it—a wealth of oil. Wealth is under there in your bosom. There is wealth in your personality—wealth in your being. But it has been clogged up and capped off by sin.

When you were born, the cap over your potential was firmly in place. Outside God's grace you will never know what is buried beneath that cap. Billions of dollars of wealth are buried within you, but you are not aware of it. You're walking along cool, but you don't know who you are. You don't understand that what you see is merely the shadow of your potential. That's why the Bible says, "nor has it entered the hearts of man the things God has under the cap for him." Oh, man!

## The Holy Spirit Connection

*But you will receive power when the Holy Spirit comes on you; and you will be My witnesses in Jerusalem, and in all Judea and Samaria, and to the ends of the earth* (Acts 1:8).

BOOK QUOTE: *Understanding Your Potential* [Chapter 5]

When you were born, the cap over your potential was firmly in place. Outside God's grace you will never know what is buried beneath that cap. Billions of dollars of wealth are buried within you, but you are not aware of it. You're walking along cool, but you don't know who you are. You don't understand that what you see is merely the shadow of your potential.

In His mercy, God has placed within each of us the answer to this dilemma. After the resurrection of Jesus Christ, God sent the gift of the Holy Spirit. That same Spirit, which we receive at our new birth, provides the connection between our spirits and God's secret wisdom.

Your capped potential is like a new battery. You came into the world full of the ability to run the whole thing. But you're just sitting there. Your stored power isn't being used. Like a battery that needs acidic water inside it before it can really fulfill its purpose, you need something to unleash the potential locked inside you. The Holy Spirit is the key that allows all the dormant power within you to come to life. Without the filling of the Holy Spirit, you can never function to your fullest potential.

> The Holy Spirit is the key that allows all the dormant power within you to come to life.

## The Holy Spirit Is the Key to Power

*For who among men knows the thoughts of a man except the man's spirit within him? In the same way no one knows the thoughts of God except the Spirit of God* (1 Corinthians 2:11).

BOOK QUOTE: *Understanding Your Potential* [Chapter 5]

The Holy Spirit is the key that allows all the dormant power within you to come to life.

Have you ever wondered why we have to be born of the Spirit? Why does the Holy Spirit come and connect with our spirits? Think for a moment about your spirit. The deepest knowledge about ourselves comes to us through our spirits—we can't know anything deeper than our spirits reveal. No one knows more about you than you know about yourself; for who can understand a man better than his own spirit (see 1 Corinthians 2:11)?

If you just got saved, your spirit doesn't know anything about you. Before your new birth in Christ, you were spiritually dead. Your spirit has been paralyzed for 15, 20, or 30 years (however long it took you to get saved). You have been dumb and ignorant about who you really are, because you can't truly know yourself until you become spiritually alive.

If you are not a Christian, you don't even know who you are. Only the spirit of a man knows the real thoughts of what a man is supposed to be, and we are born spiritually dead. We will never know who we are supposed to be until we accept Jesus as our Savior and receive God's gift of His Spirit.

If then, your spirit doesn't know any more about you than what it has learned since you got saved, look at how little it knows. Just look at you. Do you know where you would be if you had not been saved?

> We can't know anything deeper than our spirits reveal.

## he Knowledge to Bring Change

*But, "Let him who boasts boast in the Lord"* (2 Corinthians 10:17).

BOOK QUOTE: *Understanding Your Potential* [Chapter 5]

If your spirit doesn't know any more about you than what it has learned since you got saved, look at how little it knows. Just look at you. Do you know where you would be if you had not been saved?

Now don't get me wrong. You aren't perfect yet. Don't get carried away. You know there is still much that needs to be worked on—many things that need to be refined. But do you know what happens? The more we know about who we are, the more our attitude toward ourselves changes. Isn't that something? The minute we realize who we are we say, "Wait a minute now. I'm the King's kid," and we begin to put on kingly clothes. We think, "I'm a child of God now," so we start changing our language. We think, "Gosh, man. I'm a prosperous person," and we start expecting things to happen in our lives. As our knowledge about who we are grows, our lives change.

All this is possible because the Holy Spirit goes to the cap on the well of the wealth of our potential and pries it off. He comes into our lives and goes straight for the things that are clogging us up and dragging us down. Through the power of God, He pulls off that cap and starts to drill.

## Receive the Revelation

*The words of a man's mouth are deep waters, but the fountain of wisdom is a bubbling brook* (Proverbs 18:4).

BOOK QUOTE: *Understanding Your Potential* [Chapter 5]

The Holy Spirit comes into our lives and goes straight for the things that are clogging us up and dragging us down.

King Solomon described this process like a bucket drawing water out of a deep well. The Holy Spirit is the bucket that allows us to understand the wisdom and intentions of our hearts (see Proverbs 18:4). God has prepared so many deep things about who we are. Our eyes can't see them, nor can our minds conceive them, yet God is revealing them to us through His Spirit. God doesn't want us to wait until Heaven to know our full potential. He didn't give birth to us so we can develop our potential in Heaven. God wants us to realize here on this planet who we are. That is His purpose in creating us. Only the Holy Spirit searches "the deep things of God."

Some of you have received the revelation of what it cost God to love you. Others of you have not. Some of you are ready to walk into a deeper level of knowledge; others are not. God beckons you to take another step into a deeper, more relevant knowledge of your potential in Christ—though you may have been saved for years. You need to take this step because you still don't know who you are. Only the Holy Spirit can reveal this truth to you. Your eyes cannot perceive your true potential…your ears cannot hear it… neither can your mind perceive it unless the Holy Spirit gives it to the eyes and the ears and the mind. Until He does, you continue to walk around limiting your potential.

The Spirit searches all things. It's His job to search out the deep things of God and interpret them so we can understand them. How can we possibly understand God's deep things—the great mysteries He has to share with us? Can we imagine that the source of the deep things of God might be connected to us? Can we go inside God to those things that are deep within Him?

Yes, we can! God has given us His Spirit so we can understand all the things He oozed into us.

> The Holy Spirit comes into our lives and goes straight for the things that are cloggin us up, and dragging us down.

## Look What You've Got!

*We have not received the spirit of the world but the Spirit who is from God, that we may understand what God has freely given us* (1 Corinthians 2:12).

BOOK QUOTE: *Understanding Your Potential* [Chapter 5]

It's mind blowing to think that God has given us His Spirit so we can understand all the things He oozed into us!

There are things about you, concerning who you can be, that you haven't discovered yet—holy things that only the Holy Ghost can explain. God reveals His deep things to you through the Holy Spirit because He knows you would not believe them if they were simply told to you through your mind. Your mind cannot possibly comprehend all that God has prepared for you to be.

Forget what others have told you about who you can be. That's a joke. Don't even consider it. That is not all you can be, because the deepest things you can know about yourself are not in your mind or your emotions or even in your body. They are in your spirit. The deepest things you can know about yourself are what you get from your spirit.

That's why God gives you the Holy Spirit. The Spirit goes deep inside you to capture the wealth of your potential. He pulls deep from within you the answers to your spirit's cries, showing you who you are and why He created you. You will never be fulfilled until you understand why God made you.

Many people get bored coming to church. They get tired of singing and tired of praying. Why? Because there's more than coming to church…there's more than singing…there's more than praying. When you hunger for the deep things of God, a hunger that God Himself puts within you, you will not be satisfied until the Holy Spirit reveals God's secret wisdom to you. Your spirit yearns for the deep things of God that He has within Him about you. There is a deep in you crying out to the deep things in God. You will never be satisfied, even after you are saved, because there is something inside you that continually calls out for more. And the thing you are calling for is locked up in God—the wisdom of God concerning you. You will never be fulfilled until you get filled with what God has that is supposed to be in you. That's why you have to come to God. You'll never be fulfilled without God, because you are looking for what God has.

> You will never be fulfilled until you get filled with what God has that is supposed to be in you.

## od's Got It All

*Those who live according to the sinful nature have their minds set on what that nature desires; but those who live in accordance with the Spirit have their minds set on what the Spirit desires* (Romans 8:5).

BOOK QUOTE: *Understanding Your Potential* [Chapter 5]

You'll never be fulfilled without God, because you are looking for what God has.

For this reason, God gives you the Holy Spirit. The only way to get out of God and into you the deep things God knows about you is through His Spirit communing with yours. The Holy Spirit searches the deep things of God—the deep things about you that you lack. God prepared and predestined those things for you before you were created. He had them in Himself and gave them to you at birth. But you don't know those things exist, because sin has capped the well and blocked the way. Only God, through the Holy Spirit, can reveal them again.

Your potential is buried in God. We think going to the moon is great—we should see what God had planned that we didn't follow. Our eyes will never see the stuff God prepared for us, nor will our ears hear it. Only the Holy Spirit can reveal to us the deep things of God that tell us who we are.

Through the gift of the Holy Spirit, you can reestablish your relationship with God. The Holy Spirit, connected with your spirit, unravels the knots that have bound your thoughts, removes the streaks that have blurred your vision and clears the debris that has hidden your potential. Working like a sculptor, He brings out the beauty hidden deep within your being, because that is the real you.

Allow God to reveal His secret wisdom concerning you. See with your eyes and hear with your ears things you have never seen or heard before. Conceive with your mind thoughts that never before have occurred to you. Cooperate with the Holy Spirit as He sucks out of God and into you the depths of the riches that God prepared for you. Live the rest of your life building an atmosphere where it is possible for the Holy Spirit to use you as He takes His bucket of hope, dips it deep into the wells of your potential and pulls it to the top of your senses. Drink deeply, growing in the knowledge of who you really are in God. That's my dream.

> You'll never be fulfilled without God, because you are looking for what God has.

## EVIEW the Principles From This Week:

- You are in God's class.
- You will never know who you are supposed to be until you accept Jesus as your Savior and receive the gift of God's Spirit.
- The Spirit helps us find understanding and wisdom.

## od Planned Your Life

*the Lord God formed the man from the dust of the ground and breathed into his nostrils the breath of life, and the man became a living being* (Genesis 2:7).

BOOK QUOTE: *Understanding Your Potential* [Chapter 6]

If you feel good about yourself, you will feel good about other people. In other words, only after you see yourself as a worthwhile person can you appreciate others as worthwhile people.

Many people do not feel good about themselves. They look at themselves and wonder why God made them; or they doubt that anyone can find any good in them. But remember, God sees what others, and we ourselves, can't see. God looks at us and sees that we are worth feeling good about. We are special to God. We are valuable and important.

God has a good attitude toward you. He created you in His image and drew you out of Himself. Before you were born, you were in God. Part of His potential has been placed within you.

There could not be a beginning without God, because God got start started. Before start started, however, God had a finished plan for your life. Your potential is not a trial and error experience. God designed and predetermined you to be a success story.

Psalm 139 tells us that God planned each of your days before you were even born. Before you were formed, God knew you. He took great care in creating you. No part of your being was made without God's knowledge and careful concern. God wants each of us. He gives us what no other part of His creation received: His breath of life (see Genesis 2:7).

Have you ever felt like you were a mistake? Have your parents told you they wished you had never been born? Are you a child whose parents have told you: "I wish you would have died when you were a baby"?

You may be a bastard, conceived out of wedlock. Being omnipotent, God had the power to prevent your conception. Yet God allowed it because He wanted you to show up. You are here because God wanted you to be born. How you came isn't important. What matters is that you are here. And if you are here, God created you with care (see Psalm 139:13).

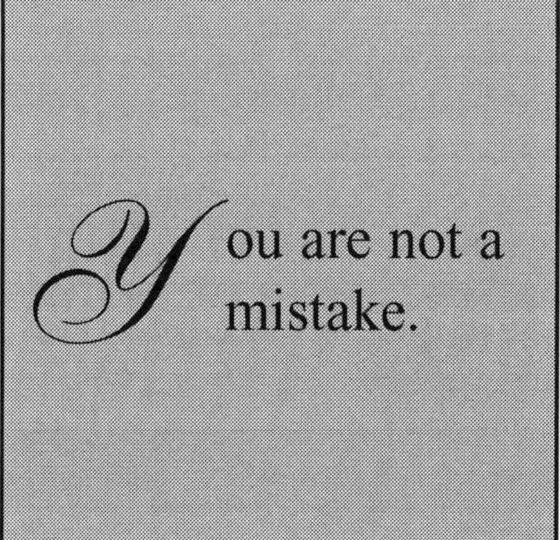

## od Designed You To Be a Success Story

*My frame was not hidden from You when I was made in the secret place...* (Psalm 139:15).

BOOK QUOTE: *Understanding Your Potential* [Chapter 6]

King David doesn't describe your mother in Psalm 139—she may have been an old alcoholic or a drug addict, a bastard or a prostitute. He is concerned with *you*. He describes how God knit you together in your mother's womb without describing what that womb was like. The womb in which you were knit together is no longer important. *You* are important. Your very existence means God wants you to exist. You are somebody special simply because you were born.

God saw you in your mother's womb when you were a tiny baby—a one-centimeter embryo. He looked into the secret place in your mother's womb and saw you. From the second your father's sperm and your mother's egg joined to form a child, God tenderly created you and watched you grow. God never would have allowed the sperm and the egg to come together if He had not planned for you to be born.

Although some parents feel their baby is a mistake, their thoughts are not true. God planned for that baby to be born. The manner in which the child was conceived may not have been in God's plan, but the child himself is surely part of God's plan.

Those of you who were brought up in a nice family with a mother and a father who love you may not understand those who have been put down by their family since the day of their birth. You may not understand how important it is for them to know that they are not mistakes. Be patient with them. Help them to see that God designed them long before they were born! Every child who comes into this world comes as a setup from God. That little boy or girl doesn't need to arrive to see what is going to happen, because the happening was already set up before he or she came.

You are here because God wanted you to be born.

## od Has a Book on You

*Before a word is on my tongue you know it completely, O Lord* (Psalm 139:4).

BOOK QUOTE: *Understanding Your Potential* [Chapter 6]

God designed you to be somebody. He looked at your unformed body and declared, "This child is good." All His plans for your life were set out long before you took a breath. He wrote out the order of your days before you lived even one day (see Psalm 139:16). There's a book on you. Some chapters God wrote about you haven't even been touched yet.

Some of you are playing around in the index or you have spent years in the table of contents. Perhaps you are 30 years old and you still don't know God's plan for your life. That's playing around on the contents page. You are 30 years old and still wondering what you are supposed to be. You haven't even started yet.

Others have jumped ahead of God's plan. Though His design calls for you to be married in chapter 17, you got married in chapter 2. You have ignored the things God wanted you to learn and experience in chapters 2 through 16 so you would be prepared for marriage in chapter 17. You have missed out on many experiences and discoveries because you moved ahead of God's schedule.

Some people are so busy peeking into chapter 17 they don't have time to live chapters 2 and 3 and 4.... Or perhaps you have pulled chapter 17 into chapter 2 so that the rest of the book is destroyed. You will never have the opportunity to experience all the chapters if you pull parts of later chapters into the early ones.

God designed you to be somebody.

## God Offers You a Rewrite

*You hem me in—behind and before; you have laid your hand upon me* (Psalm 139:5).

BOOK QUOTE: *Understanding Your Potential* [Chapter 6]

God wants to take you back to the beginning, because His plans far outreach your plans. His design for your life is so great that King David describes it as *vast* (see Psalm 139:17). You are thinking about being a teacher while God wants you to open a school. You have plans to be a clerk while God wants you to own the store. You want to work in a neighboring town while God wants you to go to Africa. You often cheat yourself because you don't realize the potential you have. Why settle to be a doorman when God wants you to own the house? David says it this way: "God, when I look at your thoughts in the book on me, it's like all the sands in the ocean. Your thoughts are endless. I can't fathom your confidence in me."

God designed you to live out the careful plans He prepared for you. You are made in God's image. The plan He wrote for you is perfect and right. No detail or part is missing. You have the potential to live out all that God has planned for your life—but only if you accept Jesus Christ as your Savior and Lord. That's the first step toward understanding why you were born.

Though you've messed up God's perfect plan for your life, He graciously offers to write another book for you. It probably won't be the best-seller the first book was designed to be, but at least God gives you the chance to start over. He comes and puts you back in chapter one so you can live the many details of His plan. That's what being born again is all about. It's the opportunity to start over—it's finally getting back to the first chapter of God's book on you. God has great plans for you—that's why He gave you life. Self-acceptance is the key to healthy self-esteem.

Accept yourself as God made you. Allow His power to transform your weakness, rather than belittling yourself when you make mistakes.

God has great plans for you—that's why He gave you life.

## Born to Expose His Nature

*...the people I formed for myself that they may proclaim my praise* (Isaiah 43:21).

BOOK QUOTE: *Understanding Your Potential* [Chapter 6]

Not only did God carefully plan for the details of your life, He also determined how your life would fit into His total plan for man. Part of the answer to the why of our birth is revealed in God's desire that we should show forth His glory. The glory of God is the excess of His nature. It's all the potential of our omnipotent God that has not yet been revealed. He's full of so much more than we can think or imagine and He's waiting to use us to realize that potential.

> *Now to Him who is able to do immeasurably more than all we ask or imagine, according to His power that is at work within us, to Him be glory in the church and in Christ Jesus throughout all generations, for ever and ever! Amen* (Ephesians 3:20-21).

Throughout the Bible, God tells us to make His name great in the earth. Praise and thanks are due God's name, which is great and awesome (see Psalm 44:8; 99:3). His name is to be proclaimed among the nations (see Malachi 1:11) as well as in Israel (see Psalm 76:1). His name is holy (see Luke 1:49; Psalm 99:3) and mighty in power (see Jeremiah 10:6). Everything is done for "His name's sake." To understand this concept, we must also understand that the Hebrew concept of "name" literally is synonymous with the object. In other words, the name of the thing is the thing. Therefore, the name of God is Himself, and He is His name. To glorify His name, then, means exposing His nature.

God created *you* to bring glory to His name. His predestined plan for *your* life was designed to bring Him glory. He knows there is more to you than we can see because He placed part of Himself in you. His plan for your life is part of His creative work—through you God wants to continue the birth of His potential. Because you share God's omnipotent nature, Jesus said you can do even greater things than He did, if you only believe (see Mark 11:23).

God created you to bring glory to His name.

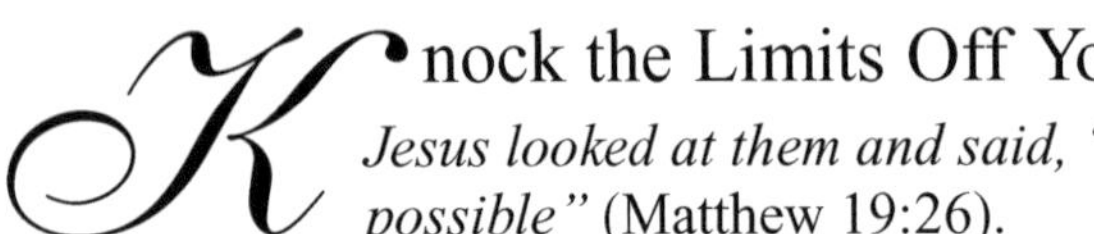

## Knock the Limits Off Your Life

*Jesus looked at them and said, "With man this is impossible, but with God all things are possible"* (Matthew 19:26).

BOOK QUOTE: *Understanding Your Potential* [Chapter 6]

The concept of Mark chapter 11 is that if you ask anything—if you can believe what you desire hard enough—God says it will be done. Somehow God gives us a little glimpse into our potential. He comes into our situation as if He's disturbed. God is disappointed in the human race. It's almost as though God looks at the ideas He stored in us and says with a voice of disappointment, "If you only knew what you can do." That's the attitude of God toward you and me. God is totally disappointed in us because He knows what we can do. But we don't. And so He says to us: "All things are possible if you'd just believe, dummy." He's always knocking the limits off our lives.

Too often we are not willing to *believe* like God defines believe. God does not say, "Everything is possible if you get the idea." Things don't become reality because we have an idea. We have to believe in the idea. We have to believe we can do it by committing ourselves to it—abandoning ourselves to it—even if it costs us our lives. That's what it takes to believe in the Lord Jesus Christ—to lose our lives…to abandon ourselves. We must say, "I'm going to go into eternity believing in Jesus. I'm not sure what's out there, but I'm going to ride on that Name and that atonement."

God isn't impressed by your dreams. Most of us never wake up long enough to do anything with our dreams. You may have great dreams for your life, but you prefer to stay asleep because when you wake up reality says, "OK, let's get to work." It's easier to dream an idea than to work it out. Everything is possible if you will abandon yourself to an idea enough that you are willing to lose your life for it. Thinking is great. But all things are possible when we *believe*. Jesus said in Mark chapter 11, "Whatever you *desire* when you pray, believe you'll receive it, and you will have it." The word *desire* is the key. Being interested in or attracted to something is not desiring it. To *desire* means "to crave for something at the expense of losing everything."

God's work in creation began with a plan. God conceived in His mind what He wanted before speaking His creations into visible form. By the time God was ready to speak, it was just a matter of taking what was in the plan and putting it on the site.

> Everything is possible if you abandon yourself to an idea enough that you are willing to lose your life for it.

## rom Thought to Action

*He replied, "...I tell you the truth, if you have faith as small as a mustard seed, you can say to this mountain, 'Move from here to there' and it will move. Nothing will be impossible for you"* (Matthew 17:20).

BOOK QUOTE: *Understanding Your Potential* [Chapter 6]

A *thought* is a silent word, so a word is an exposed thought. Everything in life starts in the thought form—it's a thought first. After it's said, it is no longer a thought. It becomes a word.

The next step is an *idea*. An idea is the concept of the thought—it has moved into a reality. Ideas are potentials.

The third level of operation is what I call *imagination*. Imagination changes an idea into a plan. If you have an idea it can come and go. You have many ideas in a day—what to cook, what to wear, what to do. You may decide the night before what you are going to wear in the morning and then wake up with a different idea. Ideas change. But if an idea develops into an imagination, it means the idea has become a plan. It is still not written or drawn, but it is in your head. Imagination is therefore a plan that is not documented. It is a visual display of your thoughts and ideas. Ephesians 3:20 challenges us to believe God is able and willing to do "*exceeding abundantly far beyond all we can think or imagine*." He dares us to use our imaginations.

If you want to be successful in life, take your ideas and turn them into imagination; then take imagination and duplicate it physically. Put it down. Let it become a plan of action.

Many people never get beyond the idea stage. That's sad. They are usually followers. The people who get to the imagination stage often talk a lot but they do nothing. They are dreamers. But when a man or woman takes his imagination and puts it on paper, you are looking at a visionary who is becoming a missionary. Visionaries see great things in their minds. Many visionaries are in the graveyard. They had visions, but their visions never made it to mission. When a visionary becomes a missionary, you have a man or woman who is going to change the world.

> Plans are documented imaginations.

## EVIEW the Principles From This Week:

- You are worth feeling good about because God wanted you to be born.
- God has a detailed plan for your life.
- The first step in living out God's plan is accepting Jesus Christ as your Savior and Lord.
- God created you with a part of His potential so you could expose and share in His glory.
- God's glory is the excess of His potential—His many plans that wait to be revealed through us.
- Develop a plan for your life that fulfills some of the possibilities God placed within you before you were born. Then believe and work them into existence.

# All Things Are Possible

*For nothing is impossible with God* (Luke 1:37).

BOOK QUOTE: *Understanding Your Potential* [Chapter 7]

For about two years now my little boy has been coming to me when he's trying to do something and saying, "I can't do this." I always respond to him by saying, "There is nothing named 'can't.'" When he comes back to me and says, "I don't know how to do it," I always reply, "There's always a way to do everything."

Several days ago my son and I were out in the yard playing bat and ball. I was throwing the ball to him and he kept on missing with the bat. Finally he became really upset and said, "I can't do that," to which I replied, "There's nothing named 'can't.'" Slowly he repeated after me, "There's nothing named 'can't.'" Then I said, "Hold the bat," and I threw the ball. He hit the ball and then said, "There's nothing named 'can't.'"

Several days later when I stopped by home to drop off my daughter, my son came running and wanted to play basketball. When I said that I had to go back to the office to do some work, he insisted that he wanted to play ball with me then. When I again replied that I had to go to the office, he said, "There's nothing named 'can't.' "

Do you see the point? If he begins to think that way at four years of age, this world is in for a winner. Too often we fail in our efforts because we have been brought up believing that we cannot do some things. The people who change the world are people who have taken impossible out of their dictionaries. The men and women who make changes in history are those who come against the odds and tell the odds that it's impossible for the odds to stop them.

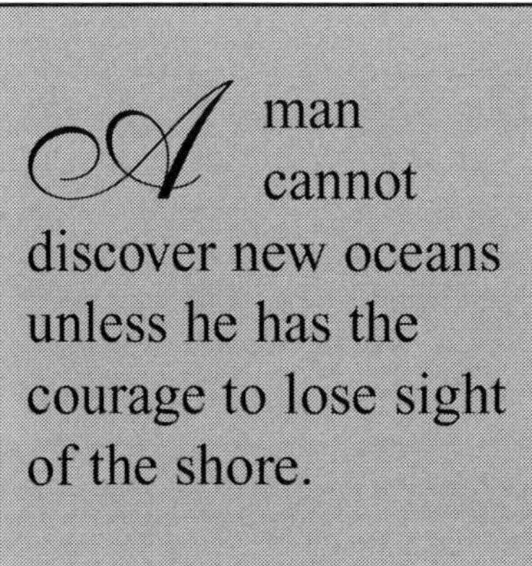

## ou Can Do All Things

*I can do everything through Him who gives me strength (Philippians 4:13).*

BOOK QUOTE: *Understanding Your Potential* [Chapter 7]

The apostle Paul, when looking back over his years in the Lord's service, stated that he could do all things through Christ who strengthens him. The Greek terminology for strengthen does not mean we are weak and God comes and props us up. Paul's words literally mean: "Christ who continues to infuse me with ability." Thus Paul is saying: "I can do all things through the potential of Christ who infuses me with the ability to do all things." This strength is not a strength that comes once in a while, but a continual ability that is infused into us because we are connected to Christ. Thus our potential is not limited to doing *some* of the things God asks us to do. We can do *all things*—whatever we believe and desire to do for God. We can do this because the ability to do so is already deposited in us. The basis for this deposit of Christ's ability goes back to God's work in creation.

God is the source of all potential because everything that is was in God. He created everything with potential and gave it the ability to fulfill itself. The potential God gave is related to the source from which He took the thing. That means whatever you came out of is an indication of your potential. Thus your potential is as great as God's potential, because when God wanted you, He spoke to Himself. When He wanted plants and animals, God spoke to the ground. But when He wanted human beings, God spoke to Himself. You came out of God. Thus the limit of your potential is God.

The people who change the world are people who have take *impossible* out of their dictionaries.

## The Demands of the Creator

*As you do not know the path of the wind, or how the body is formed in a mother's womb, so you cannot understand the work of God, the Maker of all things* (Ecclesiastes 11:5).

BOOK QUOTE: *Understanding Your Potential* [Chapter 7]

Genesis chapter 1 also teaches us that potential is determined by the demands made on it by the creator of it. This is the most amazing thing I have ever discovered about potential. The potential of a thing is determined by the demands made on it by the one who made it. A creator will not call forth from his creation something he did not put into it.

If, for example, the Ford Motor Company wanted to build a car with an engine that was supposed to have a certain degree of horsepower to get up to 200 miles per hour, they would create a car with enough spark plugs and pistons and other things to run at that speed. First they would design it. Then they would build it. Finally they would hire a professional to take it on a test track to clock its speed. Because they designed and built the car to run at 200 miles per hour, they would tell the driver: "Run this car until it hits 200 miles per hour."

Now how can they demand from that car 200 miles per hour? Simple. They built into the car the ability to produce 200 miles per hour. If all other cars can only go 198 miles per hour, they have reason to believe their car will go into a race and win. They are calling forth from the car, or demanding of it, what they created it to produce.

Or let's think about a flight of the spaceship Challenger. The people who plan a trip into space decide before the spaceship ever leaves earth when the journey will begin, where the spaceship will go, what the crew will do while in space, how long the trip will last, and where the ship will land. The men who created the spaceship and the people who trained the astronauts know what the ship and the crew can do. The demands they make are thus consistent with their potential.

Or suppose you want to take an airplane trip. If you want to fly from Nassau to Chicago, you depend upon the expertise and knowledge of others to assure you that you will get there. You may look at the airplane and say, "This thing will never get me to Chicago," but what you believe doesn't really matter because you are not the creator of either the airplane or the flight route. The folks who build and maintain the airplane would never require it to make the trip from Nassau to Chicago if they thought the plane lacked the potential to do so. The ticket agent would never schedule you for that airplane if he knew the flight didn't go to Chicago. The potential of a thing is determined by the demands placed upon it by the creator.

> The potential of a thing is determined by the demands placed upon it by the creator.

## od's "Money-Back" Guarantee

*But the Scripture declares that the whole world is a prisoner of sin, so that what was promised, being given through faith in Jesus Christ, might be given to those who believe* (Galatians 3:22).

BOOK QUOTE: *Understanding Your Potential* [Chapter 7]

The potential of a thing is determined by the demands placed upon it by the creator. This is the most amazing thing I have ever discovered about potential. The potential of a thing is determined by the demands made on it by the one who made it. A creator will not call forth from his creation something he did not put into it.

Whenever God demands something of you, don't ask whether you can do it. When you pick up the Bible and read that you can do anything if you believe, don't argue that you can't. God believes (in fact He knows) that whatever you believe hard enough, strong enough, and committed enough can come out of you because He put it in you. Your potential, like that of any other creation, is determined by the demands of your Creator.

God also graciously offers you a "Money-Back Guarantee." When you buy an appliance, a manual usually comes with it that says: "Read this before you hook it up." It also says: "You've just purchased a television that can do XYZ." You've never seen the television do that before, but the manual says it can and will because the manufacturer made it possible for it to do it. At the end of the manual, there is usually a little phrase that says: "If there is any defect, return the merchandise to the manufacturer for a free replacement." The manufacturer is guaranteeing the potential of the thing.

God mercifully says to you, "If there are any defects, return to the Manufacturer." Isn't that a blessing? If you aren't working out, take your stuff back to the Chief. The Chief will work it out. "Come unto Me," God says. "I'm the only one who can fix you." God already has guaranteed what you can do.

God already has guaranteed what you can do.

## You Can Do Everything God Asks

*...and His incomparably great power for us who believe. That power is like the working of His mighty strength* (Ephesians 1:19).

BOOK QUOTE: *Understanding Your Potential* [Chapter 7]

God is good. He has built into you the potential to produce everything He calls for. When God says, "Love your enemies," don't start listing reasons why you can't. The ability to love is built in…it's there…no excuses. God wouldn't ask for it if it wasn't available. He wired you to produce everything He demands.

God also wired everything else to produce what He demands from it. God looks at a piece of fruit and says, "In you there is a tree. There is a seed in you, and that seed is a tree. It's there, and I demand what I put in." So God says, "Plant that seed and a tree has to come out; I put a tree in that seed. Before you were given the fruit, I made the seed with the tree." That's the way God thinks. Hallelujah!

Whenever God gives you a responsibility, He also gives you the ability to meet that responsibility. In other words, *whatever God calls for, He provides for*. If God tells you to do something, He knows you can do it. So don't you dare tell God that you can't. Just because He told you to assume that responsibility means He knows you can do it. The problem isn't that you can't, it's just that you *won't*.

Whether you use the ability God has deposited within you is totally up to you. How well you assume the responsibilities God gives you is not so much a question of how much you *do*, but rather how much of the available power you use. What you are doing is not near what your ability is. What you have accomplished is a joke when compared with what you could accomplish—you are not working enough with the power of God (emphasis on work).

Whenever God gives you a responsibility, He also gives you the ability to meet that responsibility.

# f You Think It, You Can Do It

*There is surely a future hope for you, and your hope will not be cut off* (Proverbs 23:18).

BOOK QUOTE: *Understanding Your Potential* [Chapter 7]

You have a deposit of God's ability! Any person who sets a limit on what he *can* do, also sets a limit on what he *will* do. No one can determine how much you can produce except you and God. So there is nothing in this world that should stop you from accomplishing and realizing and fulfilling and maximizing your full potential.

Proverbs 23:7 tells us: If you can conceive it, you can do it. Obviously God is trying to communicate that you *can* do anything you can *think*. If you can conceive it, the fact that you can conceive it means you can do it. It doesn't matter if it's never been done—if you think it, you can do it. Likewise, if you never think it, you can't do it. God allows you to think only what you can do. If He doesn't allow you to think it, He knows you can't do it.

Think about the things you've been thinking recently. The fact that you thought them means you can do them. Now don't get me wrong. Thinking doesn't get it done. Thinking implies you can do it. See yourself doing the thing in your thoughts. Make your thought into an idea, and your idea into an imagination. Take that imagination and document it into a plan. Then go to it (of course with the proper rest periods). Put your plan into action. If you thought it, you can do it.

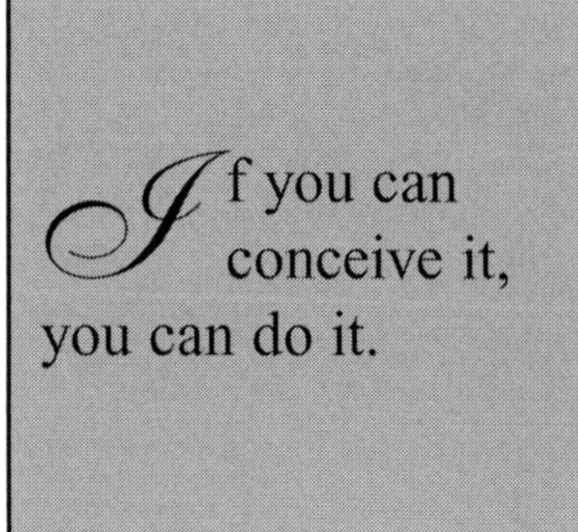

# f God Has It, You Have It

*But the fruit of the Spirit is love, joy, peace, patience, kindness, goodness, faithfulness, gentleness and self-control...* (Galatians 5:22-23).

BOOK QUOTE: *Understanding Your Potential* [Chapter 7]

Each of the fruit of the Spirit is an attribute of God. God unconditionally says, "They are you." God knows you have love. He knows you have joy—it doesn't matter what you are going through. God knows you have joy down there inside you, because Christ is joy.

Peace. How do you explain that? I used to think the Prince of Peace. "Hello, Prince." I always thought: "Others have the peace. Give me some, Jesus." But that's not what the Bible teaches. The Bible says you have peace. When you are unhappy and everything is going wrong, God says, "Have peace." He doesn't say, "I'll give you some peace," because He can't give you what you already have. Peace is not a gift; it's a fruit. Joy is not a gift; it's a fruit. If God has it, you have it.

In the beginning there was only God. All that is and all that was, was in God—everything. We came out of God. Thus, everything that is in God, is in us: love...joy...peace...patience...kindness...goodness... faithfulness...gentleness...self-control. These are in God and in us.

"Love? I can't like that person."

"You're lying to me," God says. "What do you mean you can't love? Your spirit connected to My Spirit can do all things. Since I love, you can too."

As Romans 5:5 puts it: "*...God has poured out His love into our hearts by the Holy Spirit....*" After you return to God, the Holy Spirit brings love back to your heart. He ignites the stuff that has been in your heart all along. It's not that you *can't* love; you just don't *want* to love. Love isn't a decision you make, because you already have it. That's why you can love your enemies.

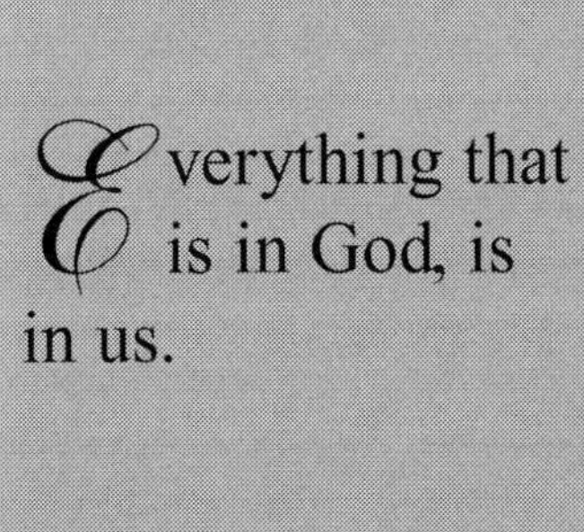

## EVIEW the Principles From This Week:

- The potential of a thing is related to its source.
- Your potential is as great as God's potential, because when God wanted you He spoke to Himself.
- Potential is determined by the demands made on it by the creator.
- If you can think it, you can do it.
- Your potential is everything that is in Christ. So if God has it, you have it.

## ominate the Earth

*Then God said, "Let Us make man in Our image, in Our likeness, and let them rule over the fish of the sea and the birds of the air, over the livestock, over all the earth, and over all the creatures that move along the ground"* (Genesis 1:26).

BOOK QUOTE: *Understanding Your Potential* [Chapter 7]

Your purpose for being is to dominate the earth. (God did not create you to go to church. You go to church because you need to relearn how to live again. Church is school, and when you graduate you will be dead. That's the perfect graduation ceremony—death. Then you finally will come back to who you really are.) You were created to dominate the earth. If God created you and commanded you to dominate the earth, God also is aware that you can do it.

God says, "Dominate the earth."

And you quickly reply, "But, but, but…"

Still God says, "Dominate the earth. I have created you to dominate the earth. I demand that you control, rule, govern, dominate, subdue, and subject this planet."

God wouldn't have made that demand if you couldn't do it. He wired you to dominate this planet. You have the potential to dominate the earth because God placed within every human being the ability to dominate the planet. That is a very serious domination. You dare not complain when you are dominated by the earth (instead of the earth being dominated by you) because God has placed within you the capacity to do whatever He asks. Don't you dare tell God that you cannot do it. He did not give you the responsibility without also giving you the ability. He created you with the ability to dominate the earth.

> Your purpose for being is to dominate the earth.

## ou Are More Than You or Others Expect

*...for everyone born of God overcomes the world. This is the victory that has overcome the world, even our faith* (1 John 5:4).

BOOK QUOTE: *Understanding Your Potential* [Chapter 7]

One morning I said to my little boy as he ran into the room and jumped on me, "You know, I'm holding in my hands all you haven't been yet." Although he didn't understand much of what I was saying, I was thinking about the vast amount of potential that lay within him just waiting to be used. Potential is like that. It's all you can be and become that you haven't yet experienced. Think about it. Potential is all you are capable of being or doing or reaching. You haven't done it yet, but you can do it.

Thus when God tells you to dominate the earth, He is pointing to a potential that lies deep within you. Although it sounds simple to say that you have the potential to dominate the earth, that fact is a salvation to happiness. It is a blessing to know that God would never demand it if you couldn't do it. God has placed in you the ability to dominate the planet.

You can overcome every habit, because God has clearly stated that you can. Isn't that amazing? That's a blessing! You are not involved in a hopeless fight. Oh, hear me if you are suffering a habit. The fact that God says "Do it!" is a joy. You can beat it.

Some of you have resolved that you are hooked for life. That's a lie. God gave you authority over that habit when He demanded that you rule the earth. Don't walk around with the hopeless idea: "I'll always be an addict. I'll always be an alcoholic. I'll always be like this."

God has placed within you the ability to dominate everything. It is there. It is in you. The problem isn't that you *can't* control your habit; the problem is that you *won't*.

People say: "I know I shouldn't be doing this." In reality that means: "I don't want to do this. Something is wrong with this but I can't help myself."

I have news for you—good news. It's more "I haven't decided to stop doing this," than "I shouldn't be doing this." You have what God demands. God will never demand anything He's not already provided for. Whatever God calls forth, He sees. God commanded you to dominate the earth, and the truth is you *can*.

## ou Are the Cream of the Crop

*God blessed them and said to them, "Be fruitful and increase in number; fill the earth and subdue it. Rule over the fish of the sea and the birds of the air and over every living creature that moves on the ground"* (Genesis 1:28).

BOOK QUOTE: *Understanding Your Potential* [Chapter 7]

No one needs to be ruled by cocaine or marijuana. Nobody needs to be the victim of alcohol and money. They are all but leaves from the trees that we are supposed to be dominating. The only way to escape these and other dominating habits is to understand your purpose for being. God did not create you to be dominated by sex or chemicals. He did not create you to be *controlled* by anything. He created you so *you could control* the earth.

You are so much more than others expect from you. You are so much more than you expect from yourself. God calls us sanctified—that means special. God calls us elite—that means cream of the crop. And what God calls you He sees in you. God's not trying to conjure up things when He affirms who you are. He already sees them in you.

God looks under all the junk and says what He sees. He says: "You are pure. You are the righteousness of God in Christ Jesus." He looks beneath our unrighteous behavior and sees righteousness. He sees it and calls it out. He'll keep calling it out until it reaches the surface. God's not trying to *make you* into something. He's trying to expose the real you He already sees. While you are walking around trying to be good and righteous, God says, "You already are righteous."

When you wake up tomorrow morning, stretch, look in the mirror and say: "You successful thing you." That's what God sees. No matter what kind of bum day is planned for you, you can decide in the morning that it's going to be a successful one. Why? Because this is the day the Lord has made. If you believe, it is possible the day will be good. It is possible to rejoice every day if you believe God has made it. Go ahead. Stretch. Look at the success that is just waiting to happen.

God's not trying to *make* you into something. He's trying to expose the real you.

## od Wants You to Know His Thoughts

*Do not conform any longer to the pattern of this world, but be transformed by the renewing of your mind. Then you will be able to test and approve what God's will is—His good, pleasing and perfect will* (Romans 12:2).

BOOK QUOTE: *Understanding Your Potential* [Chapter 7]

When God told His people: "*For My thoughts are not your thoughts, neither are your ways My ways*" (Isa. 55:8), He was not saying He doesn't want our ways and thoughts to be like His. God was telling us: "Your thoughts and ways are not like Mine, but I'm trying to get them like Mine." God wants us to have a mind like His. He told us through the apostle Paul to be transformed by the renewing of our minds. He wants you to know and obey His will—doing what is pleasing and acceptable in His sight (see Romans 12:2). Go back to the old mind in the Garden. That's the way to think.

What a blessing it is to know that you can wake up tomorrow morning and have God's thoughts. But too often you wake up and say: "Oh, God. It's Monday."

God says: "You're not thinking like Me. This is a day I made just for you. Come on, let's go out there and give 'em Heaven." Give 'em Heaven? Yeah, that's right. There's a world out there that is hurting. Let's go give them Heaven.

But we have the attitude: "Oh God. I can never be like You."

God comes to us and says, "My child, that's exactly what I want you to do. Have the mind of Christ. Think like Me." God wants you to adopt His mind and attitude toward yourself. He desires that you think about yourself the way He does. Believe His assessment of your potential.

> Believe God's assessment of your potential.

## Don't Let the World Determine Your Potential

*What is man that you are mindful of him, the son of man that you care for him?* (Psalm 8:4).

BOOK QUOTE: *Understanding Your Potential* [Chapter 7]

We have allowed the world around us to determine our potential. Teachers say to students: "You are a C student." The student then goes around believing that, and he becomes an average student for the rest of his life—an average person even. He becomes an average husband. She becomes an average wife. We become average parents and average children with average attitudes and IQs. And when we turn out to be average, our parents say: "Well, honey, you have my genes." No. They received your attitude that was transmitted to you from that teacher.

You need to shake off what people call IQs. Do you know what "IQ" means? It means Intelligence Quotient—it's what people believe your degree of intelligence is based upon some tests you take. These tests measure your motor skills, your thinking ability, your cognitive ability, your reading ability, your math ability, etc. Then based on these tests they say, "You are a D student. You are a D person." You haven't even grown up yet and they are telling you what you are going to be and do! They don't know what you are going to do.

Unfortunately, people believe what they are told based on those tests. There are thousands of examples in history of men and women who were put off and cast out as misfits. Later they turned out to be some of the world's greatest leaders. We must be careful when we start putting Intelligence Quotients on people. Your potential has nothing to do with those tests. Only God determines your potential. Your IQ is spelled *H-O-L-Y S-P-I-R-I-T.* Your IQ is something that goes far beyond the pages of a test. It goes all the way to God.

> Only God determines your potential.

## Spirits Cannot Die

*After that, we who are still alive and are left will be caught up together with them in the clouds to meet the Lord in the air. And so we will be with the Lord forever* (1 Thessalonians 4:17).

BOOK QUOTE: *Understanding Your Potential* [Chapter 7]

One day as I was talking with the Holy Spirit, He said to me, "Myles, what are you?"

I said, "Spirit."

He said, "Yea! You got that down! Do you know that spirits cannot die?"

I said, "This is true."

Then He said, "Why do humans think in terms of time only? I came back to earth to introduce humans to eternity."

I said, "Whoa!"

Then the Holy Spirit showed me how God had designed us to live forever. He said, "If you have to live forever, which you will, what are you going to do? God intended you to live forever because spirits never die. And you have to live forever being fulfilled. God never makes anything without a purpose. So you are designed to live forever and you've got to be fulfilling your purpose in life. God had to make sure He stored enough in you to last forever so you will never get bored."

That blew my mind. We are going to live forever.

Sometimes we sing: "When I get to Heaven I'm going to praise the Lord for a thousand years."

"What are you going to do after that?"

"Well, then I'll walk around the streets of gold for another thousand years."

"What are you going to do after that?" You have eternity to live. After a million years of worshiping and bowing and keeping company with the angels, what are you going to do? Your mind is so small. You think, "Wow. Look what I have accomplished."

God says, "Gosh, your life is a spot in eternity—just a drop in eternity. You will not begin really living until you leave time and enter eternity."

God has packed so much into you that the book He wrote on you is only the book for time. Your potential from birth to death is contained in that book—a book so full of expectations that David says it is "vast."

> You will not begin really living until you leave time and enter eternity.

## Created for Eternal Life

*Lord, you have been our dwelling place throughout all generations (Psalm 90:1).*

BOOK QUOTE: *Understanding Your Potential* [Chapter 7]

God is called a creator because He always has something to do. God is always busy doing something. When God took us out of Himself, He gave us part of His Spirit. God is Spirit and spirits are eternal. They cannot die. Therefore, what is spirit and comes out of God is also eternal. When God created human beings, He said, "This one will keep Us excited forever. Let's make and create a being in Our own image. Let's make one who will not fade away." Mountains will fade away and rivers will run dry. Streams will evaporate and the oceans will go away. But when God came up with man, He created something that would last forever. He took man out of Himself. God made you spirit and put so much stuff in you that it will take an eternal life to live it all. *Your true potential requires eternal life to be realized and maximized.*

There is no retirement in the Bible. Why? Because God knows you have eternity to go just like He does. God wants you to assist Him in creating and developing and dominating and ruling forever and ever and ever. That's a long time. The wealth of your potential is so rich it requires an eternal life to bring it out.

We are not going to be in Heaven for a million years bowing down around a throne. God doesn't have an ego problem. He doesn't need us to tell Him how nice He is. In fact, He was nice without us. We make Him look pretty bad. We've really messed up God. We came out of God. We are the only ones made in His image, and look what we did. God was better off without us. He doesn't need our praises to make Him feel high.

God has placed enough potential in you to last forever. Try to do as much now as you can. Pack as much as you can into the 70 to 100 years you have here. Go for it. Go for a hunk of gold. Go for the mountain that has the gold in it. Go for the whole thing. Because if you can think it, you can do it. God is the limit of your ability. He won't allow you to think it if you can't do it.

## EVIEW the Principles From This Week:

- Your potential is everything that is in Christ. So if God has it, you have it.
- God created you and commanded you to dominate the earth.
- God will never demand anything He hasn't already provided for. Whatever God calls forth, He sees.
- The wealth of your potential is so rich it requires an eternal life to bring it out.

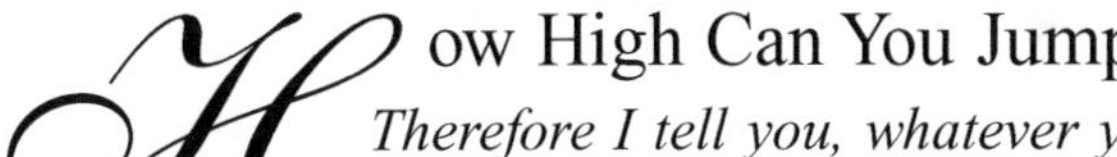

# How High Can You Jump?

*Therefore I tell you, whatever you ask for in prayer, believe that you have received it, and it will be yours* (Mark 11:24).

BOOK QUOTE: *Understanding Your Potential* [Chapter 8]

The people who are blessings to humanity are usually men and women who decide there is more to them than what other people have said. People who bless the world are people who believe there is an ability inside them to accomplish something that has never been done. Though they may not know *exactly* what they can do, they *try* because they believe they can accomplish something.

I remember the day I found out that I could jump really high—about 8 feet high.

There was a lady who lived behind our house from whose fruit trees we would occasionally feast and help ourselves. When we were little kids, we would crawl under the fence. One day while I was on her side of the fence, her very vicious dog suddenly appeared. I had just touched down after climbing the fruit tree. As I carefully considered the distance between the fence, the dog, and myself, I knew I had to make a run for it. I ran toward the fence with the dog close behind me. As the fence came closer and closer, all I could say was "O God, I'm dead." All I could think was "jump." As I left the ground, my heart was pounding and my chest felt like an arcade full of shouting people. I was so afraid! When I landed, I was safely on the other side of the fence.

I thank God for that dog. He was a blessing in my life. I never jumped that high before, and I never have since, but at least I know that I did it. I discovered that day there is a lot more potential in me than I realized was there.

The same is true for you. You aren't doing more because no one has challenged you. I want to take you from the realm of waiting for people to challenge you and encourage you to challenge yourself. Don't just look at life and say, "Well, I'm going to wait until a demand is made on me and then I will produce." Make a demand on yourself. Say to yourself, "Look, I am going to become the best in this area no matter what people have done before me." Then go after that. You will accomplish it if you set out to do it.

> The people who are blessings to humanity are usually men and women who decide there is more to them than what other people have said.

## Tell Me To Come

*...If anyone serves, he should do it with the strength God provides, so that in all things God may be praised through Jesus Christ. To Him be the glory and the power for ever and ever. Amen* (1 Peter 4:11).

BOOK QUOTE: *Understanding Your Potential* [Chapter 8]

I am reminded of a young fisherman who decided, "I'm going to take a chance and try to walk on water." One night as the disciples were crossing Lake Galilee it was hard rowing. They were being tossed about by the waves because the wind was against them. As they struggled, a man came toward them, walking on the water. In fear they cried out, "It's a ghost." Only when He spoke to them did the disciples recognize that it was Jesus. Peter then said, "*Lord, if it's you...tell me to come to you on the water*" (Matthew 14:28). And when Jesus said "Come!", Peter had the guts to respond to Jesus' order.

I believe every one of those disciples could have walked on water. The potential was in them even as it was in Peter. But only Peter succeeded, because only Peter had the guts to say, "If you challenge me, I'll take your challenge." Although we may laugh or criticize Peter for sinking, none of us has ever walked on water. He's the only guy who can say in Heaven when we get there, "I walked on water. What did you do?"

Everybody sees Jesus, but very few of us ask Jesus, "Tell me something to do. Give me something to challenge my potential." Men and women who are assets to the world and bring change for the better are those who give their potential something to maximize. *Give your ability a responsibility*; that would change the world. There is a wealth of ability in you, but you haven't given it any responsibility. Don't die without maximizing your ability—that's irresponsible. You have no right to die with what God put in you to live out.

Give your ability a responsibility; that would change the world.

## on't Wait To Be Challenged

*And God is able to make all grace abound to you, so that in all things at all times, having all that you need, you will abound in every good work* (2 Corinthians 9:8).

BOOK QUOTE: *Understanding Your Potential* [Chapter 8]

God has promised that He can do far more than you can think or imagine. His power is available to you. Is that power working in you? Are you saying to God: "I've got some power, now work it for me. Give me something to do"?

God has given you a skill or ability the world needs. He has been waiting for your birth. Perhaps He planted within you a unique ability to work for life. Imagine a dead baby turning purple in your hand. Others are thinking "undertaker," but you know that God has given you a potential to restore life. You believe God and pray, by the power of His Spirit, "God, this dear baby must live." Even though someone might overhear you, and that makes your prayer all the more difficult, you tap into the potential God planted deep within you and believe for the baby's life.

God has given you a skill or ability the world needs.

Miracles happen when we give our potential responsibility. God designed it that way. Don't allow the things within you to die with you because you did not challenge them. God planted the seed of potential within you. He made you according to the *potential principle*—like the rest of His creation. Don't waste that gift. Give your potential some responsibility.

> Miracles happen when we give our potential responsibilities.

## Beat the Odds

*I have told you these things, so that in Me you may have peace. In this world you will have trouble. But take heart! I have overcome the world* (John 16:33).

BOOK QUOTE: *Understanding Your Potential* [Chapter 8]

Men and women who make changes in history are those who have come against the odds and told the odds it is impossible for the odds to stop them. Don't throw yourself away—don't let anyone else throw you away because you are up against some odds.

The minute we see somebody in a wheelchair something happens to us. We think the person is half a person. We almost treat him as if we apologize for his condition. We look at people who are blind…who have a withered hand…who walk with a limp…who have only one arm as though they are half a person. We limit their potential to the wheelchair or the limp or the missing hand or the short arm. We reduce everybody to their bodies. You are not your body. Some of the greatest minds in the world are in wheelchairs.

I think about President Roosevelt in a wheelchair. Did you ever think an invalid could be the president of one of the greatest nations on earth?

Suppose you end up in a wheelchair next year with all the brains you have right now. Will you quit? Is your dream related to your body? Don't say "no" too fast. Some of you would just quit and get totally depressed and so sad. You'd say, "Oh, life didn't work out for me," and you'd allow all the dreams you have right now to die in the chair. You'd simply quit.

Don't give up because you are physically handicapped. Don't give up if you are facing great odds. Your potential is not determined by whether you can see the fine print of a book, walk across the street or lift heavy objects with both hands. Your potential is not destroyed because your mother is an alcoholic, your father's a junkie or you have no parents at all. There are many people in wheelchairs who have given up. There are many people who come from the wrong side of town or a bad family situation who have given up. Don't be one of them. Beat the odds.

Suppose you end up in a wheelchair next year with all the brains you have right now. Will you quit?

# Shortcuts Don't Work

*...and observe what the Lord your God requires: Walk in His ways, and keep His decrees and commands, His laws and requirements, as written in the Law of Moses, so that you may prosper in all you do and wherever you go* (1 Kings 2:3).

BOOK QUOTE: *Understanding Your Potential* [Chapter 8]

Ben Johnson is an athlete from Canada who set many world records. In 1987 he set the world record in the 100-yard dash at 9.83 seconds. In 1988 he broke his own record, winning the race in 9.79. But it is difficult to be correct in calling that a world record because the last record set was not the record of Ben Johnson. It was the record of a steroid pill. That record belongs to Ben Johnson plus the chemicals.

We will never know Ben Johnson's potential as far as running the 100-yard dash is concerned. Could he have run 100 yards in 9.79 seconds without the chemical? Possibly, but we will never know because Ben Johnson negated his potential by trying a shortcut. There was no reason for his shortcut. He had a world record. He had his name in history, and it was a good name. How sad to destroy a good name by a little bit of chemical.

I picked up a magazine on an airplane in which there was an advertisement that said, "Would you like a doctorate degree? Call us." I often read that advertisement and wonder how many have called them. If I did not realize that you cannot get something for nothing, I probably would have called them. Many have. There are people out there with doctorate degrees, or with doctorate letters in front of their names, who will never know their potential. They didn't allow themselves the chance to see what they could really do. They have the degrees, but they didn't fulfill the requirements.

There are no shortcuts to developing your potential. You will never know what you might have achieved if you use a crutch to get there. You'll never know what you may have learned if you get a degree without fulfilling the requirements. You will never know what you can do if you attempt to obtain it by a shortcut. Shortcuts negate potential. They destroy the possibilities God planted within you.

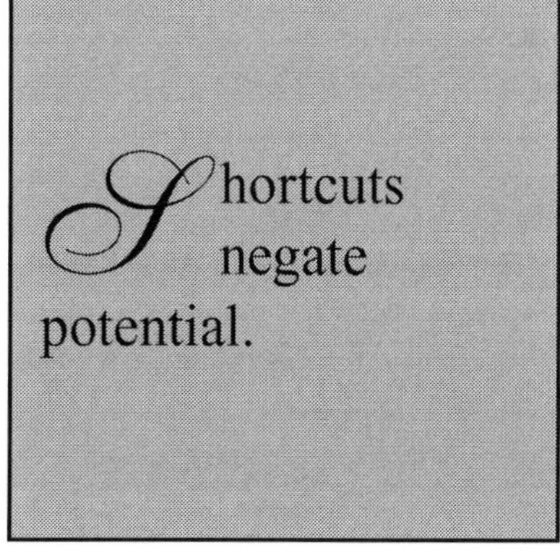

## Demand Something of Your Potential

*With this in mind, we constantly pray for you, that our God may count you worthy of His calling, and that by His power He may fulfill every good purpose of yours and every act prompted by your faith* (2 Thessalonians 1:11).

BOOK QUOTE: *Understanding Your Potential* [Chapter 8]

After God created Adam, He gave him a job. God knew Adam's potential to name all the animals would never be released unless it was challenged. Potential must be exercised to be fulfilled. Demands must be made on potential if it is to be released and fulfilled. God has given you potential. Unless you make demands on it, you will die with it. Unless you venture to try things you've never done before, you'll never experience the wealth that lives within you. Decide today, "I'm going to do something I've never done before." "I'm going to get a promotion this year in my job." "I'm going to win more people to Jesus this year than my church and my pastor ever did." If you have a business, resolve to cut the overhead and increase service. Give your potential some demands. It needs to be maximized and challenged.

The greatest works in the world will be done by people who don't care who gets the credit. I don't want to be famous, I just want to be faithful. I don't want to be well-known, I want to be well-used. I don't want to be powerful, I want to be potent. Success requires striking out on new paths instead of traveling those that are well-worn. Genius is 1 percent inspiration and 99 percent perspiration. There are many people with great ideas, but they have no desire to try. There are four steps to the accomplishment of your dream: Prepare prayerfully. Plan purposefully. Proceed positively. Pursue persistently. Failure is the path of least persistence.

Potential must be exercised to be fulfilled.

# Demand Something of Your Potential

*If the Lord delights in a man's way, He makes his steps firm; though he stumble, he will not fall, for the Lord upholds him with His hand* (Psalm 37:23-24).

BOOK QUOTE: *Understanding Your Potential* [Chapter 8]

No one can climb beyond the limitations he has placed on himself. Success is never final—failure is never fatal. It is courage that counts—courage and the willingness to move on. A great deal of talent is lost to the world for want of a little courage. Every day sends to the grave, obscure men, whom fear and timidity have prevented from making their first attempt to do something. Never tell a person that something can't be done, because God may have been waiting for centuries for someone ignorant enough to believe that the impossible could be possible.

Success is never final—failure is never fatal.

The poorest of men are men without a dream. Don't be so afraid of failure that you refuse to try. Demand something of yourself. Failure is only an incident. There's more than the failure—there's success deep behind that failure. Failure is the opportunity to more intelligently begin again. When you fail, that is a great chance to start again. Learn from it and move on. Don't be paralyzed by the failure.

One good thing about failure is that it is proof that you tried. The greatest mistake you can make is to be afraid of making one. People who do nothing in life are usually people who do nothing. People who don't make mistakes in life are usually people who didn't have a chance to make any because they never tried. Challenge your potential. Demand things of yourself that are beyond what you have already done. Expect more from yourself than the accomplishments that are easily within your reach. What you have is not all you are. The limit of your potential is God. It is better to attempt a thing and fail, than to never try and not know you could succeed.

Potential must be exercised to be fulfilled.

## EVIEW the Principles From This Week:

- Believe there is potential in you to accomplish something worthwhile.
- Unless you use your potential, you will never realize how much ability is inside you.
- Jump by your own challenge. Don't wait for someone to challenge you.
- Don't let the odds that are against you stop you from fulfilling your potential.
- Shortcuts negate your ability.
- Don't be so afraid of failure that you refuse to try.

## ll Things Have a Source

*for He knows how we are formed, He remembers that we are dust* (Psalm 103:14).

BOOK QUOTE: *Understanding Your Potential* [Chapter 9]

A grape vine is an interesting plant. The vine, which is the thick wooden part running from the ground up the pole, is the only part of the plant that contains life ability. None of the life is in the branches; all of it is in the vine. There is no life in the little green things you see on the side with the grapes hanging on them. They are getting their life from the vine. They have no root in themselves. If you were to break one of those green branches off and plant it in the ground, it would never grow because it has no life ability in it. Each small branch has to depend on the life flowing up and down the great branch, the vine, to give it life. Thus the branches cannot live without the vine. The relationship of the vine and its branches is reflected throughout God's creation. Life is not possible when a thing is separated from its source.

When God created the world, He first decided what He wanted His creation to be made out of. Then He spoke to that source, and whatever God said came out of what He spoke to. Whenever God wants to create something, He first decides what He wants the thing to be made out of. Then He speaks to whatever He wants it made out of, and whatever God speaks comes out of what He spoke to.

When God wanted plants He spoke to the soil, and out of the soil came what God spoke. Since God wanted plants to be made out of soil, every plant is dirt. When God wanted animals He spoke to the ground. Because animals came out of the ground, they are 100 percent dirt. The principle is simple. Whatever God wants He speaks to what He wants it made out of. Whatever God speaks comes out of what He spoke to.

Whatever God speaks comes out of what He spoke to.

When God wanted animals He spoke to the ground. When God wanted plants He spoke to dirt. Because God wanted man to come out of Himself, He spoke to Himself when He created man.

When God wanted man, He spoke to Himself. Therefore man is what God spoke to. Man is spirit because man came out of the spirit realm.

> The secret to a happy productive life is remaining attached to your Source.

## ource Determines Potential

*For in Him you have been enriched in every way—in all your speaking and in all your knowledge* (1 Corinthians 1:5).

BOOK QUOTE: *Understanding Your Potential* [Chapter 9]

Everything God creates has the same components as its source. Wherever something comes from determines it components. Or to say it another way: Everything is made up of the same stuff as what it came out of. Therefore plants are made up of 100 percent dirt. They consist of the same things as the dirt. Animals also are one hundred percent dirt, or whatever is in the soil.

So when a plant dies, it goes back to where it came from—you can't find it. When an animal dies, it goes back to where it came from—you can't find it. When man dies, he goes back to the spirit realm.

So whatever something comes from determines the components of which it is made. And whatever something comes from determines its potential. *Potential is related to source.* A plant can be no more than the dirt can be. Likewise, animals can be no more than the dirt can be. Since you came out of God, you have the same components as God and your potential is determined by God.

Wherever something comes from, it has to remain attached to where it came from in order to fulfill itself. All created things must be maintained by their source. Thus plants need soil to live. They can't live without the dirt. If a plant decides, "I'm tired of the soil," it also decides "I'm ready to die." Therefore, if you decide you don't need God, you have also decided never to become all you are capable of being. The potential of everything is related to source; everything must be attached to its source if it is going to fulfill its potential.

Our life depends upon our Source. We came out of God and contain a measure of His ability. But our only hope of fulfilling that ability lies in God. We must be hooked up with God if we are going to tap any of our true potential. Jesus came to bring us back to God so God's original intention when He took man out of Himself could be fulfilled. Thus the key to your full potential is staying related to God.

> If you decide you don't need God, you also have decided never to become all you are capable of being.

## Am the True Vine

*I am the true vine, and my Father is the gardener* (John 15:1).

BOOK QUOTE: *Understanding Your Potential* [Chapter 9]

As a plant cannot fulfill its potential without being in relationship with the soil, so you cannot fulfill your true potential without being related to God. Thus Jesus says in the Book of John: "*I am the true vine*" (John 15:1). Jesus calls Himself the *true vine* because there are a lot of other vines around to get hooked into: education, philosophy, science, even religion.

The word vine here literally means "source of life." Like the grape vine for its branches, Jesus is our Source of life. If you depend on education, all you are going to have is what education can offer—an intellectual stimulation. No matter how many degrees you get, you are living below your potential because you are feeding on a false vine. You will never know your true information capacity if you are stuck on education. There are people who have been out of school for 50 years who don't know any more now than they knew when they were in school. Jesus says, "I am the True Vine." By this statement He implies that there are vines or sources that are not genuine.

The potential of the branches and the vine needs the attention of the gardener. The gardener works in the vineyard trying to bring as much life as possible out of the vines. Often he prunes the vines because he knows there is more life down in the roots. Since he is aware that he isn't getting the full capacity of the vine, he begins to clip some of the branches. Cutting off the old leaves that stop the vine from producing its full potential, the gardener starts to clean up the vine.

Are there some old leaves in your life that have been hanging around for five, ten or fifteen years? Do you need to quit a habit or two so your life more truly reflects the potential of the One who made you? Are you wasting time planning, setting up, committing and feeling guilty about sin? How many hours in a day are you losing to disobedience and rebellion? Prune your life through discipline and obedience to God, who desires your potential to be maximized. Remember, all God's commands and laws are given to maximize your performance and free your potential.

> You're not measuring up to the Source from which you came.

## reed To Obey

*And this is love: that we walk in obedience to His commands. As you have heard from the beginning, His command is that you walk in love* (2 John 1:6).

BOOK QUOTE: *Understanding Your Potential* [Chapter 9]

When God placed Adam and Eve in the garden of Eden, He said, "*You are free to eat from any tree in the garden; but you must not eat from the tree of the knowledge of good and evil, for when you eat of it you will surely die*" (Genesis 2:16-17). God gives you freedom, but He also puts some limitations on you. Whenever you violate your limitations, you are in rebellion against God. The only limitations of your potential are violations of God's Word. If you do anything that doesn't violate the Word of God, you are within your freedom. God gives you freedom to do anything except disobey Him. That's a tremendous freedom. You are free to do anything within the context of God's Word. If God says it's cool, go for it, because the possibilities of your life are all connected with God.

God comes into your life with pruning shearers to free you from your disobedience and rebellion. He comes to take out those things that are stopping you from developing and growing and obeying. Anything that is contrary to the Word of God is subject to God's pruning. He comes into your life to help you clean up your act. He wants you to enjoy the freedom of obedience and life within His limitations. Bearing a pruning shear, God trims the useless and dead wood from your life so you can draw from Him the fresh fullness of your potential.

You are cleansed through the word Jesus speaks to you when you asked Him to forgive you. The lid on your well, put there through your disobedience and satan's deception, has been pried off. You are clean and free to do *anything* that doesn't violate God's Word—free to be all you were created to be and do (whatever He says you can do). What freedom!—freedom that can last, so long as you remain hooked up to God. The Son is Life and the Father is the Maximizer.

> God gives you freedom to do anything except disobey Him.

## Prerequisite for Potential

*Remain in Me, and I will remain in you. No branch can bear fruit by itself; it must remain in the vine. Neither can you bear fruit unless you remain in Me* (John 15:4).

BOOK QUOTE: *Understanding Your Potential* [Chapter 9]

Living a victorious life does not depend on us. It depends on who we are hooked up to. There are many individuals who I expected to be successful in life—their lives showed tremendous potential—but they lost their relationship with their Source. Jesus says, "If you abide in Me, you will be fruitful. But you cannot do it on your own." No branch can live by itself; it must remain attached to the vine. Neither can it bear fruit apart from the vine. Jesus is the true vine. You are a branch. If you remain in Christ and Christ in you, you will bear abundant fruit. If you do not remain in Christ, you are like a branch that withers and is thrown away. No branch can bear fruit if it is not attached. It starts going in the opposite direction. No matter how talented or gifted you are, you will never be truly fulfilled and successful apart from a personal relationship with your Creator-Source.

Thus the secret to a happy, productive life is remaining attached to your Divine Source. If you abide in Christ, His Word will abide in you. You can ask whatever you wish and it will be given to you. God will provide from the depths of His grace…freely, abundantly, victoriously. You don't have to hustle. You don't have to plead. God is always waiting to help you live a full, fruitful, complete life. From His storehouse of riches, God will supply all you can imagine, and more because *He wants you to fulfill your potential.* So long as you remain attached to the Vine and submitted to the discipline of the Gardener, you will know God's blessings. Your potential requires a relationship with its Source.

God created you to exalt and bring glory to His name. When you bear fruit, God is glorified. His name is exalted whenever you use the abilities He stored in you. The whole purpose for your being—to reflect and increase the glory of God—is fulfilled whenever you maximize your potential. God works hard to keep us hooked up with Him. He wants His glory to fill the earth through us.

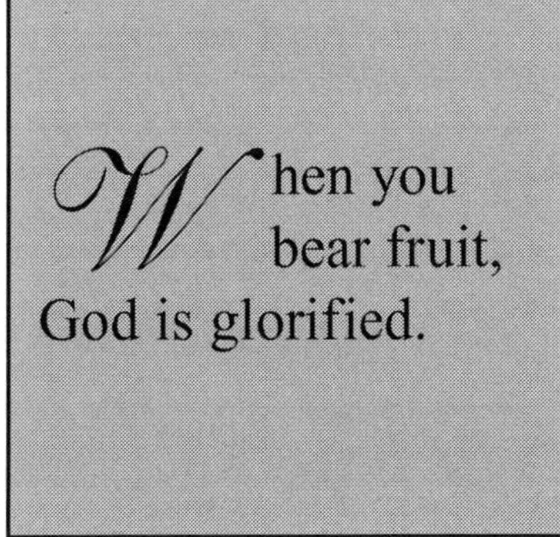

## or Disciples Only

*If you remain in Me and My words remain in you, ask whatever you wish and it will be given you* (John 15:7).

BOOK QUOTE: *Understanding Your Potential* [Chapter 9]

Jesus' words are almost frightening—whatever you wish. God will give you whatever you ask for so long as you remain in Him. What a promise! When you open your life completely to God, the Holy Spirit's crowbar firmly resists satan's attempt to recap your well. The wealth of your potential becomes limitless and free. Whatever you imagine will be done, because God won't allow you to think it unless you can do it.

What kind of life are you living? Are you in tune with Christ or are you off doing your own thing? Is there sin clogging up your pipes, preventing you from accomplishing and achieving your maximum ability? Are you constantly hustling, struggling to make your way in the world? If you are, you probably have not become a disciple of the risen Christ. You see, being a Christian is not enough to fulfill your potential. The word "Christian" was given to us by pagans. Jesus never called us "Christians." This term was given to the disciples in the early Church by the pagans in Antioch.

The Bible calls us "children of God" and "citizens of the Kingdom." We are God's offspring, a people who have been reconnected to their Source. Only disciples, those who are committed to abiding in Christ, will maximize their potential. A disciple is a learner who follows a teacher everywhere he goes. His goal is to learn and keep on learning until he resembles the teacher. Only a disciple experiences full potential. Because his greatest desire is to know and resemble the Master, he spends hours listening to His words. He seeks new visions, revelations and understandings concerning the Master's life and who He calls His disciples to be.

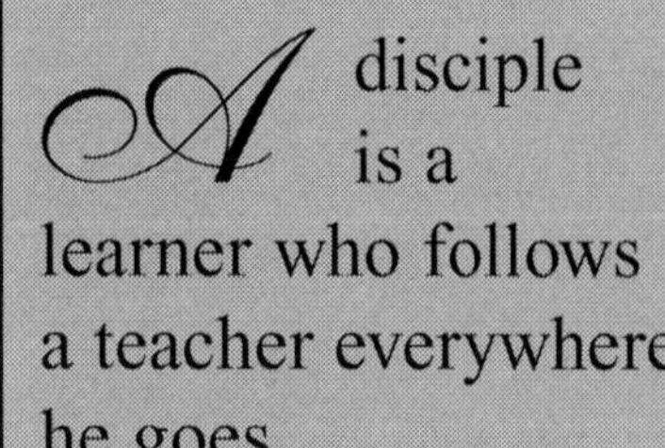

disciple is a learner who follows a teacher everywhere he goes.

## ull Potential

*Then a teacher of the law came to Him and said, "Teacher, I will follow you wherever you go"* (Matthew 8:19).

BOOK QUOTE: *Understanding Your Potential* [Chapter 9]

Only a disciple experiences full potential. Because his greatest desire is to know and resemble the Master, he spends hours listening to His words. He seeks new visions, revelations and understandings concerning the Master's life and who He calls His disciples to be.

I do not consider myself to be great or superior to anyone else, but I decided at the age of 14 that I wanted to understand everything that God has prepared for me. I invested hours in the Word of God—large chunks…sometimes half a day. After 15 years, God said to me, "That's still not enough. Follow me." Over the years He has blessed me with a greater degree of understanding and wisdom from His Word. He's given me revelations of His life, and visions of who He is and who I am and should be. I don't want to stop. I'm not great, but I want to be one of the few. I want *you* to be one of the few. I'll lay down my life to have you be one of the few. Don't fall for the limitations of the world—the lies and deceptions of the lower nature. Find your Source and get connected. Then stay connected. God has chosen you to go and bear fruit—fruit that will last. Abide in Christ, and the Father will give you whatever you wish. Refuse to live below your privileged potential. Reach for the fruit that is still within the branches of your life. Drink deep from the vine and let your life feed others.

> Reach for the fruit that is still within the branches of your life.

# EVIEW the Principles From This Week:

- What God speaks to is the source for what He creates.
- Everything has the same components as its source.
- Nothing can live without being attached to its source.
- Jesus is your Source of life.
- God prunes your life to bring you into the freedom of obedience.
- The key to fulfilling your potential is staying hooked up to God.
- Only disciples—those who are committed to abiding in Christ—will maximize their potential.
- God is glorified when you use your abilities.

## Your Power and Worth

*In a desert land He found him, in a barren and howling waste. He shielded him and cared for him; He guarded him as the apple of His eye* (Deuteronomy 32:10).

BOOK QUOTE: *Understanding Your Potential* [Chapter 10]

In discussing the awesome task of tapping our true and full potential, it is essential that we come to appreciate how important each one of us is and how special we are to God. If you were aware of how much power and worth you have, the first thing that would be affected would be your attitude toward yourself.

Many of us have a difficult time projecting a good attitude toward others because we feel bad about ourselves. Great positive thinkers and personal motivators, along with psychologists, all agree that if you feel good about yourself, then your attitude toward others will be influenced by that attitude. However, for many positive thinking programs, this is simply an attempt to convince one's self by mental assent that you are of value and worth. It's an attempt to convince you of something you don't believe.

On the contrary, what we are discussing here is something different. We are talking here about a fact grounded in truth and reality, and established by the One who created you. Your worth, value, and potential have all been given by God, and there is no formula, test, or scheme to measure the full extent of these qualities and abilities. Therefore I would like to reiterate some principles and concepts that were discussed in earlier chapters. It is essential that you understand these if you are going to tap into your true and full potential.

> The potency of your potential requires eternal life to be realized.

## Potential Unlimited

*And I heard, as it were, the voice of a great multitude, as the sound of many waters and as the sound of mighty thunderings, saying, "Alleluia! For the Lord God Omnipotent reigns!"* (Revelation 19:6 NKJV).

BOOK QUOTE: *Understanding Your Potential* [Chapter 10]

*Everything that is was in God.* In essence, everything that exists came out of God or proceeded out of His creative Spirit. He is the Source of everything. The first verse of the Book of Genesis introduces God as the Creator of all things…"*In the beginning God created the heavens and the earth*" (Genesis 1:1).

But I would again like to take you back before time began, before there was a creation. Let's consider what I call the verse before Genesis 1:1. We'll call it Genesis 1:0. Where was everything before creation came to be? I suggested that the first verse of the Bible could be written as follows:

Before there was a beginning, there was God. Before there was a creation, there was a Creator. Before anything was, there was God (see Genesis 1:0).

The above verse means God did not begin when the beginning began—He began the beginning. He did not start when start got started—He started start. There was no beginning without God. He is the Source, Creator and Sustainer of everything. Nothing exists that He did not create. If it does not exist, it is because He has not yet created it. He is the ultimate Source of everything. Anything and everything that comes after the beginning has to come out of God.

Before anything existed, God had it in Him. That is the reason we ascribe to God only the term *omni-potent*. *Potent* is the word from which we derive the word *potential*. *Omni* is defined as meaning *all* or *everything*. Therefore the ascription *omnipotent* means *one who is* ***all potential*** *or* ***all power—all ability****, seen or unseen, used or unused, manifested or yet unmanifested*. God does not only *have* potential; He is potential—and the Source of all potential. The source of all potential is in the Omnipotent One.

> The source of all potential is in the Omnipotent One.

## The Source of All Potential Is in the Omnipotent One

*...far above all rule and authority, power and dominion, and every title that can be given, not only in the present age but also in the one to come* (Ephesians 1:21).

BOOK QUOTE: *Understanding Your Potential* [Chapter 10]

Principle: the potential of a thing is related to its source. This means wherever something comes from determines the potential it has. The degree or potency of that potential can be measured by the demands made on it by the one who made it. Therefore, the potential or ability of a thing is determined by the purpose for which the creator, manufacturer or maker made it. Every product is designed and engineered by the manufacturer to fulfill its purpose. Therefore its potential is built in. The purpose establishes the demands to be placed on the product, and the demands determine its potential.

This principle is evidenced by all manufacturers who enclose a *manual* with their product detailing the expected performance and potential of their product. The manufacturer wants you to read the manual before using the product so it can tell you what demands to make on the product. They are confident you can make those demands because they have already built into the product the necessary components to fulfill the demands. The potential of a thing is therefore not determined by opinions, assumptions or prejudices, but only by the demands placed on it by the one who made it.

Your true ability and potential should not be measured by the limitations of an academic test or an Intelligence Quotient score. Nor should it be determined by the social, cultural, economic and educational "norms" of your society. Society did not create you. You are not a product of your culture. You are not the offspring of your economy. You were not created by the Department of Education. Therefore, none of these has the right to determine how much potential you really possess. If you want to know how much potential you have, first discover who created or manufactured you. Then check the demands He is making upon your life. Whatever He is demanding of you, *you can do.*

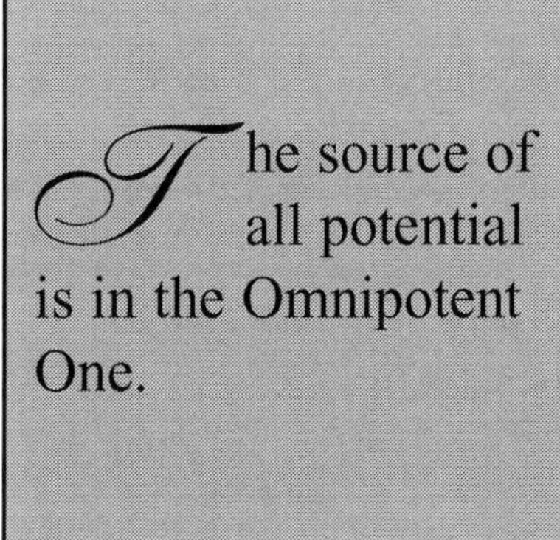

## What Are the Limits of Your Potential?

*Do you not know that your body is a temple of the Holy Spirit, who is in you, whom you have received from God? You are not your own* (1 Corinthians 6:19).

BOOK QUOTE: *Understanding Your Potential* [Chapter 10]

Principle: the potential of a thing is determined by the demands made on it by the one who made it. It seems to me that the people who change the world and significantly impact humanity are those who have discovered the limitless nature of their potential. They are people who decided to take the word impossible out of their dictionaries. If you are going to realize and maximize your full potential, you will have to understand the true nature of your potential. But to do this, you must first understand the process of your creation and the Source from which you came.

In essence, whatever God spoke to became the same material for the thing that came out of what He spoke it from. This process-principle is evidenced in the first chapter of Genesis. For example, when God wanted to create plant life and vegetation, He said: "*Let the land* [dirt, soil] *produce vegetation: seed-bearing plants and trees...*" And it was so. The land produced vegetation (Genesis 1:11-12).

When God wanted to make stars, He said: "*Let there be lights in the expanse of the sky* [the firmament of the heavens—the gasses in space] *to separate the day from the night...*" And it was so (Genesis 1:14-15).

If you examine these Scriptures from Genesis, you will discover: Whatever God wanted He spoke to the material substance from which He wanted it made. He wanted plants to be made out of soil or dirt, so He spoke them out of the earth. That is why, when a plant dies, it decomposes back to the soil. He spoke the stars from the gasses in space; therefore stars are 100 percent high density nuclear gas explosions. When a star "dies," it dissipates into gasses and returns to its original state.

Therefore, when God wanted plants and vegetation, He spoke to the soil. When He wanted stars, He spoke to the gasses. *But when God wanted* ***you*** *(man), He spoke to* ***Himself****.* It is important to understand here that whatever God speaks to produces what God says and is therefore composed of the same material substance. So as plants are soil and stars are gasses, even *so man is spirit, because he came out of God.* Man does not have a spirit, he is spirit—because of the Source from which he came.

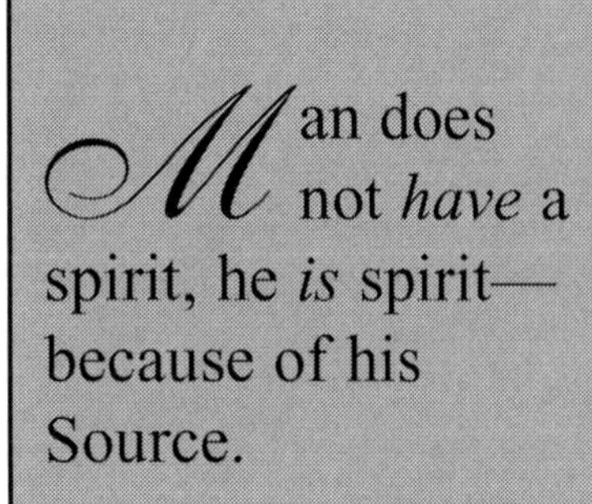

Man does not *have* a spirit, he *is* spirit—because of his Source.

## Related to the Source

*This is how you can recognize the Spirit of God: Every spirit that acknowledges that Jesus Christ has come in the flesh is from God* (1 John 4:2).

BOOK QUOTE: *Understanding Your Potential* [Chapter 10]

Man does not have a spirit, he is spirit—because of the Source from which he came.

The process-principle of creation introduces us to principles that we must understand if we are to fully appreciate the nature of our potential. These principles are evidenced in nature and are scientifically sound. They are as follows:

1. Whatever God wants He speaks to what He wants it made out of.
2. Wherever something came from, it is composed of the same material substance as where it came from. It is a composite of its source.
3. Wherever something came from, it has to be sustained and maintained by where it came from.
4. The potential of a thing cannot be fulfilled without being related to its source.

These principles are clearly demonstrated by God's system of creation in nature. The plants came from the earth and they *must* remain related (attached) to the earth in order to live and be fruitful. The stars came from the gasses in space and *must* therefore remain in space in order to remain effective. The fish came from the water and *must* remain related (submerged) in water in order to live. The animals are products of the soil from which God spoke them and must remain related (feed on) soil (dirt) products in order to live. This holds true for man also: Man (spirit) came out of God (source) and must remain related (attached) to God (his source) in order to live.

Man must remain related to God, his Source, to live.

## Man Needs God

*Jesus answered, "I am the way and the truth and the life. No one comes to the Father except through Me"* (John 14:6).

BOOK QUOTE: *Understanding Your Potential* [Chapter 10]

As the plants need dirt and the fish need water, so man needs God. If man is to realize and maximize his true potential, a relationship with God is not an option. It is a necessity. If man is to become all he was purposed to be, God is not an alternative for man, but a requirement.

This point is crucial because it helps us understand the ultimatums of Jesus and the emphatic demands of God the Father. The call of the Kingdom is not that we *should* be born of the *spirit*, but that we *must* be born of the *spirit*. Jesus didn't say, "I am *a way*," but "*I am the way*" (John 14:6). It was also He who said, "*I am the vine; you are the branches. ...apart from Me you can do nothing*" (see John 15:2-8).

This principle is also communicated in God's command to Adam in Genesis 2:17 when He stated: "*You must not eat from the tree of the knowledge of good and evil, for when you eat of it you will surely die.*" God really meant: "The day you rebel or detach yourself from your Source, you will cancel your full potential. You will never fulfill the purpose for which I created you." Sin, therefore, can be understood as man's declaration of independence from his Source. Please note that even as trees gradually die after having their roots separated from the soil, so Adam, after disobeying his Source, died spiritually. Though Adam's spiritual death was instant, the physical effects of that death were not manifested until 930 years later. This is evidence that no matter how far man progresses or how much he accomplishes, he can never experience his full potential without a personal relationship with God, his Source.

*The key to knowing your true potential is to know your Source. You will never understand, realize or maximize your true and full potential without a relationship with your Source. A man without a relationship with God (his Source) has limited his potential. He can never attain what he is capable of.*

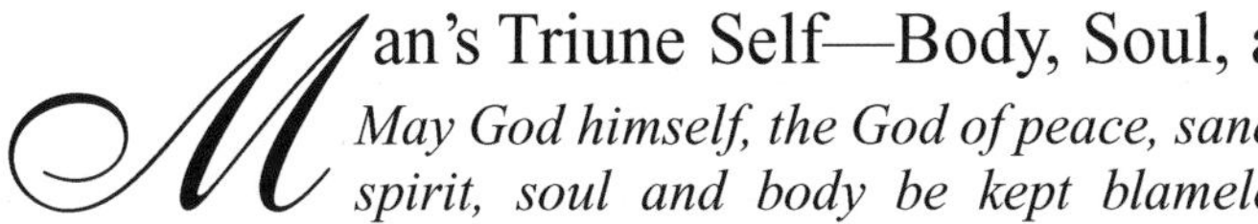

## Man's Triune Self—Body, Soul, and Spirit

*May God himself, the God of peace, sanctify you through and through. May your whole spirit, soul and body be kept blameless at the coming of our Lord Jesus Christ* (1 Thessalonians 5:23).

BOOK QUOTE: *Understanding Your Potential* [Chapter 10]

Man is a triune being created after the image and likeness of his Creator-Source. He consists of three distinct yet intricately related dimensions. Each dimension is designed to fulfill a specific purpose in God's plan for His creation. Each realm of man is designed with the potential to maximize its function and fulfill its intended purpose. But the potential of each dimension cannot be understood apart from its Source. Let us now take a closer look at each part of man and explore the untapped potential that lies buried there.

As man, in his pursuit of knowledge about his world and environment (through the disciplines of science), explores the various aspects of creation, he reaches the general conclusion that the magnificent mystery of the human body still stands at the apex of all natural forms of creation. For decades, specialists have dedicated their lives to the study of the physiological potential of the human body—its ability to handle pressure; to adjust itself to varying environmental changes; to defend itself against disease, danger or threat; to maintain its stamina under physical exertion. Yet, despite man's technological advancements and his scientific explorations of this masterpiece of creation, scientists continue to admit that they have limited knowledge concerning the potential of this mechanism of precision we call *the human body*.

The human body has been described as 80 percent water (fluid), with a degree of calcium, fiber and tissue. But to fully appreciate the true potential of the human body, we must understand the *purpose* for its creation.

Man is a triune being created after the image and likeness of his Creator Source.

## EVIEW the Principles From This Week:

When God created the earth and made the fullness of its beauty, He used the following principles:

1. He purposed and decided what He wanted.
2. He then decided what kind of material substance He wanted it made from.
3. He then spoke to the substance or material from which He wanted it made.
4. And whatever He said to what He was speaking to came out of what He spoke to—exactly what He said.
5. Whatever came out of what God spoke to was made of the same material substance from which it came.

## The Purpose of the Body

*Therefore do not let sin reign in your mortal body so that you obey its evil desires* (Romans 6:12).

BOOK QUOTE: *Understanding Your Potential* [Chapter 10]

To understand the purpose of the body, we must understand the purpose for man. When God created man, He created him a *spirit* being with a *physical* house (body). Then God placed him on the physical earth. God purposed and intended to rule and dominate the physical realm from the invisible realm through the agency of *mankind.* In essence, God desired to control the *seen* from the *unseen* through the *unseen* living in the *seen* on the *seen*. God desired to have His Kingdom extended from Heaven to earth by allowing His Spirit to reign through man's spirit as man dominated the earth through his soul and manifested His nature through the body. Therefore, the triune nature of man is designed for the following purposes:

1. Man's spirit: To relate to God (pick up the spirit world).
2. Man's soul: To relate to the mental realm (intelligence).
3. Man's body: To relate to the physical environment (pick up earth).

The human body was thus specifically designed to relate to and pick up the earth or physical realm. God did not intend the body to relate to the spiritual or supernatural world. It is essential, then, that we do not judge our true potential by the abilities or limitations of our physical bodies. For this reason, our five senses are specifically designed to "pick up" our natural environment. Our powers of sight, touch, hearing, smell, and taste are all related to the natural, physical world. The potential of our bodies is therefore governed by its physical capabilities. God never intended man to be controlled or limited by his physical body. You were not created to be intimidated by your environment.

God never intended man to be controlled or limited by his physical body.

## From Revelation to Information—From Discernment to Sense

*Since we live by the Spirit, let us keep in step with the Spirit* (Galatians 5:25).

BOOK QUOTE: *Understanding Your Potential* [Chapter 10]

Man's original state in the garden of Eden, before the fall, was one of perfect union and fellowship with God. He was designed to live from the *inside* to the *outside*, from his *spirit* to his *body*. God designed man to be *led* by his spirit, not *driven* by his environment. Man was intended to live through spiritual *discernment*, not physical *senses*. But when Adam (the first man) disobeyed God, he destroyed his fellowship and communion with the Spirit of God (see Genesis 3). The consequence was death.

Death is isolation from the spirit world of God. Through disobedience, man's spirit lost contact with the Source of Heaven. As a result, man became a victim of his *soul* (mind, will, emotions) and his *body* (five senses). His life became governed by his external environment as his five senses controlled his existence.

Immediately after Adam and Eve disobeyed God's command, "*the eyes of both of them were opened, and they* ***knew*** *that they were naked*" (Genesis 3:7 NAS). The word *knew* comes from the concept *to know*, from which we get our word *knowledge*. In essence, Adam and Eve suddenly became aware of their external environment. They began to live life from the knowledge they gained from their *senses*. That was the birth of *education*.

From that day on, man measured his life, worth and value by his environment. And the relationship between man and his environment gave birth to humanistic philosophy. In reality, the body and its sensual capacity became man's measure of reality. Man started living and interpreting his existence according to the *information* he gained through the senses of *his* body, instead of the *revelation* received through his spirit from the Spirit of God. Man's fall placed his body in a position it had not been designed to occupy. This change has caused man to limit his potential ability to the capabilities of his senses and his physical body.

God designed man to be *led* by his spirit, not *driven* by his environment.

## Dignified Dirt

*But we have this treasure in earthen vessels that the excellence of the power may be of God and not of us* (2 Corinthians 4:7 NKJV).

BOOK QUOTE: *Understanding Your Potential* [Chapter 10]

The human body was specifically designed to relate to and pick up the earth or physical realm. God did not intend the body to relate to the spiritual or supernatural world. It is essential, then, that we do not judge our true potential by the abilities or limitations of our physical bodies. For this reason, our five senses are specifically designed to "pick up" our natural environment. Our powers of sight, touch, hearing, smell, and taste are all related to the natural, physical world. The potential of our bodies is therefore governed by its physical capabilities. God never intended man to be controlled or limited by his physical body. You were not created to be intimidated by your environment.

No matter how majestic and wonderful the human body is, we must be careful to remember the reality of its composition. According to Genesis 2:7, the Manufacturer of this magnificent masterpiece made and formed it from the "*dust of the ground*." The body is 100 percent *dirt*. The apostle Paul called the body a "[heavenly] *treasure in earthen vessels*" (2 Corinthians 4:7). The principle we discussed earlier—the potential of a thing is related to its source—must be considered. If the physical body is related to the earth, it must be sustained and maintained by the earth. The body must feed on soil (dirt) in order to live (plants, animals, fish, etc.). We must, therefore, understand that our bodies—though they have tremendous potentials, powers, capabilities and values—must never become the full measure of our potential.

> Our bodies must never become the full measure of our potential.

## Physical Handicap—Myth or Master

*Therefore we do not lose heart. Though outwardly we are wasting away, yet inwardly we are being renewed day by day* (2 Corinthians 4:16).

BOOK QUOTE: *Understanding Your Potential* [Chapter 10]

There are millions of physically handicapped individuals who, because of their society's concept of potential, have resigned themselves to a life of self-pity, depression and isolation. There are many who have confused their bodies with their true selves. They have mistaken the "house" for the "resident."

But history gives ample evidence of thousands who have freed themselves of the myth that their bodies should dictate their true potential. They have defied the limitations of their "dirt houses" and soared to the unlimited heights of their soul's and spirit's potential. Many have turned their wheelchairs into the cockpits of jetliners as they explored the heights of their capabilities. Other have used their walking canes to pole-vault them into positions that changed the world. Some transformed their world of silence to produce sounds that many are enjoying today. Still others have used their blindness to see beyond the physical. They have captured sights others long to see.

Helen Keller refused to be blinded by others' opinions of her ability—she changed the attitude of the world. Sir Winston Churchill refused to be muted by his speech impediment and physical handicap—while a member of the British Parliament and later the Prime Minister of Britain, he delivered some of history's most life-changing orations.

What is your handicap? Is it a wheelchair, a bed, a walker, the socio-economic status of your family, or the color of your skin? Is it the ghetto, your parents' lifestyle, the level of your education, or a terminal illness? Are you disabled by divorce, the absence of your parents, incest, or child abuse? Are you blind or deaf? Do you have a speech impediment or a poor self-esteem? Whatever your *perceived* handicap may be, you must never allow your true potential to become a victim of the limitations of your physical body or your environment. Reach beyond your grasp. Your body is not your full potential.

> Do not allow your true potential to become a victim of the limitations of your physical body or environment.

## Reach Beyond Your Grasp

*As it is written: "I have made you a father of many nations." He is our father in the sight of God, in whom he believed... Against all hope, Abraham in hope believed and so became the father of many nations.... Without wavering in his faith, he faced the fact that his body was as good as dead...being fully persuaded that God had the power to do what He had promised* (Romans 4:17-21).

BOOK QUOTE: *Understanding Your Potential* [Chapter 10]

I encourage you to develop and maintain a correct attitude toward your body. Learn to see it from the perspective of God, its Creator, who (through the apostle Paul) calls it "*the temple of the living God*" (see 2 Corinthians 6:16). God admonishes you to keep your temple holy, clean and healthy. You are the steward of this precious earthly vessel. Its maintenance and effective operation are your responsibility. Like any essential equipment, your body needs regular checkups, proper amounts of fuel (food), periods of recuperation and recreation (rest, sleep, and fasting), and invigorating exercise. But do not allow your body to become the dictator of your potential. You are not your body.

The biblical perspective on the body is revealed in a number of clear declarations:

> *Do you not know that your body is a temple of the Holy Spirit, who is in you...? ...Therefore honor God with your body* (1 Corinthians 6:19).

> *Therefore we do not lose heart. Though outwardly we are wasting away, yet inwardly we are being renewed day by day* (2 Corinthians 4:16).

Please note that the previous reference describes the physical body as being in a state of daily disintegration. If we determine our potential by the condition of our bodies—whether we are handicapped or relatively healthy and fit—we are still relying on a premise that is constantly dissolving. You and I must not allow any physical impediment or the natural aging process to immobilize the potential that lies within us.

One of the greatest figures in history is described in the Bible as "the father of the faithful." Abraham demonstrated the tremendous potential of the soul and the spirit, in contrast to the limited potential of the body (see Romans 4:17-21).

> Do not allow your body to become the dictator or your potential.

The key to Abraham's success is related to his attitude toward his body. The demands made upon him by God were beyond the natural capacity of his physical body. He was handicapped by age and his wife was handicapped by a barren womb. But they considered not their bodies and believed that God had provided the potential to fulfill the demand being placed upon them. You must refuse to limit your true potential by the limitations of your physical body.

## The Potential of the Soul

*The mind of sinful man is death, but the mind controlled by the Spirit is life and peace* (Romans 8:6).

BOOK QUOTE: *Understanding Your Potential* [Chapter 10]

Some years ago a famous pop singer sang a song entitled "I'm a Soul Man." That title became a common phrase throughout the Western world. I suspect he was referring to the cultural-ethnic orientation of the Afro-American artistic expression. But the statement communicates both a statement of truth and a myth. As we discussed earlier in this chapter, the *soul* is the triunity of the *mind*, the *will*, and the *emotions*. The soul was created for the purpose of receiving *revelation* from the spirit-man to communicate it to the body and *information* from the physical senses to transmit it to the spirit-man. In essence, the soul was designed to be the "*servant*" of the spirit-man, and the body was designed to be the "*servant*" of the soul. Man is a spirit, lives in a body, and possesses a soul. But the fall of man changed that.

When Adam disobeyed God's words, his spirit lost fellowship with God's Spirit and was paralyzed. The soul became a victim of his body and the physical senses. When *revelation* from the spirit-man was replaced by *information* from the physical senses, man became a victim of his environment with education as his primary goal. In fact, man was reduced to a "soul man." Never allow a teacher's opinion or the score on an academic test or the fact that you didn't complete your formal education to dictate the magnitude of your potential. You are as potent as your Creator says you are. The exercise of the soul can make you smart, but not wise. Paul states in 1 Corinthians 1:25: "*The foolishness of God is wiser than man's wisdom and the weakness of God is stronger than man's strength*."

Man is a spirit, lives in a body, and possesses a soul.

## The Potential of Your Spirit

*And if the Spirit of Him who raised Jesus from the dead is living in you, He who raised Christ from the dead will also give life to your mortal bodies through His Spirit, who lives in you* (Romans 8:11).

BOOK QUOTE: *Understanding Your Potential* [Chapter 10]

The measure of your true potential is your *spirit*. God has always intended that you and I would live from the inside—from the spirit-man in communion with the eternal *Spirit of God*. Without that relationship, you are limited to the potential of your soul and your body. Paul wrote: "*The **mind** of sinful man is death, but the **mind** controlled by the Spirit is life and peace*" (Romans 8:6).

The mind controlled by the Spirit is like a fountain of life gushing forth with the potential of God through the Spirit of God. Paul also writes: "*Those who live according to the sinful nature have their minds set on what that nature desires; but those who live in accordance with the **Spirit** have their minds set on what the **Spirit** desires*" (Romans 8:5).

The Spirit of God has some desires. I believe these desires are God's original predestined will for your life as written in the book described in Psalm 139:16. If you allow the Holy Spirit to fellowship with and minister to your spirit, and you remain hooked up to the Source of your potential, then you will live according to the knowledge of God's revelation of your true potential. God has information on your ability and potential that will astonish you and your family.

The measure of your true potential is hidden in the Spirit of God. It can only be tapped by a relationship between your spirit and His. Go after the deep things in God that are related to you as the deep of your potential calls to the deep of the *Omni-potent* One. Decide to discover God's concept of your potential.

God has information on your ability and potential that will astonish you.

## REVIEW the Principles From This Week:

- The key to knowing your true potential is to know your Source—God.
- Man is a triune being: body, soul, and spirit.
- The spirit is intended to relate to God, the soul to the mental realm and the body to the physical environment.
- Death is isolation from the spirit world. We are spiritually dead at our physical birth.
- Your body is not the measure of your true potential.
- Your soul (mind, will, and emotions) is not the measure of your true potential.
- The measure of your true potential is your spirit.
- God's desires for your life are discerned by your spirit through fellowship and communication with the Holy Spirit.

## God's Instruction Manual

*Your Word is a lamp to my feet and a light for my path* (Psalm 119:105).

BOOK QUOTE: *Understanding Your Potential* [Chapter 11]

If you want a piece of equipment to operate at its maximum potential, you have to follow the manufacturer's instructions. If you don't follow the instructions, you may damage the product—or at least you won't know what you can expect from it. Only if you follow the instructions can you expect the product to meet the demands specified by the manufacturer—demands that equal what the manufacturer designed and built into the product.

We are excellent, complexly designed, tremendously built, intricately put together pieces of equipment. But we don't know what we can do. We can't even imagine the full extent of our potential. Knowing this, God sent us a manual that contains a description of our parts. He said, "Now this first part is your spirit and the second part is your soul and the third part is your body. Now here is what the body is supposed to do…here is what the soul can do…here is what the spirit can do." God also tells us the potential of this equipment called human beings. In His manual, He lists all the things we are capable of doing.

When God first presented this piece of equipment called man, something went wrong. Instead of taking it back to the manufacturer to be fixed, we took it to a second-rate, second-class, unskilled technician. And look what he did. He muddled the job. We submitted God's equipment and product to satan, who is an unauthorized dealer with no genuine parts.

But God loved us so much that, even though the warranty had run out, He decided to take back the product. Though someone else has tried to fix us and has messed us up, God is starting all over again—and He's putting in His own parts. God is rebuilding and remaking us. He knows us better than anybody else, because He is our Creator. His Word, the Bible, reveals much about His attitude toward our potential.

> God's Word, the Bible, reveals much about His attitude toward our potential.

## God's Word on Your Potential—Part 1

*Without faith it is impossible to please God...* (Hebrews 11:6).

BOOK QUOTE: *Understanding Your Potential* [Chapter 11]

You have the potential to be in God's class.

> *So God created man in His own image; in the image of God He created him; male and female He created them* (Genesis 1:27).

God sees you as being in His class. Because He made you in His image, you have the potential to be in the God class—which is spirit.

You have the potential to operate like God.

> *Then God said, "Let Us make man in Our image, in Our likeness..."* (Genesis 1:26).

When God made you in His likeness, He did not make you to *look* like Him. He made you to *function* like Him. That's what *likeness* literally means. When God created you, He made you to operate like Him. If you are not functioning like God, you are "malfunctioning," because God wired and designed you to function like Him. How does God function? His Word says, "*Without faith it is impossible to please God"* (Hebrews 11:6). God functions by faith. You and I were designed to operate by faith. Our potential therefore needs faith in order to be maximized.

God sees in you the potential to dominate, rule and subdue the whole earth.

> [God said] *"...let them rule over the fish of the sea and the birds of the air, over the livestock, over all the earth, and over all the creatures that move along the ground."...God blessed them and said to them "...Rule over the fish of the sea and the birds of the air and over every living creature that moves on the ground"* (Genesis 1:26,28).

God created you to rule over all the earth and everything that creeps in it. He will never demand anything of you He didn't already build into you. Thus, if the earth in any way is dominating you, you are malfunctioning. You were not created to give into cigarettes or submit to alcohol. God did not intend for you to be controlled by drugs, sex, money, power, or greed. If any of these are governing you, you are living below your privilege. Because God has already declared it to be so, you have the ability to dominate the earth. Everything in the earth must be under your subjection, not mastering you.

> When God created you, He made you to operate like Him.

# God's Word on Your Potential—Part 2

*For the Word of the Lord is right and true; He is faithful in all He does* (Psalm 33:6).

BOOK QUOTE: *Understanding Your Potential* [Chapter 11]

You have the ability to be fruitful and reproduce after your kind.

God blessed them and said to them, "*Be fruitful and increase in number; fill the earth and subdue it*" (Genesis 1:28).

Again God is calling forth something that's already in you. He didn't tell the man and the woman to *try* to be fruitful, He simply told them to *do* it. He knew they already had the ability to multiply and reproduce and fill the earth. You too can reproduce yourself. He always places the potential inside before He calls it forth. Whatever God calls you to do, He has already built in.

You have the ability to imagine and plan to do anything.

> *The Lord said, "If as one people speaking the same language they have begun to do this, then nothing they plan to do will be impossible for them"* (Genesis 11:6).

God gave you the ability to imagine and plan and bring into being anything you desire. Now if you read this passage in its entirety, the people to whom God was talking had planned to build a tower. God didn't stop them from building a tower by cutting off their potential. He stopped them by confusing their language, because He couldn't stop their potential.

You have the same potential God saw in those people. If you decide to do something, and you believe in it hard enough and commit yourself to work for it long enough, nothing in the universe can stop you. That's what God is saying. If you want to do anything, God already said, "You can do it." Only if you lack the commitment to follow after your dream will your dream remain unfinished. The potential to do and plan anything is in you if you will believe and persevere.

You have the potential to believe impossibilities into possibilities.

...*Everything is possible for him who believes* (Mark 9:23).

Not only are you able to plan, but you also have the ability to believe something that seems impossible and actually make it possible. If you can abandon yourself to an idea and sacrifice all you have for that idea, God says, "It's possible for that idea to come to pass."

> If you want to do anything, God already said, "You can do it."

## God's Word on Your Potential—Part 3

*Your Word, O Lord, is eternal; it stands firm in the heavens* (Psalm 119:89).

BOOK QUOTE: *Understanding Your Potential* [Chapter 11]

You have the potential to influence physical and spiritual matter.

> *I will give to you the keys of the kingdom of Heaven; whatever you bind on earth will be bound in Heaven, and whatever you loose on earth will be loosed in Heaven* (Matthew 16:19).

Jesus is talking here about your power to influence what's on earth as well as what's in Heaven. If you bind something on earth, it will be bound in Heaven. You have influence in Heaven. Likewise, if you loose something on earth, Heaven has to do the same thing—loose it. You have the power to influence things in both realms of earth and Heaven.

You have the potential to receive whatever you ask.

> *If you remain in Me and My words remain in you, ask whatever you wish, and it will be given you* (John 15:7).

God says you have the potential to receive whatever you ask. That's frightening. You have a blank check—but there is one condition on the cashing of that check: You must abide in Christ, and His words must abide in you. If that condition is met, you can ask anything in Jesus' name and it will be done for you. Jesus wants to knock the limits off your mind. But first He requires that you stay hooked up with God. Then He says, "Go ahead and ask me for anything. I'll do whatever you ask." What potential! That's God's word on *you.*

You have the potential to do greater works than Jesus did.

> *I tell you the truth, anyone who has faith in Me will do what I have been doing. He will do even greater things than these, because I am going to the Father* (John 14:12).

Jesus sees in you the potential to do greater things than He did. If Jesus says you have that potential, it's in there somewhere. Remember, whatever God says, you can do. He won't ask you to do anything He hasn't already wired you to do.

God believes in you. He knows the vastness of your potential. If He gives you an assignment, He's already given you the ability to fulfill what He asks. Along with His *demand* always comes the *capability* to meet that demand. But remember: to release your potential, you must be related to your Source. Only as you are connected to God, can you fulfill and maximize your true potential.

> God says you have the potential to receive whatever you ask.

## Say "Yes" to Jesus

*May the grace of the Lord Jesus Christ, and the love of God, and the fellowship of the Holy Spirit be with you all* (2 Corinthians 13:14).

BOOK QUOTE: *Understanding Your Potential* [Chapter 11]

Sin, or rebellion against God, clogs up our potential. Disobedience to God may have stunted your capacity for growth. But God sees and cares about that problem. He sent Jesus into the world to die for you. Jesus doesn't have a problem knowing who He is and what He can do. *You* have that problem. Jesus came to die so you can know who you are and what is the fullness of *your* potential. He came to open up the capacity of who you are—to unclog your true self.

Calvary is God's way of providing the means to unplug your true potential. Because disobedience has capped off your potential, God offers you forgiveness and hope through Jesus Christ. In your plugged up state, you can't begin to touch your true ability. Only after you say "yes" to Jesus (and your spirit begins to communicate and fellowship again with the Holy Spirit) can you start the journey of fulfilling all the potential God planted within you before you were born.

It is my earnest desire that you will realize the awesome wealth of potential residing in you. But more important than this potential is the necessity that you understand your need for a personal relationship with Your Creator through the agency He has provided, Jesus Christ.

I encourage you to pray the following prayer with me in faith:

Dear heavenly Father, Creator and Manufacturer of my life, today I submit my life to You, totally surrendering the product of my whole life to You for complete repair, maintenance and renewal in Jesus Christ. I confess Him as the only Savior of my life and submit to Him as my Lord. By faith I this moment receive the Holy Spirit, who, by His power, makes me an eternal citizen of Your Kingdom of Heaven. I commit myself to serve and acknowledge You in all my ways as I endeavor to maximize my potential for Your praise and glory…

This I pray in Jesus' Name, Amen.

Calvary is God's way of providing the means to unplug your true potential.

## Ten Keys to Releasing Your Potential – Part 1

*His divine power has given us everything we need for life and godliness through our knowledge of Him who called us by His own glory and goodness* (2 Peter 1:3).

BOOK QUOTE: *Understanding Your Potential* [Chapter 11]

Here are first five keys to releasing your full potential.

**Key #1**—You must know (be related to) your Source.

The *warranty/guarantee* agreement is set by the manufacturer if he is to take responsibility for the maximum performance, maintenance, and servicing of the product.

The same relationship exists between *God* and *man*. God guarantees the maximum performance of our potential if we submit to the conditions, specifications, and standards set by Him.

**Key #2**—You must understand how the product was designed to function.

Every manufacturer designs, develops, and produces his product to function in a specific manner.

God created man and designed him to function like He does—*by faith and love*. Our potential cannot be released without faith and love. Fear and hatred cause the short-circuit of our potential.

**Key #3**—You must know your purpose.

Every product exists for a specific purpose.

God created you and gave you birth for a purpose. Purpose gives birth to responsibility, and responsibility makes demands on potential.

**Key #4**—You must understand your resources.

All manufacturers provide access to the necessary resources for the proper maintenance, sustenance, and operation of their products.

God provided for human beings tremendous material and physical resources to sustain and maintain us as we proceed in realizing, developing, and maximizing our potential.

**Key #5**—You must have the right environment.

Environment consists of the conditions that have a direct or indirect effect on the performance, function, and development of a thing.

God created everything to flourish within a specific environment. The fall of man contaminated his environment and poisoned the atmosphere of our potential. The key to releasing your true potential is the restoration of God's original environment. Jesus came to restore us to the Father. He sent the Holy Spirit to restore our internal environment.

> God has established a plan for the maximum performance and release of your potential.

## en Keys to Releasing Your Potential – Part 2

*Therefore, my dear friends, as you have always obeyed—not only in my presence, but now much more in my absence—continue to work out your salvation with fear and trembling* (Philippians 2:12).

BOOK QUOTE: Understanding Your Potential [Chapter 11]

Here are the remaining keys to releasing your full potential.

**Key #6**—You must work out your potential.

Potential is dormant ability. But ability is useless until it is given responsibility.

Work is a major key to releasing your potential. Potential must be exercised and demands made on it, otherwise it will remain potential. Good ideas do not bring success. To release your true potential, you must be willing to work.

**Key #7**—You must cultivate your potential.

Potential is like a seed. It is buried ability and hidden power that need to be cultivated. You must feed your potential the fertilizer of good positive company, give it the environment of encouragement, pour out the water of the Word of God, and bathe it in the sunshine of personal prayer.

**Key #8**—You must guard your potential.

With all the wealth of your potential, you must be careful to guard and protect it. The Bible calls your potential a *treasure* in earthen vessels. You must guard your visions and dreams from sin, discouragement, procrastination, failures, opinions, distractions, traditions, and compromise.

**Key #9**—You must share your potential.

God created the entire heavens and earth with the potential principle, which can only be fulfilled when it is shared. True potential and fulfillment in life is not what is accomplished, but who benefits from them. Your deposit was given to enrich and inspire the lives of others.

**Key #10**—You must know and understand the laws of limitation.

Freedom and power are two of the most important elements in our lives. Potential is the essence of both. Potential is power. But freedom needs law to be enjoyed, and power needs responsibility to be effective. God has set laws and standards to protect our potential and to secure our success. Obedience is protection for potential.

All of these keys and principles are proven throughout human history to be true. Any violation of these laws limits the release and maximization of your potential. Commit yourself to obeying the Manufacturer. Then watch your life unfold as you discover the hidden ability that was always within you.

> Commit yourself to obeying the Manufacturer.

EVIEW the Ten Keys to Releasing Potential:

- Key #1—You must know (be related to) your Source.
- Key #2—You must understand how the product was designed to function.
- Key #3—You must know your purpose.
- Key #4—You must understand your resources.
- Key #5—You must have the right environment.
- Key #6—You must work out your potential.
- Key #7—You must cultivate your potential.
- Key #8—You must guard your potential.
- Key #9—You must share your potential.
- Key #10—You must know and understand the laws of limitation.

## What Are You Doing With Your Potential?

*For everyone who has will be given more, and he will have an abundance. Whoever does not have, even what he has will be taken from him* (Matthew 25:29).

BOOK QUOTE: *Understanding Your Potential* [Chapter 12]

The Bible tells us a story about people who decided to build a city with a tower that reached to the heavens. When God saw how committed the builders were to their task He said, "*...nothing they plan to do will be impossible for them*." So He came down and confused their languages so they couldn't work together (see Genesis 11:8).

Do you think God was against the tower? No. God was against the goal of the tower. They did not have a relationship with God. They were ungodly men and women who intended to build a tower to Heaven so *their* name could be great. They weren't interested in making God's name great; they wanted to make a name for themselves.

When God saw how committed they were to their task, He knew He had to stop them. Otherwise, they would be able to do anything they wanted to.

Man has accomplished many things without God. Many inventors in the world are ungodly people. Most of the people who do great feats and accomplish great exploits are ungodly people. Imagine what would happen if they were hooked up with God. Jesus came to provide that hookup. When God saw what we could and should do, it disappointed Him that we were not aware of it. So He paid the greatest price necessary—the cost of His own life—to release our full potential. Then He said, "Now go on, son. Do all you can dream. If you can think it, daughter, you can do it."

Yet many of us still live below the level of our true ability. We have settled for the standards established by the opinions of others regarding our potential. We are afraid to move beyond our dreams to action. It is more comfortable to think about all we *might* do instead of working to achieve what we *can* do. People who change the world are people who stop dreaming and wake up. They don't just wish, they act.

If you have accepted Jesus as your Lord and Savior, I'm here to encourage you to move on with the real things of God. What have you done since you were saved? What have you accomplished?

> God paid the greatest price necessary—His own life—to release our full potential.

## ife Is More Than Shelter, Food, or Security

*Therefore do not worry about tomorrow, for tomorrow will worry about itself. Each day has enough trouble of its own* (Matthew 6:34).

BOOK QUOTE: *Understanding Your Potential* [Chapter 12]

Maslow, one of the greatest influences on the thought patterns of psychology in our world, theorized that man is driven by his base needs. He believed that your most immediate need becomes your controlling factor. Therefore, your first instinct is to find shelter, second food, and third security or protection. Then you begin to move up the ladder of becoming self-realized and self-actualized, of getting self-esteem and all the rest of that stuff. According to this theory, human beings are driven by their base needs.

In the sixth chapter of Matthew, Jesus challenges that thought pattern. He instructs us to live from the perspective of what exists that we cannot see, instead of being totally caught up in the details and needs of our daily lives. God lives and thinks in the potential. He always sees things that have not yet been manifested. Faith, too, lives in the potential not in the present. Jesus simply asks us to have faith—to believe in God's goodness and care.

In teaching His followers that food, drink, clothes, and shelter are not the most important things in life, Jesus directly contradicts the psychological theories of our world. He dares you to follow God and think in the opposite. God doesn't start with your wants, but with who you are. God wants you to first know who you are. Then you will realize you deserve the things. In God's design, you deserve the things because you are somebody.

According to God, Maslow was wrong—and I go with God. There are people who have everything, but they still don't know who they are. People accumulate things with the hope that the things will make them somebody. But you don't become somebody by accumulating things. Ask the guy at the top who can't sleep. Ask the guy who has everything except peace and love and joy in his heart. Maslow was wrong. God desires to give you self-worth and self-esteem first. He wants you to know who you are *first*.

Jesus simply asks us to have faith—to believe in God's goodness and care.

## What's Really Important?

*But seek first His kingdom and His righteousness, and all these things will be given to you as well* (Matthew 6:33).

BOOK QUOTE: *Understanding Your Potential* [Chapter 12]

I have met so many people who have everything except the knowledge of who they are. Jesus said, "Why worry about these things? Life is so much more than these things about which you worry. Life is peace and love and joy and patience and gentleness..."

Seek first the things of God and everything else you need will just fall into place. The mind controlled by the Spirit of God is full of life and peace. Peace is so important to a fulfilled life. It goes hand in hand with the life Jesus came to bring. You don't have to worry when you know what is coming. When you live by the Spirit in the realm of the unseen and the invisible, there is no reason to worry. God is holding what is in store for you, because all things that are, were and are in God.

If you'll let Him, God will work it all out for you. Through your spirit talking with His Spirit, He'll assure you everything is going to be OK. You don't have to worry if God's already told you how a particular situation is going to turn out. Relax and commit yourself to maximize your potential. Preoccupy yourself with this assignment and purpose for your life, knowing that whatever God asks for He provides for.

When we are distracted by our drive for personal security and our search for identity, we rarely achieve our true potential. We are so caught up trying to make it *through* life that we don't have time to be *in* life.

You came out of God. He created you to look and think and act like Him so you would display His greatness, majesty and sovereignty. The summit of God's desires for your life is that you will show through your being who He is.

Your potential is not determined by what you look like or how far you went in school. Nor is it determined by what others think and expect from you. God, your Creator, determines the extent of your ability. Through the Holy Spirit, He enables you to develop and experience your entire potential. God makes it possible for you to do and be much more than anyone (including you) expects. You may not look smart, but if the One who made you demands smartness from you, it's in there somewhere.

> You don't need things to enjoy life—you need life to enjoy things.

## Wishing Is Not Enough—Dare to Desire

*Therefore I say unto you, What things soever ye desire, when ye pray, believe that ye receive them, and ye shall have them* (Mark 11:24 KJV).

BOOK QUOTE: *Understanding Your Potential* [Chapter 12]

Faith is not geared to what does not exist—it relates to everything that is not seen. Faith is "*being sure of what we hope for and certain of what we do not see*" (Hebrews 11:1). It deals with potential—what you yet can see, do, be and experience. Faith says, "I can't see it, but I believe it is there." Faith never deals with what you have done, but with what you yet could do.

Living by faith requires looking at the unseen, because everything that is, was in God; and *everything you could be is in you now, waiting for you to make demands on it by faith in God.*

Read Mark 11:24 above. Very often the Church has misread the word *desire*. We have expected, perhaps, that the word *desire* means "what we are dreaming about." No. *Desire* is "craving enough to sacrifice for." Only if we are willing to die for what we desire will we receive it.

God is pregnant with everything that isn't yet visible—including what you ask for in prayer. When you ask for something in faith, it is already on the way. You can't see it, but if you believe, it is already in process.

Thus, whatever you *desire* when you pray, you shall have—*but only what you desire*. Not what you *pray* for—only what you *desire when you pray.*

You must have a goal that you desire so strongly you will go after it no matter what the expense. If you are not willing to do that, you have lost already, because it is your desire for the thing that will keep you on the road of consistency. Potential needs desire to place demands upon it.

This life is full of advertisements for your attention. They come from all sides, trying to shake you from your goal. If you don't have a goal, they will provide one for you. You must know where you want to go and what you want to become. Potential needs purpose to give it direction.

When you pray, desire what you ask for. Refuse to be distracted or interrupted. The power of your potential will be revealed as you sacrifice everything to attain what you desired in prayer.

> Potential produces faith—faith is knowing potential is there.

## otential Only for the Few

*Enter through the narrow gate. For wide is the gate and broad is the road that leads to destruction, and many enter through it. But small is the gate and narrow the road that leads to life, and only a few find it* (Matthew 7:13-14).

BOOK QUOTE: *Understanding Your Potential* [Chapter 12]

Unfortunately, most of us will never fulfill the deepest desires of God's heart. Though He has done His best to free us from the false attitudes and perceptions that keep us from achieving our real potential, God is often disappointed by the lives of His creatures.

Perhaps you are a parent who has tried and tried and tried and still your kids haven't worked out. You've tried your best and given your best, but they still have disappointed you. Sometimes pastors also feel that way. They give and give and give, and the people still disappoint them. And often some of the ones who are messing up the most are the ones to whom they have given the most. Each of us feels the hurt when the people we love and have tried to help, struggle in the gutter, their lives in ruins.

In the seventh chapter of Matthew, Jesus predicts that many will hear His message, but few will follow Him and obey. Many will reject—or simply fail to accept—the abundant life He came to offer.

Read Matthew 7:13-14 above. These words have saved my sanity. I want all who read these words to fulfill their potential; but I know only a few will. Only a minute percentage of those who hear the message about who they are will ever become all they could be. Many people will never fulfill their purpose in life. They will not be who they were supposed to be or achieve what they were designed to do. It's terrible to say, but that's why I'm sharing this with you. If only I could take my desire and put it into you, I'd do it. But I can't. Some of you will end up in the gutter because you won't receive and practice what God is telling you. I'm sorry, but it will happen. Whether you fail or succeed, win or lose, does not depend on God, but on you. He is ready to do His part if you are willing to cooperate with His purpose for your life.

> God is ready to do His part if you cooperate with His purpose for your life.

## e One of the Few

*As a prisoner for the Lord, then, I urge you to live a life worthy of the calling you have received* (Ephesians 4:1).

BOOK QUOTE: *Understanding Your Potential* [Chapter 12]

Your Creator and Manufacturer built a store of miracles in you. He said you have treasures in your earthen vessel. He came to bring you abundant life. He knows there is explosive power in you waiting to be released. Through the strength of Jesus Christ you can do anything you think or imagine—and even more. But not everyone will hook up with God. Not everyone will look for the things God planted within them to be used for His glory. Not everyone will choose to fulfill their potential. Indeed, the number will be few.

Are you in the broad gate where everybody is going nowhere? Are you one of the many who aren't going to be anything? Come, join the narrow gate. Be one of the few. Decide you're not going with the crowd. Separate yourself, square your shoulders and do something. Choose to be somebody, instead of nobody. Leave your footprints in the sands of history and carry none of your potential to the cemetery.

Jesus passed judgment when He said, "The message my Father gave Me is for the world, but only a *few* will dare to take the challenge to handle abundant life." That's terrible. I wish that none should perish, but it is only a wish.

Are you a can-do person? Are you brave enough to face the challenge and take the risk to be effective? Will you dare to believe the impossible no matter what others say? I hope so. The world desperately needs some people who will go for the miracles no matter what it takes. The world needs some people who will believe God for the potential buried within them—desiring their dreams enough to move out and act. Only a few will find the kind of potential that allows them to live from the depths of their hidden ability. But for those who do, deep wells of possibilities will come to light as God reveals to them more and more of what He planned before the foundations of the world.

Join the few. Release the miracles hidden in your thoughts. Dare to try even after you've failed. Become reconnected to God and find out who you are and what you can do. Give your potential a chance, because God is waiting to do much more than you can think or imagine. He loves you. He wants you to be the beautiful person He created you to be.

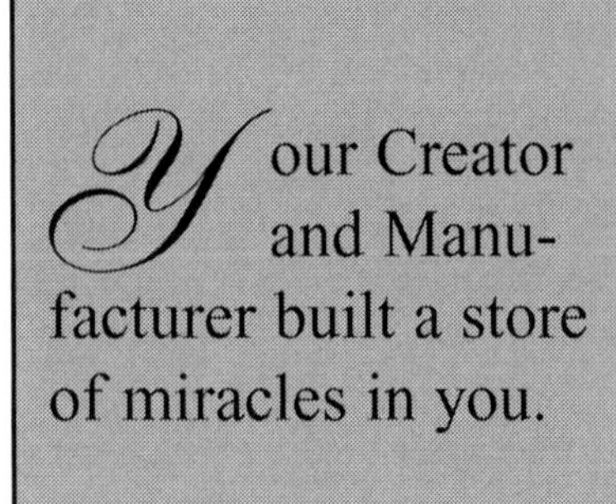

## The World Within the Third World

*For though we live in the world, we do not wage war as the world does* (2 Corinthians 10:3).

BOOK QUOTE: *Understanding Your Potential* [Chapter 12]

Today there are over five billion people on planet Earth. Over half of these people live in countries and conditions that have been labeled *Third World*. This term was invented by a French economist who was attempting to describe the various groupings of peoples throughout the world based on their socio-economic status. Whether or not this term is valid, it is generally accepted as a description or element of identification for millions of people.

I was born and live in a part of the world that is said to fall within this category. The term is defined as any people who did not benefit from or participate in the industrial revolution. A large majority of these people were not allowed to benefit from or participate in the industrial revolution because they were subjugated at that time, being used to fuel the economic base for that revolution. Many of them were reduced to slaves and indentured servants, thus robbing them of their identity, dignity, self-worth, and self-respect.

Today, despite changes in conditions and a greater measure of freedom and independence, many are still grappling with their identity and their sense of self-worth. Many of the nations that progressed and developed through the industrial revolution have reinforced (by attitudes, policies, and legislations) the notion that these Third World peoples do not possess the potential to develop the skills, intelligence, and sophistication necessary to equal that of industrialized states.

It is crucial that we do not inhibit our potential to chart a new course for the future by being destroyed by our preoccupation with the past. We have the responsibility to deposit the wealth of our potential in this generation so the next generation can build their future on our faithfulness to becoming everything we can possibly be. Just as there is a forest in every seed, so I am certain there is a new world within your world. *Whatever God calls for, He provides for.*

> We have the responsibility to deposit the wealth of our potential in this generation.

## REVIEW the Principles From This Week:

- Dare to believe in your potential.
- God paid the greatest price necessary—the cost of His own life—to release our full potential.
- We are to have faith to believe in God's goodness and care for us.
- If we seek the things of God first, everything will fall into place.
- The most important things of life come from God and His Kingdom.
- Potential produces faith. Faith is knowing potential is there.
- We must dare to dream and set goals to see the dreams become reality.

## Dreamless Poverty

*But I have raised you up for this very purpose, that I might show you my power and that my name might be proclaimed in all the earth* (Exodus 9:16).

BOOK QUOTE: *Releasing Your Potential* [Preface]

The poorest person in the world is the person without a dream. The most frustrated person in the world is the person with a dream that never becomes reality. I am certain that every individual on this planet—no matter which race, culture, nationality or socio-economic status—has had a dream of some sort. The ability of children to dream is a natural instinct instilled by the Creator. No matter how poor or rich we are, whether we were born in the bush village of an underdeveloped nation or amid the marble floors of the aristocracy of society, we all have childhood dreams. These dreams are visual manifestations of our purpose, seeds of destiny planted in the soil of our imagination. I am convinced that God created and gave us the gift of imagination to provide us with a glimpse of our purpose in life and to activate the hidden ability within each of us. Purpose is the reason why something was made. It is the end for which the means exists. It is the source of the dream and the vision you carried in your heart from childhood. It is the key to your fulfillment.

In Exodus 9, we see Pharaoh, one of earth's most powerful rulers, was in spiritual poverty because he lacked God's dream. Yet, even Pharaoh was raised up for God's purposes. How much more are we a part of God's plan and Kingdom purpose? We just need to dream a little.

The poorest person in the world is the person without a dream.

## Purpose and Potential

*For where your treasure is, there your heart will be also* (Matthew 6:21).

BOOK QUOTE: *Releasing Your Potential* [Preface]

It is a fact that every manufacturer makes a product to fulfill a specific purpose, and every product is designed with the ability to fulfill this purpose. In essence, the *potential* of a product is determined by its purpose. This is true of everything God created, including you. The purpose of a seed is to reproduce trees. Therefore, by God's design, they possess the ability or potential to fulfill this purpose. But just because a seed has the *potential* to produce a forest, does not mean it will. One of the greatest tragedies in nature is the destruction of a seed or the isolation of a seed from the soil. Consequently, the death of a seed is the burial of a forest. Having ability is good, but keeping ability is bad.

Your life has the potential to fulfill your purpose. If, however, you imprison that potential, you rob your life of its purpose and fulfillment. You and every other individual on this planet possess an awesome treasure. Too much of this treasure is buried every day, untapped and untouched, in the cemeteries of our world. Much talent, skill and creativity have been lost to the world for want of a little courage. Many obscure men and women enter eternity pregnant with potential, with a still-born purpose. Living with ability brings responsibility. Dying with ability reveals irresponsibility.

You and every individual on this planet possess an awesome treasure.

## Receiving and Releasing

*Guard the good deposit that was entrusted to you—guard it with the help of the Holy Spirit who lives in us* (2 Timothy 1:14).

BOOK QUOTE: *Releasing Your Potential* [Preface]

Everything in creation was designed to function on the simple principle of receiving and releasing. Life depends on this principle. What if the plants refused to release the oxygen they possess or if we human beings refused to release the carbon dioxide we produce? The result would be chaos and death for the entire planet. Unreleased potential is not only useless, it is dangerous—both for the person or thing who failed to release it and for everything that lives with them. Dormant potential is not healthy, advantageous, safe or effective. You must understand that your valuable deposit of potential was given to enrich the lives of others. When potential is kept, it self-destructs.

The tremendous potential you and I have been given is locked inside us, waiting for demands to be made on it. We have a responsibility to use what God stored in us for the good of the world. We dare not leave this planet with it. Many of us are aware of the ability we have inside, but we have been frustrated by our failure to release that ability. Some of us blame our historical circumstances. Others blame social status. Still others transfer the responsibility for their failure and frustration to their lack of formal education or their less than ideal opportunities.

Over the years, I have come to realize that no excuse *can* be given to justify the destruction of the seed of potential that God placed within you. You *can* become the man or woman you were born to be. You *can* accomplish the vision you saw. You *can* build that business you planned. You *can* develop that school you imagine. *You* are the only one who can stop you. No matter what your environment, you have the ability to change your attitude and your internal environment until they are conducive to the germination of your potential seed. You must not add to the wealth of the graveyard. You owe it to the next generation to live courageously so the treasure of your potential is unleashed. The world needs what God deposited in you for the benefit of your contemporaries and all the generations to follow.

Tap the untapped. Release the reservoir.

## Gone but Not Forgotten

*I cry out to God Most High, to God, who fulfills His purpose for me* (Psalm 57:2).

BOOK QUOTE: *Releasing Your Potential* [Introduction]

It was a cool, wet, rainy September Sunday afternoon in the historic city of London. I took the opportunity to steal away for a private, relaxing walk I desired. After I had walked for a few minutes, the pathway meandered to the entrance of an old cemetery. My tenacious interest in history drew me to explore the historical nature of the tombstones and the grave markers just to satisfy my curiosity. What an awesome experience it was to read and study the many names, dates, and quotes as these silent stones spoke. Names like John Hill 1800-1864, Elizabeth Robinson 1790-1830, and so on, gave evidence of the years of British history buried there.

Then I came upon a small grave, perhaps three feet in length, that read, "Markus Rogers, 1906-1910." Written below the name was the quote, "Gone but not forgotten." A brief calculation revealed that this was the resting place of a 4-year-old child. After scanning the hundreds of markers and stones, my eyes rested, once again, upon the grave of this child. Deep contemplation settled upon me. I noticed that almost all the tombstones, including the child's, had the words "Rest in Peace" inscribed on them. Many questions and thoughts raced through my mind: *Who were the child's parents? What was the cause of death? What was his purpose in being born? What special natural talents and gifts did he possess that were never displayed and never benefited anyone? What inventions or discoveries could he have shared with the human race? How many great works of art, books, or songs died in this precious infant?*

The world needs what God deposited in you for the benefit of your contemporaries and all the generations to follow.

How many great works of art, books, or songs died in this precious infant?

## Rest in Peace

*If you, then, though you are evil, know how to give good gifts to your children, how much more will your Father in Heaven give good gifts to those who ask Him!* (Matthew 7:11).

BOOK QUOTE: *Releasing Your Potential* [Introduction]

While in London, I took the opportunity to steal away to an old cemetery. I noticed that almost all the tombstones, including the child's, had the words "Rest in Peace" inscribed on them.

I wondered: *How can you rest in peace if you died with all your potential inside?* As the wet, misty rain formed dew drops on my cheeks, I walked away thinking: *What a tragedy it is for a child to die at a tender age, before he has the opportunity to realize his full potential.*

Immediately a quiet voice screamed in my head: Is it not a greater tragedy if those who lived to old age also carried their books, art, music, inventions, dreams, and potential to the grave? Suddenly the rain seemed to turn to sweat as I pondered the awesome implications of this question. One of my greatest fears is that many who still walk the streets of our world, perhaps some who are reading this book, will also deposit in the cemeteries of their communities the wealth of potential locked inside them. I trust that you will not allow the grave to rob this world of your latent, awesome *potential.*

There are five billion people on this planet. Each one is very special, unique, original, and significant. All possess a genetic combination that codes them as distinct individuals whose fingerprints cannot be duplicated. There is no one like you now, nor will there ever be another. Each of us—whether black, brown, yellow, red, or white—was conceived by destiny, produced by purpose and packaged with potential to live a meaningful, fulfilling life. Deep within you lies a seed of greatness waiting to be germinated. You have been endued with natural talents, gifts, desires, and dreams. All humanity, in all cultures, races, and socio-economic situations, lives with the natural instinct to manifest this potential.

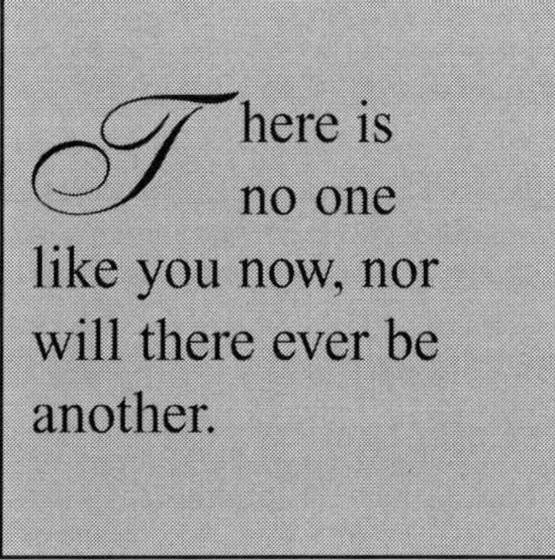

## otential to Bear Fruit

*You did not choose me, but I chose you and appointed you to go and bear fruit—fruit that will last. Then the Father will give you whatever you ask in My name* (John 15:16).

BOOK QUOTE: *Releasing Your Potential* [Introduction]

The entire creation possesses this principle of potential. Everything has the natural instinct to release its ability. The plant and animal kingdoms abound with evidences of this fact. The Creator designed everything with this principle of potential, which can be simplified to the concept of a seed. The biblical document states that God created everything with "*seed in it according to their kinds*" (Genesis 1:12). In essence, hidden within everything is the potential to fulfill itself and produce much more than we see.

Please note that when God created the earth and placed man in the garden, He did not give man a finished product. Although God knew that man would need food, clothes, shelter, transportation, and other elements of comfort, He did not make all these things instantly available. God commanded the man: "*Be fruitful, and increase in number; fill the earth and subdue it*" (Genesis 1:28). Each of these commands is based on the assumption that the *ability* to be fruitful and the *potential* to multiply and replenish and subdue were present in the man, waiting to be activated, tapped, and released. This command also implies that fruitfulness (release of hidden life) and multiplication (reproduction of hidden life) are not dependent on God, but on the individual who possesses the seed.

You have the ability to accomplish everything your God-given purpose demands. Your Creator has given you the responsibility of releasing this precious seed in obedience to His commands. The releasing of your potential is not up to God but you.

Henry Ford once said, "My best friend is the one who brings out the best in me." It is my hope that this book becomes one of your best friends as it inspires you to strive to release your hidden abilities for the benefit of the world around you and for your personal fulfillment.

You have the ability to accomplish everything your God-given purpose demands.

## Become Transformed

*And we, who with unveiled faces all reflect the Lord's glory, are being transformed into His likeness with ever-increasing glory, which comes from the Lord, who is the Spirit* (2 Corinthians 3:18).

BOOK QUOTE: *Releasing Your Potential* [Introduction]

For the last two decades, I have devoted myself to understanding, activating, tapping, and releasing my potential and the potential of others. An integral part of this devotion was the study and observation of the lives of some of this world's leading men and women—people who have affected their societies positively because they released and maximized their potential. As a result, I am convinced that every individual comes into this world with a deposit of potential that far exceeds any attempt to measure its potency. I also believe that this potential is viable in spite of the external environment in which it exists. My studies and experience have also revealed that this potential must be released by applying specific principles that are evident in every case in the lives of those people who tapped the deposit God placed within them. The presence and application of these principles was visible no matter what ethnic, social, academic, or economic situation prevailed.

Although I have said that everyone possesses great potential and the capacity to release this awesome ability, I also believe, with great sadness, that not everyone will become all the Creator intended them to be. Too many people are mere products of their environments, allowing themselves to be victimized by the opinions of others and the assessments of human analysis. They lack the will to change or challenge the limitations placed upon them by themselves and others, and thus fail to take the necessary steps to develop their potential.

I also believe, however, that anyone, of any age, and in any circumstances, can transform himself if he wants to. You can become all God designed you to be if you are willing to defy the norm and dare to believe God's assessment of your ability. It's not what you don't know that hurts you. It's what you know that just ain't so.

> One of the greatest tragedies in life is to watch potential die untapped.

## EVIEW the Principles From This Week:

- To realize your potential you must have God's dream.
- You are unique to God's purpose and plan.
- You have the ability to accomplish everything your God-given purpose demands.
- You can transform yourself if you really want to.

## our Inheritance to the World

*Therefore, since we are surrounded by such a great cloud of witnesses, let us throw off everything that hinders and the sin that so easily entangles, and let us run with perseverance the race marked out for us* (Hebrews 12:1).

BOOK QUOTE: *Releasing Your Potential* [Chapter 1]

It was my first trip to the great South American country of Brazil to address a conference of ten thousand leaders and laymen, I felt an awesome responsibility upon me. My time in this country of beautiful and complex cultures and ethnic heritages would be a lesson in humanity's oneness. It confirmed once again that despite our minor differences, we are all the same.

Seven days into my stay, my host and translator took me on a tour of their beautiful capital, Brasilia. After visiting the well-organized city and government buildings and touring the stately monuments of the picturesque city, we entered one of my favorite places to visit—the national museum.

I felt great appreciation for the beautiful and important works of art around me. As I viewed, studied, and admired the tremendous historical pieces and the priceless testimonies of the glory of this nation's past and present, I was once again reminded that each painting, sculpture, and specimen was the product of the release of someone's potential. Although many of the artists are dead, their works are not. Display after display gave evidence to potential that had not been buried with the artists. Because they had dared to expose the talent hidden within them, I and many others were enjoying, appreciating, and being inspired by their imaginative works.

Throughout time, the great and small works of individuals—be they paintings, books, music, poetry, drama, architecture, inventions, or the development of theories—have affected the lives of many. All who have helped to shape our society's destiny—the giants who teach us and inspire us—used their potential with a passion and refused to let circumstances dictate their future. The museum in Brazil, like all the museums of the world, is a constant reminder that someone lived who refused to let death have the final word on their potential. *Their released potential is the world's inheritance.*

> The death of a seed is the burial of a forest.

## ctivate Your Abilities

*Nothing in all creation is hidden from God's sight. Everything is uncovered and laid bare before the eyes of Him to whom we must give account* (Hebrews 4:13).

BOOK QUOTE: *Releasing Your Potential* [Chapter 1]

I believe earth itself is a museum. Each of us comes into this world with an assignment to fulfill. God commissions us to leave for the following generations something from which they can learn and be inspired. The abilities to complete these assignments lie within us. The tools are our natural talents, gifts, and ambitions.

Throughout time, the great and small works of individuals—be they paintings, books, music, poetry, drama, architecture, inventions, or the development of theories—have affected the lives of many. All who have helped to shape our society's destiny—the giants who teach us and inspire us—used their potential with a passion and refused to let circumstances dictate their future. Museums are a constant reminder that someone lived who refused to let death have the final word on their potential. *Their released potential is the world's inheritance.*

Unless you accept the responsibility for activating your abilities, the next generation will enter the museum of life and notice a vacant space in earth's displays. The sign below the placed reserved to display the fruit of your potential will read: "Assignment unfinished. Potential unreleased."

Each of us comes into this world with an assignment to fulfill.

## The Abortion of Ability

*So he called him in and asked him, "What is this I hear about you? Give an account of your management, because you cannot be manager any longer"* (Luke 16:2).

BOOK QUOTE: *Releasing Your Potential* [Chapter 1]

"The price of greatness is responsibility." These words were spoken by Sir Winston Churchill. They contain a truth that should be guarded and heeded. The graveyards are full of great men and women who never became great because they did not give their ability responsibility. This untapped ability is called potential. Each of us comes into the world pregnant with unlimited potential. We are capable of much more than we have already done. Unless we expose, during the course of our lives, all that God placed within us for the good of mankind, our potential will be aborted.

Abortion is one of today's most controversial issues. It is polarizing many communities. It has also become a hot political issue in many countries where it is used to manipulate the reins of power. Many people think of this concern as a recent one. Although it is causing much stir in our societies, the concern over abortion is not new. The truth is that the abortion issue is as old as time. The fact of abortion is as old as man.

Abortion is not limited to the physical termination of a fetus in a mother's womb. The first act of abortion was performed in the Garden of Eden when the first man, Adam, was given the responsibility of carrying the entire human race within his loins. In Adam was the seed of all generations and the strength of all mankind. God's instructions to Adam were very simple and clear:

> *"You are free to eat from any tree in the garden; but you must not eat from the tree of the knowledge of good and evil, for when you eat of it you will surely die"* (Genesis 2:16-17).

To *surely die* means to definitely cease from manifesting the fruitfulness that exists within a thing. Death, in its simplest form, is the termination of potential. To abort means to terminate life before its full potential has or can be realized, before the person, animal, plant, etc. is given an opportunity to fulfill its full potential.

> The graveyards are full of great men and women who never became great because they did not give their ability responsibility.

## The Termination of Potential

*But I tell you that men will have to give account on the day of judgment for every careless word they have spoken* (Matthew 12:36).

BOOK QUOTE: *Releasing Your Potential* [Chapter 1]

God created everything with the hidden ability to fulfill itself. The Bible's record of creation states that the seed of everything is in itself to produce after its kind (see Genesis 1:12). All creation possesses the hidden ability to be everything it is supposed to be:

In every seed there is a forest;
in every fish, a school;
in every bird, a flock;
in every cow, a herd;
in every girl, a woman;
in every boy, a man; and
in every man, a nation.

It is important for us to remember that *every great tree was once a seed, every woman was once a fetus, every man was once a boy, and every nation was once in the loins of a man*. It is also interesting to note that whenever God deals with man, He always speaks in terms of the generational seed within his loins. In God's calculation of life, one equals many, little equals much, small equals great, and less equals more. Therefore, to abort a seed is to kill a forest, to abort a cow is to kill a herd, to abort a boy is to kill a man, to abort a girl is to kill a woman, and to abort a man is to destroy a nation. God told Abraham, the great patriarch of history,

> *"I will make you a great nation and I will bless you; I will make your name great and you will be a blessing....and all peoples on earth will be blessed through you"* (Genesis 12:2-3).

Abortion is the ultimate tragedy. It robs life of its essence and denies the future its value.

> Death, in its simpliest form, is the termination of potential.

## bortion Through Ignorance

*So then, each of us will give an account of himself to God* (Romans 14:12).

BOOK QUOTE: *Releasing Your Potential* [Chapter 1]

Abortion is the ignorance of responsibility and the denial of obligation. Abortion is self-comfort at the expense of fruitfulness, because *all abortions sacrifice responsibility*. The abortion of potential condemns the future. This reality has caused the development of an entire discipline of science. Ecology and environmental studies, as these areas of concern are known, build their premises on the word *extinction*, meaning "the termination of the potential force within creation to fulfill itself."

It is amazing that man, with all his attempts to minimize the abortion of various species in the animal and plant kingdom by investing billions of dollars to protect animals, plants, forests, and the ozone layer, has neglected to prioritize the position of human beings in the scheme of things. While man fights to protect whales, owls, trees, and fish, he also battles for the right to terminate human babies. Perhaps the situation would improve if every doctor who performs this tragic operation would be reminded before each abortion that the opportunity to perform this surgery is his only because his mother did not abort him.

The abortion issue is, therefore, not just a problem of the taking of a life, though that is the fatal end result. Even more, abortion is the ignorance and the lack of understanding of the principle of potential that pervades our world. The majority of those who die each year are guilty of abortion because they didn't understand the basic relevance of the concept of potential to their individual lives.

Abortion is the ignorance of responsibility and the denial of obligation.

## Death of the Future

*...for all have sinned and fall short of the glory of God* (Romans 3:23).

BOOK QUOTE: *Releasing Your Potential* [Chapter 1]

*The abortion of potential is the death of the future.* It affects generation after generation. When Adam broke God's law, he aborted his seed's potential for becoming all they were intended to be. Men and women throughout all ages have fallen far short of the glory of the Creator. The word *glory* means the "true nature" or "full essence" of a thing. In other words, *to fall short of glory means to live below your true potential.* This is what God calls sin. Sin is not a behavior; it is a disposition. One of the great biblical writers states it this way:

> *I consider that our present sufferings are not worth comparing with the glory that will be revealed in us. The creation waits in eager expectation for* [the glory of] *the sons of God to be revealed* (Romans 8:18-19).

This passage states that the fall of man prevented the full glory or true potential of mankind from being revealed or manifested. All creation was affected by man's sin. God's creation is waiting for man's glory or true potential to be exposed because creation's destiny is tied to man's. Thus, any abortion, whether it's the abortion of a dream, a vision, art, music, writing, business, leadership, or inventions, affects both nature and the succeeding generations of man. *How many children yet unborn were destined to sing the song you have never written?*

To fall short of glory means to live below your true potential.

## ob the Grave

*But the gift is not like the trespass. For if the many died by the trespass of the one man, how much more did God's grace and the gift that came by the grace of the one man, Jesus Christ, overflow to the many!* (Romans 5:15).

BOOK QUOTE: *Releasing Your Potential* [Chapter 1]

When Adam aborted the vision God had placed in his heart and disobeyed the directives of the Manufacturer, he changed the lives of the entire human race that lay hidden in his loins. The Book of Romans states:

> *Therefore, just as sin entered the world through one man, and death through sin, and in this way death came to all men, because all sinned* [in Adam].... *Consequently, just as the result of one trespass was condemnation for all men, so also the result of one act of righteousness was justification that brings life for all men* (Romans 5:12,18).

It is vital that we understand the principle demonstrated in these passages. It is the awesome realization that if your potential is not released, it will affect this generation and all the generations of man yet to live. Even creation will testify against you. If you abort your potential, you will be guilty of robbing the world of the treasure you came to this planet to deliver. *The fact that you were born is evidence that God knew earth needed the potential you are pregnant with.* It is, therefore, imperative that you refuse to leave this planet without giving birth to those dreams, ideas, visions, and inventions you carry in the womb of your faith right now. Do not abort your baby of potential. *Rob the grave of the treasure you carry.* Leave the picture of your potential on the wall of history in the museum of the earth.

> Rob the grave of the treasure you carry.

## EVIEW the Principles From This Week:

- Your released potential is the world's inheritance.
- You came into the world pregnant with unlimited potential.
- You are capable of much more than you have already done.
- Creation's destiny is tied to the release of your potential.
- The fact that you were born is evidence that God knew earth needed the potential you are pregnant with.

## Knowledge of Ability is the Introduction of Responsibility

*...for acquiring a disciplined and prudent life, doing what is right and just and fair* (Proverbs 1:3).

BOOK QUOTE: *Releasing Your Potential* [Chapter 2]

Come with me in your imagination to the funeral of a loved one. Picture yourself driving to the funeral parlor or the church, parking your car and getting out. As you walk inside the building, notice the flowers and the soft organ music. See the faces of friends and family as you move through the room. Feel the shared sorrow of losing and the joy of having known that radiates from the hearts of the people there.

As you walk to the front of the room and look inside the casket, you come face to face with yourself. This is your funeral, five years from today. All these people have come to honor you and to express feelings of love and appreciation for your life. As you take a seat and wait for the service to begin, you look at the program in your hand. Five persons will speak. The first speaker is from your family, immediate and extended—your children, brothers, sisters, nephews, nieces, aunts, uncles, cousins, and grandparents who have come from all over the country to attend. The second speaker is to be one of your friends, someone who can give a sense of what you were as a person. The third speaker is from your work or profession. The fourth speaker is from your church or some community organization where you were involved in service. The fifth and final speaker is your spouse.

Now think deeply. What would you like each of these speakers to say about you and your life? What kind of husband or wife, father or mother would you like their words to reflect? What kind of son or daughter or cousin? What kind of friend or working associate?

Take a few minutes to seriously consider these questions. I firmly believe that the greatest tragedy in life is not death, but life… life that fails to fulfill its purpose and potential.

> The greatest tragedy in life is not death, but life…life that fails to fulfill its purpose and potential.

## Live Effectively

*For who knows what is good for a man in life, during the few and meaningless days he passes through like a shadow? Who can tell him what will happen under the sun after he is gone?* (Ecclesiastes 6:12).

BOOK QUOTE: *Releasing Your Potential* [Chapter 2]

I am trying to help you become aware of the great treasure you possess, which is your potential. I have addressed millions of people on this issue of living effectively. Repeatedly I have stressed that it is better to have never been born than to live and not fulfill the purpose for which you were given life. This truth is echoed in Ecclesiastes 6:3-6.

A man may have a hundred children and live many years; yet no matter how long he lives, if he cannot enjoy his prosperity and does not receive proper burial, I say that a stillborn child is better off than he. It comes without meaning, it departs in darkness, and in darkness its name is shrouded. Though it never saw the sun or knew anything, it has more rest than does that man.

This passage asserts that it would be better for an individual never to have been born than for him to live on this planet many years and not fulfill the purpose for which God gave him birth. In essence, when you become aware of the tremendous potential that resides within you, you are obligated to release that wealth to the world around you.

> Become aware of the great treasure you possess, which is your potential.

## bility and Responsibility

*Brothers, each man, as responsible to God, should remain in the situation God called him to* (1 Corinthians 7:24).

BOOK QUOTE: *Releasing Your Potential* [Chapter 2]

"What lies behind you is history and what lies before you is future, but these are both tiny matters compared to what lies within you," as Ralph Waldo Emerson said. You may not be able to change your past, and your future is yet unlived, but the present provides you with opportunities to maximize your life and the ability that lives within you. You must take responsibility for your ability—no one else can do it for you.

Are you living a stillbirth life? Are you aborting your entire purpose for living? I encourage you to take responsibility right now for your ability. Determine to activate, release, and maximize your potential for the sake of the next generation. Leave your footprints in the sands of the history of your country. *Live fully so you can die effectively. Let your life write the speech of your death and give your potential to the family of man for the glory of God.* Remember "well done" is much better than "well said." Don't just talk about your potential dreams, visions, and ideas. Step out now and determine to do them. Dare to believe that what you have already accomplished is but a minute percentage of what you can do. Move beyond the familiar patterns and experiences of your life to the dreams and plans and imaginations that wait within you to be fulfilled.

You must take responsibility for your ability.

## Will Your Abilities Be Lost to the World?

*May the favor of the Lord our God rest upon us; establish the work of our hands for us—yes, establish the work of our hands* (Psalm 90:17).

BOOK QUOTE: *Releasing Your Potential* [Chapter 2]

You possess awesome potential within waiting to be activated and released. The release of your potential demands that you refuse to be satisfied with your latest accomplishment. Only then will you tap into the vast bill of credit with which you were born. Because potential, by definition, is the large, unknown bank of resources you were given at birth, what you have accomplished is no longer your potential. Releasing your potential requires a willingness to move beyond the familiar into the realm of possibilities.

If you attempt new things and make choices that stretch your horizons, you will embark on an exciting journey. You will begin to see the marvelous being God created you to be—a being filled with more capabilities than you ever dreamed possible. The journey begins when you gain an understanding of what potential is and how you can release it. For once you understand the magnitude of the wealth God gave you, to turn from consciously and conscientiously unwrapping God's gift is to abort your potential and refuse to fulfill the purpose for which He gave you life. The knowledge of what you have failed to use to benefit yourself, your contemporaries, and the generations to follow will judge you on the great day of accountability. Potential is given to be released, not wasted.

Some men have thousands of reasons why they cannot do what they want to, when all they need is one reason why they can.

> The release of your potential demands that you refuse to be satisfied with your latest accomplishment.

## What Is Potential?

*For you have been born again, not of perishable seed, but of imperishable, through the living and enduring Word of God* (1 Peter 1:23).

BOOK QUOTE: *Releasing Your Potential* [Chapter 3]

Potential is…

…unexposed ability…reserved power…untapped strength…capped capabilities…unused success…dormant gifts…hidden talents…latent power.

…what you can do that you haven't yet done…where you can go that you haven't yet gone…who you can be that you haven't yet been…what you can imagine that you haven't yet imagined.

…how far you can reach that you haven't yet reached…what you can see that you haven't yet seen…what you can accomplish that you haven't yet accomplished.

Thus, potential is the sum of who you are that you have yet to reveal. It's a deposit that waits to be released and maximized. You are capable of much more than you are presently thinking, imagining, doing, or being. That is your potential. Unless you continually try to reach higher, go farther, see over, and grasp something greater than you now know, you will never discover your full potential.

If, for example, I hold an apple seed in my hand, I hold much more than one seed. In every seed there is a tree, and in every tree there are apples with seeds in them. And the seeds contain more apple trees that contain fruit that contain seeds and so on. In fact I hold one apple seed. In truth I hold an entire orchard. That is potential—what yet can be.

God created everything with potential. Genesis 1:12 describes how God created the plants and the trees, each "*bearing seed according to their kinds*." Each possessed the capability to be much more than they appeared to be at any one time. Each contained the seed from which future generations of plants, birds, fish and animals would come.

God also planted within you the ability to be much more than you are at any one moment. Like the apple seed, you possess hidden resources and capabilities. Most of the potential God gave you at birth still remains within you, unseen and unused. What I see when I meet you on any given day is not all you are.

> You are capable of much more that you are presently thinking, imagining, doing, or being.

## The Source of All Potential

*I am the Alpha and the Omega, the First and the Last, the Beginning and the End* (Revelation 22:13).

BOOK QUOTE: *Releasing Your Potential* [Chapter 3]

Everything that was and is was in God. Before God created anything, there was only God. Thus, God had within Him the potential for everything He made. Nothing exists that was not first in God. *God is the source of all life, because before anything was, God is.*

"*In the beginning God created the heavens and the earth*" (Genesis 1:1). He pulled everything that He made out of Himself. Indeed, the beginning was in God before it began. God started start. If the Book of Genesis had started with Genesis 1:0, it might have read, "Before there was a beginning, there was God. Before there was a creation, there was a Creator. Before anything was, there was God."

God did not begin when the beginning began. He was in the beginning before the beginning had a beginning. "*In the beginning was the Word, and the Word was with God, and the Word was God*" (John 1:1). Everything in the world we know was in God before it came to be seen. "*Through* [God] *all things were made; without Him nothing was made that has been made*" (John 1:3). Thus, God is the source of all potential. He is everything we haven't seen yet.

When we describe this characteristic of God, we say that He is omnipotent. *Omni* means "always" and *potent* means "full of power." God is always full of power. He can always do more than He has already done.

Everything that was and is was in God.

## God Gave You Potential

*My flesh and my heart may fail, but God is the strength of my heart and my portion forever* (Psalm 73:26).

BOOK QUOTE: *Releasing Your Potential* [Chapter 3]

God's process in creating the world follows an interesting pattern. *First, God planned what He wanted to create. Second, He decided what kind of material substance He wanted His creation to be made from. Third, God spoke to the substance from which the thing was to be created and, fourth, exactly what He spoke came forth from that to which He spoke.*

Thus, when God wanted to make plants, He spoke to the ground, because that is the material substance from which He wanted them to come (see Genesis 1:11). When He wanted to create animals, God again spoke to the ground because He had planned for animals to be made of dirt (see Genesis 1:24). Fish came forth from the sea when God spoke to it (see Genesis 1:20). The sun, the moon, and the stars appeared in the expanse of the sky when God called them into being (see Genesis 1:14-17). Everything came forth when God spoke to a material substance, in accordance with the plan He had developed before He spoke the world into being.

When God created human beings, He spoke to Himself. You came forth from God because God planned that human beings should be spirit even as He is Spirit. Too many people never discover God's purpose for creating them. They look everywhere but to God for the meaning of their existence. Their lives are unfulfilled and their potential is wasted. God looks at them and bemoans their loss: "If you only knew who you are. If you only knew what you can do. If you only knew why I gave you life." Perhaps that is God's attitude toward you.

Remember, few things are impossible when they are tackled with diligence and skill. Great works are performed not by strength, but by perseverance. God created you with potential. He waits to see what you will do with the remarkable gift He gave you.

> Too many people never discover God's purpose for creating them.

## EVIEW the Principles From This Week:

- God placed potential in you to benefit the world.
- Potential is the large, unknown bank of resources you were given at birth.
- Potential must be used or it will be aborted.
- Satisfaction with success kills potential.
- Potential is what yet can be.
- God created everything with potential.
- God is the Source of all potential.
- What God planned came forth from the substance to which He spoke.
- When God wanted you, He spoke to Himself.

# Review of Principles That Govern Potential—Part 1

*How many are your works, O Lord! In wisdom you made them all; the earth is full of your creatures* (Psalm 104:24).

BOOK QUOTE: *Releasing Your Potential* [Chapter 4]

Before you can begin to grasp the nature and the magnitude of your potential, you must understand the laws that control all potential. God set these laws when He tapped His creative abilities to make visible that which existed but was invisible. The first two chapters of the Bible tell the story of this unleashing of God's potential.

I want to give you six basic principles that are fundamental to *all* potential. Here are the first two principles:

**Principle #1**—What God speaks to is the source for what He creates.

An examination of the process God used to create the world reveals that everything God created was brought forth by His spoken word. Whatever God spoke to became the source for the creation God planned to bring forth. When God wanted plants, He spoke to the dirt (Genesis 1:11-12). When God wanted animals, He spoke to the ground (Genesis 1:24-25). When God wanted fish, He spoke to the waters (Genesis 1:20-21). When God wanted stars, He spoke to the gases in the heavens (Genesis 1:14-15). Throughout creation, whatever God spoke to became the source from which the created thing came, and exactly what God spoke came forth from the substance to which He spoke.

**Principle #2**—All things have the same components and essence as the sources from which they came.

The source to which God spoke during the creative process also becomes the final home of all He has created. When God's creations die, they return to the source from which He took them. Thus, plants came from the dirt and return to the dirt. Animals also came from and return to the ground. Fish came from and return to the sea, and stars came from and return to the gases of the heavens. This is possible because all things are made of the same stuff from which they came. If we take apart a plant or an animal and look at its cells beneath a microscope, we discover that plants and animals are 100 percent dirt. They are composed of dirt because they came from dirt.

Rob the grave of the potential you carry within. Release your potential.

## A Review of Principles That Govern Potential—Part 2

*It is I who made the earth and created mankind upon it. My own hands stretched out the heavens; I marshaled their starry hosts* (Isaiah 45:12).

BOOK QUOTE: *Releasing Your Potential* [Chapter 4]

I want to give you six basic principles that are fundamental to *all* potential. Here are the next two principles.

**Principle #3**—All things must be maintained by the sources from which they came.

God's world also reveals that whatever God creates must be sustained and maintained by the source from which it came. Plants that are pulled from the ground die. Animals that cease to eat plants or other animals die. Fish that are removed from water die. Flowers that are cut for arrangements wilt sooner than those that remain attached to the plant. Indeed, all living things die the instant they are removed from their sources. The signs of death and decay may not be immediately evident, but nonetheless, they are dead. None of God's living creations can survive without the resources and the nourishment provided by the substances from which they came.

**Principle #4**—The potential of all things is related to the sources from which they came.

Because all things are composed of the sources from which they came, they also contain as little or as much potential as their original substances. Animals have no greater or lesser potential than the dirt from which they came. Plants also have only the potential of the dirt. If the soil is lacking in nutrients or the ability to hold water, the plants attached to that soil are going to be adversely affected by the poor quality of the soil. Likewise, the animals that eat the plants that are growing in the unhealthy soil are going to receive less nutrients than if they had eaten plants that were growing in healthy soil.

No product can be more powerful than the source from which it came. A wooden table, for example, is only as strong as the wood of the tree from which the furniture maker built it. If you make a table from a rotten tree, you'll have a rotten table. A floor made of pine will not withstand wear as well as a floor made of oak, because pine is a softer wood than oak. The characteristics of the tree from which the flooring boards were made always affect the quality of the finished floor.

Thus, the quality of any product is dependent upon the quality of the components used in the product, which is dependent upon the quality of the materials used in the components. *The potential of something is always related to the potential of the source from which it came.* Nothing can be greater than its source.

No product can be more powerful than the source from which it came.

## A Review of Principles That Govern Potential—Part 3

*Have we not all one Father? Did not one God create us?* (Malachi 2:10a).

BOOK QUOTE: *Releasing Your Potential* [Chapter 4]

I want to give you six basic principles that are fundamental to *all* potential. Here are the last two principles.

**Principle #5**—Everything in life has the potential to fulfill its purpose.

The purpose of a thing is the original intent or desire of the one who created it. Thus, the purpose of a thing cannot be known by asking anyone other than the designer or the manufacturer. If we entered the laboratory of an inventor and you asked me what a certain contraption was supposed to do, I might guess at what service or function it could perform, but only the inventor would be able to confirm or reject my suggestion.

Likewise, *the ability of that product to fulfill its purpose is designed into the product*. No manufacturer would suggest that you use his appliance to wash clothes unless he intended for it to wash clothes. If I assume that the machine is a clothes dryer and complain to the dealer that the machine won't dry my clothes, the manufacturer will most certainly respond, "But that machine isn't supposed to dry clothes. Use it to wash clothes and it'll work fine. But don't ask it to dry clothes, because it can't. I didn't build it to dry clothes." The manufacturer determines both the product's purpose and how it will function to fulfill that purpose.

**Principle #6**—Potential is determined and revealed by the demands placed on it by its creator.

What a product can potentially do is determined by what the manufacturer of the product asks it to do. Potential is revealed by the faith of the manufacturer in his product and the expectations he places upon it. If a manufacturer of small trucks designs them to carry one-half ton, the company will not advertise their product as having the ability to carry one ton. Why? Because the manufacturer knows that he cannot require the truck to carry a full ton when the specifications under which it was built designate that the maximum capacity is one-half ton.

> Potential is revealed by the faith of the manufacturer in his product and the expectations he places upon it.

The manufacturer will not ask the product to perform more or less than he designed it to do. If a manufacturer requires a product to do something, you can be sure that he believes the ability to perform the task was built into the product.

## Keys to Maximizing Your Potential—Part 1

*...so that you may become blameless and pure, children of God without fault in a crooked and depraved generation, in which you shine like stars in the universe* (Philippians 2:15).

BOOK QUOTE: *Releasing Your Potential* [Chapter 4]

Plants are wonderful to watch. After the seeds are buried in the ground, gardeners wait with anticipation for the young shoots to push their way through the soil. Under ideal conditions, most seeds will germinate in a week or two. Although good care is essential during those early weeks of growth, the gardener will not see the full potential of the plants until they begin to bear fruit.

I want to share four keys to encouraging your garden to maturity as you liberate all the potential that God deposited in you. Here is the first.

**Key #1**—You must cultivate your potential.

Experienced gardeners know that weeds often grow faster than vegetables. If a gardener goes away for several weeks, he will return to stunted and sickly vegetable plants that yield little or no fruit. Or even worse, he may find that he has no vegetable plants at all because the weeds smothered and choked the tender shoots. Cultivation is necessary for a healthy and productive garden.

The same is true of your potential. You need to cultivate your life carefully to remove the influences and the stimulants that seek to stunt your potential or kill it completely. Seek those persons who are positive and encouraging. Remove yourself from those activities and situations that might encourage you to return to your former way of life. Cling to your Source and allow Him to cleanse you of those things that would deter you from maximizing your potential. *Much emerging potential dies for want of cultivation.* The careful and consistent nurturing of your potential will enable you to meet the full responsibilities that God planned for your life.

Much emerging potential dies for want of cultivation.

## Keys to Maximizing Your Potential—Part 2

*Be self-controlled and alert. Your enemy the devil prowls around like a roaring lion looking for someone to devour* (1 Peter 5:8).

BOOK QUOTE: *Releasing Your Potential* [Chapter 4]

Many times we are initially excited by the glimpses God gives us of the potential He planted within us. In the early weeks and months after we invite Jesus into our hearts, we may spend time in worship, prayer, and Bible study; we may attempt to look beyond our present circumstances to the unseen world of faith; we may seek God's guidance in our daily decisions as we open ourselves to His plans and purposes for our lives; we may appreciate and treasure the many blessings He showers upon us; we may carefully adjust our surroundings to make them uplifting and positive; and we may work to bring our dreams and ideas to completion. But as time passes, the garden of our potential loses its early vitality as we allow circumstances and responsibilities to crowd and choke the imaginations and the possibilities that lie hidden within us.

I want to share the second of the four keys to encouraging your garden to maturity as you liberate all the potential that God deposited in you.

**Key #2**—You must guard your potential.

Most gardeners have experienced the frustration and the disappointment that occur when rabbits, insects, or birds destroy their carefully cultivated plants. Fences, insecticides, and scarecrows are some of the many things they use to protect young plants from those things that would seek to devour them.

Satan is intent on destroying your potential. He is constantly trying to use a multitude of circumstances, attitudes, things, and people to devour your abilities. You will never see but a small portion of what you can do unless you guard your hidden wealth. The release of your full potential is directly dependent on your diligence in protecting your dreams, plans, and imaginations from the many negative influences that would block their effective fulfillment.

> The release of your full potential is directly dependent on your diligence in protecting it.

# Keys to Maximizing Your Potential—Part 3

*I planted the seed, Apollos watered it, but God made it grow. So neither he who plants nor he who waters is anything, but only God, who makes things grow. The man who plants and the man who waters have one purpose, and each will be rewarded according to his own labor* (1 Corinthians 3:6-8).

BOOK QUOTE: *Releasing Your Potential* [Chapter 4]

How well is your potential progressing? Perhaps you are tapping some of the wealth God stored in you for the world's benefit, but your progress is slowing or even stopping.

I want to share the third of the four keys to encouraging your garden to maturity as you liberate all the potential that God deposited in you.

**Key #3**—You must share your potential.

Gardening is a shared effort. While the gardener tills the ground, plants the seeds, and pulls the weeds, the plants will not bear fruit unless the bees pollinate the blossoms, the sun warms the earth, and the rain enables the soil to release its nutrients.

Maximizing your potential and the potential of the billions of people on earth is also a shared effort. *Potential is given for the benefit of many, not for the benefit of one.* There's not much gratification in writing a symphony if no musicians will share their talents to play the music. Nor will the experience of playing the music provide full satisfaction unless an appreciative audience fills the concert hall.

God made human beings to live in fellowship with Himself and other human beings. A loveless life that keeps all its accomplishments to itself will soon lose the inspiration for releasing its potential. If you give freely of your gifts, aspirations, and abilities, your potential will be magnified and maximized.

Potential is given for the benefit of many, not for the benefit of one.

## Keys to Maximizing Your Potential—Part 4

*What then? Shall we sin because we are not under law but under grace? By no means! Don't you know that when you offer yourselves to someone to obey him as slaves, you are slaves to the one whom you obey—whether you are slaves to sin, which leads to death, or to obedience, which leads to righteousness? But thanks be to God that, though you used to be slaves to sin, you wholeheartedly obeyed the form of teaching to which you were entrusted. You have been set free from sin and have become slaves to righteousness* (Romans 6:15-18).

BOOK QUOTE: *Releasing Your Potential* [Chapter 4]

I hope you are encouraged to operate in the principles that will maximize your potential. Review the first three keys that we have shared to refresh your memory.

**Key #1**—You must cultivate your potential.

**Key #2**—You must guard your potential.

**Key #3**—You must share your potential.

Here is the last of the four keys to encouraging your garden to maturity as you liberate all the potential that God deposited in you.

**Key #4**—You must know and understand the laws of limitation.

Every experienced gardener knows that there are numerous laws that affect the success or failure of a garden. Tender plants wilt in the hot sun when they are planted at noon. Inferior fruit or no fruit results when the plants are not watered regularly. Plants left to the mercy of the weeds yield a lesser crop than those that grow in a weed-free environment. While the gardener is free to ignore those laws, he does not have the power to remove the consequences of his actions.

The same is true for your potential. God has given you the freedom and the power to maximize your potential. He has established laws and commandments to protect your potential, and He has given you the freedom to choose either to obey or disobey them. God has also granted you the power to dream and plan and imagine, along with the responsibility to work those imaginations to fruition. Freedom without law results in purposelessness. Power without responsibility is ineffective. Each requires the other to forestall disaster. The outworking of your full potential requires that you understand and abide by the laws and the standards God has set to ensure the full and maximum release of your potential.

God has established laws and commandments to protect your potential, and He has given you the freedom to choose either to obey or disobey them.

God has established laws and commandments to protect your potential, and He has given you the freedom to choose either to obey or disobey them.

## EVIEW the Principles From This Week:

- Principles That Govern Potential
- What God speaks to is the source for what He creates.
- All things have the same components and essence as the source from which they came.
- All things must be maintained by the sources from which they came.
- The potential of all things is related to the sources from which they came.
- Everything in life has the potential to fulfill its purpose.
- Potential is determined and revealed by the demands placed on it by its creator.

**More Principles:**

- You came from God.
- You share the nature and essence of God.
- You will die unless you remain attached to God.
- Your potential is determined by God's potential.
- God gave you the ability to fulfill your potential.
- You can do what God demands of you because He would not require it if He had not built the power to perform it into you.

## Revealing Your Potential

*Oh, the depth of the riches of the wisdom and knowledge of God! How unsearchable His judgments, and His paths beyond tracing out!* (Romans 11:33).

BOOK QUOTE: *Releasing Your Potential* [Chapter 4]

In the great depth of God's wisdom and knowledge, He has carved a path for your potential.

Everything in creation was designed to function on the simple principle of receiving and releasing. Life depends on this principle. What if the plants refused to release the oxygen they possess or if we human beings refused to release the carbon dioxide we produce? The result would be chaos and death for the entire planet. Unreleased potential is not only useless, it is dangerous—both for the person or thing who failed to release it and for everything that lives with them.

Building potential into a product does not necessarily mean that potential will be revealed. Many of us have appliances in our homes that are capable of much more than we require of them. Perhaps you use your oven to bake but not broil because you don't know how to use the broiler. Or maybe you have a vacuum cleaner that has the ability to clean up water as well as dirt, but you haven't used that feature because you aren't aware that the manufacturer built that capability into the machine.

God has built many abilities into men and women. Too often, however, we fail to use that potential because we don't understand either the magnitude of our capabilities or the requirements that are necessary to unleash our power. In the following days, I will outline the keys to the effective release of the wealth of your potential.

> The purpose of a thing cannot be known by asking anyone other than the designer or the manufacturer.

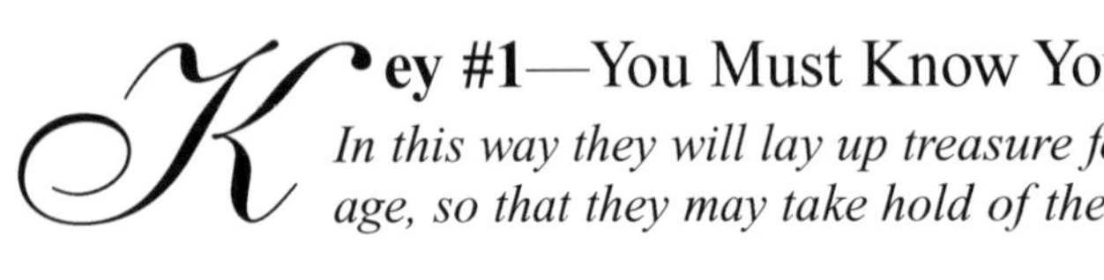

## Key #1—You Must Know Your Source

*In this way they will lay up treasure for themselves as a firm foundation for the coming age, so that they may take hold of the life that is truly life* (1 Timothy 6:19).

BOOK QUOTE: *Releasing Your Potential* [Chapter 4]

Your potential needs to be released or it will remain dormant within you. There are six keys to releasing your potential. The first one is: *You must know your Source*.

Every product you purchase includes a certain degree of guarantee based on a relationship with the one from whom you bought the product. Thus, if you want to buy a car, you will first research the integrity of the various car manufacturers and the quality of their cars. Then you will look for an authorized dealer in your area who will explain and follow the manufacturer's specifications.

> *Know that the Lord is God. It is He who made us, and we are His; we are His people, the sheep of His pasture* (Psalm 100:3).

God is your manufacturer. If you want to know your potential, you must go to Him. God, through His authorized dealer, the Holy Spirit, is the only One who can reveal to you the qualities and characteristics of your potential and the precautions you must heed to avoid wasting or abusing your abilities. Unless you get to know your Source and establish a relationship with Him through His Son, Jesus Christ, you have no hope of releasing your potential. Knowing God is the foundational key upon which all the other keys rest.

God is your manufacturer. If you want to know your potential, you must go to Him.

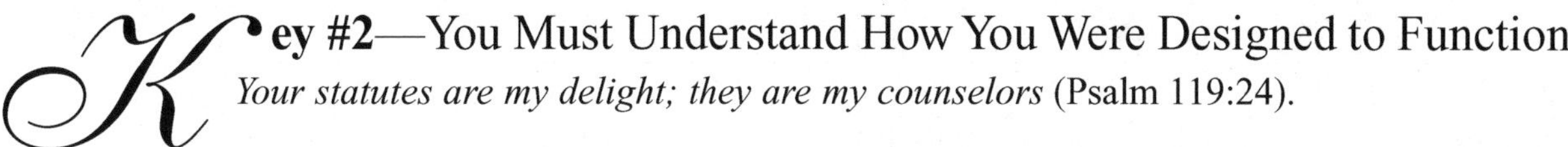

## Key #2—You Must Understand How You Were Designed to Function

*Your statutes are my delight; they are my counselors* (Psalm 119:24).

BOOK QUOTE: *Releasing Your Potential* [Chapter 4]

Potential is only as good as it is released into this world. There are six keys to releasing our potential. The first key from yesterday was: You must know your Source.

Key#2—*You must understand how you were designed to function.*

Every manufacturer designs his product with certain features and specifications. Then he gives you an instruction book that clarifies the definitions of the features so you can become familiar with both the parts of the equipment and their functions. Thus, a car manufacturer describes in the manual how the engine, the brakes, the windshield wipers, etc. are supposed to operate, because he knows that you will not get optimum performance from the car unless you understand how the various parts of the car were intended to work.

God designed you with intricate features and capabilities. If you fail to learn from God how you were designed to function, you are on your way to short-circuiting. You will never release your potential unless you learn to function by faith according to God's specifications.

To release your potential, learn to function by faith according to God's specifications.

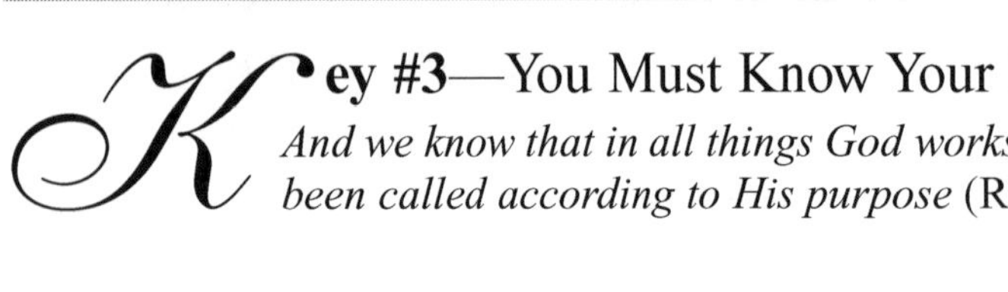

## Key #3—You Must Know Your Purpose

*And we know that in all things God works for the good of those who love Him, who have been called according to His purpose* (Romans 8:28).

BOOK QUOTE: *Releasing Your Potential* [Chapter 4]

There are six keys to releasing our potential. Today we will focus on Key #3. But remember the first two keys in order to guide your study.

Key #1—You must know your Source.

Key #2—You must understand how you were designed to function.

Key #3—*You must know your purpose.*

When a manufacturer proposes a new product, he first clarifies the purpose of that product. Then he designs the features to accomplish his intent. Therefore, a car manufacturer will first decide whether the vehicle is to be a race car, a delivery van, or a family car. Once the vehicle's purpose has been established, the engineer will incorporate various features to meet that purpose.

Before you were born, God had a plan and a purpose for your life. Then, in accordance with that plan, He gave you special abilities and aptitudes to enable you to accomplish everything that He intended. If you are going to release your potential, you must first discover God's plan for your life. Knowing and living within God's purpose is the difference between using and abusing the gifts and capabilities God built into you.

To release your potential, you must first discover God's plan for your life.

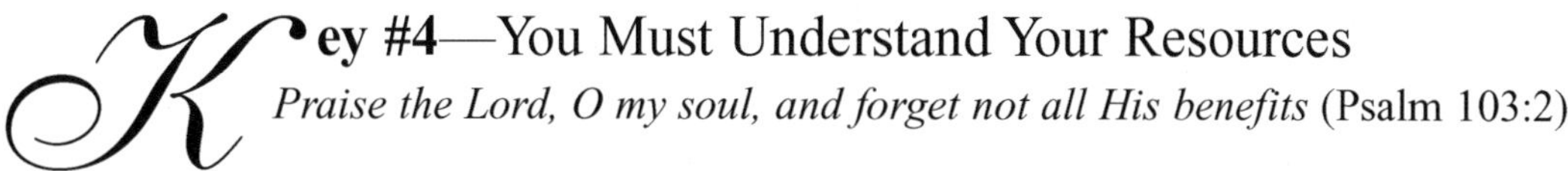

## Key #4—You Must Understand Your Resources

*Praise the Lord, O my soul, and forget not all His benefits* (Psalm 103:2).

BOOK QUOTE: *Releasing Your Potential* [Chapter 4]

There are six keys to releasing our potential. Today we will focus on Key #4. But remember the first three keys in order to guide today's study.

Key #1—You must know your Source.

Key #2—You must understand how you were designed to function.

Key #3—You must know your purpose.

Key #4—*You must understand your resources.*

Manufacturers determine the resources that are necessary for a product to perform correctly and efficiently. A car manufacturer might specify the octane of the gasoline to be used, the pressure of the air in the tires, or the weight of the oil for the engine.

God's pattern for your life also includes specifications for the spiritual, physical, material, and soul resources that are necessary for you to live a fulfilling and productive life. Until you learn what resources God has arranged for you to enjoy, and what benefits He planned for you to receive from each resource, your potential will be stunted and your performance will be less than it could be.

> God's pattern for your life also includes specifications for you to live a fulfilling and productive life.

## Key #5—You Must Have the Right Environment

*...so that you may be able to discern what is best and may be pure and blameless until the day of Christ (*Philippians 1:10).

BOOK QUOTE: *Releasing Your Potential* [Chapter 4]

There are six keys to releasing our potential. Today we will focus on Key #5. But remember the first four keys in order to guide today's study.

Key #1—You must know your Source.

Key #2—You must understand how you were designed to function.

Key #3—You must know your purpose.

Key #4—You must understand your resources.

Key #5—*You must have the right environment*

Product engineers consider carefully both the ideal environment under which a product should operate and any unfavorable conditions that might influence the product's performance. While a car manufacturer might establish the ideal conditions as a sunny day with temperatures between 32 and 70 degrees, the engineer must also plan for rainy days, fog, new moon nights, and freezing or sweltering temperatures.

When God created human beings, He placed them in the Garden of Eden, where ideal conditions for man's growth and fulfillment were present. When sin entered the world through Adam and Eve's disobedience, man's environment became polluted. But most men and women are not aware of the nature or the proliferation of the pollutants that have invaded their environment. The release of your potential requires both a knowledge of the specifications of the ideal environment God provided in the Garden of Eden, and a willingness to make the necessary changes to conform your surroundings to God's specifications.

Releasing your potential requires a willingness to conform your surroundings to God's specifications.

## Key #6—You Must Work Out Your Potential

*The wisdom of the prudent is to give thought to their ways, but the folly of fools is deception* (Proverbs 14:8).

BOOK QUOTE: *Releasing Your Potential* [Chapter 4]

There are six keys to releasing our potential. Today we will focus on Key #6, the last key to releasing your potential. But remember the first five keys in order to guide today's study.

Key #1—You must know your Source.
Key #2—You must understand how you were designed to function.
Key #3—You must know your purpose.
Key #4—You must understand your resources.
Key #5—You must have the right environment
Key #6—*You must work out your potential.*

Most products do not achieve their purpose just by virtue of their existence. They have to do something to meet the expectations of their manufacturer. A car, for example, must transport its occupants and cargo from point A to point B. Thus, its purpose cannot be fulfilled by sitting in the driveway. The potential to fulfill its purpose is present while it sits in the driveway, but the actual achievement of the manufacturer's intent occurs only when the car does what it was designed to do.

God placed Adam in an ideal environment where all the necessary resources for a productive and satisfying life were available to him. Adam enjoyed an intimate relationship with God in which the nature of God, the manner in which God functioned, and the purpose for which God had created man were known to Adam. But Adam's potential would have remained locked inside him if God had not given him a job to do. Only through work was Adam's potential to name the animals revealed. The same is true for you. Your potential will not be released until you take your thoughts, plans, and imaginations and put them into action. You must work to mine your hidden potential.

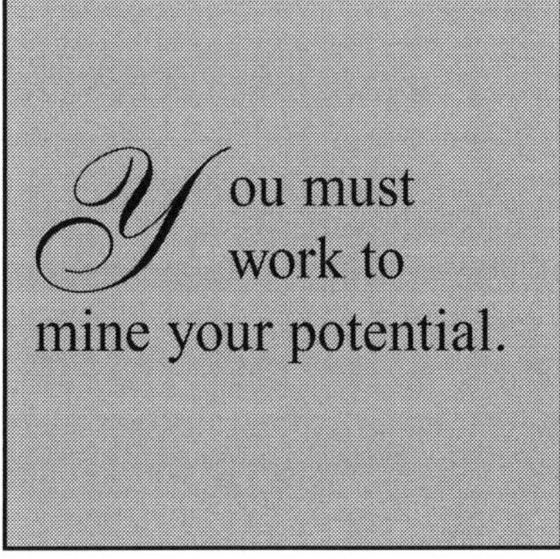

## EVIEW the Principles From This Week:

Keys to Releasing Your Potential

- You must know your Source.
- You must understand how you were designed to function.
- You must know your purpose.
- You must understand your resources.
- You must have the right environment.
- You must work out your potential.

## The Impact of Source on Your Potential

[God's] *divine power has given us everything we need for life and godliness through our knowledge of Him who called us by His own glory and goodness. Through these He has given us His very great and precious promises, so that through them you may participate in the divine nature and escape the corruption in the world caused by evil desires* (2 Peter 1:3,4).

BOOK QUOTE: *Releasing Your Potential* [Chapter 5]

Potential is determined and released by the demands made on it by its creator. These demands are based on the design and the components the manufacturer uses to create the product.

God has designed you to release and maximize your potential. But this is possible only when you are related to your Source. Apart from its source, a product cannot know what it's supposed to be or how it was designed to act.

When you became a Christian, God changed your name. He said, "I know you aren't acting like My child, but you are My child. The mess you're in is just a temporary condition. Now that your spirit and My Spirit are reconnected, I can work in you so that your behavior can catch up with your nature. Who you've been is not who you are."

When God created human beings, He intended that we should share *His divine nature.* That is still His intent, even though sin has covered over that nature. If we operate according to God's nature, we will escape all the temptations and the pressures that come against us in our daily lives. God designed us to be holy and good and forgiving, because they are characteristics of His nature, and we share that nature. When we reconnect with God, we naturally have the power to be all that He is.

Do you know what got Jesus into trouble with the religious authorities? He was too natural! He didn't keep all the rules and the regulations by which the Jewish leaders judged spirituality, yet He had the audacity to say, "God and I are tight." Jesus naturally lived from God's perspective.

You are supposed to be naturally like your Source. God's commands do not require you to live supernaturally, but naturally. If you are a Christian, your natural mode of operation is the same as God's because you came out of Him, and the product always has the nature of its source. That's why God is not impressed when you keep your body free from drugs and your mind free from impure thoughts, or when you give generously, or when you fast and pray. God expects you to act and think like He does because He is your Source/Creator and you are His child.

> God's commands do not require you to live supernaturally, but naturally.

## Your Source/Creator Determines What You Can Do

*Jesus gave them this answer: "I tell you the truth, the Son can do nothing by Himself; He can do only what He sees his Father doing, because whatever the Father does the Son also does"* (John 5:19).

BOOK QUOTE: *Releasing Your Potential* [Chapter 5]

What you can do is related to where you came from. God is serious when He says, "Without Me you can do nothing." It's not a matter of being spiritual, it just plain business sense. He created and made you. You came from Him. Therefore, the quality of your abilities is defined by God's abilities. If you want to know what you can do, find out what God can do.

*God, who is omnipotent, created you to share His potential.* When He took you out of Himself, He automatically gave you the ability to be creative and imaginative. You share God's potential to plan, design, and bring dreams into reality. God is full of more projects, ambitions, and proposals than you can imagine. He's the God of the impossible. But He has tied the revelation of His potential to your dreams, aspirations, and prayers. That's why God is constantly challenging you to ask Him for the impossible. The possible is no fun for God. He's already done that. It's the ideas, plans, and objectives the world hasn't seen yet that God wants to do.

You are the key to God's creative expression. You can do anything God demands of you because your Creator will never demand more of you than He's already built into you. God's saying to *you*, "Go ahead. Imagine anything you want. There's nothing you can imagine that I don't already have. I need your imagination to demand it. Your potential is related to My potential, and I am omnipotent."

God designed you to operate like He does. Faith is going into the realm where you demand out of God what's in Him that no one has seen yet. Are you in a situation that completely baffles you so that you don't know where to turn? You are the perfect candidate through which God can reveal His glory.

*God gets the glory when you make demands on Him.* If you want to glorify God, make Him do things He hasn't done yet. Go out on a limb and stretch your faith. That's how He created you to function. Without faith you cannot please God (see Hebrews 11:6). He demands you to perform the way He does, and He operates by faith.

> God has tied the revelation of His potential to your dreams, aspirations, and prayers.

## Your Source/Creator Determines Why You Exist

*To one he gave five talents of money, to another two talents, and to another one talent, each according to his ability (*Matthew 25:15a).

BOOK QUOTE: *Releasing Your Potential* [Chapter 5]

You will never know your purpose unless you figure out why God created you. Only God knows your purpose, because He determined it when He gave you life.

The direction you need to live a satisfying and rewarding life cannot be found in your family, your teachers, your employer, your pastor, or your coworkers. They are creatures even as you are. *The only way you can discover your purpose is through a relationship with the One who made you.* God's original desires for you shape your potential because He designed you with care to meet the demands He wants to make on you. The release of your total potential requires that you continually seek God as you try to understand what He had in mind when He laid out His plans for your life.

Jesus tells the story of a man who was going on a journey. Before he left home, the master called his servants to him and gave each of them a portion of his resources. When he returned, he asked each servant to give an accounting of what they had received. Although the master didn't expect each servant to have equal resources when he returned, he did expect that they would have used and increased the property he had entrusted to them (see Matthew 25:14-30).

God has determined the resources you need to live a happy, productive life, because He is the only One who knows what you need to meet the demands He will place upon you. If you are constantly comparing your resources with those of other people, you will be blinded both to the richness of what God has entrusted to you and the tasks He wants you to accomplish using what you have. The release of your full potential demands that you examine your life carefully so you can identify both the many assets God has given you and the purpose for which He gave them. God will not entrust you with more resources until you use wisely what He's already given you.

> God will not entrust you with more resources until you use wisely what He's already given you.

## Your Source/Creator Determines the Conditions You Need for Optimum Performance

*The Lord brought me forth as the first of His works, before His deeds of old; I was appointed from eternity, from the beginning, before the world began (Proverbs 8:22-23).*

BOOK QUOTE: *Releasing Your Potential* [Chapter 5]

Your Creator/Source is the only One who is qualified to define your optimal environment. He does so through His laws and commandments. God's laws establish the elements of your ideal environment and set the necessary requirements for consistent, healthy growth. *God's commandments help you to maintain your environment.* They serve as indicators of the state of your health and the condition of your environment. Your well-being is dependent upon your understanding of God's laws and your obedience to His commandments. You can't afford to break God's commandments because disobedience brings a polluted environment, which stunts and impedes the release of your potential.

You have the potential to perform great exploits for God. But if you fail to maintain the environment God decrees, nothing will happen in your life. It doesn't matter how much you brag about what you can do or what you would like to do, or how much you can see and dream and imagine; if God's requirements aren't met, you aren't going to expose your true self!

God not only wants to share with you His plans for your life, He also wants you to understand the variety of experiences that He deems necessary for you to effectively fulfill those plans. Many people try one thing after another as they search for the meaning of their lives. They move from one job to the next, from one church to the next, from one town to the next, and from one spouse to the next. When the going gets a little rough, they move on to something else. They never hang in there long enough to make any progress.

Jesus tells a story about a woman who swept her house and searched carefully until she found the coin she had lost (see Luke 15:8-10). She didn't just sit in her chair and mourn her loss; she got up and worked until she found it. She translated her desire into a plan, and her plan into *action*. The release of your potential requires that you stick with something until you see it through. It's not enough just to *think* about what God wants from your life; you have to get up and do it.

*Work is the method God established to release His potential.* The creation story tells us that God worked so hard creating the world that He was tired when He finished. Because you came out of God, work is also required of you to bring forth all the invisible jewels that lay hidden inside you. God established work as a priority that brings fulfillment and contentment. *He designed you to work out your potential.*

It's not enough just to *think* about what God wants from your life; you have to get up and do it.

## Lesson From Sony

*For this reason, since the day we heard about you, we have not stopped praying for you and asking God to fill you with the knowledge of his will through all spiritual wisdom and understanding* (Colossians 1:9).

BOOK QUOTE: *Releasing Your Potential* [Chapter 5]

Sony is a Japanese company that manufactures electronics. When you buy an appliance from Sony, you will find a booklet titled "Operating Instructions." You will also find a small slip of paper that says, "*Before disengaging or operating this machine, read these instructions carefully*." Because Sony wants you to experience the maximum enjoyment from its product, the company wants you to be thoroughly familiar with the quality and the capabilities of the machine *before you use it*.

The same is true of the highly sophisticated equipment God designed called men and women. You will never reach your optimal performance unless you first check God's operating instructions. The Bible is God's manual on you. You cannot operate properly until you become acquainted with everything God built into you.

One of the first pages in the Sony manual says "Owner's Record" at the top. This page instructs you to *locate the machine's serial number* and *record that number in the space provided below*.

The serial number of a product separates it from all other equipment of that same make and model. The day you invited Jesus into your heart you began a journey that is uniquely yours. Your personality traits and your life experiences have influenced both that moment of decision and your life in Christ since that day.

The early pages in the book of Sony also include a list of *specifications*. This list details each part of the equipment and tells you what to do if a certain part needs to be replaced. These instructions always include the phrase: "*If service is required, please take or send this product to an authorized dealer who will use genuine Sony parts*."

The Bible details your specifications. God designed you to be filled with the Holy Spirit. If you become filled with a demon spirit or some other foul spirit, you will not function in accordance with God's intentions. That's why a man without God is a dangerous man. He is literally insane. Even though a man's manners may be good, if his spirit is wrong, his behavior will eventually reflect his spirit.

> You cannot operate properly until you become acquainted with everything God built into you.

## Features and Precautions

*Just as you who were at one time disobedient to God have now received mercy as a result of their disobedience, so they too have now become disobedient in order that they too may now receive mercy as a result of God's mercy to you. For God has bound all men over to disobedience so that He may have mercy on them all* (Romans 11:30-32).

BOOK QUOTE: *Releasing Your Potential* [Chapter 5]

Never confuse behavior with regeneration. Your behavior is a result of the conversion of your thinking. Regeneration is the source of that conversion. You cannot demand righteousness from an unrighteous spirit. That's why God gives you His Spirit when you come back to Him. Proper behavior is impossible without the Holy Spirit because your functions arise from the nature of your spirit. If you want to function by love, you have to have the Spirit who is the Source of love.

Song, the electronics company packs a manual with new equipment. Among other things, the manual contains a list of the features Sony built into the equipment.

God has created you with certain features that He has defined and clarified in His operating manual. You have a body, a soul, and a spirit. *If you want to operate up to your full potential, you must carefully study how God designed each of these features to function.* There are certain laws that govern each characteristic. If you disregard these laws, you cannot function properly.

Sony also details the *precautions* to be observed when you operate the equipment. These are the don'ts you must avoid if you want to enjoy the highest quality and the maximum performance from the tape recorder.

When God created man, He put him in a beautiful garden and gave him authority over all that was in the garden. Then God gave man a *precaution*: "You can eat from all the trees in the garden except for this one tree. If you eat from this tree you will die." *God's precaution was an act of love.* He wanted to save man from the penalties of sin and death. But man violated God's precaution. We are still living with the consequences of that disobedience.

If God gives you a precaution, don't test it to see what will happen if you do it. *Precautions always indicate the consequences of specific actions.* Disobedience is always followed by the assessment of the penalty.

> A person without God is dangerous.

## Your Warranty

*For in Him we live and move and have our being. As some of your own poets have said, "We are His offspring"* (Acts 17:28).

BOOK QUOTE: *Releasing Your Potential* [Chapter 5]

Any operating manual for an electronic device describes the *manufacturer's warranty* and the limitations to that warranty. The manufacturer's warranty guarantees that you can return the product to the manufacturer for repair or replacement if the product fails during the specified warranty period. If, however, you violate the warranty limitations, the company is no longer responsible for the equipment. You are. These limitations refer primarily to the operation, environment, and maintenance of the equipment.

God's warranty includes a clause of grace. He'll take you in your wrecked state and throw out satan's parts. Though it may take years, God will continue to work on your memory banks until your mind is cleaned and your life is transformed. Thank God for His grace. He will pay for all the costs to fix you so long as you go to the right dealer. But you can't expect God to fix you if you are going to satan for repair.

The last thing the electronics company tells you in the operating instructions is to *retain the manual for future reference.* In other words, don't throw away your Bibles. You need God's manual to answer the operational questions you will meet in your daily life. You can function three thousand percent better than you are now functioning, so don't get rid of God's manual. The Bible contains the answers for a fulfilling, productive life.

The omnipotent God is your Source/Creator. His instruction manual details the requirements, guidelines, and warnings upon which your very life depends. God's life isn't dependent on you. He's alive without you. But your life is dependent on Him. You need Him to find true life. A relationship with God through Jesus Christ, His Son, is the gateway to a full and rich life. He is the foundational key to understanding and releasing your potential. Knowing Him and His intent for your life is the basis for an effective life.

> You can't expect God to fix you if you are going to satan for repair.

## EVIEW the Principles From This Week:

- God wants you to share His divine nature.
- You are the key to God's creative expression.
- God designed you to operate by faith.
- God has a plan for your life.
- You must have a relationship with your Creator to discover your purpose.
- You have the potential to do great things for God.
- Work is the method God established to release your potential.
- The Bible is God's manual on you. You need to know and heed the requirements, guidelines, and warnings it contains.

## Only God Knows Your Value and Potential

*But there is a place where someone has testified: "What is man that you are mindful of him, the son of man that you care for him?"* (Hebrews 2:6)

BOOK QUOTE: *Releasing Your Potential* [Chapter 6]

The basic principles that apply to the potential of all things also apply to your potential. God, your Source/Creator, is the Definer of your potential. Because you came from God and share His essence and components, your value and potential are known to Him alone.

Throughout the history of mankind, God has sought to overcome the blindness that sin has brought to our lives. He watches with sadness as His creations discount their potential and doubt their worth. He cries with and for them as they stumble along, missing the many ways He affirms and confirms the valuable persons He created them to be.

The boundaries of what God can accomplish through you were set long before you were born. He planned your days before you had lived even one of them (see Psalm 139:16). God wants you to see yourself and your abilities the way He sees you. He puts great value on you and eagerly encourages each step you take toward using even a small part of your talents and abilities. God believes in you. The Bible has much to say about your personal worth and your unique capabilities.

The Bible is the story of God's interaction with man. It contains many promises from God to His people, as well as the demands God makes on those who would live in fellowship with Him. The Bible also reveals how God sees human beings and their capabilities. God, by sending His Son, shows us the value He places on us. His willingness to send Jesus to die for our sins is the proof of how much we are worth.

When you go to the store to buy a product, you don't put a value on that product. The value of the merchandise was established long before you chose to buy it. When the courtroom of the universe demanded a price for humanity, the value that was placed on the human soul was equal to the death of God. I didn't say the value of the death of God was equal to the human soul. I said that the human soul was equal to the value of the death of God. In other words, God said, "Whatever it costs to restore the fellowship between men and women and Myself, that's the price I will pay." It's not what is paid that gives value to an item, but what it costs.

> God's willingness to send Jesus to die for our sins is the proof of how much we are worth.

## God's Word on Your Value

*But God demonstrates His own love for us in this: While we were still sinners, Christ died for us* (Romans 5:8).

BOOK QUOTE: *Releasing Your Potential* [Chapter 6]

The Bible is the story of God's interaction with man. It contains many promises from God to His people, as well as the demands God makes on those who would live in fellowship with Him. The Bible also reveals how God sees human beings and their capabilities. God, by sending His Son, shows us the value He places on us. His willingness to send Jesus to die for our sins is the proof of how much we are worth.

When you go to the store to buy a product, you don't put a value on that product. The value of the merchandise was established long before you chose to buy it. When the courtroom of the universe demanded a price for humanity, the value that was placed on the human soul was equal to the death of God. I didn't say the value of the death of God was equal to the human soul. I said that the human soul was equal to the value of the death of God. In other words, God said, "Whatever it costs to restore the fellowship between men and women and Myself, that's the price I will pay." It's not what is paid that gives value to an item, but what it costs.

God's willingness to send Jesus to die for our sins is the proof of how much we are worth.

## od's Word on Your Potential

*So don't be afraid; you are worth more than many sparrows* (Matthew 10:31).

BOOK QUOTE: *Releasing Your Potential* [Chapter 6]

Do you understand how much you are worth? You are equal to the value of your Source. You are as valuable as the God you came from! Stop feeling bad about other people's estimations of your value. You are special. You are worth feeling good about. God's word on your potential is the only evaluation that counts. You are not what your teacher or your spouse or your children or your boss say about you. *You are as valuable and capable as God says you are.* If you are going to release your full potential, you must understand and accept the value God places upon you and the confidence He has in your abilities.

Even as God is the One who set your value, so too He is the only One who is qualified to determine the extent of your potential. The possibilities that lie within you are dependent upon God, because the potential of a thing is always determined by the source from which it came. Even as the potential of a wooden table is determined by the strength of the tree from which it was made, so your potential is determined by God, because you came out of God. God's Word contains numerous statements that clearly define His evaluation of your potential.

It's not what is paid that gives value to an item, but what it costs.

## ou Are in God's Class Because You Are Spirit

*But it is the spirit in a man, the breath of the Almighty, that gives him understanding* (Job 32:8).

BOOK QUOTE: *Releasing Your Potential* [Chapter 6]

Do you remember the process by which God created the world? God first planned what He wanted to create; then He decided what He wanted it to be made from; then He spoke to what He wanted it made from; what He spoke came forth from what He spoke to. When God wanted animals, for example, He spoke to the dirt because that's what He wanted animals to be made of. Obviously, God did not want you and me to be made of dirt or water or the gases of the air, because He did not speak to the ground or the water or the air. He, who is Spirit, spoke to Himself:

> *Then God said, "Let Us make man in Our image..."* (Genesis 1:26).

The source to which God spoke when He created man reveals that God wanted us to be like He is.

Now if we further examine the stories of man's creation as recorded in Genesis chapters one and two, we discover that God used two kinds of operations when He called the world into being. He *made* things and He *created* things. The Hebrew word for "make" is *asha*, which means "to form out of something that is already there." *Brera*, the Hebrew word for "create," means "to form out of nothing." It is interesting, then, that Genesis 1:26 says, "*Let Us* ***make*** *man in Our image*..." and the following verse says, "*So God* ***created*** *man in His own image...*" The creation of man thus involved two different operations.

God *created* man out of nothing, which is Himself, then formed man's house from the dust of the ground. After man's house was completed, God took what He had created and put it inside what He had made. Therefore, man came out of God and is spirit even as God is Spirit. The house, which is your body, will decay and return to the ground from which it came. Your spirit, which is your true essence, will live forever because spirits cannot die. You share God's eternal Spirit, with all the dreams, aspirations, and desires He contains.

> You share God's eternal Spirit, with all the dreams, aspirations, and desires He contains.

## ou Can Operate Like God Operated

*With the tongue we praise our Lord and Father, and with it we curse men, who have been made in God's likeness* (James 3:9).

BOOK QUOTE: *Releasing Your Potential* [Chapter 6]

God also created us to operate like He does: *Then God said, "Let Us make man in Our image, in Our likeness…"* (Genesis 1:26).

The Hebrew word translated into the English word *likeness* means "to operate like," not "to look like." God's original design for man requires that we function like God.

Adam and Eve's fall from their initial relationship with God blinded them to their natural mode of operation. Since then, men and women have had difficulty figuring out how they are supposed to act. Instead of cooperating with God, we live in opposition to Him, following the influences of satanic forces.

God operates by faith. The light in the darkness was not visible before God called it forth, but He believed that light was present in the darkness and, by faith, He spoke it into view. Faith isn't a jump in the dark. It is a walk in the light. Faith is not guessing; it is knowing something.

God made and fashioned you to operate by faith. He designed you to believe the invisible into becoming visible. You may not see what God is calling forth from your life, but God asks you to believe it is there. He created you to operate like He does. If you aren't functioning like God, you are malfunctioning. The manual says, "*The just shall live by faith*" (Romans 1:17b), and "*everything that does* ***not come from faith is sin*** [missing the Manufacturer's standards and expectations]" (Romans 14:23b).

Faith isn't a jump in the dark…it is knowing something.

## You Can Dominate, Rule, and Subdue the Earth

*"Everything is permissible for me"—but not everything is beneficial. "Everything is permissible for me"—but I will not be mastered by anything* (1 Corinthians 6:12).

BOOK QUOTE: *Releasing Your Potential* [Chapter 6]

God's perspective on our potential says that we have the power to dominate and subdue the earth.

> *Then God said, "Let Us make man in Our image, in Our likeness, and let them rule over the fish of the sea and the birds of the air, over the livestock, over all the earth, and over all the creatures that move along the ground"* (Genesis 1:26).

Now what does it mean to be a dominator of the earth? It means that the earth should not rule or control us. If you are addicted to cigarettes, you are being controlled by a leaf. If you are ruled by alcohol, you are being controlled by grain. Leaves and grain are the earth. God created you to dominate the earth, not the earth to dominate you. If you are being controlled by any habit, you are submitting to the very things God commands you to dominate.

The apostle Paul confirms God's intent for man when he writes:

> *...I beat my body and make it my slave so that after I have preached to others, I myself will not be disqualified for the prize* (1 Corinthians 9:27).

He's telling you to use your head. There are things in the earth that will rule you if you allow them to take control of your physical body.

God's given you the potential to dominate the earth. You have the power to beat whatever habit is ruling you. It's there whether you use it or not. Your ability to release the full purpose for which God created you is dependent on your decision to use the potential God gave you to control those things that seek to entrap and subdue you. It's up to you whether you exercise the power God built into you.

God created *you* to dominate *the earth*, not the earth to dominate you.

## ou Can Be Fruitful and Multiply

*By their fruit you will recognize them. Do people pick grapes from thornbushes, or figs from thistles?* (Matthew 7:16).

BOOK QUOTE: *Releasing Your Potential* [Chapter 6]

God's perspective on our potential includes dominating, ruling and subduing the earth. His perspective also sees our potential to multiply. God gave every human being the potential to be fruitful and to reproduce after their kind.

> *God blessed them and said to them, "Be fruitful and increase in number; fill the earth and subdue it. Rule over the fish of the sea and the birds of the air and over every living creature that moves on the ground* (Genesis 1:28).

While it is true that God gave us the ability to have children, the potential God is talking about here is much more than the capacity to have babies. He has given men and women the potential to reproduce what they are. We are producing the next generation.

What kind of children are you producing? God has given you the power to influence them either for good or for evil. Will the next generation be cussing, alcoholic, illiterate people? Or will they be righteous and upright, seeking the Lord and obeying His commandments? You have the capacity to produce children who mirror your life.

> You have the capacity to produce children who mirror your life.

EVIEW the Principles From This Week:

- God believes in You and your abilities.
- You are as valuable and capable as God says you are.
- You have God's nature and qualities.
- You are to operate by faith.
- You are to dominate, rule and subdue the earth.
- You are to be fruitful and multiply.

## You Can Plan to Do and Be Anything

*It is God who arms me with strength and makes my way perfect* (Psalm 18:32).

BOOK QUOTE: *Releasing Your Potential* [Chapter 6]

The basic principles that apply to the potential of all things also apply to your potential. God, your Source/Creator, is the Definer of your potential. The Bible has much to say about your personal worth and your unique capabilities. You can dominate, rule, and subdue the earth. You can be fruitful and multiply.

God has also given human beings the capacity to imagine and plan and believe anything into reality. That's an awesome potential. The Bible reveals this power in the story of the building of the tower of Babel:

> *The Lord said, "If as one people speaking the same language they have begun to do this, then nothing they plan to do will be impossible for them"* (Genesis 11:6).

In other words, God says, "If I don't interfere, man will be able to do anything he thinks about and plans."

God did interfere in the building of that tower, but He didn't stop the people from thinking. He stopped them from understanding one another. You have the potential to think, to imagine, to plan, and to put your plan into action. Anything you carry through from thought to action is within your power to accomplish.

God has given human beings the capacity to imagine and plan and believe anything into reality.

# ou Can Accomplish Impossibilities

*...Everything is possible for him who believes* (Mark 9:23).

BOOK QUOTE: *Releasing Your Potential* [Chapter 6]

The basic principles that apply to the potential of all things also apply to your potential. God, your Source/Creator, is the Definer of your potential. The Bible has much to say about your personal worth and your unique capabilities. You can dominate, rule and subdue the earth. You can be fruitful and multiply. You have the capacity to imagine and plan and believe anything into reality.

Consistent with man's ability to make plans and bring them to completion is his power to believe impossibilities into possibilities. Jesus said to the father of a demon-possessed boy:

*...Everything is possible for him who believes* (Mark 9:23).

This ability is an extension of man's potential to operate like God.

The Gospel of Matthew tells a story of faith in which one of Jesus' disciples, for a moment, accomplished the impossible. Peter, with the other disciples, was in a boat on the Sea of Galilee when Jesus came to them, walking on the water. The disciples, thinking it was a ghost, cried out in fear. After Jesus had identified Himself, impetuous Peter replied, "*Lord, if it's You...tell me to come to You on the water*" (Matthew 14:28).

Now you and I know that the physical laws of nature should have prevented Peter from walking to Jesus. But the laws of faith are different. When Jesus told him to come, Peter got out of the boat and went toward Jesus. Only when he became fearful of the wind and the waves did he begin to sink. "*Immediately Jesus reached out His hand and caught him. 'You of little faith,' He said, 'why did you doubt?'*" (Matthew 14:31).

If you are a man or woman of faith, you have the awesome power to operate by the laws of faith. Impossibilities become possibilities when you use this potential.

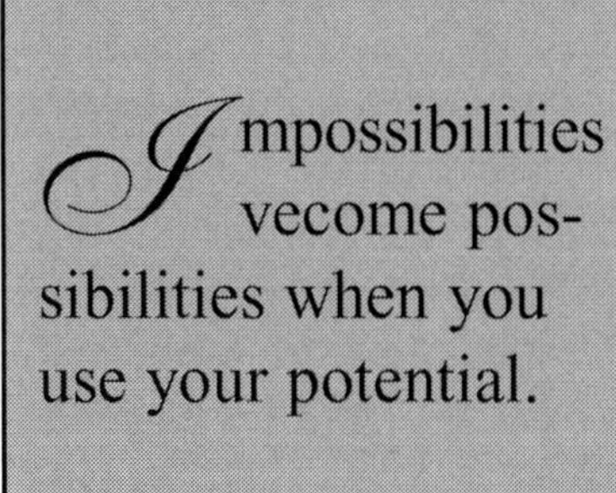

mpossibilities vecome possibilities when you use your potential.

## You Can Influence Things on Earth and in Heaven

*Then Jesus came to them and said, "All authority in Heaven and on earth has been given to Me.* (Matthew 28:18).

BOOK QUOTE: *Releasing Your Potential* [Chapter 6]

Man's tremendous potential includes the capacity to influence both physical and spiritual things. This capacity is a colossal power that we seldom use. Jesus pointed to this power when He told Peter (after Peter had confessed), "*...You are the Christ, the Son of the living God*" (Matthew 16:16).

> *Jesus replied, "Blessed are you, Simon son of Jonah, for this was not revealed to you by man, but by My Father in Heaven. And I tell you that you are Peter, and on this rock I will build My church, and the gates of Hades will not overcome it. I will give you the keys of the kingdom of Heaven; whatever you bind on earth will be bound in Heaven, and whatever you loose on earth will be loosed in Heaven.* (Matthew 16:17-19).

Jesus is encouraging us to look beyond the physical circumstances of our lives to the spiritual dimension. If you are dealing with just the physical aspects of your life, you are missing the real thing. Look beyond the problems in your job or with your spouse or in your church to the spiritual realities that underlie them. Say in the natural what you want to happen in the spiritual. The power to affect both realms is yours. You hold the keys to your effective participation in God's Kingdom, because all authority in Heaven and on earth belongs to Jesus (see Matthew 28:18), and He has shared that power with you.

> If you are dealing with just the physical aspects of your life, you are missing the real thing.

## ou Can Receive Whatever You Ask

*As for you, the anointing you received from Him remains in you, and you do not need anyone to teach you. But as His anointing teaches you about all things and as that anointing is real, not counterfeit—just as it has taught you, remain in Him* (1 John 2:27).

BOOK QUOTE: *Releasing Your Potential* [Chapter 6]

We are continuing to learn how to act like our Source. One principle we need to operate within is in the area of receiving.

During His time on earth, Jesus gave His disciples a blank check. He promised them that they could receive whatever they requested.

> *Therefore I tell you, whatever you ask for in prayer, believe that you have received it, and it will be yours* (Mark 11:24).

> *If you remain in Me and My words remain in you, ask whatever you wish, and it will be given you. This is to My Father's glory, that you bear much fruit, showing yourselves to be My disciples* (John 15:7-8).

Jesus cautioned His disciples that the evidence of fruit in their lives would be the indicator that they were His disciples. He also established the key to bearing fruit as their willingness to remain in touch with Him. Insofar as you remain in touch with your Creator/ Source, you have the power to ask whatever you wish and to receive what you request. That's God's promise concerning your potential. He's waiting to give you whatever you request, so long as you sink your roots deep into His Word and allow His words to influence and direct your entire life.

> You have the power to ask whatever you wish and to receive what you request.

# ou Have the Power to Do Greater Works Than Jesus Did

*You may ask Me for anything in My name, and I will do it* (John 14:14).

BOOK QUOTE: *Releasing Your Potential* [Chapter 6]

During His last days on earth, Jesus spent much time with His disciples teaching them, praying for them, and encouraging them to live in His power. As He spoke of His return to the Father, Jesus assured His disciples that they would continue the work He had begun because they would receive the same power they had witnessed in His ministry (see Acts 1:8).

> *Believe Me when I say that I am in the Father and the Father is in Me; or at least believe on the evidence of the miracles themselves. I tell you the truth, anyone who has faith in Me will do what I have been doing. He will do even greater things than these, because I am going to the Father. And I will do whatever you ask in My name, so that the Son may bring glory to the Father. You may ask Me for anything in My name, and I will do it* (John 14:11-14).

We usually measure those works in terms of the height of the water we will walk on or the number of people we will feed from a few groceries. That is, we interpret Jesus' words to mean that we will do *more* works, when that was not His intent.

Jesus was one man in one body with the Spirit of God living inside Him. His ministry consisted of that which He could accomplish as one person, in a specific geographic area, at a certain point in history. After Jesus' death and His return to the Father, the Spirit of God was freed to fill millions of people, not just one. The Book of Acts tells the story of the Spirit's outpouring on the early Church.

When Jesus foretold that His disciples would do greater works than He had done, He was talking about the baptism of the Holy Spirit and the power that outpouring would bring into their lives. If you have received Jesus as your Savior, and the Holy Spirit is operative in your life, you have the potential to share in the Church's commission to do greater works than Jesus did. *Therefore, the greater works did not refer to greater in quality, but in quantity and dimension.* These works were no longer limited to one body or one geographical location, but became worldwide. What potential!

"You may ask Me for anything in My Name, and I will do it."

## Your Potential is Dependent Upon God

*The grace of our Lord was poured out on me abundantly, along with the faith and love that are in Christ Jesus* (1 Timothy 1:14).

BOOK QUOTE: *Releasing Your Potential* [Chapter 6]

What does it mean when Jesus told His disciples that they would do greater works than He had done? Some people believe that God is afraid we're going to take His job. When we start talking about what we're going to do for God or what we're going to dream, some people say, "You'd better not think bigger than God." Well, you can never be bigger than your Source. *You can't think or plan or imagine something greater than God, because God is the source of your imagination.* He leaked part of His potential into you when He pulled you out of Himself. It's like owning a Sony video cassette recorder with multiple features. It cannot fulfill its purpose or potential until it is plugged into an electrical source. So it is for every man. We must plug into our Source.

It is imperative, then, that you understand the characteristics and qualities of God, as well as the provisions He has made to enable you to fulfill the purpose for which He created you. *Your ability to release your potential is directly related to your knowledge of God and your willingness to stay within the parameters He has established for your relationship with Him.*

## ou Must Know the Qualities and the Nature of God

*Be imitators of God, therefore, as dearly loved children* (Ephesians 5:1).

BOOK QUOTE: *Releasing Your Potential* [Chapter 6]

*Quality* is the degree of excellence or the essence of standard that makes one product better than another. The quality of a product can be no better than the qualities of the product's source. You can't use rotten apples to make a delicious apple pie. The pie will reveal the decay in the apples.

The quality of a product can also be defined as the characteristic attributes or elements that determine the product's basic nature. Those qualities arise out of the basic nature of the product's source. Or to say it another way, those things that occur naturally in a product also occur naturally in that from which the product was made.

*The standards of God are the standards by which your excellence is judged, because you came out of God. Likewise, the characteristics that describe God's basic nature also describe your basic nature.* If you want to know what the standards for your life are, check God's standards. If you want to know what characteristics occur in you naturally, ascertain God's inherent qualities. If God acts by a certain standard or exhibits a certain quality, that standard or quality is part of your life as well.

For example, God has the quality of faithfulness. Therefore, you have the ability to be faithful. Because God is unconditional love, you have the characteristic of love somewhere under all your hatred. Because God is merciful and long-suffering, you can be merciful and long-suffering. All the essential qualities that determine who God is and how He acts also determine who you are and how you were designed to act. Your potential is wrapped up in God because His qualities establish yours. Only when you understand and accept the nature and qualities of God can you begin to understand and accept your nature and qualities.

One of the greatest indicators of your quality and standards is expressed in God's commandments. Whatever He demands of you He knows is inside you. That's why the manual says that His "commandments are not grievous" (see 1 John 5:3).

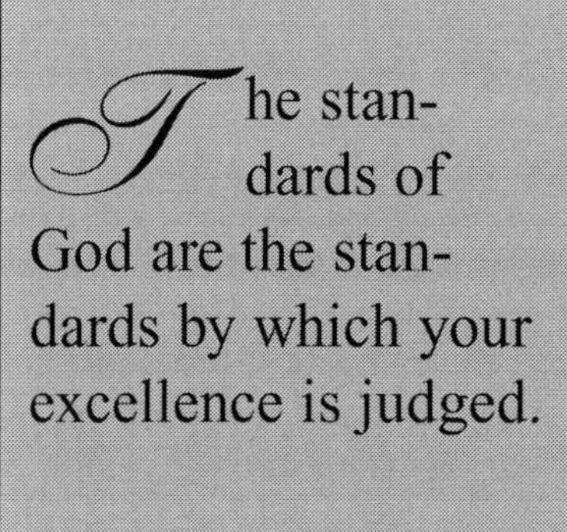

## EVIEW the Principles From This Week:

- You can accomplish anything that you carry through from thought to action.
- You can't think, plan, or imagine something greater than God, because God is the Source of your imagination.
- Your potential is dependent upon God, so you must know His qualities and nature.

## You Must Know God's Laws and Obey His Commandments

*If you fully obey the Lord your God and carefully follow all His commands I give you today, the Lord your God will set you high above all the nations on earth. All these blessings will come upon you and accompany you if you obey the Lord your God* (Deuteronomy 28:1-2).

BOOK QUOTE: *Releasing Your Potential* [Chapter 6]

In the second chapter of Genesis, God set a law about Adam's relationship with the trees of the garden: "*...when you eat of it* [the tree of the knowledge of good and evil] *you will surely die*" (Genesis 2:17). Because of this law, God also gave Adam a command: "*...You are free to eat from any tree in the garden; but you must not eat from the tree of the knowledge of good and evil...*" (Genesis 2:16-17). When Adam disobeyed God, he brought upon himself the reality of the law God had set. He died.

Now the Book of Genesis makes it clear that Adam didn't die physically at the moment of his disobedience. He lived to be 930 years old. Adam's disobedience caused his *spiritual* death.

The death of an old tree is a good word picture to describe the nature of Adam's death. When a large tree is blown down by a hurricane, the tree may lay there for weeks. Although the roots of the tree are torn from the ground and exposed to the air, the tree's leaves do not turn brown as soon as the tree is brought down by the wind. The little sap that was in the roots continues to move up the trunk, out the branches and into the leaves. When the sap is gone, the leaves turn brown. But the reality of that tree's death occurred when it fell, not when the leaves showed the evidence of its death.

Adam walked around with green leaves but no roots for many years. He was dead long before his body showed the evidence of his death. All people share Adam's death. Unless your life becomes *rerooted in God* through the salvation offered in Jesus Christ, you are going to die an eternal death. That's the law of God.

The laws of God are many and they carry with them natural results. His commandments are given for our good because they caution us not to disregard God's laws. When Adam broke God's commandment, he experienced the natural results of God's law.

> Obedience to God's commandments brings His blessings.

Obedience to God's commandments brings His blessings. In Deuteronomy chapter 28—in the words of Moses to the children of Israel—promises God's blessings for those who obey His commandments:

Your potential is limitless so long as you comprehend God's laws and purpose in your heart to obey His commandments.

## ou Must Understand God's Potential

*...so that your faith might not rest on men's wisdom, but on God's power* (1 Corinthians 2:5).

BOOK QUOTE: *Releasing Your Potential* [Chapter 6]

Daniel 11:32 promises that "*the people that know their God shall be strong, and do exploits*" (KJV). This is true because your potential is related to God's potential, and God is *omnipotent*. The combination of *omni* (meaning "always or all full of") and *potent* (meaning "power on reserve"—from which we get the word *potential*) declares that God is always full of power. Or to say it another way, all potential is in God. Thus, people who understand that God contains all the things that He's asking them to do are not afraid to do big things. It's not *what* you know but *who* you know that enables you to do great things with God.

God is God whether you choose to use His potential or not. Your decision to live with Him or without Him does not affect who He is or what He can do. He is not diminished when you choose to replace Him with other sources. God still has the stuff you need to fulfill your potential.

When you combine the knowledge of God's omnipotence with the knowledge of who you are in God, you can resist all things that seek to overcome you and to wipe out your potential. You can be strong and do great exploits. God is the Source of your potential. He waits to draw from His vast store to enable you to accomplish all that He demands of you.

> God is God whether you choose to use His potential or not.

## ou Must Have Faith in God

*He replied, "If you have faith as small as a mustard seed, you can say to this mulberry tree, 'Be uprooted and planted in the sea,' and it will obey you"* (Luke 17:6).

BOOK QUOTE: *Releasing Your Potential* [Chapter 6]

If I give you a tree as a gift and I tell you it is an avocado tree, you will tell every person who asks you what kind of tree is in your front yard that it's an avocado tree. Now you haven't picked any avocados from that tree, but you still dare to say it's an avocado tree. Why? Because you have faith in me that the tree is what I say it is. You believe that somewhere in that tree there are many avocados. Faith is simply believing and acting on the words and integrity of another. Faith in God is to believe and act on what He says.

The words of Jesus as recorded in the Gospel of Mark admonish us to have faith in God.

> *"Have faith in God," Jesus answered. "I tell you the truth, if anyone says to this mountain, 'Go, throw yourself into the sea,' and does not doubt in his heart but believes that what he says will happen, it will be done for him"* (Mark 11:22-23).

What Jesus is really saying is, "Have the God kind of faith." Don't put your faith in your own faith or in the faith of other people or in the mountains or in anything that you expect to happen because of your faith. Put your faith in God, because it's your faith in Him that will accomplish the moving of mountains. You can't speak to the mountain and expect it to move unless you are connected to God. Apart from Him you don't have the power to complete such monumental tasks.

> You can't speak to the mountain and expect it to move unless you are connected to God.

## ou Must Stay Attached to God

*He is the image of the invisible God, the firstborn over all creation. For by Him all things were created: things in Heaven and on earth, visible and invisible, whether thrones or powers or rulers or authorities; all things were created by Him and for Him* (Colossians 1:15-16).

BOOK QUOTE: *Releasing Your Potential* [Chapter 6]

The Book of Colossians describes Jesus as "*the image of the invisible God, the firstborn over all creation. For by Him all things were created: things in Heaven and on earth, visible and invisible…*" (Col. 1:15-16). Hebrews 1:3 tells us that "*the Son is the radiance of God's glory and the exact representation of His being, sustaining all things by His powerful Word.*" The King James Version of this verse says that Jesus upholds all things "*by the Word of His power…*" Not the *power of His Word*, but *the Word of His power*. God's power is released in you when you stay alive with His Word.

When God created plants, He called them forth from the soil, thereby establishing the law that plants must live off the soil. If a plant violates that word, it dies. Thus, God keeps that plant alive by the power of His Word. As long as the plant abides by the law God set at creation, it flourishes and grows. If, however, the plant chooses to disregard that law, death is inevitable.

The same is true in our lives. By taking us out of Himself, God decreed that our lives must be maintained by Him. As long as we obey God's requirement, His power is released within us and we know abundant life. That is why the writer to the Hebrews describes Jesus as the "Word of God's power." There's power in God's Word if we keep it. Jesus, through His obedience unto death, released for us the power of God's Word that brings eternal life.

Jesus looks at this same power from a different perspective when, in the fifteenth chapter of John, He describes Himself as the vine and His disciples as the branches. He used the word picture of the vine because it is the only plant that doesn't have life in its branches. If you clip a branch from a rose bush or a lemon tree, plant it in the soil and give it the proper care, the branch will root and start a new plant. This is not true for the grape vine. There is no life in the branch of a vine. No matter how rich and green it looks, a branch apart from the vine will wither and die.

God's power is released in you when you stay alive with His Word.

## ou Must Stay Connected to God

*He cuts off every branch in me that bears no fruit, while every branch that does bear fruit he prunes so that it will be even more fruitful* (John 15:2).

BOOK QUOTE: *Releasing Your Potential* [Chapter 6]

> *...No branch can bear fruit by itself; it must remain in the vine. Neither can you bear fruit unless you remain in Me* (John 15:4).

*If you cut yourself off from God, your potential is aborted.* No matter how hard you try to plant yourself in other organizations and activities, God says, "You are dead." Even if you plant yourself in religion, you are dead unless you know God and draw your nutrients from Him.

*Our need for God is not an alternative or an option.* Like the plants and the animals, which cannot be maintained without the soil, and the fish, which cannot live outside the water, *we cannot flourish and bear fruit apart from God.* When Jesus says in John 14:6, "*I am the way, the truth and the life...*," He isn't trying to convince us that He's the *best* way. He didn't use that word. Life rooted in God is a necessity. There is no option. Although you can say to a plant, "You can either stay in the soil or get out of the pot and sit on the windowsill," the plant doesn't really have a choice. If the plant chooses the windowsill, it will die. There is no alternative to the soil for the plant to meet its basic needs. So it is with human beings and God.

If you stay within God's Word, His Word takes root in your heart and becomes established. His power is released as you stay alive with His Word. *If, however, you pull yourself out of God, you shut down your productivity* and forfeit the blessings God wants to give you. You become as limited as the books, people, education, etc. that are feeding your thought patterns.

Do you want joy? Go to God. Do you need peace? Set your roots firmly in the Word and power of God. Do you need help to control your temper? Spend time with God. Jesus promises: "...*with God all things are possible*" (Matthew 19:26). God is the soil you unconditionally need.

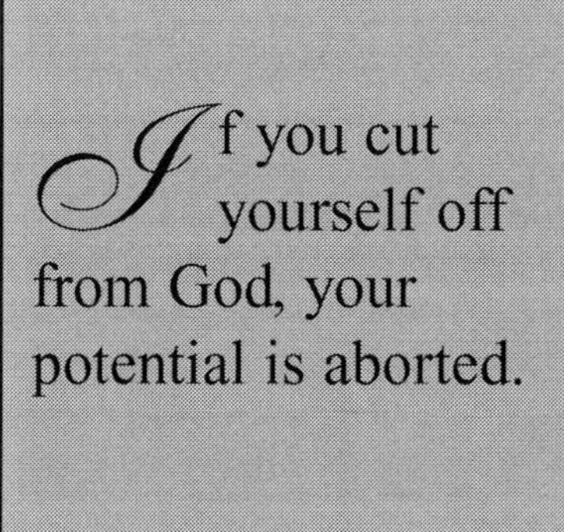

## You Must Cooperate With the Holy Spirit

*And I will ask the Father, and He will give you another Counselor to be with you forever* (John 14:16).

BOOK QUOTE: *Releasing Your Potential* [Chapter 6]

God's potential is far greater than anything we can ask Him to do. Everything that is visible came out of God. Everything that we yet will see is still within Him. Because we came out of God, that same potential is available to us. But there's a catch. God's power must be at work within us before we can tap that power.

> *Now to Him who is able to do immeasurably more than all we ask or imagine, according to His power that is at work within us, to Him be glory in the Church and in Christ Jesus throughout all generations, for ever and ever! Amen* (Ephesians 3:20-21).

When Jesus told His disciples that He was going away, He promised them that the Holy Spirit would come to be with them forever (see John 14:16). Moments before His ascension to Heaven, Jesus also promised that the *power of the Holy Spirit* (see Acts 1:8) would equip His followers to be His messengers.

Is the Holy Spirit present in your life? Are you flowing in a consistent, empowering relationship that undergirds your every thought, dream, and plan? Or are you trying to do great things without the power of the Spirit?

We may see a skyscraper or a space shuttle or a fancy computer and say, "That's something else. Man is really working here." But the Spirit says, "That's nothing compared to what man could do. That's what man is doing without Me. I want you to do something people cannot do unless they have Me. I want you to build people. I have the stuff to empower you to help people build new foundations and open new windows through which to see life. I want to give you a view from the top of life so you can see the way God sees." Wow! What power! That's the power that must be working inside you if you are going to do great things for God.

Your cooperation with the work of the Holy Spirit is the means by which God reveals the stuff He took from Himself and gave to you. When you are in tune with the Holy Spirit, you can do things this world has never seen. The power's there. It's up to you whether you make the connection that releases the power. If that power isn't working in you, your potential is being wasted.

## ou Must Use Christ's Strength

*You, dear children, are from God and have overcome them, because the One who is in you is greater than the one who is in the world* (1 John 4:4).

BOOK QUOTE: *Releasing Your Potential* [Chapter 6]

In Philippians 4:13 Paul says, I can do everything through Him who gives me strength.

*You* cannot do *all things*. You can only do *all things* through *Christ*, who gives you the ability. Even though you may shout to everybody, "I can do all things," God is asking you, "Are you with Christ?" Because if you're not, your plans, dreams, and imaginations will amount to nothing. Without Christ your efforts are futile and the result is frustration.

Romans 8:31 gives me great encouragement: "*If God is for us, who can be against us?*" Now the word *for* is really the Greek word *with*. So let's put it this way: "If God is with me, who can be against me?" The implication is that if God has given you something to do and He is with you, nothing or no one is going to stop you from accomplishing what God wants you to do. I don't care who the person is or how much influence he has, if God is with you, it's not important who is coming against you.

If you are going to release your potential, you must live each day checking out who's *with* you instead of who's against you. You may be experiencing political victimization, pressure from your boss or your spouse or your parents, or unfair treatment from your family or your employer, but these influences are not the most important factors in your life. You can spend the rest of your life fighting the many people and circumstances that come against you, or you can focus on God's presence and treat them as a temporary inconvenience. If God is with you, those who accuse or harass you have no power over you.

This week can be a good one because your protection relies not on how much power your accusers have but on how much power Christ has. Jesus promises you peace and victory if you rely on His strength:

> *In this world you will have trouble. But take heart! I have overcome the world* (John 16:33).

> If God is with you, it's not important who is coming against you.

## EVIEW the Principles From This Week:

- You must know and obey God's laws.
- You must have faith in God to release your potential.
- If you pull yourself out of God, you are dead. He is the soil you unconditionally need.

## Designed for Eternity

*For the wages of sin is death, but the gift of God is eternal life in Christ Jesus our Lord* (Romans 6:23).

BOOK QUOTE: *Releasing Your Potential* [Chapter 7]

Man has become an expert at understanding how plants and animals function. We crossbreed animals to create strains that are stronger, tastier, and more productive, and we graft stock from one tree to another to develop more compact trees that yield tastier fruit that grow larger and keep longer. But we are deficient in our understanding and application of how God designed man to function. We concentrate on our bodies instead of our spirits. This situation seriously threatens our ability to release our potential.

When God created human beings, He spoke to Himself so that men and women could be spiritual beings even as He is Spirit. He designed them to share His knowledge and wisdom and to understand His thoughts and purposes. God also assigned them part of His potential in that He gave them eternal spirits with eternal plans, ideas and projects.

Death and dirt have become such expected parts of our lives that we don't understand or appreciate the concept of free, abundant, eternal life. We assume that death is natural, and we live as though sin is natural, when in truth God designed us to be holy beings who live forever.

Adam's disobedience destroyed God's plan and brought alienation between God and man. Because man was no longer sustained by his Source, man's spirit died and his body lost its ability to continually rebuild and replenish itself. Thus, the sin that brought spiritual death also caused physical death: "*For the wages of sin is death…*" (Romans 6:23).

Man in his fallen state could no longer know and understand the thoughts and purposes of God. He became controlled by his soul instead of his spirit and began to look to his environment for the information he needed. Thus, man without God is a paralyzed spirit in dirt, walking on two legs.

All human beings since Adam sin: "*For all have sinned and fall short of the glory of God...*" (Romans 3:23). They bear in their spirits, souls, and bodies the penalty of his disobedience. You were born spiritually dead or paralyzed, and your body will eventually die. Your brain, apart from God, can know no more than those who teach you or those who write the books you read.

> Man without God is a paralyzed spirit in dirt, walking on two legs.

## Mere Dirt

*"Are you still so dull?" Jesus asked them. "Don't you see that whatever enters the mouth goes into the stomach and then out of the body? But the things that come out of the mouth come from the heart, and these make a man 'unclean.' For out of the heart come evil thoughts, murder, adultery, sexual immorality, theft, false testimony, slander. These are what make a man 'unclean'"* (Matthew 15:16-20a).

BOOK QUOTE: *Releasing Your Potential* [Chapter 7]

Your body does not need God to live. It came from the ground and needs the products from the ground to stay alive. Jesus spoke of this when He spoke to the Pharisees.

*Psyche*, the Greek word translated *heart*, literally means "the core of the spirit." It's what goes into your spirit that destroys you. Cancer may destroy your body, but it can't harm your spirit. True, your spirit may become depressed by the cancer's affects upon your body, but ultimately your spirit will live if you stay attached to God. That's why rebellion against God is such a serious matter. When you detach yourself from your Source, your spirit man dies or enters a state of eternal paralysis, void of relationship and communion with God the Holy Spirit. Then the only thing you have is a decaying body. Life from the body leads to death.

The desire to steal or covet is prompted by what you see with your physical eyes, and your sexual desires are provoked by the physical wants of your body. Indeed, life from the body discourages respect and encourages behavior that regards men and women as objects to be conquered. We are tempted to treat people like products to be manipulated instead of images of Christ to be cherished and honored.

God has a name for those who detach themselves from Him and live from the body. He calls them "mere dirt." Now that's an insult. Any person who doesn't know God is a mere man. A mere person does things unnaturally. Because they don't know their Creator and the purposes and desires He had when He created them, they focus on their *made* beings—that which came from the dust—instead of their *created* beings—that which came from God. They abuse themselves and others because they don't know how God designed them to act. Death and dirt characterize their lives.

> Any person who doesn't know God is a mere man.

## God's Plan of Redemption

*Therefore, there is now no condemnation for those who are in Christ Jesus, because through Christ Jesus the law of the Spirit of life set me free from the law of sin and death* (Romans 8:1-2).

BOOK QUOTE: *Releasing Your Potential* [Chapter 7]

The God who designed you for eternal life still desires the fellowship with you that He originally intended. He sent Jesus into the world to take away the root problem of your sin so eternity can once more be yours.

God didn't need to save you from sin and death to meet *His* needs. He was doing fine before you were saved, and He'll continue to do fine no matter what kind of relationship you have with Him in the future. Jesus was touched by *your* needs. Only when you recognize that coming to God is for your benefit, not God's, does God's grace make sense. Grace is God's reaching out when He didn't need to. Grace is God's caring enough to rework His original plan for the fallen race of man.

You were originally God's property, but satan stole you from God. Jesus paid the redemptive price through death on the cross so you could be restored to eternal life and fellowship with God. When Jesus saved you from sin and death, he rekindled your potential spirit by giving you His Holy Spirit to live in you and to be connected to your spirit. Because of that gift, you can begin to flow again in the many things He gave you before you were born. Through Jesus, God renewed your spiritual life and reconnected your soul to His fountain of wisdom and knowledge.

Although Jesus redeemed your spirit man, your body has not yet been redeemed. After Jesus rose from the dead, He promised that He would return to redeem your body.

God's making you a new home that will far exceed anything that plastic surgery can do for you. All plastic surgeons can do is patch your old body. God's in the business of giving you a new body. So don't worry if this body isn't all you'd like it to be. Patch it, fix it, do whatever you can to spruce it up. *But don't equate your life with your body.* God's going to get out of you all that He put in you. He wants you to start releasing your potential with the body you now have and to continue using your eternal capabilities long after this body has decayed. *You are much more than your imperfect, deteriorating body.*

God's going to get out of you all that He put in you.

God's going to get out of you all that He put in you.

## God's System—Faith

*...Forgetting what is behind and straining toward what is ahead, I press on toward the goal to win the prize for which God has called me heavenward in Christ Jesus* (Philippians 3:13-14).

BOOK QUOTE: *Releasing Your Potential* [Chapter 7]

God designed you to be a limitless person. He pulled you from His omnipotent Self and transferred to you a portion of His potential. He also wired you to operate like He does. When you reconnect with God through faith in Jesus Christ, He empowers you to return to your original mode of operation, which is like His own.

God thinks in terms of potential—of things that are not yet manifested. He relies on what He knows isn't visible yet, instead of what is visible. He is not excited by what you've already done.

The apostle Paul wasn't satisfied with what he had attained. He was always looking for the next step. Why? Because the past is no longer motivational. Only when you look to the future with its demands and challenges can you release more of your untapped talents and abilities.

God's waiting for your potential to be revealed. He says, "You are not what you are acting like. Because you are My child, you have the potential to act better than you're acting. My potential is flowing from Me to you."

Many of us don't appreciate how faith works. We are so used to living from what we can see, hear, and touch that we have great difficulty moving into the realm of faith. If, for example, someone asks us how we are doing, we usually respond based on the condition of our bodies or our souls. We focus on our illnesses or the depressed thoughts that are weighing us down and neglect to mention the many blessings God has promised us. These promises have a much greater impact on our lives than our physical diseases and our emotional struggles.

Faith sees what hasn't been manifested. It deals with what exists but is invisible. The minute you manifest something, it no longer requires faith, because faith is believing, conceiving, and releasing (speaking) until you receive what you desire. "*Faith is being sure of what* [you] *hope for and certain of what* [you] *do not see*" (Hebrews 11:1).

> Faith sees what hasn't been manifested. It deals with what exists but is invisible.

## The Faith Process

*It is written: "I believed; therefore I have spoken." With that same spirit of faith we also believe and therefore speak, because we know that the one who raised the Lord Jesus from the dead will also raise us with Jesus and present us with you in His presence* (2 Corinthians 4:13-14).

BOOK QUOTE: *Releasing Your Potential* [Chapter 7]

Faith begins with *belief.* Actually, faith in someone or something requires unquestioning belief that does not require proof or evidence from the one in whom you have faith. The New Testament word for faith, *pistos*, means "to believe another's testimony." Thus, faith requires you to function by believing first, instead of seeing or feeling first.

That often creates a problem, because faith requires putting your body under the control of your spirit. Your body says, "I'm not going to believe it until I see it." But God says, "If you're going to operate like Me, you aren't going to see it until you believe it!" One operates by sight, the other by faith.

Living by faith also requires that you put your soul under the control of your spirit. Your soul governs your emotions, your will, and your mind. When you live from your soul, you allow information from your physical body to govern your decisions.

After you believe God's promises, you must begin to see (conceive) them in your life. Seeing and looking are very different. Looking regards the outward appearance, while seeing considers the existence of things that are not yet visible.

After you can see something, you have to *release* it. In Genesis, God looked at the darkness and saw light. Although the light existed, it was not made visible until God spoke it into being.

Faith is required of all who want to please God. Hebrews 11:6 warns us that "*without faith it is impossible to please God, because anyone who comes to Him must believe that He exists and that He rewards those who earnestly seek Him*," and Romans 1:17 says, "*The righteous will live by faith.*" You were created to live by faith. God established faith as the only system through which men and women can touch His power. Potential demands faith, and faith makes demands on potential.

*Righteousness*, which, in the Bible, means "to enjoy a right relationship with God," is impossible without God's act of salvation in Jesus Christ. Jesus' death on the Cross freed you from eternal death, which is the penalty for your sin. For those who have received new life in Christ, God renders a verdict of "not guilty."

> Potential demands faith, and faith makes demands on potential.

## Faith Is a Requirement, Not an Option

*Jesus replied, "I tell you the truth, if you have faith and do not doubt, not only can you do what was done to the fig tree, but also you can say to this mountain, 'Go, throw yourself into the sea,' and it will be done"* (Matthew 21:21).

BOOK QUOTE: *Releasing Your Potential* [Chapter 7]

Faith is not an option for the Christian. It is a necessity. If God tells you to get moving, He doesn't want you to stand around until you see the evidence that says you should get moving. He wants you to risk, simply because He is asking you to move.

In fact, faith is not an option for human beings in general. A person who lives on anything but faith is going to live a depressing life. He will be so consumed by his environment and the circumstances of his life that he will never venture beyond the known to release the vast potential inside him. Faith is the source of hope, and no man can live without hope. Faith is the fuel of the future and the energy of anticipation.

Many people are wrecks because they try to live without faith. That's unfortunate because the Scriptures are clear that faith in God is the prerequisite for receiving what you believe, conceive, and release.

> *Therefore I tell you, whatever you ask for in prayer, believe that you have received it, and it will be yours* (Mark 11:24).

Faith is the catalyst that makes things happen. It lifts you above the outward evidence of your life and empowers you to bring light out of darkness. Remember, you will receive whatever you believe. If you expect trouble, you will get it. If you trust God and expect Him to work in the midst of your distressing circumstances, sooner or later you will see evidence of His presence.

Life without faith is foolish because life is not always what it seems. What you see or feel is not the whole story. Believe that things are going to work out. Reject the garbage that discourages you by taking your eyes off God—"You're never going to own a house. You can't even pay this rent. How're you going to afford a mortgage?"—and believe that you are going to make it. Make plans and, by faith, release your dreams by saying: "I know what I see, but I also know what I believe. I'm going to keep believing in my dreams, because all things are possible with God." Praise Him that you don't have to live by what you see. Believe in His promises and expect Him to move mountains for you.

> Faith in God is the prerequisite for receiving what you believe, conceive, and release.

## he Tragedy of Relinquishing Faith

*I have been crucified with Christ and I no longer live, but Christ lives in me. The life I live in the body, I live by faith in the Son of God, who loved me and gave Himself for me* (Galatians 2:20).

BOOK QUOTE: *Releasing Your Potential* [Chapter 7]

If things aren't working out for you, there's probably something wrong with your believing, conceiving, or speaking. Stop being intimidated by evil influences or the wicked one. Because he doesn't want you to live by faith, the evil one tries to convince you to believe wrong, conceive wrong, and speak wrong so there's no way you can receive what you have believed. Refuse to believe his lies and be careful not to worry, about the criticisms and objections of others. *If God is the source of your dream, people cannot destroy it.* You can accomplish what God wills.

Most people who are failures, are failures because they were so close to winning. Don't let that happen to you. You don't know how close you are to receiving the promise you have been waiting for. Just because things are getting worse doesn't mean that God has not heard your request. The closer you get to victory, the harder you are going to have to fight. Often when things are the worst, you are close to receiving what you seek.

Look for the positive in life and renew your voice of faith. Trust in the certainty that you can't lose when you and God are in agreement, and bear in mind that God will reward you if you put Him above all else. Commit yourself to believing, conceiving, and releasing (speaking) every day until you receive what you desire. That's how God created you to function.

*A life of faith is hard work that at times requires perseverance and patience, but you can't live any other way.* Faith is the basis upon which an abundant, satisfying life is built. It is an essential key to releasing all that God put in you to benefit yourself and the world for generations to come. Your potential needs faith to draw it out, because faith is the bucket that draws from the well of potential within you.

> Faith is the bucket that draws from the well of potential within you.

## EVIEW the Principles From This Week:

- God gave you an eternal spirit with eternal potential.
- Sin has robbed you of that potential because you are born spiritually dead.
- God redeemed your eternal potential through the death of Jesus.
- You were designed to live by faith.
- Faith is believing, seeing, releasing, and receiving.

# A Definition of Purpose

*In Him we were also chosen, having been predestined according to the plan of Him who works out everything in conformity with the purpose of His will* (Ephesians 1:11).

BOOK QUOTE: *Releasing Your Potential* [Chapter 8]

Saul was a zealous Jew who intensely persecuted the early Church and tried to destroy it. But God had another plan for Saul's life, of which Saul was ignorant. God had set Saul apart before his birth "*to reveal His Son in* [him] *so that* [he] *might preach Him among the Gentiles*" (Galatians 1:16). On the road to Damascus, Saul came face-to-face with the purpose for which God had created him. That encounter changed Saul's life forever. Saul the Pharisee became Paul the Apostle.

Although the encounter with your purpose need not be as dramatic as Saul's was, you too need to discover the purpose for which God created you. I've met many successful people who have been dissatisfied with their accomplishments. They have pursued goals and met them, but they have no fulfillment and continually ask why. Accomplishments without a sense of purpose are meaningless. Life without an understanding of life's purpose leads to disillusionment and emptiness.

The purpose of something is the reason for which it exists or the manufacturer's original intent for making it. Thus, the purpose of a thing cannot be discovered by asking another thing. Only the manufacturer knows why he created the product the way he did.

God is your Source/Manufacturer. He knows why He gave you life and endowed you with the personality, talents, and ambitions that make you unique. He wants you to discover why you were born so you can fulfill your purpose. A sense of purpose gives life meaning. It moves you beyond existence to a fulfilling and productive life.

Life without purpose is an experiment.

## Change Your Thinking

*So I tell you this, and insist on it in the Lord, that you must no longer live as the Gentiles do, in the futility of their thinking* (Ephesians 4:17).

BOOK QUOTE: *Releasing Your Potential* [Chapter 8]

Jesus had an attitude toward purpose. That attitude is expressed in the words of the apostle Paul in First Corinthians 2:11:

> *For who among men knows the thoughts of a man except the man's spirit within him? In the same way, no one knows the thoughts of God except the Spirit of God.*

Since you were born separated from God and out of touch with His Spirit, you are ignorant. Jesus pointed to the spiritual ignorance of man when He preached repentance (see Matthew 4:17). *Repent* in English primarily means "to regret, or to feel remorse or sorrow for an action, attitude or thought." In the Greek-Roman world of Jesus' day, repentance meant a "change of mind or a turning to God."

Jesus knew that admission into the Kingdom of Heaven required this complete change in thinking. His command to repent initiated God's new work of grace. Many of the religious leaders were offended by Jesus' preaching. They took it as a insult that He would imply that their thinking was wrong.

The truth is, no matter how you are thinking before you meet Jesus, your thinking is wrong. Without God you are ignorant:

> *They are darkened in their understanding and separated from the life of God because of the ignorance that is in them due to the hardening of their hearts* (Ephesians 4:18).

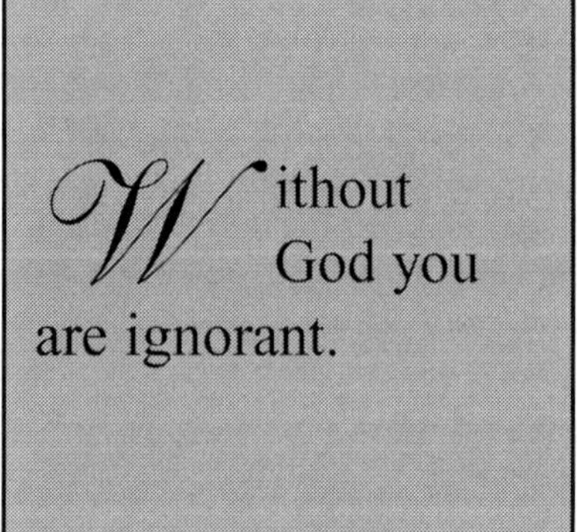

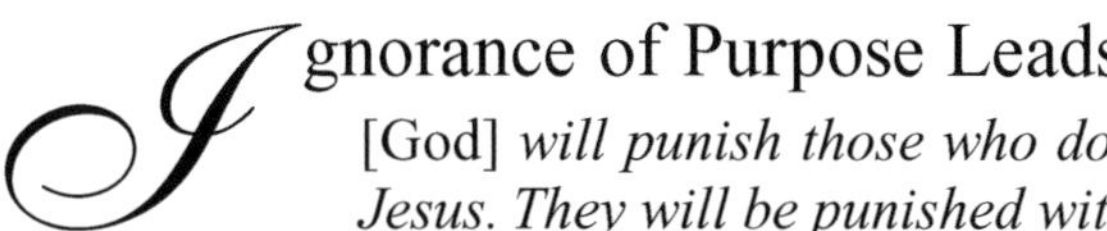

## Ignorance of Purpose Leads to Abuse

[God] *will punish those who do not know God and do not obey the gospel of our Lord Jesus. They will be punished with everlasting destruction and shut out from the presence of the Lord and from the majesty of His power* (2 Thessalonians 1:8-9).

BOOK QUOTE: *Releasing Your Potential* [Chapter 8]

Without Jesus you cannot come to God: *I am the way and the truth and the life. No one comes to the Father except through Me* (John 14:6).

Life apart from God leads to destruction. (See 2 Thessalonians 1:8-9 above.)

God doesn't want you to *perish—perish* means "to be destroyed": [The Lord] *is patient with you, not wanting anyone to perish, but everyone to come to repentance* (2 Peter 3:9b).

Out of His great love and mercy, God provides repentance as the means by which you can avoid destruction. If you don't want to be destroyed by ignorance of God and His purpose for your life, you have to change your way of thinking.

Ignorance robs you of your potential because it leads to abuse. The word *abuse* is based on two words: *abnormal* and *use*. You can't use something in its natural way unless you know why it exists and how it was designed to be used. Therefore, any time you don't know the purpose of something, you end up using it abnormally, which is abuse.

If you don't know the purpose of a wife, you'll abuse her. If you don't know what a husband is for, you'll abnormally use him. And of course, the greatest tragedy occurs when you don't know what children are for and you abuse them.

No matter how you are thinking before you meet Jesus, your thinking is wrong.

## Only the Creator Knows the Purpose of a Creation

*Many are the plans in a man's heart, but it is the Lord's purpose that prevails* (Proverbs 19:21).

BOOK QUOTE: *Releasing Your Potential* [Chapter 8]

We must go back to the mind of our Manufacturer to find out the purpose for our existence. Nobody knows the product like the creator, no matter who the creator is. If you make a dress, no one knows that dress better than you. If you build a house, you know where you used old wood that nobody else can see because it's covered by paint.

You are related to where you came from. That means nobody knows you like the One from whom you came. God who created you knows how He designed you to operate. He wants you to understand His thoughts toward you and His purposes for your life. If you try to live without God, you will completely mess up your life, because life without purpose brings abuse.

Look around you. Many people have food, houses, cars, friends, mothers, fathers, and families that they are abusing. They don't know the purpose of these people and things so they keep abusing them. If you don't know the purpose of a product, ask its manufacturer. If you don't know the purpose of your family and friends, go to God. Knowledge of purpose is the only way to avoid abuse.

Life without purpose brings abuse.

## hy Are You Doing What You Are Doing?

*If I give all I possess to the poor and surrender my body to the flames, but have not love, I gain nothing* (1 Corinthians 13:3).

BOOK QUOTE: *Releasing Your Potential* [Chapter 8]

First Corinthians chapter 13 is an example of how we can abuse things if we don't know their purpose. This chapter is often read at weddings because it talks about love. People just love this chapter, but they have a hard time living it. Why? Because they fail to look at the verses that precede it. Chapter 13 comes out of chapter 12, which talks about the baptism of the Holy Spirit.

> *There are different kinds of gifts, but the same Spirit. ...Now to each one the manifestation of the Spirit is given for the common good. ...All these are the work of one and the same Spirit, and He gives them to each one, just as He determines. ...And now I will show you the most excellent way. ...Love is patient, love is kind* (1 Corinthians 12:4,7,11,31b; 13:4a).

If don't have the Holy Spirit in your life, you will abuse love and the one you desire to love. You can't get the result without the living presence of the Holy Spirit in your life. Without Him you will be impatient, unkind, envious, boastful, proud, rude, self-seeking, and easily angered in your relationship with your lover. In fact, your love will fail because you don't understand love as an outgrowth of God's power in your life.

It doesn't matter what you do, if you don't understand why you are doing it you are wasting your time. If you give everything you have to the poor or you sacrifice your body to be burned, but you don't understand the purpose for doing it, all you will have is a dead body (see 1 Corinthians 13:3). God's not impressed by religious or moral acts unless you know why you are doing them.

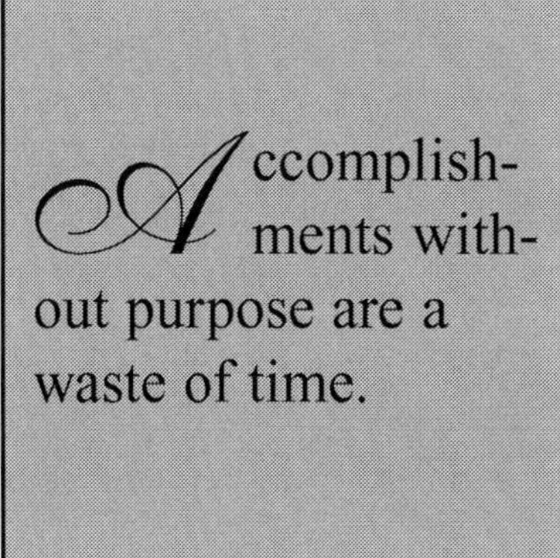

## Man Without God Is Lost and Confused

*...the people living in darkness have seen a great light; on those living in the land of the shadow of death a light has dawned* (Matthew 4:16).

BOOK QUOTE: *Releasing Your Potential* [Chapter 8]

Psalm 82 describes man's situation without God:

> *They know nothing, they understand nothing. They walk about in darkness; all the foundations of the earth are shaken. I said, "You are 'gods'; you are all sons of the Most High." But you will die like mere men...* (Psalm 82:5-7a).

We are children of the Most High, but we are living like mere flesh and blood who did not receive the Spirit of God. We are completely without purpose and direction: We don't know anything. We don't understand anything. We (and our world) are totally out of line going nowhere fast. This is the lot of those who do not understand why God created them. Confusion and abuse characterize their lives. You may think God created you to get a good education or to go to church or to make a living. In truth, none of those achieve God's purpose for creating you.

God's reasons for creating human beings:

- To express God's image.
- To enjoy fellowship with God.
- To dominate the earth.
- To bear fruit.
- To reproduce ourselves.

We are children of the Most High, yet living like mere flesh and blood.

# God's Purpose for Man: Expressing His Image

*For those God foreknew He also predestined to be conformed to the likeness of His Son, that he might be the firstborn among many brothers* (Romans 8:29).

BOOK QUOTE: *Releasing Your Potential* [Chapter 8]

If you don't know your purpose, it is impossible to fulfill it. Thus the release of your potential requires that you learn why God created you. The Bible clearly defines God's reasons for creating human beings:

- To express God's image.
- To enjoy fellowship with God.
- To dominate the earth.
- To bear fruit.
- To reproduce ourselves.

*Created to Express God's Image*

The first chapter of Genesis tells us that God intended for man to express His image:

> *Then God said, "Let Us make man in Our image..."* (Genesis 1:26).

Everything you are is related to your purpose—your height, race, natural talents, gifts, and deep desires. God did not create you so you could hate yourself so much that you try to change what you look like. God gave you beauty when He made you. He wants you to look like yourself. Fashionable clothes, cosmetics, and hairstyles are fine so long as you know why you are choosing to look like you do. If you just want to look your best or you're trying to make your hair and clothes easier to care for, then go for it. But if you are trying to look like someone else, you're in big trouble. God doesn't want you to look like someone else. He planned that you would be different. He wants you to look like you and act like Him.

God wants you to look like you and act like Him.

## EVIEW the Principles From This Week:

- Purpose is the creator's original intent for making something.
- God knows the purpose for your life.
- You have been created to:
  1. Express God's Image.
  2. Enjoy Fellowship With God.
  3. Dominate the Earth.
  4. Bear Fruit.
  5. Reproduce Yourself.

# God's Purpose for Man: Acting Like God

*Through these He has given us His very great and precious promises, so that through them you may participate in the divine nature and escape the corruption in the world caused by evil desires* (2 Peter 1:4).

BOOK QUOTE: *Releasing Your Potential* [Chapter 8]

The Bible clearly defines God's reasons for creating human beings:

- To express God's image.
- To enjoy fellowship with God.
- To dominate the earth.
- To bear fruit.
- To reproduce ourselves.

Expressing God's image has to do with the way you act, not the way you look. He wants you to mirror His character. He fashioned you so that His nature could be revealed through your uniqueness.

The essence of God's nature is succinctly defined in the "love" chapter we looked at earlier. He is the wonderful things this chapter describes.

> [God] *is patient,* [God] *is kind.* [He] *does not envy,* [He] *does not boast,* [He] *is not proud.* [God] *is not rude,* [He] *is not self-seeking,* [He] *is not easily angered,* [He] *keeps no record of wrongs. God does not delight in evil but rejoices with the truth.* [God] *always protects, always trusts, always hopes, always perseveres.* [God] *never fails* (1 Corinthians 13:4-8a).

This is how you were created to live. God made you to act like He does. Having God's nature is the difference between *looking* lovely and *being* lovely. One refers to your outward appearance, the other to your nature. You may look good, but be mean. You may dress nicely, but speak unkindly. You may look religious, but act like the devil. God wants you to express His nature. That's one reason He created you.

God fashioned you so that His nature could be revealed through your uniqueness.

## od's Purpose for Man: Enjoying Fellowship With God

*God is spirit, and His worshipers must worship in spirit and in truth* (John 4:24).

BOOK QUOTE: *Releasing Your Potential* [Chapter 8]

Here are God's reasons for creating human beings:

- To express God's image.
- To enjoy fellowship with God.
- To dominate the earth.
- To bear fruit.
- To reproduce ourselves.

God's first question to Adam after Adam's disobedience was "*Where are you*?" (see Genesis 3:9). God had come to the garden in the cool of the day to enjoy fellowship with the man and the woman He had created. The opportunity for fellowship was part of the reason God had created human beings.

Any being that worships or fellowships with God must be spirit. Men and women are the only beings on this planet that God created from His Spirit in His own image. But man lost the fellowship God had designed him to enjoy when he sinned and allowed distance to come between himself and God.

Fellowship is companionship—a mutual sharing of an experience, an activity, or an interest. You cannot enjoy fellowship with God unless you have received Jesus as your Savior, because sinful human beings cannot know and understand God's experiences, activities, and interests. A reconnection of God's Spirit and your spirit is the prerequisite for the establishment of this companionship. The fulfillment of your purpose to love God and enjoy Him forever is impossible until you reclaim your spiritual heritage, for those who seek to worship God must worship Him in spirit and in truth (see John 4:24).

Reconnect God's spirit for eternal companionship.

# God's Purpose for Man: Dominating the Earth

*You have made him to have dominion over the works of Your hands; You have put all things under his feet* (Psalm 8:6 NKJV).

BOOK QUOTE: *Releasing Your Potential* [Chapter 8]

We are continuing to study God's reasons for creating human beings:

- To express God's image.
- To enjoy fellowship with God.
- To dominate the earth.
- To bear fruit.
- To reproduce ourselves.

The Genesis description of man's creation includes God's intent that man should have dominion over the earth:

> *Then God said, "Let Us make man in Our image, in Our likeness, and let them rule over the fish of the sea and the birds of the air, over the livestock, over all the earth, and over all the creatures that move along the ground"* (Genesis 1:26).

God created us to dominate the entire earth. But when we lost touch with our Source, we became confused and allowed the earth to dominate us. Every problem that we are experiencing is the result of our not fulfilling our purpose to dominate the earth. We've allowed ourselves to be so dominated by leaves and fruit that they tell us what to do. "It's time for a smoke now. You can't do without me."

But more serious than the domination itself is the deception that goes along with the domination. We are tremendous self-deceivers. Social drinkers say, "I can hold my liquor. I'm not under any pressure to have another drink." But the truth is that every alcoholic started as a social drinker.

When we become dominated by the things we were supposed to dominate, all the earth goes off course. Our world is filled with the violence that revolves around the printed paper that comes from trees. *Money* controls our lives. We kill, rob, steal, cuss, and do many other despicable things to get our hands on that sliver of wood.

> All the earth goes off course when we allow things to dominate us.

Even as the domination of people by things destroys our world, so too the domination of people by people creates pain and violence. Husbands abuse their wives. Women abuse their children. Races discriminate against other races. These problems and many more arise from our failure to understand that God gave us dominion over the earth, not over other people.

## ffective Release of Your Potential

*The wrath of God is being revealed from Heaven against all the godlessness and wickedness of men who suppress the truth by their wickedness* (Romans 1:18).

BOOK QUOTE: *Releasing Your Potential* [Chapter 8]

The lack of knowledge or the loss of insight into the purpose of a person or a thing always leads to confusion and pain. Homosexuality is an excellent example of the resulting turmoil. God created the woman to be a suitable helpmeet to the man. He did not design the male to be a helpmeet to the man or the female to be a helpmeet to the woman. God made them male and female, giving the female to the male. So the purpose of the woman is the man, and the purpose of the man is the woman. Anything else is abnormal use.

The apostle Paul spoke of this abnormality when he wrote to the church at Rome:

> *The wrath of God is being revealed from Heaven against all the godlessness and wickedness of men who suppress the truth by their wickedness.... For although they knew God, they neither glorified Him as God nor gave thanks to Him, but their thinking became futile and their foolish hearts were darkened.... Because of this, God gave them over to shameful lusts. Even their women exchanged natural relations for unnatural ones. In the same way the men also abandoned natural relations with women and were inflamed with lust for one another...* (Romans 1:18,21,26-27).

God abhors abnormal use. He destroyed the cities of Sodom and Gomorrah for such evil (see Genesis 18-19). Satan, on the other hand, wants you to justify your sin by thinking it is natural. *No amount of rationalizing and spiritualizing can erase the penalties of abuse.* Degradation and corruption wait for those who misuse what God blessed and pronounced as good because "*they* [receive] *in themselves the due penalty for their perversion*" (Romans 1:27b). *Twisting the truth to fit your desires does not change the truth; it only opens you further to the father of lies.*

Understanding God's purposes for creating male and female, husband and wife, parent and child is essential for the effective release of your potential and theirs. God created you to dominate the earth. Check your life to see where you are dominating people. Then repent and reestablish those relationships according to God's purposes. Your life depends on it.

> Twisting the truth does not change the truth; it only opens you further to the father of lies.

## God's Purpose for Man: Bearing Fruit

*This is to My Father's glory, that you bear much fruit, showing yourselves to be My disciples. ...You did not choose Me, but I chose you and appointed you to go and bear fruit—fruit that will last* (John 15:8,16a).

BOOK QUOTE: *Releasing Your Potential* [Chapter 8]

Review God's reasons for creating human beings:

- To express God's image.
- To enjoy fellowship with God.
- To dominate the earth.
- To bear fruit.
- To reproduce ourselves.

If you have an apple tree in your backyard that never produces any apples, you're going to get tired of that tree taking up space without bearing any fruit and you'll cut it down. The same is true of God's relationships with people. No tree should ever be without fruit, because God created every tree with its seed inside it. God has a way of moving unproductive people to the side and raising up productive people. *A productive person is simply somebody who will respond to the demand.*

Jesus teaches us in the Gospel of John that God created us to bear fruit (see above).

Your fruitfulness is related to the food you are eating. If your spiritual source is not of top quality, your productivity will show it. No matter where you go or what you do, apart from God you will be an ornamental plant without fruit. You are what you eat.

God wants you to reveal all the potential He buried inside you. He offers you tremendous opportunities to share in His work on this earth. Your ability to fulfill God's demand is connected to your relationship with Him because the fruitfulness He desires is the manifestation of His Spirit in your life:

> *But the fruit of the Spirit is love, joy, peace, patience, kindness, goodness, faithfulness, gentleness and self-control. Against such things there is no law. Those who belong to Christ Jesus have crucified the sinful nature with its passions and desires. Since we live by the Spirit, let us keep in step with the Spirit* (Galatians 5:22-25).

God created you to bear abundant, life-giving fruit. That's part of your purpose. The presence of the Holy Spirit in your life is the key to fulfilling that purpose.

> God created you to bear abundant, life-giving fruit.

## od's Purpose for Man: Reproducing Ourselves

*Anyone who believes in the Son of God has this testimony in his heart. Anyone who does not believe God has made him out to be a liar, because he has not believed the testimony God has given about His Son* (1 John 5:10).

BOOK QUOTE: *Releasing Your Potential* [Chapter 8]

We continue to study God's reasons for creating human beings:

- To express God's image.
- To enjoy fellowship with God.
- To dominate the earth.
- To bear fruit.
- To reproduce ourselves.

God created you to multiply and replenish the earth (see Genesis 1:28). This ability to have children is sometimes seen as a curse rather than a blessing. Sin is at the root of these feelings.

When God gave Adam and Eve the command to fill the earth, pain was not associated with childbearing. It was not until after sin entered the world that God told the woman:

> *...I will greatly increase your pains in childbearing; with pain you will give birth to children. Your desire will be for your husband, and he will rule over you* (Genesis 3:16).

But more important that your ability to physically reproduce is your power to instill in others your values and attitudes. Your life influences your children, your spouse, your friends, your boss, your coworkers, and so on, for good or evil. They watch your actions and hear your words. The effect of your presence in their lives can be either encouraging or discouraging, upbuilding or degrading, positive or negative.

> More importantly than physical reproduction is your power to instill your values and attitudes in others.

## hat (or Who) Is Controlling You?

*...who, by the power that enables Him to bring everything under His control, will transform our lowly bodies so that they will be like His glorious body* (Philippians 3:21).

BOOK QUOTE: *Releasing Your Potential* [Chapter 8]

The release of your potential is directly related to your willingness to know, understand, and submit to God's purposes for your life. The wisdom and power to accomplish this task is available to all who have the gift of God's indwelling Spirit. For He is the channel through which you can freely communicate with God until your heart and vision become one with His.

The corollary is also true. Life apart from God subjects you to control by other things, people, and spirits and conceals the purpose for which you were born. Under those circumstances, you and your potential will be abused. Indeed, much that you have to offer will die with you.

Take time now to examine your life. Who or what is controlling you? Are you releasing your potential by discovering God's purpose for your life?

You have the ability to fulfill that purpose because God built it into you. Determine now to find God's intent for your life.

> Your potential is directly related to knowing, understanding, and submitting to God's purposes for your life.

## EVIEW the Principles From This Week:

- Apart from God you are ignorant of your purpose.
- Ignorance produces abuse.
- You must understand why you do what you do.
- You must submit to the control of the Holy Spirit, or something or someone else will control you.

# Poverty and Wealth—Biblical Viewpoint

*Do not love sleep or you will grow poor; stay awake and you will have food to spare* (Proverbs 20:13).

BOOK QUOTE: *Releasing Your Potential* [Chapter 9]

You can never change the world by being controlled by the earth. All resources should lead to God, their ultimate Source.

Most of us at some point in our lives have wished that we had more resources than we actually have. We have looked at another person's resources and envied them, bemoaning our apparent poverty. This attitude is a stumbling block to releasing our full potential because God's view of poverty and wealth is very different from ours. He is more concerned with what we *do* with what we have, than with how much we *have*.

Many people believe that God favors the rich and keeps things from the poor, but that is not what the Bible teaches. God loves and cares for all people, rich or poor:

> *The poor man and the oppressor have this in common: The Lord gives sight to the eyes of both* (Proverbs 29:13).

Therefore, it is not that God makes rich people and poor people. Rather God makes all people—some who become rich and some who become poor. The key is what you do with the resources God gives you.

> *Lazy hands make a man poor, but diligent hands bring wealth* (Proverbs 10:4).

Poverty is a not a gift from God but the result of your actions. The degree of wealth or poverty in which you find yourself is to a large extent related to the way you are using what you have. A hardworking person becomes rich, while a lazy person becomes poor. Your success is not determined by what you have, but by what you do with what you have.

It doesn't matter what your family is like economically. You can decide that you aren't going to stay where your family is. You can resolve to try new things and to work hard. God wants energetic, diligent people. He's always searching for men and women who will look beyond their circumstances to their possibilities.

> Your success is not determined by what you have, but by what you *do* with what you have.

## od's Provisions for All

*And my God will meet all your needs according to His glorious riches in Christ Jesus* (Philippians 4:19).

BOOK QUOTE: *Releasing Your Potential* [Chapter 9]

God created a potent man and supplied him with resources with unlimited potential. Nothing we have today was added to or subtracted from God's original provisions in the Garden. But those resources are not equally divided among the peoples of our world. Hardworking, diligent people got their hands on most of the wealth, while lazy, sluggard people watched them take it. Thus, our world knows the rich, the poor, and those who are in transit—some gaining wealth and others losing it.

When God gives you resources, He wants you to care for them, cultivate them, and work them. All of these require effort. An inventor is a thinker who takes his idea and makes it visible. He doesn't create anything new, he just uses his potential to imagine, plan, and work so you can see what you were looking at that you didn't know was there. Thus, the people who get ahead in life are those who have learned to understand and use their resources.

Everything has a purpose. Whether or not you work to discover the purpose of your resources determines how effectively or ineffectively you will use them, because understanding must precede use. Use *with* understanding releases potential. Use *without* understanding kills potential. In other words, the proper use of resources maximizes potential, and the abnormal use (abuse) of resources destroys potential.

Thus, the release of your potential hinges directly on your ability to know the purpose of your resources, to understand their properties, to obey the laws governing them, and to open yourself to their limitless potential. If you learn what your resources are and how they were designed to operate, you will have limitless potential. But if you use them in an abnormal way, you will destroy your potential.

Cocaine, for example, is used in hospitals to bring healing. But if you misuse it, your thinking will be distorted and you'll end up losing many of the things that are dear to you. Or consider drugs like aspirin and Tylenol, which relieve pain. If you use these drugs according to the directions on the bottle, they have a positive influence. But if you disregard the warning to limit their use, you can kill yourself or make yourself very ill.

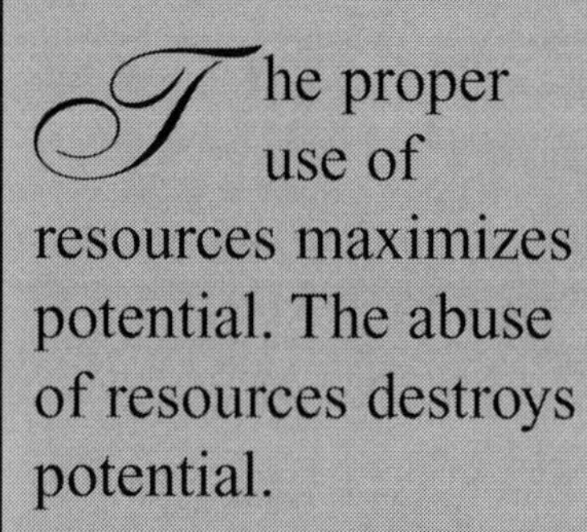

## The Effective Use of Resources

*...in order that satan might not outwit us. For we are not unaware of his schemes* (2 Corinthians 2:11).

BOOK QUOTE: *Releasing Your Potential* [Chapter 9]

One of the greatest problems facing the Church is not the lack of resources but the *lack of use* of resources. Every resource God gave to Adam is available to us. But we don't use all those resources. Instead of seeing the possibilities in everything God has given us, we categorize our resources and refuse to use some of them because we are threatened by the world's use of them.

What the world is doing or building is not the problem. Worldly people don't have any more resources than those they are currently using to solve the world's problems. This is not true for the Church. The Church is not solving the world's problems because we misunderstand the resources that are available to us.

The Bible affirms that all things were made by God, and "*without Him nothing was made that has been made*" (see John 1:3). That means everything belongs to God. The Bible also affirms that "*God saw all that He had made, and it was very good"* (see Genesis 1:31). That means every resource God has given man is good.

The Scriptures are clear that God is the Creator and satan is a perverter. Satan cannot create anything. He can only pervert what God created. Therein lies the source of our problem. Counterfeits abound in our world. They are the result of satan's misuse and abuse of God's resources.

God gives you resources so you can accomplish what He put you here to do. He gives them to you to live *on*, not *for*. When you start living for money you're in trouble. When your job becomes the most important thing in your life, you're in for hard times. Whenever a resource becomes more important than the purpose for which God gave it, you have crossed the line between using it and abusing it.

God gives you resources so you can accomplish what He put you here to do.

## our Available Resources—Spiritual

*...Man does not live on bread alone, but on every word that comes from the mouth of God* (Matthew 4:4).

BOOK QUOTE: *Releasing Your Potential* [Chapter 9]

There are five types of resources you must understand and control if you are going to become a successful person: spiritual, physical, material, the soul, and time.

*Spiritual Resources*

First, God has given you spiritual resources. Because God created you in His own image, He gave you the ability to tap into Him.

Spiritual food is available to you in a variety of forms. First and foremost, you must feed your spirit from the Word of God:

> *Blessed are those who hear the Word of God and obey it* (Luke 11:28).

Stay in a good place where they teach the Word of God. Keep staying there until you get what they are feeding you. You may fall as you learn to walk according to the Spirit, but that's OK. Just pick yourself up and try again. As long as you're feeding yourself spiritual food, you're growing, changing, and getting stronger. You may not see that growth, but it's happening whether you see it or not.

*The gifts of the Spirit* are also resources to feed you: *Now to each one the manifestation of the Spirit is given for the common good* (1 Corinthians 12:7).

These resources include the word of wisdom, the word of knowledge, faith, miracles, healings, tongues, interpretation of tongues and prophecy. God gave these wonderful gifts to build up the Church. If you have accepted Jesus as your Lord and Savior, they are available to you.

God also provides *His armor* to protect you (see Ephesians 6:13-18).

Truth, righteousness, peace, faith, salvation, prayer. What wealth! Add to them fasting, giving, and forgiving. If your spirit and God's Spirit are in touch, each is yours to use. They can make the difference between a good day and a bad day, between a dismal life and a successful life. Your circumstances may not change as quickly as you'd like, but I guarantee you that your attitudes will.

> If your spirit and God's Spirit are in touch, each is yours to use.

## our Available Resources—Physical and Material

*Then God said, "I give you every seed-bearing plant on the face of the whole earth and every tree that has fruit with seed in it. They will be yours for food"* (Genesis 1:29).

BOOK QUOTE: *Releasing Your Potential* [Chapter 9]

We will continue to study the five types of resources you must understand and control if you are going to become a successful person: spiritual, physical, material, the soul, and time.

*Physical Resources*

God's provisions include physical resources. When God created you, He created your spirit and put it into your body. Because of God's gift of life, your wonderful, physical machine can breathe, move, eat, and heal itself. Many of the pleasures you enjoy in life are yours because God took the dust of the ground and fashioned your body. You can see the beauty of flowers, a sunset or a rainbow. You can taste the sweetness of honey or of fruit fresh from the tree. You can feel the love of your children as their little arms encircle your neck and your ears hear those sweetest of words: I love you Mommy. I love you Daddy.

As wondrous as your body is, you may not use it however you desire. Choose carefully the kind of fuel you give your body. Be aware that your body is for food, and food is for your body. Like any of God's resources, improper care and inappropriate attitudes toward your body can result in misuse and abuse:

> *"Everything is permissible for me"—but not everything is beneficial. "Everything is permissible for me"—but I will not be mastered by anything. "Food for the stomach and the stomach for food"—but God will destroy them both. The body is not meant for sexual immorality, but for the Lord, and the Lord for the body. ...Do you not know that your bodies are members of Christ Himself?* (1 Corinthians 6:12-13,15a)

*Material Resources*

The third kind of resource God has given you is material resources. God's conversation with Adam in the Garden of Eden shows that God provided well for Adam's needs (see Genesis 1:29 above).

Genesis 1 also reveals that God also provided gold, aromatic resin, onyx, and a river for watering the earth. Indeed, the vast geological and geographical resources of this earth are all part of God's gracious provision for your life.

> Because of God's gift of life, your physical machine can breathe, move, eat, and heal itself.

## Your Available Resources—Soul and Time

*What good will it be for a man if he gains the whole world, yet forfeits his soul? Or what can a man give in exchange for his soul?* (Matthew 16:26).

BOOK QUOTE: *Releasing Your Potential* [Chapter 9]

We are studying the five types of resources you must understand and control if you are going to become a successful person: spiritual, physical, material, the soul, and time.

*The Resources of the Soul*

You are spirit and you have a soul. The assistance you receive from your mind, your will, and your feelings are the resources of the soul that God has given you.

Think what life would be like without these resources. They are the primary means by which you express who you are. Your spirit depends on your soul, as does your body. The Scriptures recognize the importance of the soul: "*Dear friends, I urge you, as aliens and strangers in the world, to abstain from sinful desires, which war against your soul*" (1 Peter 2:11).

Jesus came after the soul because the spirit is easy. It is through your will, your feelings, and your mind that satan seeks to attack you. If you guard your soul, your spirit and your body will be well. Their condition depends on the state of your soul. This is clearly revealed in the Bible: "*For as* [a man] *thinketh in his heart, so is he*" (Proverbs 23:7a KJV).

Belief takes place in the spirit, but thinking takes places in the soul. You can believe one thing and think something completely different. What you think is what you become, not what you believe. That's why Jesus came preaching repentance. He knew that our thoughts influence us much more than our beliefs.

The resources of your soul are not available to you unless you allow God to transform your mind.

*The Resource of the Time*

Time is a temporary interruption in eternity. It is a commodity that can be neither bought nor sold. The only thing you can do with time is use it. If you don't use it, you lose it. The apostle Paul encouraged members of the early Church to "[redeem] *the time* (Ephesians 5:16 KJV) or "[make] *the most of every opportunity*" (NIV).

The only time you have is now. Get busy and use it wisely. Say, "God, I am going to use every minute of my day constructively, effectively, and efficiently." Time is God's gift—one of His precious resources. Refuse to be one of those who waste time and then complain because they don't have enough time. Make the hours of your day count.

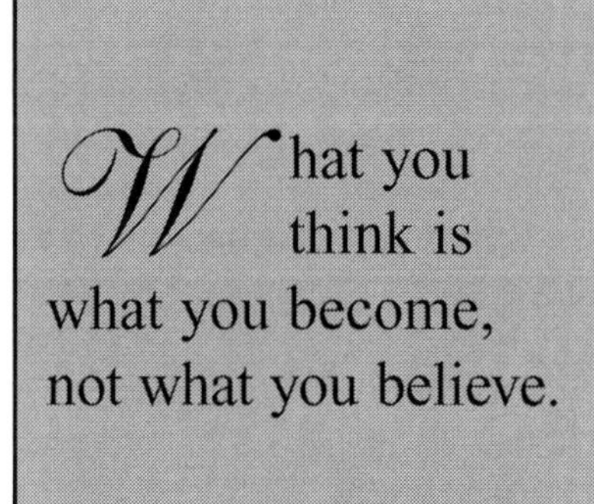

## What Are You Doing With What You Have?

*For surely, O Lord, you bless the righteous; you surround them with your favor as with a shield* (Psalm 5:12).

BOOK QUOTE: *Releasing Your Potential* [Chapter 9]

God provides many resources beyond those of spirit, body, material things, soul, and time to challenge your potential. How are you using these resources? Or are you even aware that you have these assets?

The wealth of your resources is limitless if you will allow God to open your eyes to their possibilities. Give from your abundance. Choose wisely when you buy something. *View your resources as gifts to be used in God's service instead of property to be hoarded for your benefit and ease.* Repent (change your thinking) from the "I need more" mentality and use what you already have.

God wants to enlarge your vision of what you have. He wants you to see the storehouses of blessing that presently surround you. Use the anointing God has poured upon the Church and its ministers. Move beyond your shame and let them minister to your needs. Spend time reading God's Word until the Bible becomes for you a treasure of knowledge and inspiration.

No matter how rich or poor you are financially, you are accountable to God for the wealth of your resources. You have the responsibility to discover, enhance, and cultivate the precious gifts you have received from God's hand. The accomplishment of that task begins with the recognition that you are indeed wealthy—perhaps not by this world's standards, but certainly by God's standards. He carefully scrutinizes your attitudes and anxiously watches your use (or abuse) of the resources He has given you.

Determine now to use to the fullest all that God has given you. Refuse to allow the standards and attitudes of this world to influence your efforts to use wisely and effectively the wealth of resources you now own.

> *For everyone who has will be given more, and he will have an abundance. Whoever does not have, even what he has will be taken from him* (Matthew 25:29).

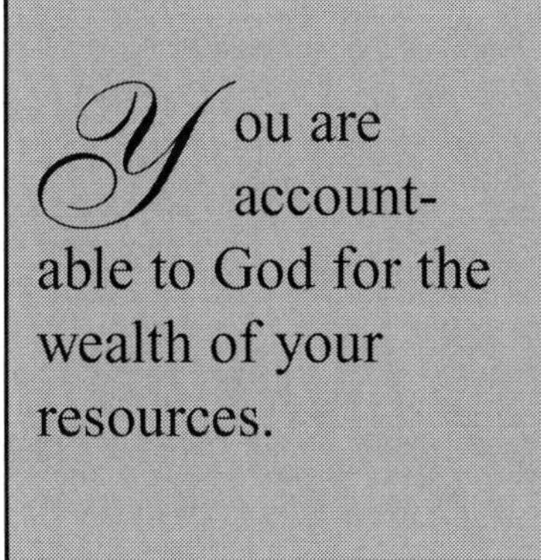

## EVIEW the Principles From This Week:

- God makes and provides for all people. Some become rich and some become poor.
- Wealth and poverty are primarily based on what you do with what you have.
- God gives you resources to live on, not for.
- The proper use of resources releases potential.
- The improper use (abuse) of resources kills potential.
- You have many resources that you aren't presently using.

## God's Care in Setting Ideal Environments

*He also says, "In the beginning, O Lord, you laid the foundations of the earth, and the heavens are the work of your hands"* (Hebrews 1:10).

BOOK QUOTE: *Releasing Your Potential* [Chapter 10]

You are what you eat, and what's eating you.

The story is told of a small boy who wanted to play with his pet fish. So he reached into the fish tank, caught the squirming fish and placed it on the floor beside him. Then he returned to playing with the cars and trucks that were scattered on the floor around him. As he played, he talked to the fish about everything he was doing until he became so engrossed in his toys that he forgot about the fish. Many minutes later, he remembered the fish and turned toward his pet. The fish no longer moved when he touched it. Frightened, the boy ran to his mother with the fish in his hand.

When his mother saw the fish, she quickly took it and put it in the fish tank. The boy watched tearfully as his pet floated on the top of the water. It was dead. When the mother asked her son what had happened to the fish, the boy innocently replied, "Why, we were playing together on the floor when I noticed that he wasn't moving."

Compassionately, the mother replied, "Honey, didn't you know that the fish can't live on the floor? God made fish to live in water."

This story illustrates how much God's creatures depend on the correct environment to live and grow. Even as fish need water to live, so we need the particular environment that God designed for men and women. Too often, however, we are unaware of the impact our environment has on our lives. We flop about like fish on the floor and wonder what's wrong.

When God created the heavens and the earth, He was very careful to give all that He made an ideal environment. This care is evident, for example, in the earth's placement three planets away from the sun.

The earth's relationship to the sun allows the sun to draw water from the surface of the earth, which then freezes and becomes clouds. When the clouds become heavy, they release the water, which returns to earth as rain. Thus, God's precise positioning of the earth and the sun both affords the earth protection from the sun's radiation and provides the moisture earth's plants and animals need to continue living.

> God's creatures depend on the correct environment to live and grow.

## Your Environment Can Onstruct Your Miracle

*"Whether He is a sinner or not, I don't know. One thing I do know. I was blind but now I see."..."Nobody has ever heard of opening the eyes of a man born blind. If this man were not from God, He could do nothing"* (John 9:25,32-33)

BOOK QUOTE: *Releasing Your Potential* [Chapter 10]

Violation of environment always produces death. Vegetation that is planted in parched ground will eventually whither and decay. Wildlife that lives in drought areas will die from dehydration and starvation. Fish that live in polluted waters will become sickly and die. The Bible tells a story that illustrates this principle.

Jesus was called to the home of a ruler whose daughter had died. When He entered the house, Jesus found that the professional mourners had arrived and the funeral, with its cacophony of sounds, was in progress. After He had put the noisy crowd outside, Jesus entered the room where the girl lay. In the quietness, He took her by the hand and she got up. The unbelief and mockery of the crowd produced the wrong environment for a resurrection, so Jesus changed the environment.

The Gospel of Mark tells of another occasion when Jesus encountered an environment that obstructed the manifestation of His power:

> *When the Sabbath came,* [Jesus] *began to teach in the synagogue, and many who heard Him were amazed. "Where did this man get these things?" they asked. "What's this wisdom that has been given Him, that He even does miracles...." And they took offense at Him.* [Unbelief and skepticism so filled the minds of Jesus' friends and neighbors that] *...He could not do any miracles there, except lay His hands on a few sick people and heal them* (Mark 6:2-3,5).

The Gospel of John tells the story of a blind man who was healed by Jesus. When the Pharisees tried to discount the miracle of his restored sight by questioning the integrity and power of the One who had healed him, the blind man refused to be sucked into their attitudes of unbelief (see Scripture above).

> Violation of environment always produces death.

## verything Has an Ideal Environment

*Now the Lord God had planted a garden in the east, in Eden; and there He put the man He had formed. And the Lord God made all kinds of trees grow out of the ground—trees that were pleasing to the eye and good for food. In the middle of the garden were the tree of life and the tree of the knowledge of good and evil. A river watering the garden flowed from Eden* (Genesis 2:8-10a).

BOOK QUOTE: *Releasing Your Potential* [Chapter 10]

Everything was designed to function within a specific environment. The conditions of that environment are the specifications that affect the creature's ability to fulfill its purpose. Thus, your potential is directly related to your environment. If your environment is ideal, the possibilities for fulfilling your potential are limitless.

God planted a treasure in you. That treasure will never be released unless you learn the conditions of your ideal environment and make the effort to keep your environment in line with those conditions. God set your ideal environment when He created a garden in Eden and put Adam in the garden.

An examination of the garden's description reveals that:

1. God created the garden.
2. God planted the garden.
3. God organized the garden.
4. God's presence was in the garden.
5. God provided everything man needed to live in the garden, including faith.

God is at the center of man's ideal environment. That's why life without God is unproductive and unfulfilling. You cannot live outside the environment God designed for you, because you need God's presence. You need a relationship with Him that encourages fellowship and obedience. You need the assurance that He will provide for you and direct your steps. You need the guidance and challenge His laws and commandments provide. Anything less will retard and cancel your ability to develop according to God's plans and purposes.

Life outside the garden does not include these ingredients. Since Adam and Eve's disobedience, we cannot benefit from God's presence and fellowship. Nor can we draw from His creative ability. Our lives are planted in foreign soil that was not planted and organized according to God's intricately designed plans. Chaos and disorganization result when we disobey the laws and commandments He set for our good. Man is a wreck outside of God's environment.

> Man is a wreck outside of God's environment.

## The Disruption of the Garden Environment

*The eye is the lamp of the body. If your eyes are good, your whole body will be full of light. But if your eyes are bad, your whole body will be full of darkness* (Matthew 6:22-23a).

BOOK QUOTE: *Releasing Your Potential* [Chapter 10]

Our present world is designed to destroy your potential. This attack on your environment has been around since Adam and Eve experienced similar pressures in the Garden.

Satan's attack came as mental pollution: "Did God really say...?" When the woman repeated what God had said, the serpent went one step further to devastate the woman's faith in God and His words:

> *"You will not surely die," the serpent said to the woman. "For God knows that when you eat of it your eyes will be opened, and you will be like God, knowing good and evil"* (Genesis 3:4-5).

Thus, the serpent completely undermined the woman's faith in God. The progression of the corruption that controlled Eve also seeks to ensnare you.

Pollution starts with the eyes. Seeing isn't sinning, and looking won't kill you. Seeing is the opening through which sinful thoughts and actions begin to take hold. If you don't want to eat, don't look.

> *When the woman saw that the fruit of the tree was...pleasing to the eye...* (Genesis 3:6).

Your trouble deepens when you move from considering the right or wrong of your action to an analysis of the relative merit of what you want. This is particularly true if your good doesn't equal God's good.

Desire pollutes the environment because it makes you want something at any expense. Your eyes get cloudy and your vision becomes blurred until everything looks right, even though it may be wrong. When desire makes you crave what you want no matter what the consequences, sit tight. You may grab something that will burn you!

Sin enters your life when your environment becomes so corrupt that you disobey God's commands and experience the brokenness that follows your disobedience. Suddenly you're in a mess and you're on your own. You no longer have a relationship with God that allows you to rely on His power and wisdom to deal with your problems. That's when your sanity starts to go. That's when pain and heartache fill your days. God doesn't have to convict you of sin because the polluted atmosphere of guilt and excuses will.

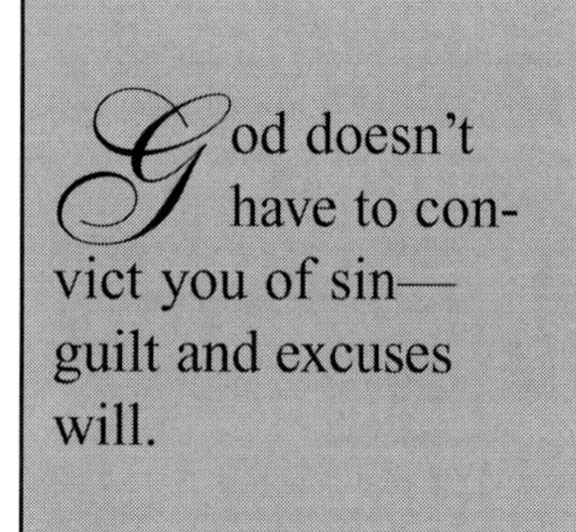

## The Effects of a Wrong Environment

*The wrath of God is being revealed from Heaven against all the godlessness and wickedness of men who suppress the truth by their wickedness, since what may be known about God is plain to them, because God has made it plain to them. For since the creation of the world God's invisible qualities—His eternal power and divine nature—have been clearly seen, being understood from what has been made, so that men are without excuse* (Romans 1:18-20).

BOOK QUOTE: *Releasing Your Potential* [Chapter 10]

After their banishment from the Garden, Adam and Eve entered a world gone awry. The first evidence of this confusion emerges when Cain murders his brother, Abel.

Several generations later, we again see the dysfunction that arises from a polluted environment. Lamech, one of Cain's descendants, marries two women (see Genesis 4:19) and unfaithfulness enters the world.

By the time of Noah, the world was so out of control that "*the Lord saw how great man's wickedness on the earth had become, and that every inclination of the thoughts of his heart was only evil all the time*" (Genesis 6:5). So grieved was God by this situation that He destroyed the earth and all people.

Some time later, men decided to make a name for themselves by building a tower to the heavens (see Genesis 11:3-4). Their selfishness further reveals the consequences of a wrong environment. You want everything for yourself with no thought for God or your neighbor.

The evil that characterized the world described in the Book of Genesis also plagues our world. A man shoots his wife and children. A woman aborts her child. A teenager jealously stabs another girl to death because of the lost affections of her boyfriend. These horrors and many others reveal our corrupt value system that places little or no worth on human life. They expose the disastrous results of sin and the consequences of our banishment from the Garden. Adrift in a world that is riddled with abnormal behavior, we witness and experience a multitude of tragedies.

So overwhelmed is our world by the forces of evil that the love and peace God intended mankind to know have been replaced by hatred, jealousy, immorality, and anger. The pain of broken marriages and families has touched us all. The fear and anxiety that make us see even our own flesh and blood as enemies shadow our lives. The consequences of sexual promiscuity stare us in the face. Our environment is out of control and we are powerless to restrain it.

> Our environment is out of control and we are powerless to restrain it.

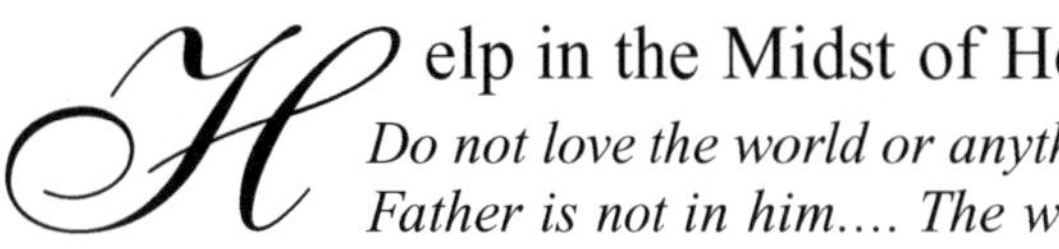

## Help in the Midst of Helplessness

*Do not love the world or anything in the world. If anyone loves the world, the love of the Father is not in him.... The world and its desires pass away, but the man who does the will of God lives forever* (1 John 2:15,17).

BOOK QUOTE: *Releasing Your Potential* [Chapter 10]

Jesus told a story that points to the solution of our messed up environment: A father had two sons. One day not long after he had asked his father for his share of the inheritance, the younger son left home and went to a distant country where he wasted his wealth in wild living. After he had spent everything, he became so hungry that he longed to eat the pigs' food.

> *When he came to his senses, he said, "How many of my father's hired men have food to spare, and here I am starving to death! I will set out and go back to my father and say to him: Father, I have sinned against heaven and against you. I am no longer worthy to be called your son; make me like one of your hired men." So he got up and went to his father* (Luke 15:17-20a).

What a telling phrase: "*When he came to his senses...*" It reveals both the son's awareness of his poverty and his belief that his need could be met. He trusted his father's goodness enough to return and ask for forgiveness.

God is well acquainted with the insanity of your world. He offers Himself as the solution to your problems. Through Jesus, He has taken the initiative to restore the garden atmosphere with its gift of His presence, His fellowship, and the freedom to obey Him. But He will not force you to accept the new environment that He offers. Like the father of the wayward son, He waits for you to come to your senses and admit your sin and your need of His forgiveness. Only then can He make sense of your world.

God dealt with the problem of a polluted environment in Abram's life by asking him to leave everything (see Genesis 12:1-4a). Why? Because God knew that Abram's relationship with Him would be compromised by the negative influence of his family and friends.

> God is well acquainted with the insanity of your world.

## hat's the State of Your Environment?

*These commandments that I give you today are to be upon your hearts. Impress them on your children. Talk about them when you sit at home and when you walk along the road, when you lie down and when you get up. Tie them as symbols on your hands and bind them on your foreheads. Write them on the doorframes of your houses and on your gates* (Deuteronomy 6:6-9).

BOOK QUOTE: *Releasing Your Potential* [Chapter 10]

Take a few moments to examine your environment. Is it uplifting or degrading? Does it enrich your spiritual life or detract from the work of God's Spirit in your heart? Is obedience to God the norm for those with whom you spend your days or do rebellion and disobedience characterize the lifestyles of your closest friends?

Moses instructed the Israelites to immerse themselves in God's commandments in Deuteronomy 6:6-9 (see above).

I recommend the same practice to you. For out of a heart centered on God flow His gifts of faith, forgiveness, and obedience. These essential ingredients of your God-designed environment testify to a relationship with the Risen Christ that clings to the promise of His presence and delights in the joy of His fellowship. They are the heritage of those who maintain a positive environment so their potential can be released, because a relationship with God always provides the right environment.

A Checklist for Your Environmental Conditions:

1. Who are your friends?
2. What books do you read?
3. What movies do you watch?
4. What magazines fill your shelves?
5. What are your hobbies?
6. What are your recreational activities?
7. Who feeds your musical appetites?
8. Who are your heroes?
9. Who feeds you spiritually?
10. Are the conditions of your home, school, work, or play conducive to your goals in life?

All the above should be carefully screened, analyzed, and adjusted to feed, activate, enhance, and foster the release of your potential.

> God is well acquainted with the insanity of your world.

## EVIEW the Principles From This Week:

1. God designed everything to function in a specific environment.
2. The conditions under which you function properly include: the presence of God, a relationship with God, fellowship with God, and the freedom to obey God.
3. Trust, faith, forgiveness, and obedience are necessary ingredients of your ideal environment.
4. Keep God's Word on your lips to create a positive atmosphere.
5. A wrong environment destroys potential.
6. Leave a wrong environment or change it.

## What Rules Your Life?

*Misfortune pursues the sinner, but prosperity is the reward of the righteous. A good man leaves an inheritance for his children's children, but a sinner's wealth is stored up for the righteous* (Proverbs 13:21-22).

BOOK QUOTE: *Releasing Your Potential* [Chapter 11]

Many workers see their jobs as dull, laborious, repetitious, tedious, and irritating. This attitude toward work has become of great concern to governments, corporations, and the media. As major problems with poor quality work, reduced productivity, and declining services cripple economic growth, the need and the desire to offer incentives and motivational exercises grow. Thus, aerobics classes, fitness rooms, and running tracks have become the focus of much effort and expense in the work place.

No matter how we dissect things, the power in our society can be reduced to two basic elements: *God* and *money*. They are the major forces in our world. Jesus warned that we would serve one or the other:

> *No one can serve two masters. Either he will hate the one and love the other, or he will be devoted to the one and despise the other. You cannot serve both God and money* (Matthew 6:24).

Which one you serve has a significant impact on the release of your potential, because the basic power in your life determines what motivates you. If money motivates you, greed will control your actions. If God empowers you, His purposes for your life will control you. The Scriptures promise that God will meet the needs of those who give their first allegiance to Him:

> *Therefore I tell you, do not worry about your life, what you will eat or drink; or about your body, what you will wear. Is not life more important than food, and the body more important than clothes? For the pagans run after all these things, and your heavenly Father knows that you need them. But seek first His kingdom and His righteousness, and all these things will be given to you as well* (Matthew 6:25-26,32-33).

*They also warn that allegiance to money brings trouble and financial bankruptcy: The greedy man brings trouble to his family...* (Proverbs 15:27).

> Some dream of worthy accomplishments, while others stay awake and do them.

This is true because the love of money promotes corrupt morals and perverted values. The need to accumulate more and more material wealth overshadows God's concerns of truth and honesty until deception and dishonesty determine what you do and how you do it.

## o You Work or Go to a Job?

*The wages of the righteous bring them life, but the income of the wicked brings them punishment* (Proverbs 10:16).

BOOK QUOTE: *Releasing Your Potential* [Chapter 11]

The love of money promotes corrupt morals and perverted values. The need to accumulate more and more material wealth overshadows God's concerns of truth and honesty until deception and dishonesty determine what you do and how you do it.

> *The wicked man earns deceptive wages, but he who sows righteousness reaps a sure reward.... Whoever trusts in his riches will fall, but the righteous will thrive like a green leaf* (Proverbs 11:18,28).

This conflict between God and money is very evident in our attitudes toward work.

Most of us want jobs, but we don't want to work. We want the money, but we don't want to expend the energy. Nothing is as depressing and frustrating as having someone on a job who's not interested in working. People who want a job without the work are a detriment. They are more interested in being job keepers than workers. They are more concerned with receiving a paycheck than in doing good work.

This attitude is completely contrary to God's concept of work. God wants you to be a good worker, not a good job keeper. He is more interested in your attitude toward work than the status of your checkbook. He has the power to increase your bank account balance, but He can't force you to have a positive attitude toward work.

God wants you to be a good worker, not a good job keeper.

## ur Negative View of Work

*Moreover, when God gives any man wealth and possessions, and enables him to enjoy them, to accept his lot and be happy in his work—this is a gift of God* (Ecclesiastes 5:19).

BOOK QUOTE: *Releasing Your Potential* [Chapter 11]

Thomas Edison was a great inventor. Many of the things we enjoy today, including the electric light, are the fruit of his willingness to be responsible for the possibilities hidden within him. He was not afraid to roll up his sleeves and work out his potential to make visible that which existed but we couldn't see. His life mirrored his words: "Genius is 1 percent inspiration and 99 percent perspiration."

Too often we allow the pain and perspiration of work to hide its blessings. We assume that work is a necessary evil without looking for the good it brings. The source of our misconceptions lies in the fact that we equate sin and work. Although work does not exist because of sin, sin did change the conditions of work.

> *Cursed is the ground because of you; through painful toil you will eat of it all the days of your life. It will produce thorns and thistles for you, and you will eat the plants of the field. By the sweat of your brow you will eat your food until you return to the ground, since from it you were taken* (Genesis 3:17b-19a).

Work as God planned it was given to man before sin entered the world. The account of Adam naming the animals precedes the account of Adam and Eve's disobedience. Work as we know it—with its pain, sweat, and struggle—reveals the devastation of Adam and Eve's disobedience.

When God told Adam, "Dominate this world I made. Rule this planet," life was new and fresh, and Adam had no knowledge of the power God had built into his brain. So God required Adam to come up with a different name for every animal. As he started naming the birds of the air and the beasts of the field, Adam discovered his potential. Thus, work is a blessing that reveals what you can do. It is the master key to releasing your potential.

"Genius is 1 percent inspiration and 99 percent perspiration."

## isconceptions About Work

*Six days do your work, but on the seventh day do not work, so that your ox and your donkey may rest and the slave born in your household, and the alien as well, may be refreshed* (Exodus 23:12).

BOOK QUOTE: *Releasing Your Potential* [Chapter 11]

Most of us don't understand the importance of work. We prefer rest and relaxation to a good day's work. The release of our potential requires that we acknowledge and move beyond the fallacies that characterize our view of work.

Six Days You Shall Labor…

We are a rest-oriented society. We believe that holidays, vacation and weekends are better than work days. This adoration of time free from work reflects our assumption that rest is to be preferred over work. This is a false assumption. Rest is not better than work.

When God created the world, He worked six days and rested one (see Genesis 2:2). He also instructed us to work six days and rest one (see Exodus 23:12). The result of our desire to work one day and rest six is evident in the boredom and unhappiness that plague our world.

*Work always produces more personal growth and satisfaction than rest does.* It stirs up your creative abilities and draws from the hidden store of your potential. If you are unfulfilled, you are probably resting too much. You're getting bored because you aren't working. You can't run from work and expect to be happy. Work is the energy that keeps you alive. It's the stuff that gives life meaning. Having six weeks of vacation is not the supreme measure of success or the ultimate prescription for happiness.

> If you are fulfilled, you are probably resting too much.

## etirement Isn't Part of God's Plan

*Sow your seed in the morning, and at evening let not your hands be idle, for you do not know which will succeed, whether this or that, or whether both will do equally well* (Ecclesiastes 11:6).

BOOK QUOTE: *Releasing Your Potential* [Chapter 11]

A fallacy that affects our view of work is the assumption that retirement is the goal of work. You were not designed to retire. You came out of God, and God hasn't retired. He's been working ever since He spoke the invisible into the visible. Therefore, retirement is not part of His plan for your life. Because God created man by giving him an immortal spirit with eternal potential, God planned enough work to keep you busy forever. Oh, you may retire from a specific organization or job, but you can never retire from life and work. *The minute you quit working, you begin to die, because work is a necessary part of life.*

Have you ever met a retired person who was uncomfortable, bitter, rowdy, and senile? He became that way because He retired from work. The lack of work made him crazy because it took away his means of finding fulfillment.

Just like a car runs on gasoline, you run on work. God created you to feel healthy and happy when you are expending energy to reveal all that He put in you. He designed you to find satisfaction in looking at the fruit of your labor. That's why *inactivity often brings depression and discouragement.* God didn't intend for you to sit around and loaf.

God rested when He became tired. He didn't retire. So He says to you, "I'm still working. Why aren't you? There are still things in you that I need." May God deliver you from the spirit of retirement, because retirement is ungodly, unscriptural, and unbiblical. Retirement is foreign to God's plan for human beings.

Another fallacy that adversely affects your understanding of work is the belief that you can get something for nothing. Nowhere is this fallacy more evident than in our fascination with lotteries. Advertisements for magazine sweepstakes fill our mail boxes. Daily numbers are announced every evening on TV and radio newscasts. Mail order houses promise great wealth if you buy their products. Get-rich-quick schemes, casinos, and TV game shows captivate millions and feed them this attitude. The messages of our world encourage our desire to get something for nothing. Sadly, we are taken in by their hype. Until we let go of our hideous attempts to receive benefits without effort, we will forfeit the blessings of work, because work is God's pathway to a satisfying, meaningful existence.

Work is God's pathway to a satisfying, meaningful existence.

## You Cannot Fulfill Your Purpose Without Work

*...his work will be shown for what it is, because the Day will bring it to light. It will be revealed with fire, and the fire will test the quality of each man's work. If what he has built survives, he will receive his reward* (1 Corinthians 3:13-14).

BOOK QUOTE: *Releasing Your Potential* [Chapter 11]

*You cannot fulfill your purpose without work.* Trying to get money by winning the lottery bypasses personal fulfillment. Neither can you achieve God's intent for your life by reaping the benefits of someone else's efforts. Those who win the lottery often testify that they are more unhappy after they receive all that money than before. Why? Because they lose their reason for getting up in the morning.

Without purpose, life becomes meaningless. Life on "easy street" is not really easy because satisfaction requires effort. In fact, winning a million dollars could very well kill you if you stopped working. Oh, your body might live for a while, but your potential—the real you—would die from lack of use. The joy of life would be gone.

*God gives you work to meet your need for personal fulfillment.* When you try to get something for nothing you miss the opportunity to find gratification, because effort is the key to satisfaction. Life bears this out in many ways. *Benefits without work short-circuit fulfillment* because you usually have more appreciation for something you worked hard to get. You remember all you went through to obtain it, and from your remembering flows the impetus to treasure and care for the products of your labor. Handouts meet your desire for material possessions, but they deny you the pride of gaining through effort. This is the weakness of a welfare system that robs the individual of the personal responsibility, gratification and pride that comes from self-development and self-deployment.

Benefits without work short-circuit fulfillment.

## Work and Responsibility

*Blessed are all who fear the Lord, who walk in his ways. You will eat the fruit of your labor; blessings and prosperity will be yours* (Psalm 128:1-2).

BOOK QUOTE: *Releasing Your Potential* [Chapter 11]

The love of work is the secret to a productive life. *Without work, you will lose direction and gradually succumb to atrophy*. Your very survival will be threatened as the various facets of your life fall apart from a lack of purpose. So crucial is your need to work that the absence of work is often the issue that underlies problems in interpersonal relationships.

If, for example, a man marries without thinking beyond the pleasures of marriage to the responsibilities of a family, he begins to resent those things that naturally go with marriage and the establishment of a home—things like rent, utility bills, car payments, and grocery bills; things like the expenses and obligations that go with children. And, in time, the reasonable responsibilities of a home and a family begin to look unreasonable, and the duties of husband and father become burdens. That's when the problems start, because the man begins to look for a way out of his seemingly intolerable situation. In essence, he begins to call responsibility pressure.

Work is God's way to draw out your potential. Through work He opens the door into your inner storehouse and teaches you how to use your talents and abilities to meet the many responsibilities of life. Work and the ability to handle responsibility go hand in hand because work requires you to take on new challenges, dares you to risk failure to show your capacity for success, and prompts you to take the steps to make your dream a reality.

God wants you to fulfill all that He created you to do and be. That's why He is constantly giving you tasks that reveal more and more of the wealth that lies hidden within you. Little by little, He's chipping away at your storehouse of riches, trying to release all that He put in you. But you must cooperate with His efforts. You must refuse to allow the rest/retirement/I-can-get-something-for-nothing mentality to rob you of your need to work. When you accept your responsibility to work and allow God to change your perceptions of work, you will see a difference in your life because God set work as a priority for personal gratification. Work is the *master key* to releasing your potential.

Benefits without work short-circuit fulfillment.

## EVIEW the Principles From This Week:

- God or money will rule your life.
- An allegiance to money brings physical, financial, social, emotional, and spiritual problems.
- God wants you to be a good worker, not a good job keeper.
- Work is a blessing that reveals what you can do.
- Work always produces more personal growth and satisfaction than rest does.
- Retirement isn't part of God's plan for your life. You will die if you quit working.
- God gives you work to meet your need for personal fulfillment.

## Potential Is Never Realized Without Work

*For we are God's fellow workers; you are God's field, God's building* (1 Corinthians 3:9).

BOOK QUOTE: *Releasing Your Potential* [Chapter 12]

Have you ever noticed who God uses? God uses busy people. Truly God loves busy people because their busyness shows that they are willing to work. Jesus' preference for busy people is evident in His choice of four fishermen who were preparing their nets, to be His first followers.

The priority Jesus put on work is also evident later in His ministry as He went through the towns and villages of Galilee and Judea, teaching in the synagogues and healing the sick. He saw there many people who were so helpless and harassed that He likened them to sheep without a shepherd. With compassion, He instructed His disciples to pray for workers to meet their needs:

> *Then* [Jesus] *said to His disciples, "The harvest is plentiful but the workers* [laborers] *are few. Ask the Lord of the harvest, therefore, to send workers* [laborers] *into His harvest field"* (Matthew 9:37-38).

Jesus needed *workers*. He needed people who would give their best to bring others into the Kingdom of God. He told His disciples to pray that God would send somebody to work.

God uses busy people.

## Don't Be a Reluctant Worker

*One who is slack in his work is brother to one who destroys* (Proverbs 18:9).

BOOK QUOTE: *Releasing Your Potential* [Chapter 12]

When Jesus was on earth, He needed *workers*. He needed people who would give their best to bring others into the Kingdom of God. He told His disciples to pray that God would send somebody to work.

God hasn't changed. Work is still a priority for Him. Nor have the needs of our world changed. Helpless, harassed people still need what God stored in us for them.

But we don't appreciate God's ways. We want results without the process. We seek promotion without responsibility. We desire pay without work. You will not participate in the creative power of the One who says, "I've given you the ability to produce. Now work to see what you can do" until you cease to be a reluctant worker. You must stop refusing to work, unless someone is standing over you, giving you the work, and making sure that you do it. When God commanded Adam to work in the garden, there was no supervisor, manager, or time clock to motivate Adam or to force him to work.

God expects us to understand our natural need to work. The Church, and the world at large, must recover God's principle of work because there can be no greatness without work. We must accept the truth that we need to work because God worked and He created us to work.

God expects us to understand our natural need to work.

## od Worked

*So on the seventh day He rested from all His work. And God blessed the seventh day and made it holy, because on it He rested from all the work of creating that He had done* (Genesis 2:2b-3).

BOOK QUOTE: *Releasing Your Potential* [Chapter 12]

God set the priority of work when He called the invisible world into view. Before there was anything, there was God. Everything we now see existed first in God, but it was invisible. If God had done nothing to get started, the world we know would not exist. The universe would have stayed inside Him. But God chose to deliver His babies by *working*. He took His potential and, through effort, changed it from potential to experience.

God's efforts in making the world are noteworthy. He determined the number of stars and called them by name (see Psalm 147:4). He covered the sky with clouds, supplied the earth with rain, and made grass to grow on the hills (see Psalm 147:8). He formed the mountains by His power see (see Psalm 65:6) and set the foundations of the earth (see Psalm 104:4). The moon marks the seasons by His decree and the sun sets at the appointed time (see Psalm 104:19). So vast and marvelous are God's works in creation that He pronounced them good when He stopped and looked at what He had made. He savored the joy of seeing the wondrous beauty He had brought forth.

> *God saw all that He had made, and it was very good.... Thus the heavens and the earth were completed in all their vast array. By the seventh day God had finished the work He had been doing* (Genesis 1:31; 2:2a).

God took His potential and, through effort, changed it to experience.

## God's Effort in Creation

*God saw all that He had made, and it was very good.... Thus the heavens and the earth were completed in all their vast array. By the seventh day God had finished the work He had been doing* (Genesis 1:31; 2:2a).

BOOK QUOTE: *Releasing Your Potential* [Chapter 12]

God's efforts in making the world are noteworthy. He determined the number of stars and called them by name (see Psalm 147:4). He covered the sky with clouds, supplied the earth with rain, and made grass to grow on the hills (see Psalm 147:8). He formed the mountains by His power see (see Psalm 65:6) and set the foundations of the earth (see Psalm 104:4). The moon marks the seasons by His decree and the sun sets at the appointed time (see Psalm 104:19). So vast and marvelous are God's works in creation that He pronounced them good when He stopped and looked at what He had made. He savored the joy of seeing the wondrous beauty He had brought forth.

God didn't create the world by dreaming, wishing, or imagining. He created it by working. Indeed, God worked so hard that He had to rest.

> *So on the seventh day He rested from all His work. And God blessed the seventh day and made it holy, because on it He rested from all the work of creating that He had done* (Genesis 2:2b-3).

Rest is needed after a long, laborious experience, not a tiny task that requires little effort. God's effort in creation was so extensive that He rested.

Too often we think that coming back to God means we don't have to work anymore. How wrong we are! God loves to work. He delights in pulling new things from His Omnipotent Self. He also requires you to work.

God delights in pulling new things from His Omnipotent Self.

## God Created Adam to Work

*A curse on him who is lax in doing the Lord's work! A curse on him who keeps his sword from bloodshed!* (Jeremiah 48:10).

BOOK QUOTE: *Releasing Your Potential* [Chapter 12]

After God finished creating the world and planting and organizing the garden, He put Adam in the garden and gave him *work* to do. Indeed, God had work on His mind before He even created human beings.

> *When the Lord God made the earth and the heavens—and no shrub of the field had yet appeared on the earth and no plant of the field had yet sprung up, for the Lord God had not sent rain on the earth and there was no man to work the ground, but streams came from the earth and watered the whole surface of the ground—the Lord God formed the man from the dust of the ground and breathed into his nostrils the breath of life, and the man became a living being* (Genesis 2:4b-7).

When God created Adam, He gave him dominion over the fish of the sea, the birds of the air, and the living creatures that move on the ground. Although we understand dominion to be sitting on a throne while others obey our every command, that is not God's intent. *God equates dominion with work. Every assignment God gave Adam required work.* The care and protection of the garden required work. The naming of the animals required work. The subduing of the earth required work. Work was an essential part of Adam's life.

God equates dominion with work.

## God Created You to Work

*...nor did we eat anyone's food without paying for it. On the contrary, we worked night and day, laboring and toiling so that we would not be a burden to any of you* (2 Thessalonians 3:8).

BOOK QUOTE: *Releasing Your Potential* [Chapter 12]

When God created Adam, He gave him dominion. Adam had dominion over:

- Fish (water)
- Birds (air)
- Living creatures (land)

This dominion meant that Adam had to work. Work was an essential part of Adam's life.

The same is true for you. God created you to work. He didn't create you to rest or retire or go on vacation. He didn't create you to punch a time card or to stand under the eagle eye of a boss or supervisor. He gave you birth to experience fulfillment by completing tasks through effort.

Work is a gift from God. Every assignment God has ever given required work. Noah worked to build the ark (see Genesis 6). Joseph worked to provide for the Egyptians during a seven-year famine (see Genesis 41:41ff). Solomon worked to build the Temple (see 2 Chronicles 2-4). As each accomplished what God asked of him, he fulfilled God's purpose for his life. His willingness to do the work God gave him blessed himself and others. Through work these people and many others have met the various responsibilities of their lives.

Work is a gift from God.

## ou Need to Work

*All hard work brings a profit...*(Proverbs 24:23).

BOOK QUOTE: *Releasing Your Potential* [Chapter 12]

Work is honorable. God designed you to meet the needs of your life through work. When you refuse to work, you deny yourself the opportunity to fulfill your purpose, because God created you to act like He acts, and God worked. The release of your potential demands that you admit that you need work.

*Work Profits the Worker*

*The plans of the diligent lead to profit…* (Proverbs 21:5) …by providing for physical needs.

> *Make it your ambition to lead a quiet life, to mind your own business and to* ***work*** *with your hands...so that your daily life may win the respect of outsiders and so that* ***you will not be dependent on anybody*** (1 Thessalonians 4:11-12).

Work profits the worker by allowing him to meet his financial responsibilities. The apostle Paul provided for his own needs by making tents (see 1 Thessalonians 2:6-9). He did not rely on the provisions of others, but whenever possible, worked for his living.

The same is required of you. Don't become a burden on others. Work to provide for yourself and your family. Settle down and get a job. Put your roots down and do not allow yourself to be easily deterred from your responsibilities. God gave you work to earn the bread you eat.

God designed you to meet the needs of your life through work.

## EVIEW the Principles From This Week:

- God worked when He created the world.
- God created you to work.
- Subduing and dominating the earth requires work.
- You need to work because it is profitable for you.

## Work Profits the Worker

*Do your best to present yourself to God as one approved, a workman who does not need to be ashamed and who correctly handles the Word of truth* (2 Timothy 2:15).

BOOK QUOTE: *Releasing Your Potential* [Chapter 12]

Work profits the worker…

…by revealing potential.

God also ordained that work would show you your potential. Although all work brings profit, the reward is not always a financial one. You may feel like you are working hard but you're not getting paid what you are worth. Keep working so you can reap the profits of your work. God does not lie. Even if no one ever pays you, your work profits you because you discover what you can do. It is better to deserve an honor and not receive it than to receive an honor and not deserve it.

…by unveiling the blessings of work.

Work is much more important than honor because it brings the learning that releases your talents, abilities, and capabilities. It is also more valuable than a paycheck. When you stop working for money, you'll discover the blessing of work.

*The laborer's appetite works for him; his hunger drives him on* (Proverbs 16:26).

…by giving the opportunity to rejoice in achievement.

A commitment to work will also permit you to develop a perspective that rejoices in achievement more than pay. Then you can find happiness in your work even when the pay is less than what you expect or deserve. Administrators give those who are busy more to do because they know the busy people are willing to work. *If you want to be promoted, get busy. Become productive.* When you work, work because you want to know what you can do, not because you are trying to get paid. You may not be noticed immediately, but your promotion will come. Excellent work always profits the worker.

…by building self-esteem.

Finally, work profits you by enhancing your self-esteem. If you feel worthless, find some work. Get busy. When you have something to do, your ability to feel good about yourself can change overnight. As you take the opportunity to focus on the results of your labor instead of the losses in your life that tempt you to feel unloveable and incapable, your estimation of yourself will grow. Work keeps you healthy, physically and emotionally.

> Keep working so you can reap the profits of your work.

## Work Blesses Others

*...I have never seen the righteous forsaken or their children begging bread. They are always generous and lend freely; their children will be blessed* (Psalm 37:25b-26).

BOOK QUOTE: *Releasing Your Potential* [Chapter 12]

> *Share with God's people who are in need. Practice hospitality* (Romans 12:13).

Work affords the opportunity to help others. Indeed, the Gospel of Matthew records a parable in which our willingness to help meet the needs of others is the basis on which our faithfulness or unfaithfulness to Christ is judged (see Matthew 25:31-46). The apostle Paul notes the benefits of sharing when he commends the Corinthian church for their willingness to help sister churches in need (see 2 Corinthians 8-9). He advises them to give generously, not grudgingly, with the promise that what they give and more will be returned to them:

> *Remember this: Whoever sows sparingly will also reap sparingly, and whoever sows generously will also reap generously. Each man should give what he has decided in his heart to give, not reluctantly or under compulsion, for God loves a cheerful giver.... Now He who supplies seed to the sower and bread for food will also supply and increase your store of seed and will enlarge the harvest of your righteousness. You will be made rich in every way so that you can be generous on every occasion...* (2 Corinthians 9:6-7, 10-11a).

> Our willingness to help meet the needs of others is the basis on which our faithfulness or unfaithfullness to Christ is judged.

## So Who's Stealing?

*...I have never seen the righteous forsaken or their children begging bread. They are always generous and lend freely; their children will be blessed* (Psalm 37:25-26).

BOOK QUOTE: *Releasing Your Potential* [Chapter 12]

If I were to ask you to describe a thief, you would probably talk about someone who entered your home and took your possessions. This is certainly a legitimate definition, but the thief doesn't always have to sneak in and out to take what isn't his.

Many of us go to work and steal from our bosses. We come to work late, take extra long lunch hours, and go home early. Or we take home the pencils, paper, pens, and paper clips that belong to the company, we make private copies on the boss's copy machine, and we conduct personal business on company time. These actions are no better than those of a thief who enters your home and takes your possessions because both result in the loss of goods that someone else worked to provide.

In an even broader sense, a thief is anyone who relies on the productiveness of another to provide for his needs because he is too lazy to meet them himself. If you are able to work and you're not working, you are stealing from those who are working. You're requiring them to provide what you could get for yourself if you would work. If you are eating but not working, or you are living in a house but not working, you are a thief. *Taking the benefits of work without participating in the effort is theft.*

> If you are able to work and you're not working, you are stealing from those who are working.

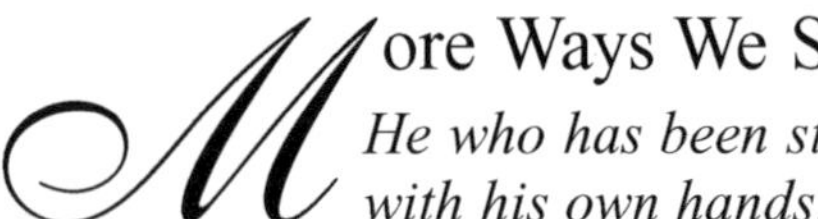

## More Ways We Steal

*He who has been stealing must steal no longer, but must work, doing something useful with his own hands...* (Ephesians 4:28).

BOOK QUOTE: *Releasing Your Potential* [Chapter 12]

If you are able to work and you're not working, you are stealing from those who are working.

A son who plays baseball all day then comes in and messes up the house his mother spent all day cleaning is a thief. He has stolen her energy. Likewise, an adult child who is out of school, but lives at home, steals from his parents if he goes into the kitchen and eats from the pot that is on the stove without helping to provide what's in the pot.

Theft goes even farther than relying on another's effort. You are pregnant with babies that need to be born. You have talents, abilities, and capabilities that God wants you to share with the world. But you will never see them unless you begin to understand God's definition of work and His purpose for giving you the opportunity to share His creative powers. Your potential is dying while you are sitting around doing nothing.

If you steal something, you don't stop and look at it. Instead of admiring your efforts, you worry about who's going to take your things from you. Or you are so busy seeing how little work you can do without being caught that you have accomplished nothing at the end of the day that merits the pride of accomplishment. *The absence of work is stealing. Likewise, the cure for stealing is work—doing something useful with your hands.*

(See Ephesians 4:28 above.)

Usefulness is more than a job. It's making a profitable contribution to the world. It's gaining so you can give. It's finding wholesome, legal work that helps and blesses another, instead of immoral degrading behavior that harms and destroys. Usefulness recognizes the accomplishments of others and tries to complement them.

> The cure for stealing is work—doing something useful with your hands.

## he Penalties of Laziness—Part 1

*Even when we were with you, we gave you this rule: "If a man will not work, he shall not eat"* (2 Thessalonians 3:10).

BOOK QUOTE: *Releasing Your Potential* [Chapter 12]

Sitting around is no more acceptable to God than taking what does not belong to you. You rob yourself and others when you are lazy. Like any theft, laziness carries many penalties. The first of these is *hunger*:

> *The sluggard craves and gets nothing, but the desires of the diligent are fully satisfied* (Proverbs 13:4).
>
> *Laziness brings on deep sleep, and the shiftless man goes hungry* (Proverbs 19:15).

A second penalty of laziness is *isolation* and *shame*:

> *In the name of the Lord Jesus Christ, we command you, brothers, to keep away from every brother who is idle.... Do not associate with him, in order that he may feel ashamed* (2 Thessalonians 3:6,14b).
>
> *A poor man is shunned by all his relatives—how much more do his friends avoid him!* (Proverbs 19:7).

A third penalty of laziness is *others' reluctance to take you seriously*, because lazy people always have an excuse why they aren't working.

> *The sluggard says, "There is a lion outside!" or, "I will be murdered in the streets!"* (Proverbs 22:13).

You rob yourself and others when you are lazy.

## The Penalties of Laziness—Part 2

*Do you see a man skilled in his work? He will serve before kings; he will not serve before obscure men* (Proverbs 22:29).

BOOK QUOTE: *Releasing Your Potential* [Chapter 12]

Like any theft, laziness carries many penalties. The first of these is *hunger*. A second penalty of laziness is *isolation* and *shame*. A third penalty of laziness is *others' reluctance to take you seriously*, because lazy people always have an excuse why they aren't working.

A fourth penalty of laziness is *lost opportunities for advancement* because jealousy and over concern for the progress of others prevents you from doing your work.

> *Be sure you know the condition of your flocks, give careful attention to your herd; for riches do not endure forever and a crown is not secure for all generations* (Proverbs 27:23-24).

A fifth penalty of laziness is *the inability to see your own need to get up and work*:

> *The sluggard is wiser in his own eyes than seven men who answer discreetly* (Proverbs 26:16).

A sixth penalty of laziness is an increasing *loss of ambition*:

> *The sluggard buries his hand in the dish; he is too lazy to bring it back to his mouth* (Proverbs 26:15).

> *Go to the ant, you sluggard; consider its ways and be wise! It has no commander, no overseer or ruler, yet it stores its provisions in summer and gathers it food at harvest* (Proverbs 6:6-7).

A seventh penalty of laziness is the *desire to sleep*:

> *As a door turns on its hinges, so a sluggard turns on his bed* (Proverbs 26:14).

An eighth penalty of laziness is *the inability to take pride in what you have accomplished* because you haven't accomplished anything.

> *The lazy man does not roast his game, but the diligent man prizes his possessions* (Proverbs 12:27).

A ninth penalty of laziness is *slavery*:

> *Diligent hands will rule, but laziness ends in slave labor* (Proverbs 12:24).

An tenth penalty of laziness, and the most severe, is *poverty*. Poverty is the cumulative result of all the other penalities.

> *All hard work brings a profit, but mere talk leads only to poverty* (Proverbs 14:23).

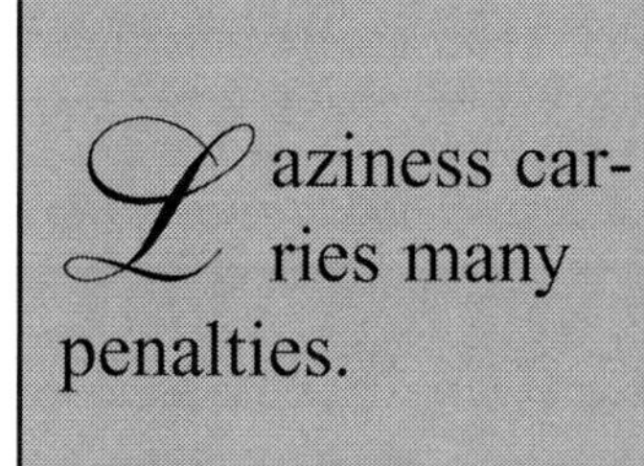

Laziness carries many penalties.

## The Most Severe Penalty for Laziness—Poverty

*Go to the ant, you sluggard; consider its ways and be wise! It has no commander, no overseer or ruler, yet it stores its provisions in summer and gathers it food at harvest* (Proverbs 6:6-8).

BOOK QUOTE: *Releasing Your Potential* [Chapter 12]

A tenth penalty of laziness, and the most severe, is *poverty*. Poverty is the cumulative result of all the other penalities.

> *All hard work brings a profit, but mere talk leads only to poverty* (Proverbs 14:23).
>
> *How long will you lie there, you sluggard? When will you get up from your sleep? A little sleep, a little slumber, a little folding of the hands to rest—and poverty will come on you like a bandit and scarcity like an armed man* (Proverbs 6:9-11).
>
> *Lazy hands make a man poor...* (Proverbs 10:4).

A sluggard is a lazy bum—my mother used to call them "grassy bellies." When I was young I didn't understand what my mom meant. But one day when I was sitting in the library at the university I realized that Mom called sluggards grassy bellies because they lay on their bellies long enough for grass to grow on them. The Greek word for *poor*, as used by Jesus, is *poucos*, which means "nonproductivity." That's what poverty is. To be poor doesn't mean you don't *have* anything. It means you aren't *doing* anything.

Poverty is cured by hard work. If you don't work you will end up begging. Or you'll become a slave to your boss because you refuse to work for your own satisfaction in completing the job and wait for him to force you to work.

Look at the birds. God provides food for them, but they have to go and look for it. They have to dig and pull it out of the ground. So it is with you. God has given you many talents and ambitions to bring satisfaction and fulfillment into your life. But you have to go and look for that fulfillment. You can't sit back and wait for it to come to you, because it will never come. Work is God's path to an abundant, fulfilling life that reveals the wealth of your potential. *God established your need to work when He worked out His potential in creation and demanded the same of Adam.*

## EVIEW the Principles From This Week:

- When you refuse to work, you deny yourself the opportunity to fulfill your potential.
- The absence of work is stealing.
- You rob yourself and others when you are lazy.
- Poverty is cured by hard work.

## orking for Fulfillment

*Share with God's people who are in need. Practice hospitality* (Romans 12:13).

BOOK QUOTE: *Releasing Your Potential* [Chapter 13]

A study of history reveals that all great empires were built on the sweat and blood of a labor force, whether the energy of the workers was given voluntarily or through force. The civilizations of Egypt, Greece, Rome, and Assyria were built on the backs of subjugated peoples.

The power of productivity is evident today in the influence of labor unions. Because unions control the workers, who control the productivity, they can cripple a country, destroy an economy and control a government. And once you control productivity, you control wealth.

Do you know how countries measure their strength and wealth? They measure it not by the money they have in their treasury, but by their GNP, which means Gross National Product. Thus, the relative strength or weakness of a country is measured by the level of employment and productivity. The power of productivity is work. You can't run a country where the people aren't working because you can't force people to work. Governments can't legislate obedience, nor can they force people to cooperate without question. Everybody has rights, a will and a conscience. Sooner or later, workers will rebel if they feel they are working for nothing. Out of sheer desperation they will try to control their own destiny. There's power in work—much more power than churches, governments, or other social organizations have—because the workers control productivity and, therefore, the destiny of the nation.

When people decide they aren't going to work, the back of a nation is broken. We have seen this in the recent past as the former Soviet Union and other countries have changed dramatically through the power of the worker. Thus, the demise of world-class companies is not the fault of the board or the president. The cause rests with the little guys who push wheels on a plane or weld car parts together. Our countries are falling apart because our people are refusing to work, and work well. We must change our attitudes toward work. Our only hope is to rediscover God's definition of work and the benefits He intends work to bring to our lives.

> Working for fulfillment is better than working for money. The purpose of a job is work, not money.

## God's Definition of Work

*Why spend money on what is not bread, and your labor on what does not satisfy? Listen, listen to me, and eat what is good, and your soul will delight in the richest of fare* (Isaiah 55:2).

BOOK QUOTE: *Releasing Your Potential* [Chapter 13]

Our definition of work and God's are very different. Work is not the same as a job. Work releases potential; a job provides a paycheck. While you may work at your job, work does not always result in a financial reward. Work arises out of a desire to contribute to the world's wealth and well-being by giving of yourself. It moves beyond effort under the force of another and avoids the "I'm not going to work because you can't make me work" mentality.

Frequently we make work overly sophisticated. We need to get labor back into work. We need to *labor* in the office, not just go to the office. God didn't say, "Six days you shall go to your job," but "six days you shall work." Until we change our attitude toward work we will not obey this commandment.

Labor isn't so much *doing things* as *delivering hidden stuff*. It's delivering the babies you will die with if you don't work them into sight. It doesn't matter what kind of job you have, whether you are an executive, a salesman, a factory worker, or a housewife. Work as though your life depended on it, because it does.

Jesus commanded us to pray for *laborers*. This term is also used to describe the process of a woman in childbearing. The process of delivering the pride and joy of a new baby—the hidden potential—involves conception, time, development, adjustments, labor, pain, and cooperation. All are necessary for the manifestation of a child. This process is the same for all humanity. Labor delivers!

Work is God's way of revealing your talents, abilities, and capabilities. It helps you to discover the satisfaction of accomplishment and the results of perseverance. Without work you'll never see the results of your potential. Without effort you'll never feel the satisfaction of accomplishment.

Work releases potential; a job provides a paycheck.

# ork Is Activated Strength and Energy

*Diligent hands will rule, but laziness ends in slave labor* (Proverbs 12:24).

BOOK QUOTE: *Releasing Your Potential* [Chapter 13]

Jesus worked while He was on the earth. He gave sight to the blind and hearing to the deaf. He preached the good news of God's coming Kingdom and welcomed sinners into God's family. Again and again He called on His strength and energy to meet the demands of lonely, harried, fearful, needy people. Had He chosen to withhold the potential He possessed to better the lives of those He met, His power would have remained hidden and His purpose would have been lost. But Jesus knew that He had been sent to redeem a suffering, dying world. He accepted the task God gave Him and worked to change the course of history. Indeed, the results of His work were the clues Jesus pointed to when He was questioned whether He was the One to be sent from God.

> *Jesus said to them, "My Father is always at His work to this very day, and I, too, am working"* (John 5:17).

You have a similar responsibility to release the strength and energy God gave you for the good of the world. You can accomplish this through work. The Greek word *ergon*, which means "to activate," is often translated *work*. From *ergon* comes our word "energy." Thus, work is the activation of stored energy. If a car is parked, it is inoperative. But the minute you start the engine, the pistons begin working and the car has the power to move. Work is the God-given method that empowers you to operate. Through work you can do and become all that God intended for your life.

This concept of becoming is further clarified in another Greek word for work, *energia*, which means "to become." No matter what God requires of you, if you don't do it, you can't become what He sees in you. *Potential is the existence of possibilities. Work is the activation of possibilities.* Potential without work remains potential—untapped, untouched, untested!

God created you to be a genius. He endowed you with enough thoughts, ideas and desires to fulfill every expectation He has for your life. But the presence of potential does not make you a genius. You are not *born* a genius. You *become* one by working to release what you have. Geniuses are people who work relentlessly to accomplish what they believe can be done. They try again and again until they receive in the physical what they see in their imaginations. They activate their hidden strength and energy to become what they are and to accomplish what they already possess. Geniuses use God's gift of work to achieve what no one else has done. God planned for you to be a genius. Remember, "Genius is 1 percent inspiration, and 99 percent *perspiration*."

> Through work you become what you are.

*Potential is what you have. Work is what you do*. What you do with what you have makes the difference between a life of strength and energy, and a life of weakness and defeat. God gives you work to activate your power. Through work you become what you are.

## Work Is Bringing Something to Pass

*And we pray this in order that you may live a life worthy of the Lord and may please Him in every way: bearing fruit in every good work, growing in the knowledge of God,* (Colossians 1:10).

BOOK QUOTE: *Releasing Your Potential* [Chapter 13]

A fantasy is a dream without labor. It is also a vision without a mission. When God gives the potential for something, He also demands that it be worked out. The story of Abraham is a good example of this principle.

One day when God and Abraham were on top of a mountain, God told Abraham that He would give him everything as far as he could see to the north, south, east, and west. Then God told him to *walk* the length and breadth of the land to *receive* what he had been promised (Genesis 13:14-17). Along with the promise came the command to work. Before Abraham could take possession of his inheritance, he had to fight those who lived in the land. The promise would not be possession without effort.

The same is true for you. Every time God gives you a promise, He also gives you the command to work to receive what He has promised. God doesn't just deliver like Santa Claus. You have to fight to get what is yours. The potential to possess what God has given is within you, but you will not obtain the promise until you put forth the effort to claim it.

So if you need money to pay your bills, don't wait for someone to drop the dollars into your hand. Get up and take the job God sends.

*Every job, no matter how much you dislike it, is working for you.* If you can educate yourself to work no matter what the conditions are, you will learn discipline, because the work is more important than the conditions. Work is also more important than the job. If a child always gets what he wants, he learns to expect his wants to be met without any effort on his part. Our world is full of adults who act like spoiled children. They never learned the value of work.

We do well when we learn the lesson early in life that God requires us to work for what we want. One of the greatest things parents can do for their children is to demand that they learn the responsibility of work at an early age. If your child has to work for his spending money, he will soon learn that he can't get something for nothing. *Work brings potential to pass.* Without work, all you have is potential.

> Every job, no matter how much you dislike it, is working for you.

# Work Is Using Your Abilities and Faculties to Do or Perform Something

*So we rebuilt the wall till all of it reached half its height, for the people worked with all their heart* (Nehemiah 4:6).

BOOK QUOTE: *Releasing Your Potential* [Chapter 13]

When God wanted a place to live, He could have created a magnificent dwelling by speaking it into place. But He chose to have man build the house for Him. Thus, God instructed Moses to gather offerings for the Tabernacle and to employ skilled craftsmen to create its various parts. After Moses had collected the materials and the workers, the work began. Silversmiths, goldsmiths, carpenters, glass cutters, weavers, embroiderers, and gem cutters all contributed their *skills* until the dwelling place of God was completed. Then the Lord, through His presence in the cloud by day and the pillar of fire by night, entered and filled the Tabernacle *they had prepared.*

God has given you a wealth of skills, talents, and abilities. Work is the means to discovering those resources. Persistent, consistent effort polishes the gems within you, making your life a suitable dwelling place for our holy God. It activates your potential and enables you to share your expertise and proficiency. The release of your gifts will benefit the world for generations to come.

When the Israelites returned from exile in Babylon, Nehemiah, the governor of Jerusalem, led the people in repairing the walls of the city. Because he had a burden to repair the gates destroyed by fire and to rebuild the buildings that lay in rubble, he toured the ruins and asked the officials of Jerusalem to work with him. When scoffers ridiculed them, Nehemiah replied, "*The God of Heaven will give us success*" (Nehemiah 2:20). He believed that the dream was from God and, therefore, trusted Him for the attainment of his goal. His efforts were aided by those who "*worked with all their heart*" (Nehemiah 4:6). Time and again God frustrated the plots of those who would have threatened Nehemiah's dream, thus proving that He will fight for those who undertake to fulfill His purposes.

Work coupled with a mind to do what God desired brought victory for the Israelites who were committed to the rebuilding of the wall of Jerusalem. *Committed work toward a desired result is also a key to your success.*

Commited work toward a desired result is a key to your success.

## Potential and the Benefits of Work

*As God's fellow workers we urge you not to receive God's grace in vain* (2 Corinthians 6:1).

BOOK QUOTE: *Releasing Your Potential* [Chapter 13]

Work provides the means through which the knowledge you gained through the study of the other keys can be activated. It takes you from knowing that you must live by faith to acting on what you know. Knowledge is not profitable until it is translated into action. Work is the translator God has provided.

A fantasy is a dream without work. It is also a vision without a mission. You can have all the vision you want, but until you get a mission, your vision will be no more than a wishful thought. Work is the means to make what you see into what you receive. Visionaries must become missionaries to be effective and successful.

Work is part of your design. If you're not working, you're not fulfilling your purpose. In God's system, everyone *needs* to work. *You* need to work. Your ability to dominate and subdue the earth is related to the effort you put forth to accomplish the tasks God gives you. If you refuse to work, your potential to express God's image and to bear fruit are sealed inside you, dormant and useless. Without labor there is no fruit, and the blessings God wants to give you are forfeited. Your refusal to work destroys the possibilities you possess to cooperate with God's work of creation.

It's not how many resources you have but how much work you generate with those resources that will control your poverty or wealth. Potential without work is poverty because your willingness to work is the key to the realization of your potential. Everybody has potential—which is dormant ability, hidden strength, untapped strength and unused resources—but not everybody works to release what they have.

Work is crucial to the care and multiplication of your resources. If you are faithful over little, God will make you ruler over much. But He can only give as much as you are willing to accept. Work is the means to multiply what God has already entrusted into your care, be it great or small.

People tend to gravitate to those who think and act like they do. This is certainly true of those who avoid work. Lazy people don't like to be in the company of diligent people because their non-productivity is readily visible.

> Until you start working, your power to benefit mankind will remain untapped.

## How to Work Out Your Potential

*The plans of the diligent lead to profit as surely as haste leads to poverty* (Proverbs 21:5).

BOOK QUOTE: *Releasing Your Potential* [Chapter 13]

Are you hungry to accomplish something? Are you so committed to a vision that you will do anything to see that vision come to life? Then make plans and follow them.

There's a difference between plans and haste. Haste is trying to get something for nothing. Haste leads to poverty. But the hard worker make plans and expends the effort to see those plans pay off.

Do you want to be a lawyer, a doctor, a teacher, a carpenter, a policeman, a minister, a secretary, an accountant, or a politician? Put some work behind that dream. Burn the midnight oil and study. Make the acquaintance of a person who is working in your chosen field and work with him to learn the trade, business, or profession. The completion of your plans is related to your willingness to work, as is your prosperity. Likewise, *the release of your potential is dependent upon your expenditure of the necessary effort to change your thoughts into visible realities. Work of your own initiative. Don't wait for life to force you to work.*

Work is the key to your personal progress, productivity, and fulfillment. Without work you can accomplish nothing. God assigns you work so you can release your possibilities and abilities by putting forth the effort to accomplish each task. The responsibilities God gives you are presented to provoke your potential and to challenge you to try new things. Until you stop being a reluctant worker, you will miss the vitality and meaning that God intended work to bring to your life.

Accept today God's gracious gift of work. Refuse to allow a pessimistic attitude toward work to rob you of your potential. Then look forward to the joy of accomplishment and the delight of discovering all God put in you for the world. You will truly find that work is a blessing.

Work is the key to your personal progress, productivity, and fulfillment.

## EVIEW the Principles From This Week:

- The achievement of greatness requires work.
- Labor delivers your potential.
- Work is…activated strength and energy, the effort required to bring something to pass, the use of your abilities and faculties to do or perform something, and the means to produce a desired result.
- Faith without work is unproductive.
- God designed you to fulfill your purpose by working.
- Work multiplies your resources, be they large or small.
- Idleness invites the company of lazy people.
- The release of your potential is dependent upon your expenditure of the necessary effort to change your thoughts into visible realities.

## he Definition of Responsibility

*The disciples, each according to his ability, decided to provide help for the brothers living in Judea* (Acts 11:29).

BOOK QUOTE: *Releasing Your Potential* [Chapter 14]

One of the most beautiful sounds to ever enter the human ear is the first cry of a newborn baby—the sound of life! Millions of people over the years have experienced much joy, elation, celebration, and relief at this sound. Yet, a newborn's cry also signals the arrival of responsibility. Not only do the parents have the responsibility for the new infant but the child himself becomes accountable for the awesome potential he possesses at birth.

*Responsibility* is defined as a state of being reliable, dependable, accountable, answerable, and trustworthy. Responsibility also involves entering into a contract or an obligation. All of these indicate the transfer of something valuable, with the implication that the receiver of the trust is to achieve some positive result. Responsibility also embraces self-reliance, effectiveness, faithfulness, and capability. In essence, responsibility is simply *the ability to respond.*

All human beings come to this world pregnant with potential. Each person, like a computer, has a tremendous capacity to compute, analyze, assimilate, compare, and produce. But this ability is useless until it is programmed and demands are made on it. Your potential, ability, and natural talent were given by Divine Providence for the purpose of preparing the next generation to fulfill its potential. No one comes to this earth empty. Everyone comes with something. Just like a seed has a forest within it, so you have much more than was evident at your birth.

Unlike the seed, however, you are not dependent on a farmer to plant and cultivate your potential. You are accountable for the time you spend on this planet. The responsibility for activating, releasing, and maximizing this hidden, dormant ability is yours alone. The fact that you were born is evidence that you possess something that can benefit the world. No matter what you have done or accomplished, there is still much more inside you that needs to be released. Only you can release it.

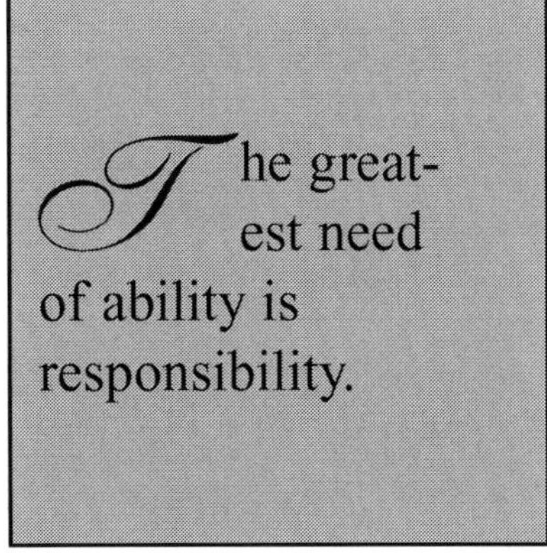

## The Definition of Responsibility

*The Lord God took the man and put him in the Garden of Eden to work it and take care of it. ...Now the Lord God had formed out of the ground all the beasts of the field and all the birds of the air. He brought them to man to see what he would call them; and whatever the man called each living creature, that was its name. So the man gave names to all the livestock, the birds of the air and all the beasts of the field...* (Genesis 2:15,19-20).

BOOK QUOTE: *Releasing Your Potential* [Chapter 14]

I am convinced that life was designed to create environments that make demands on our potential. Without these demands our potential would lie dormant. This thought is reflected in the saying, "Necessity is the mother of invention." How true! Most of us respond to life creatively and innovatively only when circumstances *demand* that response. The many technological, medical, and social breakthroughs that have been achieved because problems or circumstances demanded a response vividly illustrate this truth. The book of Genesis also clearly reveals this principle in the account of man's first encounter with creation in the Garden of Eden.

Man, as God first created him, was one hundred percent unreleased potential. He was an adult with full capabilities, talents, and gifts. His physical, mental, intellectual, emotional, and spiritual powers were fully developed. But man's powers and abilities were totally unused, untapped, unmanifested, unchallenged, and unemployed. The Creator's plan for releasing this hidden ability is recorded in Genesis 2:15,19-20 (see above).

God's first action after creating this totally new man—a man with muscles that had never been exercised, a brain that had never been stimulated, emotions that had never been aroused, an imagination that had never been ignited, and creativity that had never been explored—was to give him assignments that placed demands on his hidden abilities. By giving Adam's ability responsibility, God placed demands on Adam's potential. In a similar manner, your potential is released when demands to fulfill an assignment in God's greater purpose for your life are placed on you. This is why *work* is called *employment*—it employs your abilities for the purpose of manifesting your potential.

> The greatest need of ability is responsibility.

## ying Empty

*For I testify that they gave as much as they were able, and even beyond their ability. Entirely on their own...* (2 Corinthians 8:3).

BOOK QUOTE: *Releasing Your Potential* [Chapter 14]

God's command to *work* required Adam to use his physical potential. Likewise, God's commands to *cultivate the garden* and to *name the animals* activated his intellectual, mental, and creative potential. The demands God makes on you accomplish the same thing in your life. The release of your potential demands that you accept the responsibility to work, because the greatest need of ability is responsibility. You will never know the extent of your potential until you give it something to do. The greatest tragedy in your life will not be your death, but what dies with you at death. What a shame to waste what God gave you to use.

Have you ever noticed the deep peace and contentment that come over you when you fulfill a responsibility? Nothing is more rewarding and personally satisfying than the successful completion of an assigned task. The joy and elation that fill you at such times are the fruit of achievement. The experience of fulfillment is directly related to this principle of *finishing*.

An old Chinese proverb says: "The end of a thing is greater than its beginning." In other words, finishing is more important than starting. The beginning of a task may bring a degree of anxiety and apprehension, but the completing of a task usually yields a sense of relief, joy, and fulfillment.

History is filled with great starters who died unfinished. In fact, the majority of the five billion human beings who inhabit the earth will die unfinished. What a tragedy! What counts is not how much a person starts, but how much he or she finishes. The race is not to the swift, but to him that endures to the end.

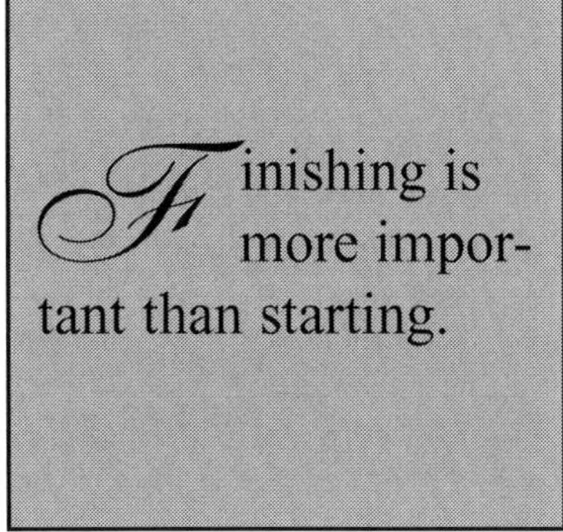

## he Principle of Finishing

*For I am already being poured out like a drink offering, and the time has come for my departure. I have fought a good fight, I have finished my race, I have kept the faith* (2 Timothy 4:6-7).

BOOK QUOTE: *Releasing Your Potential* [Chapter 14]

Jesus finished His task on earth. The words He spoke on the Cross clearly indicate that He fulfilled an assignment, completed a task and satisfied a requirement. They resonate with a deep sense of peace. In fact, they confirm that He was not killed but simply died.

> *When He had received the drink, Jesus said, "It is finished." With that He bowed His head and gave up the His spirit* (John 19:30).

Because He had released and maximized His potential to successfully fulfill the purpose for which God had sent Him into the world, Jesus saw death not as something to be feared, but as the natural next step. In other words, Jesus went to the grave empty.

This principle of *finishing* is also expressed very clearly by the apostle Paul in his second letter to Timothy (see above).

Paul faced death with complete confidence and peace because he knew that he had fulfilled God's purpose for his life. When he spoke of being "poured out," which suggests emptying some contents from oneself, he pointed to an accurate and important concept that must be understood by all who would release their potential.

You, like Paul and our Lord Jesus Christ, were born for a purpose. The ability to fulfill that purpose resides deep inside you screaming to be released. Perhaps you yearn to write books, compose songs, scribe poetry, obtain an academic degree, paint on canvas, play music, open a business, serve in a political, civic or spiritual organization, visit other countries, or develop an invention. Think how long you've carried your dream. Recall how many times you have postponed satisfying your desire. Count the many times you began to realize your goal only to quit.

God did not intend that the cemetery would be the resting place of your potential. The grave irresponsibility of taking your precious dreams, visions, ideas, and plans to the grave is not part of His design. You have a responsibility to release your potential. Join Jesus, Paul, and many others who robbed death of the pleasure of aborting their potential. Remember, the wealth of the cemetery is the potential of the unfinished.

> The wealth of the cemetery is the potential of the unfinished.

# Potential and the Next Generation

*A good man leaves an inheritance for his children's children...* (Proverbs 13:22).

BOOK QUOTE: *Releasing Your Potential* [Chapter 14]

*God designed everything not only to reproduce itself but also to transfer and transmit its life and treasure to the next generation.* Consider a seed. Every seed comes into this world to deliver a tree, which in turn delivers more seeds, which produce more trees, and on and on it goes. All aspects of creation possess this generational principle.

In the biblical record, God continually stresses the generational principle in all His dealings with man. He instructed Adam and Eve to be fruitful and multiply. He told Abraham that his "seed" would be great and bless the earth. He advised Moses to teach the people to pass on every law and experience to their children and their children's children. He also expressed it through Solomon in Proverbs 13:22 (see above).

If all the seeds in the world withheld the potential of the trees within them, a natural tragedy would be the result. The bees would suffer, the birds would die, and the animals would starve to death. The genocide of man would also occur as oxygen disappeared from the atmosphere. All this would occur because one element in nature refused to fulfill the purpose for which it was created.

No man is born to live or die unto himself. God gave you the wealth of your potential—your abilities, gifts, talents, energies, creativity, ideas, aspirations, and desires—for the blessing of future generations. You bear the responsibility to activate, release, and deposit them. This generational principle of God, the Father of creation, is crucial to your full appreciation of the principle of potential. Tragedy strikes whenever a person fails to die empty.

> No man is born to live or die unto himself.

## Your Potential Benefits the Future

*...consider well her ramparts, view her citadels, that you may tell of them to the next generation* (Psalm 48:13).

BOOK QUOTE: *Releasing Your Potential* [Chapter 14]

God gave you the wealth of your potential—your abilities, gifts, talents, energies, creativity, ideas, aspirations, and desires—for the blessing of future generations. You bear the responsibility to activate, release, and deposit them. This generational principle of God, the Father of creation, is crucial to your full appreciation of the principle of potential. Tragedy strikes whenever a person fails to die empty.

I wonder how many hundreds of people—perhaps thousands or millions—were born or are yet to be born who need to benefit from the books you have neglected to write, the songs you have failed to compose, or the invention you have continued to postpone. Perhaps there are millions who need the ministry you have yet to begin or the business venture you have not yet started.

The next generation needs the treasure of your potential. Think of the many inventions, books, songs, works of art, and great accomplishments others in past generations have left for you. Even as their treasures have become your blessings, so your treasures must become your children's unborn children's blessings. You must not die unfinished and let the grave steal the gems of the future. Deliver your potential to inspire the children of our world to release theirs.

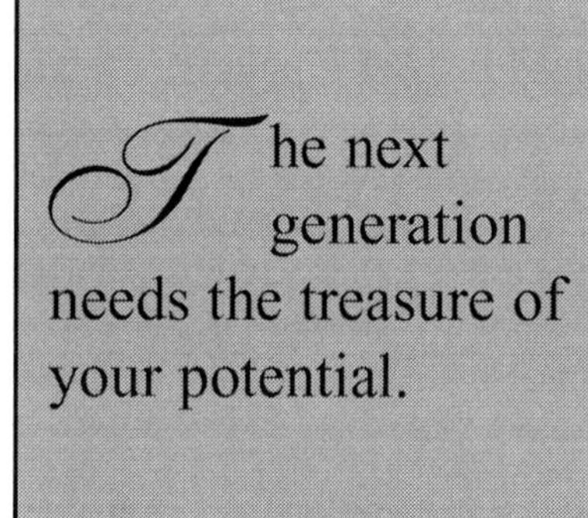

The next generation needs the treasure of your potential.

## A Word to the Third World Mind

*Give, and it will be given to you. A good measure, pressed down, shaken together and running over, will be poured into your lap. For with the measure you use, it will be measured to you* (Luke 6:38).

BOOK QUOTE: *Releasing Your Potential* [Chapter 14]

History reveals the truth that any people who are robbed by oppression, suppression, depression, and subjugation of the opportunity to activate, release, and maximize their potential suffer from the loss of generational thinking. Their oppression forces them to think in terms of self-preservation and personal security with little thought for posterity and the future. This mentality pervades many Third World nations today, manifesting itself in an attitude and a lifestyle that encourages *immediate gratification at the expense of the future.* This mind-set ultimately leads to fear, distrust, suspicion, and resentment among members of the same ethnic community.

This lack of generational consciousness traps individuals in a cycle of self-maintenance and retards creativity, inspiration, and innovation. Consequently, the release of the tremendous abilities that lie within every individual is forfeited. Third World people everywhere must be delivered from this mentality. It is essential that they understand the responsibility they have to their children and their children's children. *Until a man can see beyond his own loins, the future is in danger.*

*The essence of potential is not preservation but liberation.* Although we cannot change the past, we have the potential to chart our destiny and arrange a better future for our children. The opportunity to blame others for the past is often before us, but we can never transfer responsibility for the future to others. You and I have been given by God all that we need to fulfill His purpose for our lives. We possess the ability to impact our homes, our communities, our cities, our nations, and perhaps the world if we dare to challenge ourselves and place demands on the vast wealth of potential buried deep within us.

Decide today to do something with your dreams. Disappoint procrastination and commit yourself to releasing your potential. Stop wishing and start willing. Stop proposing and start purposing. Stop procrastinating and start planning. Determine to die empty and leave the earth an inheritance that gives life to others. Remember, few things are impossible to diligence and skill. Great works are performed by perseverance.

Until a man can see beyond his own loins, the future is in danger.

## EVIEW the Principles From This Week:

- The fact that you were born is evidence that you possess something that can benefit the world.
- God gave you potential for the blessing of future generations.
- The greatest need of ability is responsibility.
- God places demands on your potential by giving your ability responsibility.
- Fulfillment is directly related to the successful completion of a task.
- God has given you everything you need to fulfill His purpose for your life.

## Write Your Last Chapter

*By faith Abraham, even though he was past age—and Sarah herself was barren—was enabled to become a father because he considered Him faithful who had made the promise* (Hebrews 11:11).

BOOK QUOTE: *Maximizing Your Potential* [Chapter 1]

It was four o'clock on a cold, wet, winter morning. The snow had turned to mush, the wind blew with a vengeance, and the entire day seemed destined to be a source of depression. The small town appeared to be drugged as farmers, storekeepers, and street sweepers dragged themselves to their places of business. Suddenly, a young boy about 12 years of age appeared on the time-weathered, cobblestoned sidewalk, skipping along as he clutched an old cello case. The smile and quick stride revealed his anxiety and anticipation of reaching his intended destination.

The little boy's name was Pablo Casals. His interest in and commitment to music at such an early age inspired even his teacher and proved to be the seed of destiny for one of the world's greatest cellists. Through the years, his work, accomplishments, and achievements have been testimonies of greatness that stand worthy of emulation. Millions have enjoyed his live performances; history will always hold a place for his ineffable work.

Yet, after a lifetime of distinguished achievements, Pablo Casals, at age 85, continued to rise early and spend most of the day practicing his cello. When he was asked during an interview why he continued to practice five hours a day, Casals replied, "Because I think I'm getting better."

Pablo Casals reminds us of the monumental character of men and women such as Abraham, the biblical patriarch who at 70 years of age, childless and frustrated, married to a barren woman, and being, with his wife, beyond the biological age of conceiving a child, accepted the vision of a baby destined to change the world and believed it would come to pass. Abraham saw the fruit of his faith when he was 100 years old.

> Nothing is more irritating, guilt-producing, and incriminating than an unfinished book: live to your last chapter.

## Live To Your Last Chapter

*I have worked much harder, been in prison more frequently, been flogged more severely, and been exposed to death again and again* (2 Corinthians 11:23b).

BOOK QUOTE: *Maximizing Your Potential* [Chapter 1]

Great minds and souls, knowing always that what they have done must never be confused with what they can yet do, never settle for great work. As a matter of fact, the concept of retirement is a great myth that traps the untapped potential buried in millions of talented, gifted, and valuable individuals. This Western concept has caused many great men and women to settle for the average and to succumb to the mediocrity of the socially accepted standards of success. Please note, however, that all individuals throughout history who have left their footprints in the sands of destiny were driven by a passion greater than the desire for personal comfort.

Abraham, the biblical patriarch who at 70 years of age, childless and frustrated, married to a barren woman, and being, with his wife, beyond the biological age of conceiving a child, accepted the vision of a baby destined to change the world and believed it would come to pass. Abraham saw the fruit of his faith when he was 100 years old.

Moses, at midlife, changed careers from a sheep-herding fugitive to a deliverer and national leader of over three million people; by age 120 he had guided them safely to the brink of their destiny. David, the great king of Israel, worked in the twilight of his many years of excellent leadership to make plans for the construction of a magnificent temple for worship, a temple that was eventually built by his son Solomon.

The apostle Paul wrote in Second Corinthians 11:23b-27 a brief description of his challenges (see excerpt above). Though he suffered many times, Paul wrote the epistles in the final "chapter" of his life.

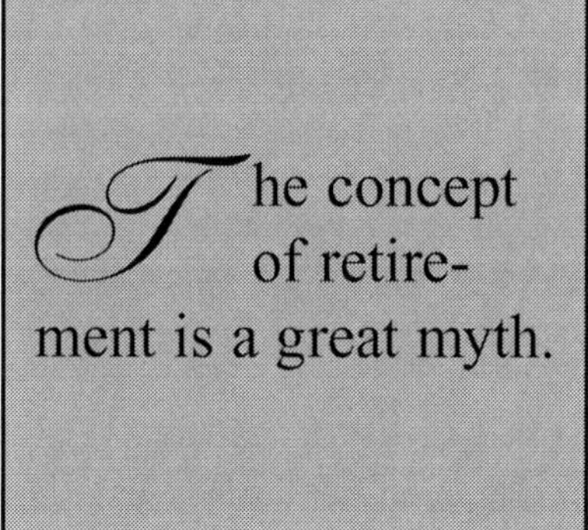

## Complete the Race

*I have fought the good fight, I have finished the race, I have kept the faith* (2 Timothy 4:7).

BOOK QUOTE: *Maximizing Your Potential* [Chapter 1]

Paul, the unrivaled apostle of the Church, after many years of tremendous hardship, wrote a brief description of his challenges in a letter to the church at Corinth. He stated:

> *I have worked much harder, been in prison more frequently, been flogged more severely, and been exposed to death again and again. Five times I received from the Jews the forty lashes minus one. Three times I was beaten with rods, once I was stoned, three times I was shipwrecked, I spent a night and a day in the open sea, I have been constantly on the move. I have been in danger from rivers, in danger from bandits, in danger from my own countrymen, in danger from Gentiles; in danger in the city, in danger in the country, in danger at sea; and in danger from false brothers. I have labored and toiled and have often gone without sleep; I have known hunger and thirst and have often gone without food; I have been cold and naked* (2 Corinthians 11:23b-27).

Then this great leader exclaims: "*Who is weak, and I do not feel weak?*" (2 Corinthians 11:29a).

The apostle Paul believed that no matter what he had done, accomplished, achieved, or experienced in the past, there was always so much more left within to develop, release, and express. He believed that the enemy of better is best, and the tomb of the extra-ordinary is the ordinary.

> Retirement is never a concept in the minds of world changers.

# Life Is But a Cup of Drink

*"This is my blood of the covenant, which is poured out for many," He said to them* (Mark 14:24).

BOOK QUOTE: *Maximizing Your Potential* [Chapter 1]

Paul's perception of life, and the responsibility of each of us to maximize life to its fullest potential, is expressed in his final letter to Timothy. To this favorite young student, he wrote:

> *For I am already being poured out like a drink offering, and the time has come for my departure. I have fought the good fight, I have finished the race, I have kept the faith* (2 Timothy 4:6-7).

Paul likened his life to the ceremonial drink offering administered by the priest in the Old Testament rituals of the temple, in which the priest filled a cup with wine and ceremonially poured it out at intervals in the service until the cup was completely empty. Using this example, Paul gives a very effective illustration of how our lives should be lived.

Your life is like a cup of drink served to the world by our great Creator. The drink is the awesome, untapped, valuable, destiny-filled treasure, gifts, and talents of potential buried within you. Every minute, day, month, and year is an interval of opportunity provided by God for the pouring out of another portion of yourself until you have exposed all His precious treasure that makes you unique. This is called *maximum living.*

True success is not a project but a journey. The spirit of achievement is guided by the notion that success is an installment plan on which we make daily payments until we maximize ourselves. This success begins when we understand and accept that life is a process of growing and developing. Thus, life is meant to be a never-ending education, a journey of discovery and adventure, an exploration into our God-given potential for His glory.

## The Maximum of Mediocrity

*Arise, shine, for your light has come, and the glory of the Lord rises upon you* (Isaiah 60:1).

BOOK QUOTE: *Maximizing Your Potential* [Chapter 1]

What does it mean to maximize? What is maximum? The word *maximum* may be defined as "supreme, greatest, highest, and ultimate." It is synonymous with such concepts as pinnacle, preeminence, culmination, apex, peak, and summit. It implies the highest degree possible. Just a brief look at these concepts immediately convicts us of the many opportunities we have abused and forfeited because we have failed or have refused to give our all.

This failure to do our best, to go beyond the expectations of others, to express ourselves fully, to live up to our true potential, to extend ourselves to the limit of our abilities, to give it all we have, to satisfy our own convictions, is called *mediocrity*. Simply put, *mediocrity* is living below our known, true potential. It is accepting the norm, pleasing the status quo, and doing what we can get by with. Therefore, to *maximize* is to express, expose, experience, and execute all the hidden, God-given abilities, talents, gifts, and potential through God's vision breathed in our souls to fulfill His purpose for our lives on earth.

How tragic that most of the nearly six billion people on this planet will settle for an average life limited only by their unwillingness to extend themselves to the summit of their own selves. Anything less than maximum is mediocrity. In other words, *mediocrity* may be defined as the region of our lives bounded on the north by compromise, on the south by indecision, on the east by past thinking, and on the west by a lack of vision. Mediocrity is the spirit of the average, the anthem of the norm, and the heartbeat of the ordinary. Mediocrity is so common and pervasive that those who are labeled as genius or exceptional have to do only a little extra.

Remember, we were created to be above average, unnormal, and extraordinary. God never intended for success in our lives to be measured by the opinion of others or the standards set by the society in which we live. In fact, the Scriptures instruct us *not* to "*conform any longer to the pattern* [standards] *of this world, but* [to] *be transformed by the renewing of* [our] *mind*" (Romans 12:2a). To maximize ourselves, we will find it necessary to declare independence from the world of the norm and to resist the gravity of the average in order to enjoy the outer limits of the new frontiers of our abilities. Why do so many of us settle for mediocrity? The answer is found in what I call the curse of comparison.

> Mediocrity is living below our known, true potential.

## The Curse of Comparison

*We do not dare to classify or compare ourselves with some who commend themselves. When they measure themselves by themselves and compare themselves with themselves, they are not wise* (2 Corinthians 10:12).

BOOK QUOTE: *Maximizing Your Potential* [Chapter 1]

The autobahn is a network of roads, without speed restrictions, that crisscross Germany and many other neighboring countries. One day as we were traveling from a city in northern Germany to the south, my host asked if I would like to experience driving without a speed limitation.

At first I was excited, thrilled, and anxious as I felt adrenaline rush through my entire body. The feeling of having the responsibility for power without externally imposed limits also brought other mixed emotions, including temporary confusion. All I had learned from my past concerning speed limits, fear of violation, and restrictions imposed by the law as I knew it began to wrestle with my newly found freedom. In essence, the possibility of using maximum power was challenged by my learned knowledge of limitation. I was trapped by the conditioning of my past and handicapped by the fear of unlimited possibilities.

As the pressure of my foot accelerated the engine, I felt the thrill of a car traveling at 115 mph. Words cannot describe the awesome power and pride I felt controlling the speed and direction of such ability. I was on top of the world. Who could catch me now? I had arrived. I was the king of the road, master of the highway.

This feeling of supremacy was further enhanced every time I passed another vehicle. In fact, I heard myself saying every time we passed another car, "Why don't they pull over, park, and let a real driver through?" There I was. I had achieved the ultimate. I had set a record for myself. I had passed everyone else. I was the best.

Suddenly, after approximately 20 minutes of driving, a Mercedes-Benz cruised past me at 150 mph, seemingly coming out of nowhere. Instantly, I felt like I was standing still. My host turned to me and said with a chuckle, "So you see, you are not traveling as fast as you can, but only as fast as you will."

As his words lodged in my mind, I quickly began to understand the curse of comparison and the limitations of self-pride. From this experience, I learned three lessons that have become the foundations of my thinking concerning success and effective living: the principle of capacity, the principle of comparison, and the principle of experience.

> We can be trapped by the conditioning of our past.

## he Principle of Capacity

*I know that when I come to you, I will come in the full measure of the blessing of Christ* (Romans 15:29).

BOOK QUOTE: *Maximizing Your Potential* [Chapter 1]

The true capacity of a product is determined not by the user but the manufacturer. An automobile is built with the capacity to travel at 180 mph; therefore its full potential was determined by the manufacturer. The true potential of the car is not affected by my opinion of its ability or by my previous experience with driving. Whether or not I use the full capacity of the car's engine does not reduce its potential capacity.

The same principle applies to your life. God created you like He did everything else, with the capacity to fulfill your purpose. Therefore, your true capacity is not limited, reduced, or altered by the opinion of others or your previous experience. You are capable of attaining the total aptitude given to you by your Creator to fulfill His purpose for your life. Therefore, *the key to maximizing your full potential is to discover the purpose or reason for your life and commit to its fulfillment at all cost.*

The apostle Paul, in a letter to the church at Corinth, spoke of the hidden secret wisdom of our destiny that is invested in each of us by our Creator God.

> *No, we speak of God's secret wisdom, a wisdom that has been hidden and that God destined for our glory before time began. None of the rulers of this age understood it, for if they had, they would not have crucified the Lord of glory. However, as it is written: "No eye has seen, no ear has heard, no mind has conceived what God has prepared for those who love Him"* (1 Corinthians 2:7-9).

The implication in verse 9 is that no human has the right or the ability to fully determine or measure the capacity of the potential you possess.

> Your true capacity is not limited, reduced, or altered by the opinion of others or your previous experience.

## EVIEW the Principles From This Week:

- Retirement is not a biblical concept.
- Our potential is to be poured out for the sake of the Kingdom of God.
- Mediocrity is living below our known, true potential.
- We have the capacity for a tremendous destiny.

# The Principle of Comparison—Part 1

*The Lord does not look at the things man looks at. Man looks at the outward appearance, but the Lord looks at the heart* (1 Samuel 16:7b).

BOOK QUOTE: *Maximizing Your Potential* [Chapter 1]

One of the most significant mistakes humans make is comparison—the measuring of oneself against the standards, work, or accomplishments of another. This exercise is fruitless, demeaning, and personally tragic because it places our true potential at the mercy of others, giving them the right to determine and define our success.

Once, while I was in Germany, I drove a car on the autobahn. This network of roads has no speed limit. The lack of limitations allowed me to accelerate beyond what I had ever done before. When I was driving, I was in a position of great success and achievement if I compared myself to the drivers I overtook. Yet, even though I was leading all the others, I was still not operating at *my car's* full potential. The car's true capacity was 180 mph, and I was traveling at 115 mph. When I compared my car's performance to all the others, I was leading the pack; I could have been considered a success in their eyes because I was traveling faster than all of them. When I compared my car's performance to its true capacity, however, I was not truly successful because I was traveling below the maximum speed built into the car by the manufacturer.

The lesson here is that true success is not measured by how much you have done or accomplished compared to what others have done or accomplished; true success is what you have done compared to what you could have done. In other words, living to the maximum is competing with yourself. It's living up to your own true standards and capabilities. *Success is satisfying your own personal passion and purpose in pursuit of personal excellence.* In fact, you must always remember to perform for an audience of one, the Lord your Creator.

Success is satisfying your own personal passion and purpose in pursuit of personal excellence.

## The Principle of Comparison—Part 2

*If anyone thinks he is something when he is nothing, he deceives himself. Each one should test his own actions. Then he can take pride in himself, without comparing himself to somebody else, for each one should carry his own load* [responsibility] (Galatians 6:3-5).

BOOK QUOTE: *Maximizing Your Potential* [Chapter 1]

From the early years of childhood, we are compared to our sisters and brothers, the neighbor's children, or some other person. This comparative spirit continues on into our teen and adult years, developing into a sophisticated dehumanizing state of competition. The result is traumatizing because we spend most of our lives trying to compete with others, comparing our achievements with those of our peers, and attempting to live up to their standards of acceptance. Instead of being ourselves, we become preoccupied with being who others dictate we should be.

If we succumb to this temptation, we will be reminded that there will always be some people whom we exceed and others who outpace us. If we compete with ourselves and not with others, then it does not matter who is behind us or ahead of us; our goal is to become and achieve all we are capable of being and doing, and this becomes the measure of our satisfaction.

The apostle Paul, the great leader of the Church, commented on this critical issue:

> *We do not dare to classify or compare ourselves with some who commend themselves. When they measure themselves by themselves and compare themselves with themselves, they are not wise. We, however, will not boast beyond proper limits, but will confine our boasting to the field God has assigned to us...* (2 Corinthians 10:12-13).

These statements strongly admonish us not to compete with others or to compare our talents with their abilities or potential, since we are responsible only for our potential, not theirs. The story of the servants with the talents clearly confirms this personal responsibility (see Matthew 25:14-30). Therefore, our principal goal in life should be to discover God's will and purpose for our lives and to complete our assignment with excellence.

> Our goal is to become and achieve all we are capable of being and doing, and this becomes the measure of our satisfaction.

## he Principle of Experience—Part 1

*If we claim to have fellowship with Him yet walk in the darkness, we lie and do not live by the truth* (1 John 1:6).

BOOK QUOTE: *Maximizing Your Potential* [Chapter 1]

*Experience* may be defined as "the observation of facts as a source of knowledge and skill gained by contact with facts and events." By its very nature, experience is a product of the past and is, therefore, limited to and controlled by previous exposure. In spite of the fact that experience may be valuable for making decisions and judgments concerning the future, it is important to know that any significant measurement of growth, development, expansion, or advancement will require experience to submit to the substance of the unknown through faith.

Unfortunately, experience has compelled many promising people to cower in the shadows of fear and failure because they were not willing to venture out into the uncharted frontiers of new possibilities. Experience is given not to determine the limits of our lives, but to create a better life for us. Experience is a tool to be used!

My experience with driving over the years has conditioned me to drive a car monitored by the speed limits established by the society. Therefore, my driving capacity has become subject to the accepted norms of 45-60 mph. The fact that I have driven my car at 45-60 mph for over 25 years does not cancel the automobile's capacity to travel at 100-180 mph. *In essence, experience does not cancel capacity.* Therefore, my car's capacity is determined not by my use of that capacity but by the capacity built into the car by the manufacturer.

Experience does not cancel capacity.

## he Principle of Experience—Part 2

*By faith Enoch was taken from this life, so that he did not experience death; he could not be found, because God had taken him away. For before he was taken, he was commended as one who pleased God* (Hebrews 11:5).

BOOK QUOTE: *Maximizing Your Potential* [Chapter 1]

Experience is given not to determine the limits of our lives, but to create a better life for us. Experience is a tool to be used!

*In essence, experience does not cancel capacity.* At any point in our lives, we are the sum total of all the decisions we have made, the people we have met, the exposure we have had, and the facts we have learned. In essence, every human is a walking history book. Nevertheless, we must keep in mind that our personal history is being made and recorded every day, and our past experience was once our future. Therefore, we must be careful not to allow our past to determine the quality of our future. Instead, we must use our experience to help us make better decisions, always guarding against the possibility that it may limit our decisions. *Remember, your ability is never limited to your experience.*

This world is filled with millions of individuals who are capable of traveling at a maximum capacity of 180 mph, but they have settled for 55 mph. Because they have overtaken some folks or have exceeded the expectations of a few others, they have compared their lives to these persons and have accepted mediocrity as excellence.

Determine not to let your past experience limit your capacity. Be grateful for the lessons of the past, then accelerate with confidence on to the autobahn of life, being careful to obey only those signs that have been established by your Creator, who admonishes you, "*All things are possible if you only believe*" (see Mark 9:23).

Your ability is never limited to your experience.

## Dissatisfaction With a Fraction

*...for it is God who works in you to will and to act according to His good purpose* (Philippians 2:13).

BOOK QUOTE: *Maximizing Your Potential* [Chapter 1]

One of life's great tragedies is that the majority of the world's population is composed of individuals who have negotiated an agreement with mediocrity, signed a contract with the average, and pledged allegiance to the ordinary. They have resolved never to be more than society has made them or do more than is expected. What a tragedy of destiny. God expects more!

Inside of every human being is a deep call of destiny to do something worthwhile with our lives. The urge to accomplish great things and engage in significant endeavors is the germ of purpose planted by God in the heart of man. Why then do we settle for so little? Why do we abandon our dreams and deny our purpose? Why do we live below our privilege, buried in the cemetery of wishful thinking and empty regrets?

As we have seen, one reason we fail to progress in fulfilling our purpose is satisfaction with our present measure of success. The belief that we have arrived is the deterrent that keeps us from getting to our destination. A second part of the answer lies in the fact that we have accepted the present state of our lives as the best we can do under the circumstances.

Inside of every human being is a deep call of destiny to do something worth-while with our lives.

## Under the Circumstances

*...equip you with everything good for doing His will, and may He work in us what is pleasing to Him, through Jesus Christ, to whom be glory for ever and ever. Amen* (Hebrews 13:21).

BOOK QUOTE: *Maximizing Your Potential* [Chapter 1]

One reason we fail to progress in fulfilling our purpose is that we have accepted the present state of our lives as the best we can do under the circumstances.

This concept, "under the circumstances," serves to imprison us and to immobilize our God-given ambition because too many of us have surrendered to the status quo and have become prisoners of the war for our minds. We forget that "circumstances" are simply temporary arrangements of life to which we are all exposed. We overlook or disregard the fact that these circumstances are designed to identify, expose, develop, refine, and maximize our true potential. It's not what happens to us that matters, but what we do with what happens. Much of the time we are not responsible for our circumstances, but we are always responsible for our response to those circumstances. *One key to maximizing your potential is to become dissatisfied with the circumstances that restrict, limit, and stifle your potential.*

Many people know that they possess great potential, that they have a significant purpose in life, but they still fail to move beyond good intentions to experience the fullness of their lives. Why? Their comfort is greater than their passion. They are more concerned with fitting in than with standing out.

Remember, *you will never change anything that you are willing to tolerate*. Your Creator wants you to consciously choose to fulfill your purpose and maximize your potential because in so doing you will bring glory to His name. Unfortunately, history gives evidence of only a few rare individuals who, driven by a passion to achieve a cherished vision in their hearts, initiated their own deliverance, rose above the tide of the norm, and impacted their generation and ours.

A second significant key to maximizing potential is the unassuming benefits of "crisis." Crises, as defined by author Dick Leider, are life's "wake-up" calls. These alarms are often the catalysts that impel us to become fully conscious of our mediocre lives.

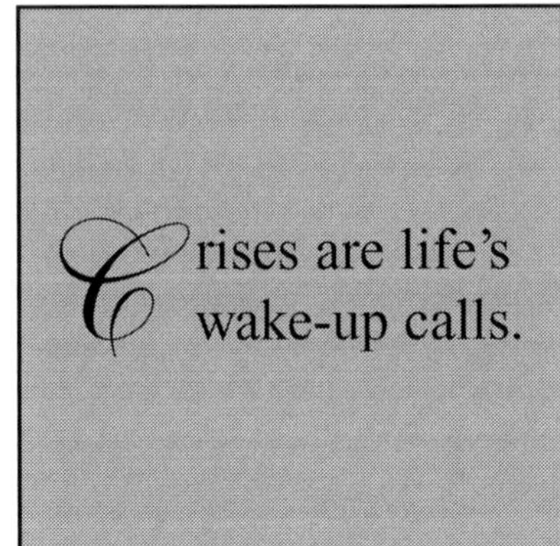

## Move Beyond Your Comfort Zone

*Like an eagle that stirs up its nest and hovers over its young, that spreads its wings to catch them and carries them on its pinions. The Lord alone* [leads you] (Deuteronomy 32:11-12a).

BOOK QUOTE: *Maximizing Your Potential* [Chapter 1]

How many stories have you heard about individuals who, after a close call with death or disease, suddenly change their lifestyles and their attitude toward life? Often their priorities, and sometimes their entire value system, change. The biblical record bears witness to the efficacy of a crisis to get people back on track. Beginning with Abraham, and continuing on to Joseph, Moses, David, Jonah, Peter, and most significantly the apostle Paul, God used the interjection of a major crisis to lead these heroes of faith to move beyond mediocrity to life at the maximum.

Remember, *we cannot become what we were born to be by remaining what we are*. Just as the mother eagle removes the comforts of her feathery nest to "disturb" the young eaglets into flying, so our Creator moves us beyond our comfort zones so that we are forced to fly. Without this stirring, most of us would never fly.

An eagle that doesn't fly cannot fulfill its purpose. Likewise, your life will lack purpose and focus until you discover your wings. This discovery will require both wisdom and courage because the thrill of flying always begins with the fear of falling. Yet you are not left alone to find your wings because God, through the prophet Moses, promises to undertake for you.

He will give definition to the crises of your life and inspire you to move on into all He has planned for you. Indeed, the greatest gift God can offer you is to push you into a crisis of temporary discomfort that requires you to try your wings. This pushing into crisis is His supreme act of love, akin to that of a mother eagle that pushes her young from the nest to force them to fly.

> Don't be a pigeon if you were born to be an eagle. Experience God's altitude for your life.

## EVIEW the Principles From This Week:

- What you have done does not equal the sum of what you can do.
- Success is a journey of discovery and adventure as you explore your God-given potential.
- Mediocrity accepts the norm, pleases the crowd, and does what it can get by with. Maximum living pushes the norm, pleases God, and sets the standard of excellence.
- The capacity of your potential is not determined by what you have done or what others think about what you have done.
- The performance or opinions of others cannot measure your success.
- Your past experience cannot measure your future success.
- Circumstances and crises are God's tools to move you into your purpose and the maximizing of your potential.

## Treasure in Clay Pots

*...set His seal of ownership on us, and put His Spirit in our hearts as a deposit, guaranteeing what is to come* (2 Corinthians 1:22).

BOOK QUOTE: *Maximizing Your Potential* [Chapter 2]

The great writer Paul refers to this hidden wealth within as "*treasure in jars of clay*" (2 Corinthians 4:7). The jar may not look like much, but the treasure inside it is valuable and priceless. In other words, *what people see when they look at you is not who you truly are. You can become much more than you now are.*

Who would have thought that Saul of Tarsus, a fervent Jew who vigorously opposed the followers of Jesus, would become Paul the apostle, the greatest missionary the Church has ever known? Certainly not the Christians he persecuted—they did not expect anything good from him (see Acts 9:20–21)—nor Saul himself. Not in his wildest imaginings would he have seen himself as a servant of the One he despised. Yet, like the old house, Saul contained a dormant wealth that was not evident under the outer trappings of his misguided religious fervor.

That same wealth is present in you. You are capable of more than others expect of you—even beyond your own most extravagant dreams. Unexposed, dormant potential rests beneath the surface of your daily existence, waiting to be discovered and released. Although access to this great treasure has been clogged by sin, the strength and beauty of your potential can be reclaimed. The destruction, decay, and neglect of years need not continue to hold captive the reality of who God created you to be.

This untold wealth within you is uniquely yours because God creates no two people for the same purpose. Your personality, abilities, and resources are God's gifts, bestowed on you before He gave you the breath of life, and they contain the possibility for bringing meaning and fulfillment into your life. They are available, however, only to those who put forth the effort to recover them and to use them according to their God-given specifications. *Learning to tap the hidden wealth of your potential is the greatest task and the most pressing need of your life* because if you do not discover how to expose and use this treasure, you will die with it. This wealth, which is the all-surpassing power of God within you, is never given to be buried. God wants you to release all He gave you for the benefit of others and the blessing of your own life.

> You are capable of more than others expect of you—even beyond your own most extravagant dreams.

# Keys to Releasing Your Potential—Know Your Source

*May you be blessed by the Lord, the Maker of Heaven and earth* (Psalm 115:15).

BOOK QUOTE: *Maximizing Your Potential* [Chapter 2]

If you are going to move from who you now are to whom God created you to be, you too must seek to understand the nature of God's original design for you, before sin ravaged your life. That understanding is not available to you unless you become reconnected with God, your Creator. Apart from Him, you cannot and will not release your full potential because He gave you this potential and He designed you to fulfill it. *You must know God, your Source, if you want to experience a satisfying, abundant life.*

Saul of Tarsus met his Source on the road to Damascus when Jesus Christ spoke to him from a bright light that left him blind. For three days he remained blind and did not eat or drink. He simply waited before God, wondering what would happen next. Then God sent a man named Ananias to place his hands on Saul to restore his sight and to bring the Holy Spirit into his life. Immediately, something like scales fell from Saul's eyes and he could see again. It was during this period that the purpose for Paul's life was revealed to him by his Creator/Source. After that, Saul spent several days with the disciples in Damascus, preaching that Jesus is the Son of God and proving that Jesus is the Messiah.

What a change! Few of us will experience a change as dramatic as that which occurred in the man Saul who became Paul, but a change just as radical—from being self-centered to God-centered—must occur in all who would discover and use their full potential. This is true because *the foundation key for releasing potential is always a relationship with the source or maker of a product.* You must have a life-changing encounter with the One who made you if you want to become who you were created to be.

Like the young man who could not restore the house to its former grandeur without understanding the builder's original design and intent, you cannot expose the gifts, talents, and natural abilities that God put into you if you do not become reconnected with Him. All you do and are apart from God will always fall short of the true value and capacity of your potential. Therefore, fulfillment and value are impossible without Him. Only by returning to your Source/Manufacturer/Creator can you hope to unlock His power within you. You must know your Source to become your potential. This is the foundation key.

> You must know God, your Source, if you want to experience a satisfying, abundant life.

## Keys to Releasing Your Potential—Understand Your Function

[I] *live by faith, not by sight* (2 Corinthians 5:7).

BOOK QUOTE: *Maximizing Your Potential* [Chapter 2]

The mode of operation for maximum performance of any product is determined and established by the manufacturer/creator, and must be obeyed for maximum benefit. Thus, the second key to releasing your potential is knowing how God created you to function and applying that knowledge to your life. No builder can successfully restore a house unless he first knows the specifications determined by the builder and the features provided by the original blueprints. A shower, for example, may fulfill part of the designer's intent for the bathroom, but it cannot match all the functions of a tub. Thus, installing a shower in place of a tub would change not only the room's appearance but also its ability to provide the intended functions that were built into the original design.

Man was designed to live by faith. *God's original design for men and women calls for them to live from the perspective of faith with eternity in their hearts.* The Book of Hebrews defines faith as "*being sure of what we hope for and certain of what we do not see*" (Hebrews 11:1). This is God's mode of operation. He is not influenced by outward appearances; neither is His power diminished by seemingly impossible obstacles.

The apostle Paul learned the importance of looking beyond what is immediately visible and evident. Although he encountered many situations that seemed to stand in the way of his mission to share the good news of Jesus with those outside the Jewish world, he persevered by focusing on His God-given task and by relying on the Holy Spirit to guarantee the completion of God's plans. Thus, Paul testified, "[I] *live by faith, not by sight*" (2 Corinthians 5:7).

Your ability to unleash your potential is tied to your willingness to consistently live from God's perspective, which saw Paul the apostle in Saul the murderer. He created you to share His viewpoint. If you allow the obstacles that clutter your path and the expectations of others to discourage you and to send you on time and energy-consuming detours, your God-given talents and abilities will be wasted. *Learning to function by looking beyond what you now see to what is yet possible is an important key to releasing your potential. You must resolve to live by faith.*

> God is not influenced by outward appearances; neither is His power diminished by seemingly impossible obstacles.

## Keys to Releasing Your Potential—Understand Your Purpose

*...God, who set me apart from birth and called me by His grace, was pleased to reveal His Son in me so that I might preach Him among the Gentiles...*(Galatians 1:15-16).

BOOK QUOTE: *Maximizing Your Potential* [Chapter 2]

To fully release your potential, you must discover your corporate and specific reason for existence and the accompanying assignment. One of the first tasks of a builder who wants to restore an old house is to determine the purpose for each room. Although this purpose may not be immediately evident, the rebuilding cannot accurately and effectively duplicate the original building if the purpose for each room is not established.

In a similar manner, you cannot effectively release your potential if you do not discover God's purpose for giving you life. Your potential and your purpose are perfectly related because God never requires you to do or be something that is not part of His purpose. Likewise, He never requires something of you that He did not provide for when He created you. Your potential enables you to fulfill your purpose, and your purpose reveals the potential hidden within you.

From his encounter with Christ on the road to Damascus to the end of his life, the apostle Paul knew that he had been called and saved by God for a specific purpose: "*...God, who set me apart from birth and called me by His grace, was pleased to reveal His Son in me so that I might preach Him among the Gentiles...*" (Galatians 1:15-16). Similarly, the apostle Peter discovered his purpose when Jesus told him three times, "*Take care of My sheep*" (John 21:16; see also John 21:15-18). Both remained faithful to God's purpose, dedicating their lives to its accomplishment and conforming their actions to its fulfillment.

You are like these apostles. You too have a purpose set forth by God and the skills, talents, abilities, and characteristics that enable you to fulfill His plan. Your responsibility is to discover *what* God designed you to do and *how* He planned that you would accomplish it. Until you discover God's blueprint, you will not have the motivation to uncover the potential that will empower you to accomplish it, nor will you be happy and fulfilled. *Discovery of purpose is discovery of potential.*

Success without an understanding of purpose is meaningless. Knowing and cooperating with your God-given purpose is the third key to releasing your potential. He alone knows why He created you with the specific combination of personality, abilities, and dreams that make you the unique individual you are. *You share the purpose of humanity to glorify God by fulfilling your individual purpose and by releasing the power, beauty, and possibilities hidden within you.*

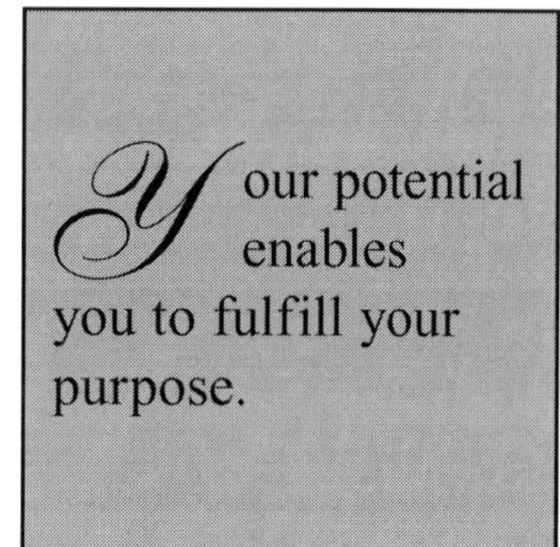

# Keys to Releasing Your Potential—Know Your Resources

*Command those who are rich in this present world not to be arrogant nor to put their hope in wealth, which is so uncertain, but to put their hope in God, who richly provides us with everything for our enjoyment* (1 Timothy 6:17).

BOOK QUOTE: *Maximizing Your Potential* [Chapter 2]

Provisions are given for the fulfillment of vision. Every builder, before he starts a project, both estimates what materials he will need to complete the job and determines what resources are available to him. God functions in a similar manner. As He forms and fashions each person for a specific purpose, He also provides the necessary resources to accomplish His plans.

The apostle Paul knew that God had given him certain resources to help him fulfill his purpose and release his potential. Varied in nature and use, these resources included his tent-making skills, his Roman citizenship, his Jewish education and upbringing, and, most importantly, his faith in Jesus Christ and his confidence that God, through the Spirit, had given him a message for the world. (See Romans 15:15-19.)

Paul was careful, however, to view these resources only as tools given by God to accomplish His plans. Therefore, he always treated his resources as being less important than the One who gave them. His education and upbringing as a Jew, for example, had to be refined and redirected before Paul could use, not abuse, them. Thus, he came to see the law, which had been all-important to him as a Pharisee, as God's gift for showing men their sin and their need of a Savior. (See Romans 3:20.) Resources cannot and should not be substituted for the Source.

You too possess God-given resources. The proper use of these resources will release your potential, but their misuse will destroy you. Hence, you cannot fulfill your limitless potential unless you learn what resources you have, how God intended them to function, and why He gave them to you. *The effective use of your resources is the fourth key to releasing your potential.*

> Resources cannot and should not be substituted for the Source.

## Keys to Releasing Your Potential—Maintain the Right Environment

*"I* [the Lord] *will live with them and walk among them, and I will be their God, and they will be My people. Therefore come out from them and be separate, says the Lord. Touch no unclean thing, and I will receive you. I will be a Father to you, and you will be My sons and daughters, says the Lord Almighty." Since we have these promises, dear friends, let us purify ourselves from everything that contaminates body and spirit, perfecting holiness out of reverence for God* (2 Corinthians 6:16b–7:1).

BOOK QUOTE: *Maximizing Your Potential* [Chapter 2]

All potential demands conditions conducive to the maximum fulfillment of purpose. Consequently, all life forms have ideal conditions in which they grow and flourish. The apostle Paul clearly understood that the conditions in which we live affect the nature of our living. Light that is continually surrounded by darkness is in danger of losing its brilliance. Righteousness that repeatedly associates with wickedness may, in time, be tarnished. Thus, Paul writes 2 Corinthians 6:16b-7:1 (see above).

Paul's observations are as applicable today as they were when he wrote them. "*For what do righteousness and wickedness have in common? Or what fellowship can light have with darkness?*" (2 Corinthians 6:14b). You cannot consistently spend time with ungodly people, or be surrounded by unrighteous behavior, and maintain your fellowship with God. That's serious business, since *fellowship with God and obedience to His laws and commandments are essential ingredients of your ideal environment.* Life outside that environment will destroy your potential because a wrong environment always means death.

All manufacturers establish the ideal conditions required for the maximum performance of their products. In the same manner, you were created to function under specific conditions established by your Creator. Any violation of the Manufacturer's specific conditions minimizes His intended effect. The laws of God are given not to restrict us but to protect us by maintaining the ideal environment for maximum performance. Obedience protects performance. Disobedience diminishes potential.

As fish cannot live in polluted waters and plants die in parched ground, so you cannot live in conditions that do not acknowledge God as the central, all-important factor of daily life. Creating and sustaining a God-centered environment is as important for your growth and satisfaction as designing houses that fit their climates and settings is for the reputation and the success of an architect. *Maintaining your ideal environment* is the fifth key to releasing your potential.

> Life outside your ideal environment will destroy you potential.

## Work—The Master Key

*For we are God's workmanship, created in Christ Jesus to do good works, which God prepared in advance for us to do* (Ephesians 2:10).

BOOK QUOTE: *Maximizing Your Potential* [Chapter 2]

Dreams without work accomplish nothing. The apostle Paul could not have reached the non-Jewish world with the gospel of Jesus Christ if he had only rejoiced in his new relationship with God, learned to live by faith, surveyed his resources, and sought a healthy environment in which to live. Paul had to work to release his potential and to achieve his purpose.

The New Testament is filled with stories of Paul's efforts to share God's gift of salvation with those who had not heard the gospel. (See particularly Acts 13–20.) When one door closed, he looked for another. Again and again, Paul worked hard—fighting discouragement, misunderstandings, and distrust—to fulfill his commission from God.

Work as God planned it was given to man before he sinned. *It is His tool to make us productive and fruitful.* Because God's assignments and activities always involve work, He designed men and women to share in His creativity by giving them the opportunity to work. Even as God worked through His spoken word to make the unobservable visible, so too we must work to reveal the invisible possibilities that exist in us. Although the *conditions* of work changed after sin—becoming painful and requiring great effort—the *purpose* of work did not. *Work is not a result of sin.*

Work releases potential and empowers success. It uses innate abilities and natural talents to share experience and proficiency. It also energizes the world's productive ability and activates man's creative power. In essence, *work brings forth from a man or a woman the possibilities that will die with that individual unless they are activated, performed, produced, and fulfilled.* In the absence of work, strength and energy waste away, dreams and visions wither and die, God-given skills and talents degenerate, and productivity wanes. In essence, laziness, which is the absence of work, aborts potential and sacrifices possibilities.

Therefore, God's purpose for giving you work is to bless you by calling forth from you all that He sees in you. He designed you to meet your needs and the needs of others through your ability to work. When you see work from this perspective, and you accept your opportunities to work as the gifts of a loving God who wants to draw from you the wealth of your hidden potential, you will find that work becomes an anticipated pleasure to be embraced as an opportunity to find happiness and fulfillment. *Work is the master key to releasing your potential.*

> God works the vision in; man works the vision out.

## EVIEW the Principles From This Week:

- What God speaks to is the source for what He creates. God spoke to Himself when He created you, so you came from God.
- All things have the same components and essence as the sources from which they came.
- Because you came from God, who is Spirit, you also are spirit.
- All things must be maintained by the sources from which they came. You must be maintained by God, your Source. Apart from Him you will die.
- The potential of all things is related to the source from which it came. Your potential is related to God's potential.
- Everything in life has the ability to fulfill its potential. God built into you the ability to fulfill your potential.
- Potential is determined and revealed by the demands placed on it by its creator. God reveals what He created you to do by placing demands on you. You are capable of doing everything God asks of you.

**Keys to Releasing Your Potential:**

- You must know your source. God is your Source.
- You must understand how you were designed to function. God designed you to operate by faith.
- You must know your purpose. God created you to express His image, to enjoy fellowship with Him, to dominate the earth, to bear fruit, and to reproduce yourself.
- You must understand your resources. God has given you resources of spirit, body, soul, time, and material things.
- You must have the right environment. God created you to live with Him in a relationship of fellowship and obedience that is established and maintained by His presence, assurance, guidance, and direction.
- You must work out your potential. Work is God's blessing to challenge and expose your potential.

## The Enemy of Your Potential

*The Lord is exalted, for He dwells on high; He will fill Zion with justice and righteousness. He will be the sure foundation for your times, a rich store of salvation and wisdom and knowledge; the fear of the Lord is the key to this treasure* (Isaiah 33:5-6).

BOOK QUOTE: *Maximizing Your Potential* [Chapter 3]

When God placed man in the Garden, He commanded him to work the garden and take care of it. This requirement of God is given to man before he breaks fellowship with God through disobedience. Man is in his ideal environment, being filled with God's power and anointing, living in perfect holiness and purity, and enjoying God's fellowship and presence. Thus, this commandment implies that something or someone was waiting to take or attack what man had been given to keep. John 10:9-10 warns us of this thief.

Satan is our enemy. He wants to destroy the power of God within us so that God's glory is not revealed in us. He's out to destroy all we could be because he knows that those who become rerooted in God have the ability to act like God, showing His nature and likeness. Consequently, satan comes as a thief to steal our potential because he cannot boldly challenge God's power within us. Our outward container, which is our body, reveals nothing of the treasure inside us. This all-surpassing treasure is God's power and wisdom.

In other words, the key to releasing God's power within you is reverencing Him, which is living with Him in a relationship of obedience and submission. *You are filled with heavenly wisdom, but you have to follow God's program to benefit from it.* Jesus spoke of this need to live in relationship with God in John 15:4-7.

No wonder satan tries to steal our potential. He fears God's power within us because it is greater than he is. Therefore, our dreams, plans, and ideas are targets of his evil forces. The minute we have a good idea, the deceiver will send someone to criticize our dream because he cannot permit us to accomplish our vision. As long as we are only dreaming, he is safe and he'll let us alone. When we begin to act on our dream, he'll hit us full force.

> Our dreams, plans, and ideas are targets of satan's evil forces.

You are responsible to guard your dream and bring it to reality by safeguarding and protecting it from injury and loss. To do so you must understand how satan seeks to rob you of your destiny.

## he Enemy of Disobedience

*Let us, therefore, make every effort to enter that rest, so that no one will fall by following their example of disobedience* (Hebrews 4:11).

BOOK QUOTE: *Maximizing Your Potential* [Chapter 3]

Satan's methods for stealing dreams are many and varied, according to the vision and the personality of the dreamer. Let us identify some of these enemies of potential so you will recognize them for what they are, the deceiver's activity in your life.

1. Disobedience.

The Bible repeatedly states that disobedience withholds God's blessings and rains His curses upon us. This is true because disobedience brings into our lives the natural (God-ordained) consequences of our actions. Teenagers who experiment with sex destroy the beauty of the first intimacy that is to be enjoyed between a husband and a wife, open themselves to AIDS and other diseases, and risk losing the joys of youth due to the birth of a child. They also forfeit their dreams to problems in marriage in later years, to serious illnesses and possible death, and to the responsibilities of raising a child before they have matured into the task.

Jonah learned the consequences of disobedience when he boarded a ship going in the opposite direction from the city to which God was sending him. He nearly lost his life by drowning. In a similar situation, Lot's wife, in spite of God's commandment not to look back, sacrificed her life for one last look at the city she was fleeing from. *Disobedience always wastes potential and retards the attainment of goals. You cannot persist in disobedience and maximize your potential.* To maximize your life you must submit to God's will in everything.

Disobedience withholds God's blessings and rains His curses upon us.

## The Enemy of Sin

*Blessed is the man whose sin the Lord will never count against him* (Romans 4:8).

BOOK QUOTE: *Maximizing Your Potential* [Chapter 3]

We are looking at the enemies of potential. We have already seen the effects of disobedience. The second enemy we face is:

2. Sin.

Although the effects of disobedience and sin are similar, sin is a more basic ill because it is total rebellion against the known will of God—or to say it another way, a declaration of independence from your Source. The resulting alienation from God destroys potential because we cannot know God if we do not have His Spirit, and His Spirit is the password to unlocking our potential. Sin, in essence, says, "I know better than you do, God, how to run my life."

King David experienced the desolation and death that result from a rebellious spirit when he violated another man's wife and tried to cover up his action by having the woman's husband killed in battle and taking her for his wife. The son born to David from this affair died, and David endured the agony of separation from the God he loved. What the child could have done in his lifetime was sacrificed, as were David's energy and vitality during the months before he confessed his sin. It is no wonder David prayed:

> *Hide Your face from my sins and blot out all my iniquity. Create in me a pure heart, O God, and renew a steadfast spirit within me. Do not cast me from Your presence or take Your Holy Spirit from me. Restore to me the joy of Your salvation and grant me a willing spirit, to sustain me* (Psalm 51:9-12).

Destroying your relationship with God through sin is always suicide. *You cannot become who God created you to be if you persist in rebelling against Him.* Without God's Spirit living and working in you, you will die with your potential. Sin caps the well of your potential. To maximize your life you must avoid compromise with ungodliness.

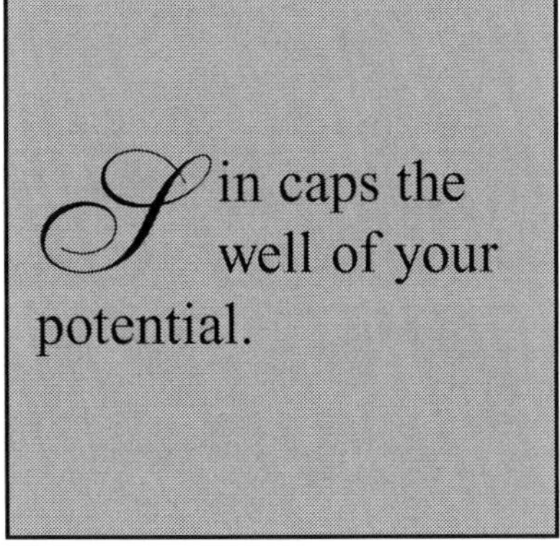

## The Enemy of Fear

*For you did not receive a spirit that makes you a slave again to fear, but you received the Spirit of sonship. And by him we cry, "Abba, Father"* (Romans 8:15).

BOOK QUOTE: *Maximizing Your Potential* [Chapter 3]

We are continuing to look at the enemies of potential. We have already seen the effects of disobedience and sin. The third enemy we face is:

3. Fear.

Fear is having faith in the impossible. It's dwelling on all that *could go wrong* instead of what *will go right*. Although, for example, accidents do happen and cars must be carefully maintained and driven, fear that prevents us from driving or riding in a car immobilizes our potential because it severely limits where we can go.

When as a lad, David met the giant Goliath with a slingshot and three stones, he most likely was afraid. Yet because he mastered his fear by trusting in God instead of thinking about all that could go wrong, he freed the Israelites from the oppression of their enemies and honored the name of God. (See First Samuel chapter 17.) His faith in God moved him beyond timidity to power. Fear is seeing Goliath too big to hit. Faith is seeing Goliath too big to miss. Paul wrote to Timothy about this ability to move beyond fear:

> *...fan into flame the gift of God, which is in you through the laying on of my hands. For God did not give us a spirit of timidity, but a spirit of power, of love and of self-discipline* (2 Timothy 1:6-7).

A spirit of self-discipline submits the information we receive through our bodies and our minds to the knowledge we receive from God's Spirit. It refuses to allow our minds to run wild imagining everything that *could* happen and chooses instead to apply God's promises to the situation and to depend on God's love and power for the outcome. Faith, our God-given mode of operation, combats fear and encourages the maximizing of potential. He who fears to try will never know what he could have done. He who fears God has nothing else to fear. To maximize your life you must neutralize fear with faith.

> He who fears to try will never know what he could have done.

## The Enemy of Discouragement

*Be strong and very courageous. Be careful to obey all the law my servant Moses gave you; do not turn from it to the right or to the left, that you may be successful wherever you go. Do not let this Book of the Law depart from your mouth; meditate on it day and night, so that you may be careful to do everything written in it. Then you will be prosperous and successful* (Joshua 1:7-8).

BOOK QUOTE: *Maximizing Your Potential* [Chapter 3]

We are continuing our study on the enemies of potential. We have already seen the effects of disobedience, sin and fear. The fourth enemy we face is:

4. Discouragement.

Most things worth having require patience and perseverance. No pianist plays perfectly the first time she touches the keys, nor does an athlete win a race the first time he runs. Many discouraging moments exist between an initial experience and the perfecting of a skill.

Unfortunately, *much potential is sacrificed on the altar of discouragement.* Perhaps you've experienced this enemy as too many sour notes hindered your ambition to practice or the failure to win a prize took you from the race. Replaying the music until it's right and running every day are the only ways to fulfill your potential. Concert pianists and Olympic athletes aren't born. They move beyond their discouraging moments to perfect their innate skills.

The same attitude is required of you to maximize your potential. *God will not give you a dream unless He knows you have the talents, abilities, and personality to complete it. His commands reveal the potential He gave you before you were born.*

God commanded Joshua to be courageous (see Deuteronomy 31:7; Joshua 1:7-8). Even though Joshua didn't feel courageous, God knew courage was in him and commanded him to show what was there.

Those who are under command—military command, for example—just do what they are told. No matter how they feel about the command, they just obey it.

You must respond the same way to God's commands. Even if you are feeling discouraged about completing the task, you must start it. Do what needs to be done no matter how difficult or impossible God's commands feel. Then discouragement will have no opportunity to destroy your potential. To maximize your life you must neutralize discouragement with hope.

To maximize your life you must neutralize discouragement with hope.

## The Enemy of Procrastination

*If you wait for perfect conditions, you will never get anything done* (Ecclesiastes 11:4 LB).

BOOK QUOTE: *Maximizing Your Potential* [Chapter 3]

This is the next part of our study on the enemies of potential. We have already seen the effects of disobedience, sin, fear and discouragement. The fifth enemy we face is:

5. Procrastination.

How many times have you delayed so long in making a decision that it was made for you, or in completing a project that it was too late for your intended purpose? Most of us do this more often than we'd like to admit.

*Procrastination, the delaying of action until a later time, kills potential.* The Israelites discovered this when they found many reasons why they couldn't obey God and enter the land He was giving them. When they saw that the land was good, with an abundance of food, and finally decided to take the land as God had commanded them, they discovered that the opportunity to obey God was past. Disregarding God's warning that He would not go with them, they marched into battle and were soundly defeated. God left them alone to fight for themselves.

Procrastination often grows out of discouragement. When we become discouraged, we stop finding reasons for doing what we know we can do. Then God allows us to go our own way and suffer the consequences. Sooner or later, we will discover that we've lost much because we refused to act when God required it. Very often He will find someone else to do the job. Procrastination is a serious enemy of potential. It eats away at the very core of our time and motivation. To maximize your life you must destroy procrastination by eliminating all excuses and reasons for not taking action. Just do it!

> Procrastination eats away at the very core of our time and motivation.

## The Enemy of Past Failures

*...I press on to take hold of that for which Christ Jesus took hold of me. Brothers, I do not consider myself yet to have taken hold of it. But one thing I do: Forgetting what is behind and straining toward what is ahead, I press on toward the goal to win the prize for which God has called me heavenward in Christ Jesus. All of us who are mature should take such a view of things.... Only let us live up to what we have already attained* (Philippians 3:12-16).

BOOK QUOTE: *Maximizing Your Potential* [Chapter 3]

We are continuing our study on the enemies of potential. We have already seen the effects of disobedience, sin, fear, discouragement and procrastination. The sixth enemy we face is:

6. Past Failures.

Too often we are unwilling to take risks in the present because we have failed in the past. Perhaps the first story you sent to a magazine wasn't published, so you never wrote another story. Perhaps your first garden didn't produce many vegetables, so you never planted another garden. Perhaps your first business proposal didn't win the bank's approval, so you never started your own business, and you're still working for someone else.

*Failure is never a reason to stop trying. Indeed, failure provides another opportunity to enjoy success.* The apostle Paul discovered the truth of this when he met Jesus and turned from persecuting Christ to preaching the good news of God's salvation in Him.

Paul was not unaware of his failures, but he refused to allow them to keep him from doing what he knew he could do. He believed that the God who had called him to serve Him would accomplish within and through him all that He had purposed. He trusted in a power higher than himself.

> *...I consider everything a loss compared to the surpassing greatness of knowing Christ Jesus my Lord, for whose sake I have lost all things. I consider them rubbish, that I may gain Christ and be found in Him, not having a righteousness of my own that comes from the law, but that which is through faith in Christ—the righteousness that comes from God and is by faith* (Philippians 3:8-9).

Failure is another opportunity to enjoy success.

Paul had messed up, but in Christ he found the reason and the strength to pick himself up and move on. You must do the same or you will never see your full potential. Refuse to be a loser no matter how many times you lose. It is better to try and fail than never to try at all. Remember, you cannot make progress by looking in the rearview mirror. To maximize your life you must let the past be past and leave it there.

## REVIEW the Principles From This Week:

- Vision can be aborted.
- Satan is your enemy. Your dreams, plans, and ideas are targets of his evil forces.
- Beware of the enemies of your potential:
    1. Disobedience
    2. Sin
    3. Fear
    4. Discouragement
    5. Procrastination
    6. Past Failures

## he Enemy of Others' Opinions

*But Jesus would not entrust Himself to them, for He knew all men. He did not need man's testimony about man, for He knew what was in a man* (John 2:24-25).

BOOK QUOTE: *Maximizing Your Potential* [Chapter 3]

We are continuing our study on the enemies of potential. Last week we learned about the effects of disobedience, sin, fear, discouragement, procrastination, and past failures. The next enemy we face is:

7. The Opinions of Others.

Most of us have had the experience of sharing a great idea with friends only to have them tell us 50 reasons why it won't work. *Forsaking dreams because others belittle them or say we are crazy for trying them wastes potential.* Satan uses those closest to us, whose opinions we value, to get to our potential.

No human being can be trusted to defend *your* potential. You alone are responsible. By refusing to allow the disparaging comments of others to discourage you, by removing yourself from their influence when your vision becomes threatened, and by clinging to God's commandments and directions, you can unleash the totality of God's power within you.

Jesus demonstrated the importance of disregarding the opinions of others when He went to Jerusalem one Passover and the crowds believed in Him because of the miracles He performed. Jesus would not entrust Himself to them, for He knew all men (see John 2:24-25 above). He had a good reason to be cautious about accepting the affirmation of the crowd: He knew the fickle nature of people. He didn't trust their cheers and their pats on the back. Accolades should be appreciated but never required.

The events of the week preceding His death confirm the wisdom of His decision. One day the people in Jerusalem received Him with great joy and hailed Him as the Messiah. Several days later they clamored for His death.

You too must beware of allowing the opinions of others to influence your decisions. Remember, you are required to perform for an audience of one, the Lord Jesus Christ. When He applauds, then you are successful.

> Satan uses those closest to us, whose opinions we value, to get to our potential.

*Get your encouragement and promotion from God.* Tap into the heavenly realm and receive the confirmation of your plans from Him because His opinion is the only one that counts. The opinions of others can destroy your potential if you permit them to touch your dreams and visions. To maximize your life you must declare independence from the opinions of others.

## The Enemy of Distractions

*But Martha was distracted by all the preparations that had to be made. She came to him and asked, "Lord, don't you care that my sister has left me to do the work by myself? Tell her to help me!"* (Luke 10:40).

BOOK QUOTE: *Maximizing Your Potential* [Chapter 3]

We have been studying the enemies of potential. Yesterday, we looked at how the opinions of others affect us. The next enemy we face is:

8. Distractions.

This is one of the principal enemies of maximizing potential. All of us have had the experience of walking into another room and saying, "Now, why did I come here?" We had a purpose when we decided to go into the other room, but something between our decision to go and the moment we arrived sidetracked us from our original intention.

Satan uses distractions to stop our progress toward a goal, or at least to change the speed of that progress. If he cannot convince us that our dream is wrong, he'll throw other things into our path to slow the development of our vision or he'll push us and induce us to move ahead of God's timetable. One of satan's most successful devices is to preoccupy us with "good" things to distract us from the "right" things.

Perhaps God has planted the seed of a dream that He wants you to accomplish 20 years from now. Between then and now He has many other plans for your life. Let that seed incubate, and proceed cautiously. As you stay open to God's leading in that area, He will reveal when the timing is right. Never sacrifice the right thing for a good thing.

Everything that doesn't help our progress, hinders it. This is true because obeying God too soon or too late is disobedience. Therefore, we must be careful not to get drawn into good activities that distract us from our overall purpose. God requires our prompt response to Him throughout the journey. Obedience part of the way is really disobedience. We must be true, then, to our whole vision over the long haul because true obedience to God is doing what He says, when He says, the way He says, as long as He says, until He says "stop."

Because distractions take us off course, we cannot maximize our potential if we allow ourselves to be distracted from faithfully obeying Him every step of the way. Even if God, in His love and mercy, permits us to get back on course, we cannot recover the time and effort we wasted being distracted.

God is the only One who knows where you are going and what is the best way to get there. The fulfillment of your potential is His hope and joy. To maximize your life you must stay focused on your purpose and avoid distractions through discipline.

> Because distractions take us off course, we cannot maximize our potential.

## The Enemy of Success

*I, even I, have spoken; yes, I have called him. I will bring him, and he will succeed in his mission* (Isaiah 48:15).

BOOK QUOTE: *Maximizing Your Potential* [Chapter 3]

We have been studying the enemies of potential. The next enemy we face is:

9. Success.

Success is another enemy of potential. When we complete a task and quit because we think we've arrived, we never become all we are. If, for example, you graduate from college and teach first grade for the rest of your life when God wanted you to be a high school principal, you forfeit much of your potential because you stopped at a preliminary success. *Leave your success and go create another. That's the only way you will release all your potential.*

Remember, satan is afraid of our potential. He knows that God created us to do something great. Therefore, he will allow us a small success and try to convince us that we have arrived. Then, we will not want to move on to greater successes. We must beware that a small success does not keep us from accomplishing our larger goal or purpose.

In a similar manner, we must be careful to judge our successes by God's standards, not the world's. Success in the world's eyes is not really success because the world does not know what true success is. True success is being right with God and completing *His* assignment and purpose for our lives. It's knowing God and obeying Him. Thus, *we cannot succeed without discovering and doing what God asks of us*. Without God, everything we do is nothing.

Therefore, do not be intimidated by your lack of achievement in the world's eyes. The power of God within you is greater than any other power. When you're hooked up to God and you're obeying *His* directives, you will achieve success by His standards. Refuse to allow the world's measurements of success to encourage or discourage you because God's standards are the only criteria that matter. Follow Him as He leads you from success to success. To maximize your life you must never allow temporary achievement to cancel eternal fulfillment.

Leave your success and go create another.

## he Enemy of Tradition

*You have let go of the commands of God and are holding on to the traditions of men* (Mark 7:8).

BOOK QUOTE: *Maximizing Your Potential* [Chapter 3]

We have been studying the enemies of potential. The next enemy we face is:

10. Tradition.

*Traditions are powerful enemies of potential because they are full of security.* We don't have to think when we do something the way we've always done it. Neither do we receive the incentive to grow and be creative because our new ideas may interfere with the conventional way of doing things.

The tragedy is that the tradition, which probably served its purpose well when it was started, prevents the accomplishment of the purpose for which it was established. When the manufacturing company was small, it made sense to have the receptionist open all the mail and stamp it received because she also served as the secretary for the various departments. Now that the company has grown and each department has secretaries and clerks within it, the continuation of that tradition is self-defeating. Disorganization, rather than efficiency, is the result.

Remember, no matter how good the present system is, there's always a better way. Don't be imprisoned by the comfort of the known. Be an explorer, not just a passenger. Don't allow yourself to become trapped by tradition or you will do and become nothing. Your present level of success will be your highest level of success, and God, who is not trapped within tradition, will find someone else to do what you could have done. *Use your imagination. Dream big and find new ways to respond to present situations and responsibilities.* Then you will uncover never-ending possibilities that inspire you to reach for continually higher achievements. We are sons of the "Creator," who created us to be creative. Nowhere in Scripture did God repeat an identical act.

Refrain from accepting or believing, "We've never done it that way before." Now is the time to try something different. The release of your full potential demands that you move beyond the present traditions of your home, family, job, and church—in essence, throughout your life. To maximize your life you must be willing to release ineffective traditions for new methods.

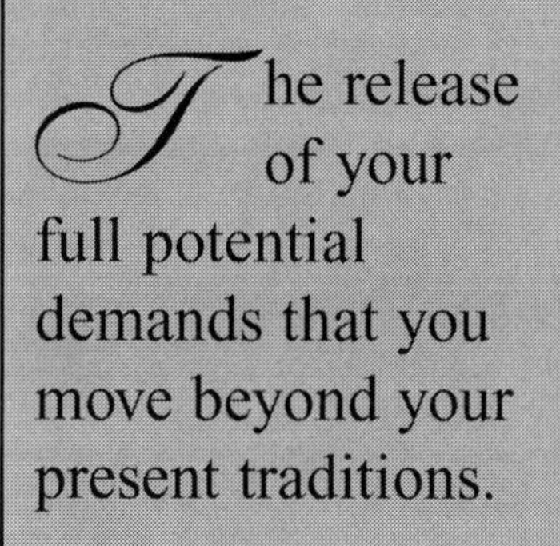

# The Enemy of A Wrong Environment

*Bad company corrupts good character* (1 Corinthians 15:33b).

BOOK QUOTE: *Maximizing Your Potential* [Chapter 3]

We have been studying the enemies of potential. The next enemy we face is:

11. A Wrong Environment.

Nutritious vegetables cannot grow in poor soil and healthy fish cannot thrive in polluted waters. Neither can we maximize our potential in a wrong environment. The apostle Paul speaks to this principle when he says, "*Bad company corrupts good character*" (1 Corinthians 15:33b). That means, no matter how good our intentions may be, if we get in with bad company, we will eventually think and act as they do. We will not change them, they will change us.

*Many dreams die because they are shared with the wrong people.* Joseph learned that lesson the hard way. Indeed, he landed in a pit and was sold into slavery because his brothers were jealous of their father's favoritism toward him and they were offended by his dreams that placed him in authority over them. This is really not so surprising because older brothers rarely enjoy being dominated by younger ones. Had Joseph kept his dreams to himself, his brothers' resentment may not have developed into a plan to murder him.

Remember, others do not see what you see. They cannot completely understand the vision God has given you. Protect your potential by choosing carefully those with whom you share your dreams and aspirations, and by maintaining an environment in which your potential can be fulfilled. To maximize your life you must manage your environment and the quality of the people and resources that influence you. Your greatest responsibility is to yourself, not others.

Many dreams dies because they are shared with the wrong people.

## The Enemies of Comparison and Opposition

*For what was glorious has no glory now in comparison with the surpassing glory. And if what was fading away came with glory, how much greater is the glory of that which lasts!* (2 Corinthians 3:10-11).

BOOK QUOTE: *Maximizing Your Potential* [Chapter 3]

We have been studying the enemies of potential. The next two enemies we face are comparison and opposition:

12. Comparison.

Many parents struggle with the temptation to compare their children's strengths and weaknesses with the skills and temperaments of other children. This tendency to compare can be lethal to potential because it may produce either discouragement or false pride. Both prevent us from becoming all we can be. Discouragement keeps us from trying new things because we lack the confidence that we can succeed. False pride short-circuits our potential by giving us the illusion that we have arrived.

Whenever you compare your skills and abilities with others—either favorably or unfavorably—you forfeit the opportunity to become your potential because you try to make equal but different people the same. God created you with your specific blend of personality, skills, and abilities to fulfill your purpose. To maximize your life you must understand that you are unique, original, and irreplaceable. There is no comparison.

13. Opposition.

Satan has a way of snuffing out our great dreams by causing us to compromise. Most often this occurs because we give in to opposition. If he can't stop us, he'll push us to make a deal that is not God's deal. Then we have no hope of attaining our goal because we are trying to accomplish our God-given vision with human values and specifications. Opposition is natural to life and necessary for flight. If everyone agrees with your dream, it's probably a nightmare.

To fulfill your vision in life you will usually have to swim upstream against the tide of popular opinion. Opposition is proof that you're swimming, not floating.

*Compromised vision always kills potential because a vision that is attempted outside God's guidelines cannot reveal His power.* Take your dream and be willing to die for it. This is a requirement for maximizing potential. To maximize your life you must accept and understand the nature and value of opposition.

Be willing to die for your dream.

## The Enemy of Society's Pressure

*We are hard pressed on every side, but not crushed; perplexed, but not in despair; persecuted, but not abandoned; struck down, but not destroyed* (2 Corinthians 4:8-9).

BOOK QUOTE: *Maximizing Your Potential* [Chapter 3]

We have been studying the enemies of potential. The next enemy we face is:

14. Society's Pressure.

Pressure from society's standards and expectations is a threat to potential. The people we associate with, if they make judgments based on age, race, financial status, ancestry, and education, may pressure us to relinquish a dream because they do not believe we can accomplish it:

*Many dreams are killed by laughter and ridicule, but your dream doesn't have to die. Dare to be different. Accomplish something.* Trust God's word rather than society's expectations. Never *is as old as the first time it changes*. It only lasts as long as the person who refuses to allow society's dictates to squash his or her dream.

Those who say "I can" no matter how many people say "you can't" transform dreams into realities. They have learned the priority of remaining true to their vision and they have developed the inner strength to trust God when society pushes them to abandon their goal. They are those who maximize their potential.

When the apostle Paul described our potential as treasure in clay pots (see 2 Corinthians 4:7), he recognized that discovering and exposing that treasure is not always an easy task.

You too must trust God and cooperate with Him to fulfill all the dreams He gives you and to reach all the goals He sets before you. Yes, satan will use the enemies of your potential to destroy God's power within you, but you are not captive to his ways. You can choose to protect yourself from his attack; to cultivate the possibilities you yet can accomplish; to use your talents, skills, and abilities for the good of others; and to live within the laws of limitation that govern who you can become. These keys to maximizing potential, together with the keys to releasing potential, acknowledge both your dependence on God and your responsibility to trust Him and cooperate with Him as He works in and through you.

> Pressure from society's standards and expectations is a threat to potential.

As we expect a plant or tree to grow from a seed because we know it exists in it, so God calls forth from us the wealth of our potential. He wills that we should bear fruit that shows His potency. Practicing the keys that maximize potential and recognizing the enemies of potential are essential steps in our journey of becoming who we are.

## EVIEW the Principles From This Week:

- You must guard and protect your potential.
- You must cultivate and feed your potential.
- You must understand and obey the laws of limitation that govern your potential.
- You must share your potential.
- Beware of the enemies of your potential:
  1. The Opinions of Others
  2. Distractions
  3. Success
  4. Tradition
  5. A Wrong Environment
  6. Comparison
  7. Opposition
  8. Society's Pressure

## An Audience of One

*Be on your guard; stand firm in the faith; be men of courage; be strong* (1 Corinthians 16:13).

BOOK QUOTE: *Maximizing Your Potential* [Chapter 4]

The boy sighed with satisfaction as the last of the four towers stood firm and tall. Now all he had to do to finish the sand castle was to draw the design on the top of the walls. As he worked, he watched the approaching waves. Before long they would be up to the castle. The surf had been far down on the sand when he started building four hours before, but he had known that the time would come when the waves would approach where he worked. Hence, he had built a large moat with an opening toward the sea to help the water stay in the moat instead of coming up over the entire castle. He hoped the moat would protect his castle for a few minutes before the waves completely destroyed it.

As he finished the last of the walls, the boy also kept an eye on his younger sister. Twice she had come to "help him." The first time she had smashed an entire section of the wall with her shovel before he could stop her. The last time he had been on guard and had seen her coming. Thus, he had protected the castle from major destruction by catching her hand.

The boy building the sand castle was wise. He recognized the approaching waves and the misguided help of his sister as enemies of his goal to build a castle and to play with his boats in its moat, and he defended against them.

The defense of something occurs in two stages. *Guarding* is preventive in nature. It occurs while the *possibility* of an attack is present but before the threat is active and near. Recognizing the existence of an enemy who wants to steal or destroy the treasure, the one who guards watches over the treasure to safeguard it from injury or loss. He does so by taking precautions against an attack and by keeping watch so the enemy cannot slip up on him and catch him unaware. Guarding leads into the second step of defense, which is the action necessary when an enemy steps over the established boundary and threatens the treasure.

This second step of defense is *protecting*. *Protection* is active defense in the midst of an assault. It implements the pre-established plan to preserve the treasure from danger or harm. The boy protected his castle when he caught his sister's hand to keep her from ruining it.

> You were created to perform for an audience of one, the Lord Jesus Christ!

## We Are Responsible for Defending Our Treasure

*Fight the good fight of the faith. Take hold of the eternal life to which you were called when you made your good confession in the presence of many witnesses* (1 Timothy 6:12).

BOOK QUOTE: *Maximizing Your Potential* [Chapter 4]

The defense of something occurs in two stages. *Guarding* is preventive in nature. It occurs while the *possibility* of an attack is present but before the threat is active and near. Guarding leads into the second step of defense, which is the action necessary when an enemy steps over the established boundary and threatens the treasure.

This second step of defense is *protecting*. *Protection* is active defense in the midst of an assault. It implements the pre-established plan to preserve the treasure from danger or harm.

Protecting and guarding work together. One without the other presents a weakened resistance to the thief who is trying to steal the treasure. The responsibility for this resistance lies with the recipient of the treasure. God didn't tell Heaven or the angels to protect the garden. He told Adam to protect it. In a similar manner, the apostle Paul admonished Timothy, not his mother or his grandmother, to defend the treasure he had received:

> *Timothy, my son, I give you this instruction in keeping with the prophecies once made about you, so that by following them you may fight the good fight, holding on to faith and a good conscience. Some have rejected these and so have shipwrecked their faith* (1 Timothy 1:18-19).

This defense begins with an understanding of the treasure we have received from God and is worked out in our fight to keep what we have received. This treasure is both God's wisdom and power within us (our potential) and the gift of His Spirit.

> Defense begins with an understanding of the treasure we have received from God.

## What Are We to Defend?

*"Now if you obey me fully and keep my covenant, then out of all nations you will be my treasured possession. Although the whole earth is mine, you will be for me a kingdom of priests and a holy nation." These are the words you are to speak to the Israelites* (Exodus 19:5-6).

BOOK QUOTE: *Maximizing Your Potential* [Chapter 4]

The defense of something occurs in two stages. *Guarding* is preventive in nature. *Protection* is active defense in the midst of an assault. It implements the pre-established plan to preserve the treasure from danger or harm. Protecting and guarding work together.

Defense begins with an understanding of the treasure we have received from God and is worked out in our fight to keep what we have received. This treasure is both God's wisdom and power within us (our potential) and the gift of His Spirit.

As we have seen, God deposits a treasure in each person He creates. This treasure is a) God's wisdom and knowledge concerning who He is, who we are, and how we are to live in relationship with Him; b) God's power that worked in creation through the spoken word and even today brings forth beauty from chaos; and c) God's Spirit who lives within our hearts. Thus, God reveals Himself to us and crowns us with His potency—His power, authority, and strength to effectively accomplish what He wills.

> *But we have this treasure in jars of clay to show that this all-surpassing power is from God and not from us* (2 Corinthians 4:7).

This potency of God within us—our potential—is the treasure we must defend. The treasure is the God-invested vision and purpose for our lives, designed both to show His glory and to bring Him glory.

The potency of God within us is the treasure we must defend.

## The Treasure of God's Wisdom

*The fear of the Lord is the beginning of knowledge, but fools despise wisdom and discipline* (Proverbs 1:7).

BOOK QUOTE: *Maximizing Your Potential* [Chapter 4]

The prophet Isaiah recognized God's wisdom as a treasure, as did the psalmists and King Solomon. They also agreed that the fear of the Lord is the key to this treasure:

> *He will be the sure foundation for your times, a rich store of salvation and wisdom and knowledge; the fear of the Lord is the key to this treasure* (Isaiah 33:6).

> *The fear of the Lord is the beginning of wisdom; all who follow His precepts have good understanding...* (Psalm 111:10).

> *My son, if you accept my words and store up my commands within you, turning your ear to wisdom and applying your heart to understanding, and if you call out for insight and cry aloud for understanding, and if you look for it as for silver and search for it as for hidden treasure, then you will understand the fear of the Lord and find the knowledge of God. For the Lord gives wisdom, and from His mouth come knowledge and understanding* (Proverbs 2:1-6).

What does it mean to fear God? The psalmists liken those who fear God with those who "*hope...in His unfailing love*" (Psalm 33:18), who "*understand* [His] *statutes*" (Psalm 119:79), and who "*walk in His ways*" (Psalm 128:1). They also compare fearing God with trusting Him (see Psalm 40:3; 115:11) and advise those who would learn what it means to fear the Lord to "turn from evil and do good; seek peace and pursue it" (see Psalm 34:11,14). Solomon equates fearing the Lord with shunning evil (see Proverbs 3:7; 8:13) and hating knowledge with *failing* to fear the Lord (see Proverbs 1:29). *Thus, to fear the Lord is to trust and obey Him. In so doing we defend the deposit of His wisdom and knowledge within us.*

The apostle Paul speaks of God's wisdom within us as a "*secret wisdom*" (1 Corinthians 2:7) because sinful man can neither know nor understand the thoughts and the heart of God toward His children. Only as we come to God through faith in Jesus Christ, "*and Him crucified*" (1 Corinthians 2:2), and through the presence of the Holy Spirit in our hearts (see 1 Corinthians 2:9-16) are we privileged to understand God's thoughts toward us.

> Only as we come to God through faith in Jesus Christ through the presence of the Holy Spirit in our hearts are we privileged to understand God's thoughts toward us.

## The Treasure of God's Knowledge

*Timothy, guard what has been entrusted to your care. Turn away from godless chatter and the opposing ideas of what is falsely called knowledge, which some have professed and in so doing have wandered from the faith...* (1 Timothy 6:20-21).

BOOK QUOTE: *Maximizing Your Potential* [Chapter 4]

We don't think like God. Isaiah acknowledged this difference between God's thoughts and ours:

> *"For My thoughts are not your thoughts, neither are your ways My ways," declares the Lord. "As the heavens are higher than the earth, so are My ways higher than your ways and My thoughts than your thoughts. As the rain and the snow come down from heaven, and do not return to it without watering the earth and making it bud and flourish, so that it yields seed for the sower and bread for the eater, so is My Word that goes out from My mouth: It will not return to Me empty, but will accomplish what I desire and achieve the purpose for which I sent it"* (Isaiah 55:8-11).

This wisdom of God is a treasure to be cherished and defended. His thoughts toward us are good and His knowledge of us is perfect. He sees beyond our vessels of clay to His wisdom within us and calls forth from us what He sees. As we learn to see as God sees and to live from His perspective, we begin to understand this treasure of His wisdom and the importance of safeguarding it from the snares of the evil one. Paul wrote of this to Timothy (see above):

God's wisdom will never match the ways of the world:

> *For it is written: "I will destroy the wisdom of the wise; the intelligence of the intelligent I will frustrate." Where is the wise man? Where is the scholar? Where is the philosopher of this age? Has not God made foolish the wisdom of the world?* (1 Corinthians 1:19-20)

We must be careful to safeguard His knowledge within us so we can see the perfection and beauty of His plans and purposes for our lives.

Sadly, satan influences many people to close their eyes and walk away from their visions because they don't believe what they see. He knows the potential they contain—what they can become, the many goals they can meet, and the ideas they can accomplish—but they don't. This is why the apostle Paul instructs us to "*take captive every thought to make it obedient to Christ*" (2 Corinthians 10:5).

> God sees beyond our vessels of clay to His wisdom within us and calls forth what He sees.

*When we bring our thoughts to Jesus and make them subject to Him, we combat satan's strategy and unmask his deception.* Jesus, who knows both satan's works and the potential God builds into every human being, cleanses our sight and enables us to see rightly through the eyes of faith and hope. This is the beginning of wisdom.

## The Treasure of God's Power

*...and said: "O Lord, God of our fathers, are you not the God who is in Heaven? You rule over all the kingdoms of the nations. Power and might are in Your hand, and no one can withstand You.* (2 Chronicles 20:6).

BOOK QUOTE: *Maximizing Your Potential* [Chapter 4]

God has also deposited His power within us. The apostle Paul spoke of this power as the means by which God works salvation in us—"*I am not ashamed of the gospel, because it is the power of God for the salvation of everyone who believes...*" (Romans 1:16)—and he carefully portrayed this salvation as "*a demonstration of the Spirit's power, so that* [our] *faith might not rest on men's wisdom, but on God's power*" (1 Corinthians 2:4-5).

In a similar manner, Peter and John understood God's power to be the secret behind their power:

> *..."Men of Israel, why does this surprise you? Why do you stare at us as if by our own power or godliness we had made this man walk?...By faith in the name of Jesus, this man whom you see and know was made strong..."* (Acts 3:12,16a).

God doesn't want us just to *know* who we are in Him; He wants us to *become* it. This occurs as we take hold of His power and make it our own. We must always be careful "*...to show that this all-surpassing power is from God and not from us*" (2 Corinthians 4:7). Even when we do not understand how God is working in our lives or what He is trying to accomplish, we can do great things when we cooperate with His power. This is true because potential is vision in a dormant state that can be activated by our faith in God's power. If we are children of God, our greatest goal in life should be to resemble our Father.

Whenever we see ourselves being something, doing something, or going somewhere, and we believe that God's power in us will bring this glimpse of our potential to pass, we tap into God's power to accomplish His will. This power of God is at work in us to save us and to call us to a holy life in Christ Jesus (see 1 Corinthians 2:1-5 and 2 Timothy 1:8-10).

Satan knows that God "*is able to do immeasurably more than all we ask or imagine, according to His power that is at work within us*" (Ephesians 3:20) and he is threatened by potential that is transformed by this power. Therefore, we must diligently defend God's power within us so that our vision can be changed into mission and God's potency may be revealed in us. God's power in us is a second treasure to be defended from the schemes of the evil one.

> God doesn't want us just to *know* who we are in Him; He wants us to *become* it.

## he Treasure of the Holy Spirit

*But thanks be to God, who always leads us in triumphal procession in Christ and through us spreads everywhere the fragrance of the knowledge of Him* (2 Corinthians 2:14).

BOOK QUOTE: *Maximizing Your Potential* [Chapter 4]

Paul identifies the Holy Spirit Himself as the deposit or treasure within us that we must guard and protect.

> *Now it is God who makes both us and you stand firm in Christ. He anointed us, set His seal of ownership on us, and put His Spirit in our hearts as a deposit, guaranteeing what is to come...* (2 Corinthians 1:21-22).

> *Now it is God who has made us...and has given us the Spirit as a deposit, guaranteeing what is to come* (2 Corinthians 5:5).

The Holy Spirit both reveals God's wisdom and power in us and guarantees that we will receive all God has planned for those who seek His wisdom and live by His power. His presence in our lives is an important deposit because He is the key to tapping into God's storehouse of wisdom and power. We cannot understand and apply God's wisdom without the Holy Spirit; neither can we live by His power. He is the Counselor to teach us all things (see John 14:26), the Searcher of our hearts to reveal to us the deep things of God (see 1 Corinthians 2:9-11), and the One who testifies that we are God's children (see Romans 8:16). Through Him we know God's thoughts and understand what God has given to us:

> *We have not received the spirit of the world but the Spirit who is from God, that we may understand what God has freely given us* (1 Corinthians 2:12).

> The Holy Spirit is the key to tapping into God's storehouse of wisdom and power.

## EVIEW the Principles From This Week:

- You are responsible to guard and protect your potential.
- The treasure you must defend is:
  1. God's wisdom.
  2. God's knowledge.
  3. God's power.
  4. The presence of God's Spirit in your life.
  5. This potency of God within you is your potential.

## The Treasure of Potential

*Guard the good deposit that was entrusted to you—guard it with the help of the Holy Spirit who lives in us* (2 Timothy 1:14).

BOOK QUOTE: *Maximizing Your Potential* [Chapter 4]

In essence, God's wisdom, power, and Spirit are the treasure we must safeguard. They are a deposit of Himself in us so that we can act and function like Him, sharing in His work. Together they are our potential, the source of our dreams and visions. We must remember, however, that having this deposit of God does not mean that we will keep it.

All the great things God has put inside us—our visions, dreams, plans, and talents—are satan's targets. He is afraid of men and women who have faith in God's wisdom and power, because they take their visions and translate them into action. They not only set goals, they make them happen.

The deceiver fears the treasure we possess. His destructive tactics and deceptive influences come into our lives to nullify and entrap all God has given to us. He isn't going to let us fulfill our potential without encountering resistance from him. Indeed, his attack is so severe that Paul advised Timothy to seek the help of the Holy Spirit to meet and overcome it:

Have no fear! God has given us everything we need to safeguard our hidden wealth from the schemes and deceit of the evil one. We must be careful, however, not to rely on weapons of human strength and wisdom. We cannot whip the enemy by ourselves, "*for the foolishness of God is wiser than man's wisdom, and the weakness of God is stronger than man's strength*" (1 Corinthians 1:25). Only as we are "*strong in the Lord and in His mighty power*" (Ephesians 6:10) can we withstand satan's onslaught against us. The Holy Spirit, sent by Jesus when we receive Him as Savior, is our Helper.

All the great things God has put inside us—our visions, dreams, plans, and talents—are satan's targets.

## God's Plan of Defense

*Therefore put on the full armor of God, so that when the day of evil comes, you may be able to stand your ground, and after you have done everything, to stand* (Ephesians 6:13).

BOOK QUOTE: *Maximizing Your Potential* [Chapter 4]

The description of the armor of God in Ephesians chapter 6 details a plan to *guard* and *protect* your life against satan's invasion. You must understand the provisions of this plan and put them into practice if you want to defend your potential.

First, recognize your enemy as the spiritual forces of evil, *"for our struggle is not against flesh and blood, but against...the powers of this dark world and against the spiritual forces of evil..."* (Ephesians 6:12). What looks to be a conflict in personalities or a difference in values may well be a struggle on a more basic level. Discouragement, opposition, criticism, and the other enemies of potential are the work of evil forces through those who are close to you. Learn to recognize and combat these obstacles for what they are.

The Scriptures are filled with examples of satan's work. Moses' mother and sister relied on God's power to save him from death when Moses' life was threatened by the Pharaoh of Egypt's decree that all Hebrew boys should be killed at birth.

Joseph was but a youth when his brothers plotted to kill him. After they had sold him into slavery instead of killing him, Joseph endured many hardships that could have prevented his potential from being unveiled and exercised. He didn't allow the enemies of discouragement, opposition, and the negative opinions of others to destroy the dreams God had given him.

King Saul tried to kill David many times. Discouragement, fear, loneliness, distractions, negative opinions, and pressure from others were all part of those years. Yet, David trusted God to fulfill the promise he had received when Samuel had anointed him to be king. In time, David fulfilled his potential and became the greatest king in Israel's history.

Although death is a favorite way for satan to destroy potential, he will most likely try to ensnare you with one of the enemies of potential. Be alert to recognize these enemies for what they are—satan's attacks on your potential.

> Learn to recognize and combat the enemies of potential.

## Expect satan's Attack

*For our struggle is not against flesh and blood, but against the rulers, against the authorities, against the powers of this dark world and against the spiritual forces of evil in the heavenly realms* (Ephesians 6:12).

BOOK QUOTE: *Maximizing Your Potential* [Chapter 4]

The apostle Paul knew that the attack of satan is inevitable. Thus, he told the Ephesians to put on the full armor of God so they could withstand when the evil day came. He wanted them to expect trouble so they would be prepared to meet it when it came.

No matter what you do, you will always have critics. This is true because some people cannot bear to see others succeed. When you aren't doing anything, you're not a problem for them; but when you start fulfilling your dreams and visions, you'll attract attention. People don't care about you until you start doing something big.

This opposition often occurs because your critics aren't doing anything. Those who are working out their own dreams don't need to be threatened by your accomplishments. They are too busy to be jealous and too confident to worry how your success might affect them. Thus, you must be careful of those who are doing nothing with their potential. They will be your greatest critics.

Learn to expect their opposition and to rise above it. Refuse to get drawn into their petty quarrels or to allow their words and actions to influence your self-esteem or your behavior. *Every dream you share has the potential to cause jealousy*, so be careful with whom you share your dreams. Sometimes you must keep your dream to yourself because no other person can understand it. Indeed, your dreams may sound funny or pretentious to others.

Just stick with what you're supposed to do until you achieve what you're after, and let those who are going nowhere go there without you. Others who are pursuing their purpose and maximizing their potential will understand your behavior, even if they can't see your particular vision. Find them and enjoy their company, for those who are going somewhere are more likely to support you in your journey. This is an essential factor in guarding your potential.

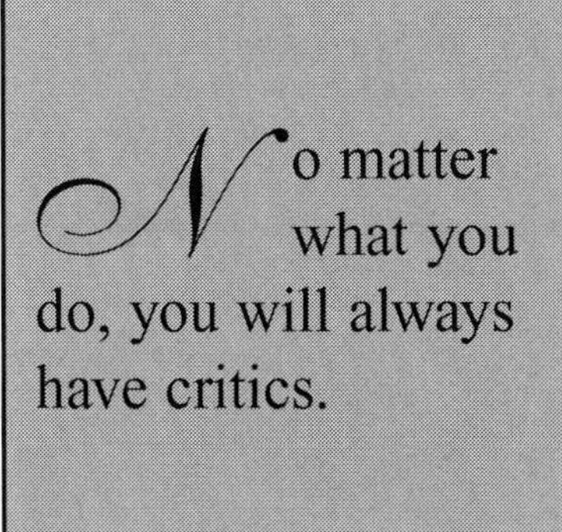

## repare to Overcome satan's Attack

*Put on the full armor of God so that you can take your stand against the devil's schemes* (Ephesians 6:11).

BOOK QUOTE: *Maximizing Your Potential* [Chapter 4]

We need to learn how to defend our potential. *One way you can prepare to defend your potential is to make wise choices.* Consider carefully with whom you associate and where you spend your time. Examine your reading material and how you fill your day. Be cautious with whom you share your dreams—if you share them at all.

*A second priority in preparing to meet satan's attack is to be sure that your vision is from God.* Don't conjure up your own ideas. If they contradict God's Word, you know your ideas are not from Him. God will not deny His Word. False dreams and fake prophecies are sure ways to lose your potential. Satan will distract you any way he can. Prepare for his attack by staying in close fellowship with God and by seeking His knowledge and wisdom.

*A third method for fortifying yourself against the assault of evil is to seek God's discipline and direction in your life.* Be truthful in your dealings. Act with justice and virtue. Live at peace with others in so far as it is within your power, being careful, however, not to compromise your loyalty and obedience to God and His Word. Seek His chastening when you have failed and "*rejoice in* [your] *sufferings, because...suffering produces perseverance; perseverance, character; and character, hope. And hope does not disappoint us...*" (Romans 5:3b-5). God will honor your efforts to obey Him and, in so doing, you will guard your potential.

Sooner or later, satan is going to step over the boundaries of your defense and you are going to be under attack. Then it is time to move from *guarding* your potential to *protecting* it. Paul admonished the Ephesians to stand their ground and, after doing everything else, still to stand. Perseverance is the key. You may not win the war in one battle, but you can stand firm in the midst of each assault.

Abraham, Joseph, Moses, David, Paul—all persevered through numerous battles to emerge victorious. At times they faltered and failed, but they always returned to the battle. You too must persevere when the forces of evil threaten to overwhelm you to destroy your potential. The story of Nehemiah offers some hints on how to do this.

> One way you can prepare to defend your potential is to make wise choices.

## How To Protect Yourself From Attack

*Stand firm then, with the belt of truth buckled around your waist, with the breastplate of righteousness in place, and with your feet fitted with the readiness that comes from the gospel of peace. In addition to all this, take up the shield of faith, with which you can extinguish all the flaming arrows of the evil one. Take the helmet of salvation and the sword of the Spirit, which is the Word of God* (Ephesians 6:14-17).

BOOK QUOTE: *Maximizing Your Potential* [Chapter 4]

Nehemiah was sent by the King of Persia to return to Jerusalem and rebuild the city. Even though Nehemiah was trying to do something beneficial, certain people were angered by his plans. So they started to make trouble for him (see Nehemiah 2:19b).

But Nehemiah was not to be deterred. He gathered workers and began the work. This incensed his enemies so that they began to ridicule the Jews (see Nehemiah 4:2b-3b).

Nehemiah did not reply to their ridicule. Instead, he turned to the Lord in prayer (see Nehemiah 4:4-5) and kept on with the work. This illustrates the first guideline for protecting your potential. *Don't answer your critics.*

At first your critic may be annoyed by you, but if you persist in your work, he becomes incensed. Nehemiah's enemies became increasingly hostile. Nehemiah responded to this new threat the same way he had answered the last one. He prayed to God and added a second line to his defense (see Nehemiah 4:15).

This reveals a third means of protecting your potential from attack. Allow God to fight for you. The workers stood guard, but God frustrated the plans of the attackers (Nehemiah 4:20).

For a while, Nehemiah and his helpers worked in peace. Yet, they did not let down their guard (Nehemiah 4:16-18a). Thus, they employed a fourth means for protecting their potential from attack. *Don't allow a lull in the battle to convince you that the war is over. Don't confuse quiet with peace.*

Finally, when Nehemiah's enemies received word that the wall had been completely rebuilt, they requested a meeting (Nehemiah 6:2b). Nehemiah wisely countered this as well, recognizing it as a different kind of attack (Nehemiah 6:2c-3).

This reveals a fifth and a sixth means of protecting your potential from attack. First, Nehemiah refused to meet with his enemies. *Stay away from the opposition.* Second, he refused to stop his work to talk. *Don't waste time talking.*

Even when the opposition tried to intimidate Nehemiah by suggesting that he would soon be in trouble with the king in Persia, Nehemiah remained firm in his stance. You too must *remain firm in your decisions and refuse to be intimidated by your oppressors.* These are the seventh and eighth factors in protecting your potential when you are under assault.

> Stand firm in the midst of attack.

Nehemiah used many methods to fight for his vision. You must employ the same methods to preserve your potential from attack.

## ight For Your Vision

*Folly delights a man who lacks judgment, but a man of understanding keeps a straight course* (Proverbs 15:21).

BOOK QUOTE: *Maximizing Your Potential* [Chapter 4]

There will always be people who are committed to destroying you. They will criticize you, ridicule you, and become angry with you. Let them. You are not responsible for their actions, only your own.

Fight for your vision. Share your dream only when you must, and choose carefully with whom you share it. Do the background work and stay on course when the going gets rough. Expect opposition and be careful not to allow the threats and accusations of your enemies to intimidate you. Stick with your decisions and remain committed to your goal. Don't let quietness fool you so that you are caught unprepared by a later attack. Talk to God about your needs and allow Him to respond to your oppressors. Never answer them yourself.

Finally, keep yourself busy. *Don't allow the battle to interfere with your work.* You may not be popular, but you will be successful because God works with those who put forth the effort to stay with the vision He has given them. Thus, *your opposers will learn that they are not as important as what you are doing*, and you will remain focused on your vision with renewed wisdom and strength to accomplish it. Your potential is worth the effort of overcoming its enemies.

Don't allow the battle to interfere with your work.

## et Moving

*We work hard with our own hands. When we are cursed, we bless; when we are persecuted, we endure it* (1 Corinthians 4:12).

BOOK QUOTE: *Maximizing Your Potential* [Chapter 4]

*God helps those who help themselves.* This familiar saying expresses an important truth. Paul told Timothy to seek the help of the Holy Spirit (see 2 Timothy 1:14), not to expect Him to run the whole show. The Holy Spirit will not take over our lives, but He will assist *us* in running them. He is our helper or assistant. He doesn't guard our potential. He helps us to do so by guiding our decisions and by empowering us to withstand and triumph in the midst of trials.

If you want God to guard your potential, you have to start using it. If you want Him to protect it, you have to start protecting it. That first step you take may not be the right one, but God can't help you until you do something. He can't close a door you haven't opened or affirm a decision you haven't made. *If you aren't doing anything to accomplish your goal, He isn't doing anything either. The Holy Spirit can't work for you unless you are working.*

The same principle is true for protecting your potential. When you do something to remove the attack against your vision, God will aid your efforts. Nevertheless, *the initiative must come from you.*

God won't take a bad habit or an inappropriate lifestyle from you because He didn't give it to you. He *will* affirm your decisions and strengthen your efforts when you start taking positive steps to *rid yourself* of the negative influences, the wrong attitudes, or the poor choices that are threatening your potential.

If you stay stuck in your present rut with no attempts to get out of it, your dreams will wither and die. *Start moving and the gentle touch of God will begin changing you and helping you to achieve seemingly impossible dreams. God is your partner.* You must work together to protect your potential. When you start contributing to your own protection, the Holy Spirit starts to protect you as well. He empowers what you begin and redirects your efforts when they don't match His expectations. Then you can begin to discover your potential and to protect what you see.

> God is in the business of maximizing potential.

Guarding potential is a daily task that requires more wisdom and power than we possess. God is in the business of maximizing potential. He'll empower our efforts if we cooperate with Him, but He will not do the work for us. Begin today to follow the guidelines for guarding and protecting your potential. The future of your dreams and visions is at stake.

## REVIEW the Principles From This Week:

**Guidelines for safeguarding your potential:**

- Recognize your enemies as the forces of evil.
- Expect satan's attack.
- Prepare to overcome his attack.
- Stand firm in the midst of attack.

**Guidelines for protecting yourself from attack:**

- Don't answer your critics.
- Post a guard to deter attack and to warn of impending danger.
- Allow God to fight for you.
- Don't allow a lull in the battle to convince you that the war is over.
- Stay away from your opposition.
- Don't waste time talking.
- Refuse to be intimidated by your critics' threats and accusations.

# A Prizewinning Flower—Your Potential

*But grow in the grace and knowledge of our Lord and Savior Jesus Christ. To Him be glory both now and forever! Amen* (2 Peter 3:18).

BOOK QUOTE: *Maximizing Your Potential* [Chapter 5]

The old woman smiled as she entered the small, hot room. A blaze of color met her eyes. African violets of many colors filled the room.

After the last of their children had left home, the woman had become very depressed, missing the children and having very little to do. That's when a friend had given her clippings from her African violets and had persuaded her to turn the playroom into a greenhouse. The idea had been a good one, giving her renewed interest in life.

When the first plants not only lived but flourished under her touch, she gained the confidence to add other colors by getting more clippings from her friend. She also began reading books and magazine articles about the care of African violets and talking with others who loved plants.

She had spent part of every day in this room, watering her plants, checking for insect pests, rooting new cuttings, fertilizing the plants that were about to bloom, picking off old blossoms, and rotating the plants so each one received sufficient light. Even the day her husband had died, she had wandered in here to find solace among her friends—as she had come to think of her plants.

In the evening, she often read gardening and horticulture magazines here, having moved her favorite chair from the living room when her husband was no longer there to spend the long hours with her. After nearly 40 years of hard work and extensive reading, the riotous color that surrounded her revealed the success of her efforts.

Now, her skill in cultivating and breeding African violets was known throughout the community, and over the years she had found great joy in teaching others the art of cultivating plants. Every year her conservatory was considered to be the highlight of the garden tour. Plant collections throughout the town—in gardens and rooms—were testimony to her skill.

The successful fulfillment of your potential is similar to the task of growing prizewinning flowers. Both require careful attention and diligent effort to produce winning results.

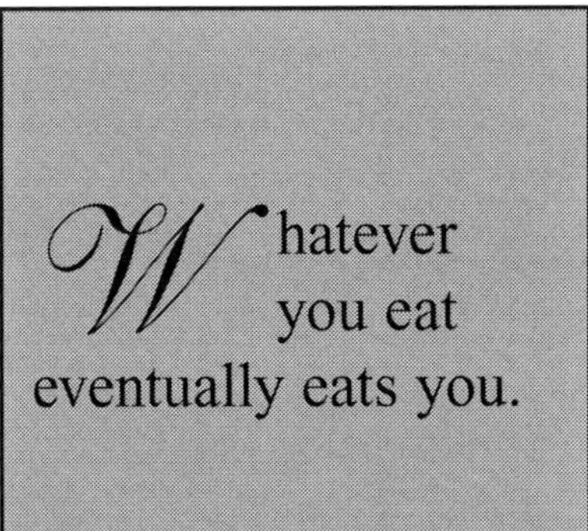

## Potential Doesn't Guarantee Performance

*He has lost connection with the Head, from whom the whole body, supported and held together by its ligaments and sinews, grows as God causes it to grow* (Colossians 2:19).

BOOK QUOTE: *Maximizing Your Potential* [Chapter 5]

God made everything with the ability to produce fruit or to reproduce itself. Yet, the potential to produce does not guarantee performance, nor does the quantity of fruit guarantee its quality. You may have a good idea that produces mediocrity-laden results. Or you may have big dreams that amount to very little. This is true because pregnancy is no guarantee of fruitfulness, and performance is not ensured by plans and dreams. Pregnancy and performance match when the potential to produce is properly cared for and developed.

You may have the potential to be a world-class architect, but your ability does not guarantee that you will reach this level of success. You may never progress beyond drawing doll house plans for your daughter or designing a model train layout for your son. An important key to producing what you are capable of is spending the necessary time and effort to promote the development of your talent. *You must cultivate and feed your potential.*

When God made man, shrubs had not yet appeared on the earth and plants had not yet sprung from the ground. Only after man's creation did God plant a garden and give it a river to water it. Why? Until then *"there was no man to work the ground"* (Genesis 2:5). The earth was pregnant but nothing was coming out because there was no one to care for the soil's babies.

Thus, we see that God created all life to depend on cultivation to maximize its existence because potential cannot be released without work. In essence, God said, "I can't allow these trees and plants to grow yet because they need cultivation when they start growing and there is no one to care for them." The fruit and seeds of many plants and trees were present in the ground, but the soil did not produce them until Adam cultivated the garden.

The New International Version of the Bible says that God gave Adam the responsibility of *working* the garden. The Revised Standard Version and the King James Version describe man's task as that of *tilling* the garden, and the Good News Bible speaks of *cultivating*. All point to man's assignment to help the garden produce to its fullest capacity. Thus, man was created to have a cultivating ministry by making the earth grow richer as he gives to it, feeds it, and adds to it.

> Pregnancy is no guarantee of fruitfulness, and performance is not ensured by plans and dreams.

## Winning the Prize Requires Running the Race

*You were running a good race. Who cut in on you and kept you from obeying the truth?* (Galatians 5:7).

BOOK QUOTE: *Maximizing Your Potential* [Chapter 5]

Potential is like soil. It must be worked and fed to produce fruit. King Solomon referred to this process of releasing the fruitfulness of man when he said, "*The purposes of a man's heart are deep waters, but a man of understanding draws them out*" (Proverbs 20:5). Notice, the drawing out of man's potential requires effort. Like the fisherman who brings forth the treasures of the sea by hard work and the farmer who harvests the fruit of the ground by the sweat of his brow, so man must labor to tap even a portion of God's potential within him.

The apostle Paul understood this need to put forth the effort to release his fruitfulness.

> *Do you not know that in a race all the runners run, but only one gets the prize? Run in such a way as to get the prize. Everyone who competes in the games goes into strict training. They do it to get a crown that will not last; but we do it to get a crown that will last forever. Therefore I do not run like a man running aimlessly; I do not fight like a man beating the air. No, I beat my body and make it my slave so that after I have preached to others, I myself will not be disqualified for the prize* (1 Corinthians 9:24-27).

Understanding and wisdom are the keys to the success of man's mission. His race to maximize everything God has given him begins with knowing what God requires of him and how He expects him to reach the finish line. The primary principle in cultivating one's life for maximum living is to destroy ignorance by the pursuit of knowledge, wisdom, and understanding.

Potential is like soil. It must be worked and fed to produce fruit.

## nderstanding Promotes Growth

*By wisdom a house is built, and through understanding it is established* (Proverbs 24:3).

BOOK QUOTE: *Maximizing Your Potential* [Chapter 5]

Maximizing our potential requires a process. Think of it this way. Suppose I wanted to create a beautiful vase to place in my living room, but I knew nothing about making pottery. My first step would need to be a visit to a master potter, or at least to the local library, to learn all I could about working clay into beautiful pieces. I would have to learn about the selection and preparation of the clay, the throwing and shaping of the vase on the potter's wheel, the length of time and the conditions for seasoning the raw pot, the proper temperature and duration for firing the pot in the kiln, etc. Much work, including many hours of practice on much lesser pots than the vase I hoped to create, would precede my reaching the goal of making a vase to place in my living room.

This procedure is not unlike the process we must undertake to maximize our potential. Knowledge and effort must coexist, but knowledge is the foundation for success. As we saw in the last chapter, God's wisdom and knowledge become available to us when we are connected to Him through the presence of His Spirit. An understanding of His ways and the discovery of His purposes are part of the treasure He has given us.

> *For the Lord gives wisdom, and from His mouth come knowledge and understanding. He holds victory in store for the upright, He is a shield to those whose walk is blameless, for He guards the course of the just and protects the way of His faithful ones. Then you will understand what is right and just and fair—every good path. For wisdom will enter your heart, and knowledge will be pleasant to your soul* (Proverbs 2:6-10).

Understand God's ways and discover the treasure He has given us.

## Knowledge Promotes Growth

*Apply your heart to instruction and your ears to words of knowledge* (Proverbs 23:12).

BOOK QUOTE: *Maximizing Your Potential* [Chapter 5]

The search for knowledge requires effort. You must seek it like a treasure that is precious to you. You cannot touch God's knowledge, however, without diligence and exertion.

> *My son, if you accept my words and store up my commands within you, turning your ear to wisdom and applying your heart to understanding, and if you call out for insight and cry aloud for understanding, and if you look for it as for silver and search for it as for hidden treasure, then you will understand the fear of the Lord and find the knowledge of God* (Proverbs 2:1-5).

> *By wisdom a house is built, and through understanding it is established; through knowledge its rooms are filled with rare and beautiful treasures. A wise man has great power, and a man of knowledge increases strength; for waging war you need guidance, and for victory many advisers* (Proverbs 24:3-6).

Building a house and waging war require great effort. They do not just happen. The same is true for storing up things. If you've ever canned or frozen fruits and vegetables in the summer to provide for your family in the winter, you know that many long, hot hours precede the final act of putting the finished jars on the shelf.

In a similar manner, removing treasures from the earth is also arduous and time-consuming. Wells must be drilled before oil can be pumped from the depths of the earth, and great shafts or tunnels must be dug before the mining of diamonds, silver, and other precious metals can be achieved. These are the images Solomon used to illustrate the strength and the dedication you will need to exercise if you hope to gain the knowledge that will advance the unleashing of your potential.

*Knowledge* must always precede action or much time and effort will be wasted through misguided efforts and dead-end directions. God, who planned your life and granted you the potential to fulfill His plans, works for and with you when you seek to know Him and to understand and follow His ways.

> Knowledge must always precede action.

## The Penalties of Neglecting Knowledge

*Wise men store up knowledge, but the mouth of a fool invites ruin* (Proverbs 10:14).

BOOK QUOTE: *Maximizing Your Potential* [Chapter 5]

Sadly, we often forfeit our potential because we neglect the wisdom, knowledge, and understanding that come from God alone. Solomon spoke of the consequences of this neglect, as did the prophet Hosea:

> *The teaching of the wise is a fountain of life, turning a man from the snares of death. Good understanding wins favor, but the way of the unfaithful is hard. Every prudent man acts out of knowledge, but a fool exposes his folly* (Proverbs 13:14-16).

> *My people are destroyed from lack of knowledge. "Because you have rejected knowledge, I also reject you as My priests; because you have ignored the law of your God, I also will ignore your children"* (Hosea 4:6).

A lack of knowledge is not the same as the unavailability of knowledge. Hosea says that God's people perish because they have *rejected* knowledge. Knowledge may surround us, but unless we apply it to our situation or use it to inform our decisions, it is useless to us. We cannot really excuse ourselves before the Lord saying, "I didn't know," because opportunities to gain knowledge abound in our world. We live in an age of an information explosion with libraries, tape ministries, teaching videos, television, and radio bombarding us on every side with opportunities to stretch our horizons and increase our knowledge. What we can confess to God is, "I rejected the opportunity to learn."

The saying, "What you don't know can't kill you," is simply not true. Too often we suffer loss because we did not take the opportunity to learn the facts about a particular subject. We perish because of what we don't know. *No matter how great your dream is, if you don't have the information relative to your plan, forget it.*

> Unless we apply knowledge to our situation, it is useless.

## The Penalties of Ignorance

*My people are destroyed from lack of knowledge. "Because you have rejected knowledge, I also reject you as My priests; because you have ignored the law of your God, I also will ignore your children"* (Hosea 4:6)

BOOK QUOTE: *Maximizing Your Potential* [Chapter 5]

The devil doesn't destroy God's people…the government doesn't destroy God's people…the economy doesn't destroy God's people…cocaine and marijuana don't destroy God's people. Ignorance destroys God's people. This one thing is behind every destructive influence in our lives.

*God rejects those who reject His knowledge*. Ignorance affects how God answers our prayers because we ask for things we don't need or shouldn't want. To ask rightly we must understand how we operate, how the devil operates, how the world operates, and how God operates. Asking God to do something for us before we understand these aspects of our situation is wasting our time and God's. He must reject everything we request because our prayers and His ways, will, and desires for us do not line up.

Research your dream before you start working to achieve it. Learn everything you can about the business you want to start or the people you want to reach. You need good information to make right decisions.

*God also ignores the children of those who ignore His knowledge*. This is true because your children learn what you know. If you don't know anything, they aren't going to learn anything, and they will thus make the same mistakes and have the same values and attitudes you have.

*Ignorance messes up the next generation*. It destroys not only your fruitfulness but your children's as well. Thus, you and your children reap what you sow, and *your* lack of information harms *them*. Our world is experiencing a multitude of human disasters that give evidence to this fact. Abortion, AIDS, environmental issues, drugs—all reveal the consequences of the rejection of knowledge by this generation and those that preceded us. In essence, ignorance is generational and transferable. The decision to pursue knowledge, improve understanding, and gain wisdom is a personal decision but not a private issue. Every book you read affects your grandchildren, so read and cultivate yourself for posterity.

> Ignorance affects how God answers our prayers.

## EVIEW the Principles From This Week:

- The potential to produce fruit does not guarantee either fruitfulness or the quality of the fruit.
- Potential must be worked (cultivated) and fed to produce fruit.
- Ignorance messes up the next generation because God rejects both those who reject knowledge, and their children.

## Twisted Values

*The teaching of the wise is a fountain of life, turning a man from the snares of death. Good understanding wins favor, but the way of the unfaithful is hard. Every prudent man acts out of knowledge, but a fool exposes his folly* (Proverbs 13:14-16).

BOOK QUOTE: *Maximizing Your Potential* [Chapter 5]

So many of us ignore the knowledge of God and His will. *Our ignorance of God's will and His ways has twisted our world. We devalue what God values and elevate what is insignificant to Him.* He sees the tremendous ability we have and we look at the earth houses that contain that treasure (see 2 Corinthians 4:7). He created us to show forth His power, but we are more interested in success by the world's standards. He affirms our ability to tap into His wisdom, but we make decisions based on the information we receive from our physical senses and our education.

Our poverty of knowledge is revealed by our inability to fulfill God's potential on our own. We live aimlessly without purpose, flitting from one thing to another and never accomplishing anything. Such life is a waste of time. Without a sense of purpose we are like stillborn babies.

Your potential will be wasted if you do not allow God to cleanse your sight and redirect your values. Then you can escape this purposeless existence. This occurs as you become aware of the world's standards and compare them carefully with God's. You may be surprised by what you find.

Allow God to cleanse your sight and redirect your values.

## Potential Under Attack

*Jesus said, "My kingdom is not of this world. If it were, My servants would fight to prevent My arrest by the Jews. But now My kingdom is from another place"* (John 18:36).

BOOK QUOTE: *Maximizing Your Potential* [Chapter 5]

The Bible says, "*Man looks at the outward appearance, but the Lord looks at the heart*" (1 Samuel 16:7c). It's time you and I reevaluate the standards of the world. Our cars are faster but weaker. Our clothes are sharper, but they come apart at the seams. Our vinyl shoes shine nicely, but they lack the durability of leather. What appears to be better may indeed be a compromise on value and worth. These upside-down values are attacking your potential.

Sadly, we are more concerned about the destruction of the earth's atmosphere than we are about the poisoning of our children by the airwaves they breathe in our homes. We are interested in the purity of the water we drink, but we do not monitor the pollutants that fill our minds. Our world is sick because we value the wrong things.

The values and standards of our world are not so different from those of the Pharisees. We save whales and try to protect endangered species, but we allow babies to be aborted. We cannot shoot flamingos, but we can take a scalpel and kill human fetuses.

We are sick. Therefore, we need to rethink our values and redefine the definition of pollution. *The most damaging pollutants that are poisoning our communities are not coming from cars, factories, and toxic waste dumps. They come from bookshelves, televisions, movie houses, and rental videos.* They come from our schools and colleges where teachers who do not believe in God teach our children that God is a crutch or a figment of their imaginations. Don't tell me not to shoot flamingos when teachers are shooting my children by teaching them corruption, error, evolution, and Godless philosophies!

The only way to combat this pollution is to examine what we are feeding our children and to cultivate with care the environments in which they grow. Then we can activate and stimulate their potential, and ours, with the proper nutrients and fertilizers. God determined this need to care for our potential when He placed Adam in the garden and commanded him to work, till, and cultivate it.

> We need to rethink our values and redefine the definition of pollution.

## A Twofold Process: Cultivating and Feeding Your Potential

*He is like a tree planted by streams of water, which yields its fruit in season and whose leaf does not wither. Whatever he does prospers* (Psalm 1:3).

BOOK QUOTE: *Maximizing Your Potential* [Chapter 5]

Potential must be cultivated and fed to produce fruit. But how do we do this? How do we cultivate and feed the talents, skills, and abilities we possess?

The definitions of cultivate include: a) to prepare and work to promote growth; b) to improve growth by labor and attention; c) to develop and refine by education and training; and d) to seek or promote, such as a friendship. To *feed* something means that we a) supply with nourishment; b) provide as food; c) furnish for consumption; and d) satisfy, minister, and gratify. All these definitions imply that the process is to be beneficial, not harmful. If the provisions do not supply nourishment that is essential for growth, they are not truly feeding us. Likewise, if the activity and attention do not help us to develop, refine, improve, and promote our abilities, skills, and talents, they cannot truly be called cultivation.

Even as seeds do not become plants overnight, so the wealth of our potential cannot be exposed and fulfilled in an instant. We must exert effort to cultivate what God has given us, and we must exercise care to fertilize and water it properly. As specific plants require certain nutrients and conditions to grow, so we must provide the right nourishment and environment to encourage the maximizing of our potential. These specifications have been set by God, who created us. To ignore them is to invite death.

> We must exert effort to cultivate what God has given us.

# Cultivating and Feeding the Three Dimensions of Potential

*Consecrate yourselves and be holy, because I am the Lord your God* (Leviticus 20:6).

BOOK QUOTE: *Maximizing Your Potential* [Chapter 5]

We are like a fallow field. We contain much fruit, but our fertility will not become evident until and unless we cultivate and feed our bodies, souls, and spirits. These are the three dimensions of potential. Cultivating and feeding work together to promote maximum growth and fulfillment. If we activate and stimulate our potential through challenging work and experiences, but we neglect to provide the appropriate fertilizers that will sustain and maintain it within those situations, before long growth will become stunted and eventually stop. Likewise, if we feed our bodies, souls, and spirits according to our Manufacturer's specifications, but we fail to foster and develop occasions when we can try new things and reach for new goals, we will still diminish the effective release of our potential. Both cultivating and feeding are necessary for wholesome growth.

Each dimension of our potential—body, soul, and spirit—has definite specifications and materials for cultivation and explicit requirements in fertilizers. These specifications or requirements prescribed by our Manufacturer ensure that each part of our being operates at peak performance and achieves maximum fruitfulness. They are essential ingredients for unveiling who we can be and what we can do.

You are what you eat. This is true for all three dimensions of potential. If you eat excessive fatty foods, you will gain weight and your face will be covered with pimples. If you feed your mind with trash, your thoughts will be in the gutter. If you feed your spirit the information received through the senses of your body and the education of your soul, neglecting God's wisdom and knowledge, you will operate from worldly standards and values.

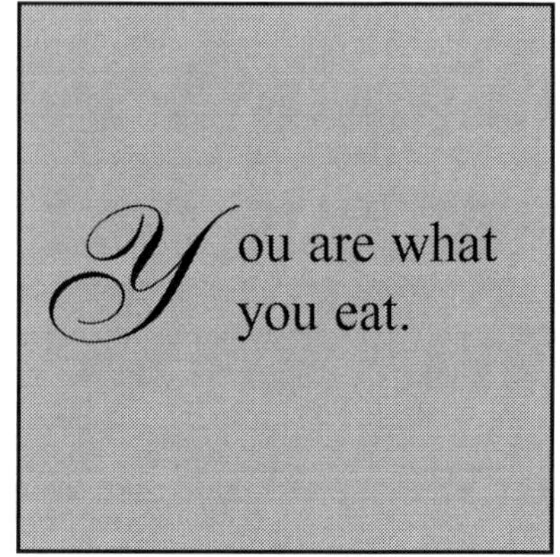

# Cultivate and Feed Your Body

*...offer your bodies as living sacrifices, holy and pleasing to God—this is your spiritual act of worship* (Romans 12:1).

BOOK QUOTE: *Maximizing Your Potential* [Chapter 5]

Your body is a precise machine that requires proper food, exercise, and rest. Healthy food, regular exercise, and scheduled periods of rest are essential for it to operate at its maximum potential. Physical health deteriorates when sweets, fats, or other harmful foods are stuffed into the body, and the body's strength and endurance are lessened if exercise (work) is missing from your daily routine. Likewise, the absence of rest depletes the body's resources until exhaustion and even collapse eventually occur. Cultivate and feed your body by living within a healthy routine that includes nutritious food, moderate but systematic exercise, and regular sleep and relaxation.

*Second*, the cultivation and feeding of your body requires that you use it with discretion, setting it apart for its intended uses. Consider the proper use of your body when you are working or exercising. For example, safeguard your back by bending your knees to lift a heavy load.

This requirement to use your body with discretion also means that you should treat it with respect and exercise caution not to abuse it. Take care not to allow cigarettes, alcohol, and other harmful substances to enter it. As the apostle Paul warns us:

> *For we must all appear before the judgment seat of Christ, that each one may receive what is due him for the things done while in the body, whether good or bad* (2 Corinthians 5:10).

Each person will have to give an account for what he did with his body.

*Third*, you must cultivate your physical body by preserving it and protecting it from pollutants. If you are going to do something for the world, if you are really going to contribute to the effectiveness and the productivity of your nation, you cannot be sick because you cannot be effective if you are sick. As the apostle Paul says:

> *Do you not know that your body is a temple of the Holy Spirit, who is in you, whom you have received from God? ...Therefore honor God with your body* (1 Corinthians 6:19-20).

For something to be a sacrifice, it must be valuable and worth giving. You cannot effectively honor God if your body is too heavy or your heart is weak because you have filled your body with cholesterol-producing foods. Preserve your body by understanding and obeying the Manufacturer's directions. You are responsible to protect your physical temple. Cultivate your body.

> You are responsible to protect your physical temple.

## ultivate Your Soul

*Finally, brothers, whatever is true, whatever is noble, whatever is right, whatever is pure, whatever is lovely, whatever is admirable—if anything is excellent or praiseworthy—think about such things* (Philippians 4:8).

BOOK QUOTE: *Maximizing Your Potential* [Chapter 5]

Your soul consists of your mind, your will, and your emotions. *What goes into your mind always influences what comes out.*

Be careful, then, to *convert your mind* by filling it with godly, uplifting materials. Use your moments of leisure to uplift rather than tear down.

Likewise, *cultivate your mind.* Use the resources available to your mind to inspire you to activate your dreams and reach for new goals. Your mind is a powerful tool created by God for the good of mankind.

It's a pity to die with water when people are dying of thirst. Yet it happens every day as people who have the answers to the world's problems refuse to feed and cultivate their minds so they can reach into the deep wells of their possibilities and pull out what the world needs. Look to the careful cultivation and feeding of your mind. Remember, the person who *doesn't* read is no better off than the person who *can't.*

*The cultivation of your soul also includes the discipline of your will.* Discipline is training or teaching someone or something to obey a particular command or to live by a certain standard. The discipline of your will is particularly important because the will is the decision maker. If you refuse to discipline your will, you won't be successful in fulfilling your potential because your will determines your decisions, which govern your potential.

*The cultivating of your soul also requires that you control your emotions.* Too often we allow our emotions to control us instead of our controlling them.

Jesus said that *the soul is the most important dimension of our make-up because the soul is both our receiving center and our distribution center.* It receives information through our physical senses and discernment through our spirits and it sends directions back to both our bodies and our spirits. Thus, our souls process information from both the physical and the spiritual worlds.

Too often the soul is neglected and permitted to pick up information that is not good for the spirit. Maximize your potential by cultivating and feeding your soul so that your spirit may fellowship with God, who is the source of all potential.

> It's a pity to die with water when people are dying of thirst.

## Cultivate and Feed Your Spirit

*Jesus answered, "It is written: 'Man does not live on bread alone'"* (Luke 4:4).

BOOK QUOTE: *Maximizing Your Potential* [Chapter 5]

Maximizing your potential begins with your decision to accept Jesus Christ as your Lord and Savior because the measure of your true potential is your spirit. Until you become reconnected with God through faith in Jesus Christ and the presence of His Spirit in your heart, you are spiritually dead, and the potential of your spirit is unavailable to you. Then your mind can only be controlled by what you receive through your senses and your mind.

> *Those who live according to the sinful nature have their minds set on what that nature desires; but those who live in accordance with the Spirit have their minds set on what the Spirit desires. The mind of sinful man is death, but the mind controlled by the Spirit is life and peace* (Romans 8:5-6).

The secret wisdom of God concerning your potential (see 1 Corinthians 2:7-11) cannot influence your life if His Spirit is not present in your heart because only God's Spirit knows and understands God's plans and purposes for you. These were written long before your birth. They contain the information you need to live to the fullest and to achieve everything you were sent to do. Attaining your maximum potential is impossible if you do not cultivate and feed your spirit by hooking yourself up to God and abiding in Him. (See John 15:1-8.)

Cultivating and feeding your potential is a second key to maximizing your potential. As you pay attention to the fertilizer you give your body, soul, and spirit, and the work you do to keep them healthy by the Manufacturer's specifications, you will be surprised and delighted by the many things you can accomplish and the satisfaction and joy in life you will experience. *You must cultivate and feed your potential according to God's specifications and with His materials.*

> Show me your friends, and I will show you your future.

## REVIEW the Principles From This Week:

- God designed the potential of your body, your soul, and your spirit to be maximized by specific fertilizers and environments that promote positive growth and development.
- Cultivate and feed your body by getting the proper food, exercise, and rest, by using it with discretion, and by preserving and protecting it from pollutants.
- Cultivate and feed your soul by feeding your mind positive, Godly information, by disciplining your will to discover and live by God's wisdom and purposes, and by governing your emotions with God's truth.
- Cultivate and feed your spirit by living from God's secret wisdom dispensed through His Holy Spirit.

# Sharing Maximizes and Fulfills Potential

*Command them to do good, to be rich in good deeds, and to be generous and willing to share* (1 Timothy 6:18).

BOOK QUOTE: *Maximizing Your Potential* [Chapter 6]

Silently the orchestra waited. What would this new masterpiece of their beloved conductor be like? He had promised that it would be different from anything he had ever written. As each player received his part, he looked at it in surprise. Although each score contained some notes, there were many more rests than notes. All assumed the other instruments must have the lead part for the piece.

When they started to play, however, it soon became evident that no one had the lead. The trumpets would play for a few measures, then the trombones, after which the clarinets or the flutes picked up the tune. Although it was true that the parts had some resemblance to each other, no clear melody was evident. The longer the musicians played, the stranger the music became, but they kept playing because it seemed to be what the conductor expected.

Then the maestro passed out another set of music. This time when he lifted his baton, anticipation filled each face. Although the scores still contained rests, they were considerably fewer and they seemed to be at fitting places.

After the orchestra had played for a few minutes, the conductor stopped them and asked, "Do you understand what I have done? If you look at the notes on the two scores, you will notice that they are the same. It is the rests that are different. The first time, one of you played a little, then another, then a third player. You never played together. I did this to show you that each part is important, but it is meaningless without the others. When we all play the right notes at the right time, blending the music and sharing the unique sounds of each instrument, a beautiful melody emerges. Unlike the strange awkwardness of the first score, the second score highlights each instrument at the appropriate time, with the other instruments playing the supporting chords and the countermelodies. This is the way music is supposed to sound."

> The wealth of our potential is minimized when we do not share it with others.

This blending and support is also the way potential is meant to be used. Even as the beauty of a symphony is minimized when each instrument's part is played in isolation, so the wealth of our potential is minimized when we do not share it with others. Potential is maximized and fulfilled only when it is shared. This sharing of potential is God's way of bringing to pass His plans and purposes for men and women.

## You Share God's Potential

*In a large house there are articles not only of gold and silver, but also of wood and clay; some are for noble purposes and some for ignoble. If a man cleanses himself from the latter, he will be an instrument for noble purposes, made holy, useful to the Master and prepared to do any good work* (2 Timothy 2:20-21).

BOOK QUOTE: *Maximizing Your Potential* [Chapter 6]

Everything God called into being He gave a purpose that meshes with the larger purpose of the world. Every animal, bird, fish, insect, reptile, plant, and tree is connected to the whole of creation. If one species becomes extinct, its death disrupts and impacts the entire ecosystem. In essence, each part of God's world in some way balances and enriches the rest.

Human beings are God's crowning creative act. The treasure He put in us He took from Himself. He chose to give us part of His potential so we could use it for Him. God could have run the world by Himself, but He brought us into His plan so we could bring glory to Him by revealing all He is. He doesn't need our involvement to accomplish all He is capable of doing and being, but He wants us to enjoy the blessing of participating in His purpose. *Your gifts, talents, and abilities are your share of the endowment God gives to mankind to bless all creation.*

God finds satisfaction in watching you discover and use your potential. In essence, you show forth God's nature and reveal His potency when you fulfill your potential. *Your purpose is equal to your potential, and your potential is equal to your purpose.* The more you understand your purpose, the more you will discover what you can do.

Thus, God gets excited when you take authority over your bad habits. He enjoys watching you discover and use the deposit of His power and wisdom within you. Sometimes it would be easier for God to just snap His fingers and take over, but then He'd lose the joy of watching you order your life and the pleasure of seeing you expose His potential.

There are some things He'd like to do for you, but He's holding back so you can enjoy your success when you do them yourself. God has shared His potential with you, now He wants to enjoy the benefits of that gift. His joy overflows when you release all He has given you.

> God finds satisfaction in watching you discover and use your potential.

## Potential Is Never Given for Itself

*Therefore, as we have opportunity, let us do good to all people, especially to those who belong to the family of believers* (Galations 6:10).

BOOK QUOTE: *Maximizing Your Potential* [Chapter 6]

When I was in college, I went on a tour of Europe. After several days, I lost interest in all I was seeing because my fiancée, who is now my wife, was not there to share it with me. On that trip I learned the truth of this principle: *Potential is never given for itself. Whatever God gives to you, He gives for others.*

Even as a solitary instrument cannot produce the majestic music of a symphonic orchestra, so human beings cannot glorify their Creator in isolation. I need your potential to maximize mine, and you need my potential to maximize yours. All we have been given is meant to be shared.

After man had finished naming all the animals and no suitable helper for him was found among them, God performed another significant act of creation. Why? "*It is not good for the man to be alone*" (Genesis 2:18).

God did not make woman because man asked for a wife, nor because a helper for man was a good idea. Man *needed* a companion because he could not realize his potential without sharing it with someone. His solitary existence was not good.

To be solitary or alone is not the same as being single. To be alone is to be isolated and cut off from others. Communication is impossible because you have no one like yourself to share with. This is what God says is not good.

To be single is to be unmarried. Marriage is not a requirement or a prerequisite for the fulfillment of your potential. You do not necessarily *need* a husband or a wife. What you do need, however, is someone with whom you can share your potential. This is true because *your personal satisfaction is connected to your fulfilling God's purpose for your life, and your purpose cannot be achieved in isolation*. You need those people who will call forth your potential and into whom you can pour your life. *You may be wired to be single, but you are not designed to live isolated and alone.*

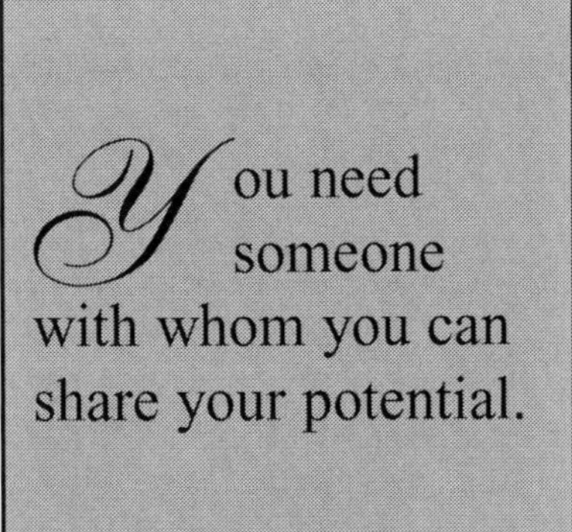

## Caution on Sharing

*Do not envy wicked men, do not desire their company* (Proverbs 24:1).

BOOK QUOTE: *Maximizing Your Potential* [Chapter 6]

You must be careful when, how, and with whom you share your potential. Sharing your hidden wealth in a manner that transgresses God's laws of limitation is not good. All your natural abilities, all the gifts you have cultivated, and all the knowledge you have accumulated are yours to share within the context of God's principles, plans, and purposes. *God created everything to fulfill its potential within the limitations of certain laws*. In other words, He specified the boundaries within which all things can perform to their maximum capabilities.

Neither two males nor two females can produce a baby because man's potential is fulfilled by sharing it with a woman, and woman's is fulfilled by sharing it with a man. For their potential to be fruitful, men and women must share their physical potential within the context of a male-female relationship that is within the bonds of marriage.

What is known today as an alternative lifestyle is truly the abuse of natural destiny and the violation of human nature because it prevents this fulfillment of purpose. Woman was created to receive, and man was created to give. Thus, their shared potentials complement each other. A man cannot be fruitful without a woman, nor can a woman be fruitful without a man. Two givers or two receivers cannot work together to produce fruit. Be careful that you share your physical potential with the right person.

*Your soulical potential is fulfilled by sharing it within the context of the family*. Here a child learns to give and receive love and affection. Very often psychological and emotional problems arise when love is not felt and expressed in the formative years. If a boy never feels loved by his mother, he may become confused later in life if a male starts meeting some of those needs. Then his ability to give and receive affection, affirmation, and attention seeks to be fulfilled in the wrong context.

Men can enjoy deep and lasting friendships with men, but they must be careful what they share within that relationship. Certain things are good to share; others are not. The same is true of friendships between women. God intends that you will fulfill your basic soulical potential within the context of the family.

> Your soulical potential is fulfilled by sharing it within the context of the family.

# otential Is Fulfilled When it Is Released

*Give to him as the Lord your God has blessed you* (Deuteronomy 15:14b).

BOOK QUOTE: *Maximizing Your Potential* [Chapter 6]

*Potential is fulfilled only when it is given to others. You cannot enjoy or fulfill your potential if you keep it to yourself.* Everything God gave you, He gave for me and everyone else. He blesses you with additional gifts when you use the blessings you have already received to bless others. In other words, *fruitfulness is always given to make you a blessing to others. You are blessed when you take what you have and give it away*. This is true because sharing your potential both reveals hidden possibilities and releases additional gifts.

A seed produces nothing if it does not surrender its potential to the soil. If it says, "I'm going to keep what I have," its potential to produce a tree is lost. Only as the seed relinquishes its outer shell and puts down roots that permit it to receive nourishment from the soil can it release its potential to be a tree. Through self-giving, the seed is transformed and gives birth to new possibilities. Then the tree, having been blessed by the gift of the seed, begins to push out blossoms, showing forth some of its fruit. In time, it yields fruit with more seed that can continue the cycle of giving. If anything along the way chooses to withhold its potential—be it the seed, the tree, or the fruit—the cycle is broken and much potential is lost.

This same truth is evident in the music of an orchestra. The instruments' potential to produce music cannot be fulfilled until the individual notes are released by the players. If even one player refuses to release what he possesses, the loss extends far beyond the one who withholds his contribution because the withheld potential of one affects the potential of all. Indeed, the music either remains hidden and dormant or it emerges misshapen and incomplete. All suffer loss—musicians and music—if even one person or one instrument refuses to cooperate. Only as all give of what they possess can the potential of the music be released.

> Everything God gave you, He gave for me and everyone else.

## Giving Exposes Potential

*"In everything I did, I showed you that by this kind of hard work we must help the weak, remembering the words the Lord Jesus himself said: 'It is more blessed to give than to receive'"* (Acts 20:35).

BOOK QUOTE: *Maximizing Your Potential* [Chapter 6]

Treasures that are hidden and locked up benefit no one. Say, for example, that your grandmother gave you a beautiful necklace that she wore as a bride. If you keep it locked in a safe and never wear it, its beauty is wasted.

Or perhaps you have wedding gifts of beautiful china, sterling silver, and fine crystal that you have never used to serve a meal. You're wasting the potential of those dishes. They cannot do what they are supposed to do sitting on a shelf. People bought them for you to use. *Treasure is useless unless you expose it.* Potential can never be attained if it has no opportunity to give.

This was the power of John F. Kennedy's words, spoken at his inauguration to be the president of the United States: "Ask not what your country can do for you, but what you can do for your country." Kennedy's words prompt us to focus on what we can give instead of what we can get. It is through our giving that we discover what we can do and be.

This was also the wisdom shared by the apostle Paul, "*It is more blessed to give than to receive*" (Acts 20:35). Releasing what you have received benefits you and others. Holding on to a treasure forfeits the blessing inherit in the treasure, and no one profits from it. Like the seed, *you must release what God has stored in you for the world.* You do this by releasing seeds into the soil of the lives of others.

Potential can never be attained if it has no opportunity to give.

## od Is a Giver

*How great is the love the Father has lavished on us, that we should be called children of God! And that is what we are! The reason the world does not know us is that it did not know Him* (1 John 3:1).

BOOK QUOTE: *Maximizing Your Potential* [Chapter 6]

God is constantly releasing seeds into the soil of your life. He is a giver and He created you to be like Him. The foundation of God's giving nature is revealed in His purpose for creating men and women.

God made Adam and Eve so He would have someone to love and bless—more children like Christ, His Incarnate Son. Although God possessed all He had created, those things were useless to Him until He created man to release their potential by using His creations and, thereby, showing off His fullness.

In essence, God, who is love, created man to fulfill His potential to love. Love is worthless until it is given away. It must have an object to be fulfilled. Therefore, God needed something on which He could lavish His love, something that could understand and appreciate what He had to give. Of all God's creatures, only men and women share God's Spirit and, thus, can appreciate His love.

You are the object of God's love. Because love can be fulfilled only when the receiver of love is like the giver, He created you like Himself, to be loved by Him and to love as He loves.

> God, who is love, created man to fulfill His potential to love.

## EVIEW the Principles From This Week:

- Potential cannot be maximized and fulfilled unless it is shared.
- God shares with you so you can share with others.
- Isolation is not good because it prevents sharing.
- You must share your potential within the limits of God's laws.

## The Mutuality of Giving

*They are always generous and lend freely; their children will be blessed* (Psalm 37:26).

BOOK QUOTE: *Maximizing Your Potential* [Chapter 6]

Think about the last time you bought a card or a gift for a spouse or a close friend. Much of the pleasure in giving the gift is found in choosing something that will delight the one to whom you are giving it. The gift's meaning is found in the shared love of the giver and the recipient.

This is the meaning of Jesus' words:

> *Do not give dogs what is sacred; do not throw your pearls to pigs. If you do, they may trample them under their feet, and then turn and tear you to pieces* (Matthew 7:6).

A pet cannot appreciate a diamond ring, but your sweetheart will. Why? She understands the thoughts and the feelings that both prompted the gift and are revealed in it. The one who receives a gift must understand and appreciate the giver before the gift can have meaning. Through giving love is released.

You have been physically birthed by the giving of your parents and spiritually birthed by the giving of Christ. Even as your parents gave the seed of their bodies to release their potential to produce another human being, so Jesus Christ gave the seed that brings new life by releasing His potential to be a Savior. Their giving brings you life and the opportunity to continue the cycle of giving. Joy is found in participating in the pattern of giving, receiving, and giving again. This pattern of releasing potential by giving and receiving is particularly visible in the biblical concept of a blessing.

## Blessed to Be a Blessing

*The fruit of the righteous is a tree of life, and he who wins souls is wise* (Proverbs 11:30).

BOOK QUOTE: *Maximizing Your Potential* [Chapter 6]

The giving of a blessing is an important image in Scripture. Whether it is God, a father, or some other person giving the blessing, it is a gift that exposes possibilities and releases power. In each case, the blessing confirmed what God had already purposed for the one who received the blessing.

Blessings are never given solely for the benefit of the one who receives them. That means all God has given you—your clothes, food, house, car, bike, education, intelligence, personality, etc.—are given to you so you can maximize them by sharing them. You cannot release the full potential of anything if you do not share it.

Abraham not only received a blessing from God; he was also made a blessing to others:

> *I will make you into a great nation and I will bless you; I will make your name great, and you will be a blessing. I will bless those who bless you, and whoever curses you I will curse; and all peoples on earth will be blessed through you* (Genesis 12:2-3).

God operates from this perspective: "I'm going to share with you so you will be blessed by My sharing and you, in turn, will bless others by your sharing." He gives to you so you can share His potential by being motivated to pass on all He gives you. Therefore, *the task of humanity is to emulate the attitude of God by drawing from each person all he or she possesses*. You exist to pull things from me, and I exist to pull things from you.

God finds joy in giving to you so you can give to others. He blesses you to bless another. No matter what your circumstances are, there is some way you can share your potential with others. If you are homebound, give yourself through prayer or the ministry of encouragement through cards, letters, and phone calls. Or perhaps you are retired with few financial resources but much time. Pour yourself into a child.

Whatever your blessings, find some way to share them. This is God's intention for giving them to you. Your gifts may be different from mine, but their value is equal if we serve the same Lord with the same Spirit (see 1 Corinthians 12:1-7). *Your gifts are for me and my gifts are for you. Together we can bless the world.* This is how potential is released.

> Blessings are never given solely for the benefit of the one who receives them.

## Receiving Without Giving Results in Destruction

*Look at the birds of the air; they do not sow or reap or store away in barns, and yet your heavenly Father feeds them. Are you not much more valuable than they?* (Matthew 6:26).

BOOK QUOTE: *Maximizing Your Potential* [Chapter 6]

*True joy is found not in what you accomplish but in who benefits from your success*. Dying to yourself and giving for me and others will reap for you the joy of seeing your efforts reproduced many times over in us. Your sharing will give life to many.

If, however, you refuse to share, you will destroy both God's joy in giving to you and your joy in passing on what He gives. You will also forfeit His blessings because those who wish to receive from the abundance of God must use wisely all He gives. This is true because selfishness concerns itself only with its own prosperity and well-being. It lacks interest in the concerns and needs of others.

You cannot emulate the giving nature of God if you retain all you have for your own wants and needs; neither can your bucket draw from the deep waters in me. Such selfishness kills potential and lessens the likelihood that you will be blessed by my potential.

True wisdom is understanding this interdependence: "*The purposes of a man's heart are deep waters, but a man of understanding draws them out*" (Proverbs 20:5). This cannot occur, however, if we are consumed by thoughts of ourselves.

True joy is found not in what you accomplish but in whom benefits from your success.

## Selfishness Destroys Personal Happiness and Satisfaction

*Now all has been heard; here is the conclusion of the matter: Fear God and keep His commandments, for this is the whole duty of man. For God will bring every deed into judgment, including every hidden thing, whether it is good or evil* (Ecclesiastes 12:13-14).

BOOK QUOTE: *Maximizing Your Potential* [Chapter 6]

You were created to give. When you lavish your potential on yourself, your potential and all you accomplish by using it lose their meaning. King Solomon learned this when he went through life doing one thing after another for himself.

> *"Meaningless! Meaningless!" says the Teacher. "Utterly meaningless! Everything is meaningless." What does man gain from all his labor at which he toils under the sun?*
>
> *I undertook great projects.... I made gardens and parks and planted all kinds of fruit trees in them. I made reservoirs.... I bought male and female slaves.... I also owned more herds and flocks than anyone in Jerusalem before me. I amassed silver and gold for myself....*
>
> *I denied myself nothing my eyes desired; I refused my heart no pleasure. My heart took delight in all my work, and this was the reward for all my labor. Yet when I surveyed all that my hands had done and what I had toiled to achieve, everything was meaningless....*
>
> *So I hated life, because the work that is done under the sun was grievous to me. All of it was meaningless, a chasing after the wind. I hated all the things I had toiled for under the sun, because I must leave them to one who comes after me* (Ecclesiastes 1:2-3; 2:4-8,10-11,17-18).

Work and effort that focus on self are meaningless. It doesn't matter what you accomplish, none of it will bring you satisfaction unless you give from what you have. Nor will your accumulated riches bring you happiness, for they are useless and meaningless if you don't understand and seek to fulfill God's purpose for giving them to you.

You must share what you earn before it can bring you pleasure and satisfaction because sharing ensures that the blessings you have received will be passed on and others will also be blessed. This basic principle of sharing is foundational for maximizing your potential.

*If you refuse to share, your potential will kill you* because you cannot enjoy freedom in your conscience when you are acting against your natural design to give. *Pleasure will end, but conscience abides until it has completed its assignment.* It works on you until you acknowledge the error of your ways. Only by releasing all God has given you can you have a pure and holy conscience before Him and find meaning in life. Pursuing selfish pleasure always destroys the one who seeks it. In a similar manner, unshared potential consumes the person who seeks to hold it tightly for selfish gain.

> Work and effort that focus on self are meaningless.

## Selfishness Destroys the Joy of Giving

*By Myself I can do nothing; I judge only as I hear, and My judgment is just, for I seek not to please Myself but Him who sent Me* (John 5:30).

BOOK QUOTE: *Maximizing Your Potential* [Chapter 6]

*First, selfishness destroys God's pleasure in watching you pass on all He has given you.* Near the end of His life, Jesus reminded His disciples that they could not accomplish anything apart from Him. The same is true for our lives. Without this consistent association with God, our fruitfulness suffers and we become no more than a branch to be thrown into the fire. The power of potential is gone. (See John 15.)

This absence of power hurts both the person who has withdrawn from God and God Himself. He created us to bear fruit that reflects His nature and glory. When we neglect to fulfill this purpose, we grieve the heart of God.

God's pleasure in Jesus was evident when He spoke from a cloud at the time of Jesus' baptism and again on the mountain of transfiguration (see Matthew 3:17 and 17:5). The source of His pleasure was Jesus' willingness to fulfill the purpose for which He had been sent into the world and to release His potential (see John 8:29 and 17:4-6,10,13).

> *Let us fix our eyes on Jesus, the author and perfecter of our faith, who for the joy set before Him endured the cross, scorning its shame, and sat down at the right hand of the throne of God* (Hebrews 12:2).

Obedience. Jesus found joy in doing what God asked of Him. This is also the source of God's pleasure in us. As we obediently share all that God has given us for the world, we will find that He delights in us. If, however, we decline to fulfill His plans and purposes and refuse to allow His nature and likeness to govern our thoughts and actions, we destroy the fullness of joy we could have brought Him had we sought His purposes and obeyed His principles.

*Second, selfishness destroys the joy of giving.* When we hoard and hide what we receive from God, we deny ourselves the delights of passing on God's gifts. It is not the magnitude of our gift but simply the act of sharing that produces joy. When we refuse to share we deny ourselves this benefit.

*Third, selfishness destroys the joy of seeing others share what we have given them.* The apostle Paul also speaks of this joy.

> *In all my prayers for all of you, I always pray with joy because of your partnership in the gospel from the first day until now, being confident of this, that He who began a good work in you will carry it on to completion until the day of Christ Jesus* (Philippians 1:4-6).

Sharing is a privilege to be sought and enjoyed.

## Selfishness Destroys the Gift

*This is how we know what love is: Jesus Christ laid down his life for us. And we ought to lay down our lives for our brothers* (1 John 3:16).

BOOK QUOTE: *Maximizing Your Potential* [Chapter 6]

> *In all my prayers for all of you, I always pray with joy because of your partnership in the gospel from the first day until now, being confident of this, that He who began a good work in you will carry it on to completion until the day of Christ Jesus* (Philippians 1:4-6).

Partnership speaks of sharing. When we fail to share our potential, this partnership is forfeited and the fruit for which we were chosen and appointed is lost.

> *You did not choose Me, but I chose you and appointed you to go and bear fruit—fruit that will last. Then the Father will give you whatever you ask in My name* (John 15:16).

God mourns for this loss because the loss of potential limits His activity on earth and destroys the joy of sharing—for God, for ourselves, and for those with whom we might have shared. Selfishness always destroys the joy of giving.

God is often hurt because people are pregnant with great treasure but they keep it to themselves. Say, for example, that you are a medical researcher who discovers a cure for leukemia. Instead of sharing the results of your research with others, you carefully guard your secret knowledge so no one else can take credit for your discovery. Meanwhile, many people needlessly die. In time, your God-given talent to heal will be destroyed. Because you are so concerned that someone may receive the recognition you deserve, you will lose the desire to study and to receive new medical insights. Your selfishness in keeping the treasure to yourself ultimately destroys the very gift that is the source of your wealth. *Potential that is not shared self-destructs.*

> When we fail to share our potential, our partnership is forfeited and the fruit for which we were chosen and appointed is lost.

## elfishness Stops the Flow of God's Blessings

*For where you have envy and selfish ambition, there you find disorder and every evil practice* (James 3:16).

BOOK QUOTE: *Maximizing Your Potential* [Chapter 6]

*Selfishness destroys the cycle of giving initiated by God.* Very often you have not because you lavish upon yourself all you have received. God will give you all things if you ask to receive so you may pass it on to others. I'm blessed because I have a passion to pass on to you all that God has given to me.

God expects you to pass on to another all He has poured into you. Get rid of it. Make room for more of the vast quantity He has prepared to pour into you. You hold up God's plans and purposes when you cling to your blessings, and you cap off your potential when you refuse to share all you have received. Jesus said:

> *Give, and it will be given to you. A good measure, pressed down, shaken together and running over, will be poured into your lap. For with the measure you use, it will be measured to you* (Luke 6:38).

Some of you are blessed with tremendous talents, gifts, and knowledge. I wonder what is happening to them. Flow with your God-given abilities. Use them to bless others and to glorify God. Don't worry if your gifts and talents aren't as grand as you'd like. Use them to benefit others, and you will see them grow. *Sharing all God has given you is a must if you want to maximize your potential.*

> God expects you to pass on to another all He has poured into you.

## EVIEW the Principles From This Week:

- Giving transforms and reveals potential.
- God's blessings in your life expose His power within you and the possibilities that are your potential.
- The selfish retention of God's gifts destroys:
  1. God's joy in giving.
  2. Your personal happiness and fulfillment.
  3. Your joy in giving to others.
  4. Your joy in watching others share what they have received from you.
  5. The gifts that are given.
  6. The continuing evidence in your life of God's blessings.
- Giving your potential to others is a basic key to maximizing all that God has given you for your blessing and the benefit of others.

## Live for Tomorrow

*One generation will commend your works to another; they will tell of your mighty acts* (Psalm 145:4).

BOOK QUOTE: *Maximizing Your Potential* [Chapter 7 and Preface]

*The greatest threat to being all you could be is satisfaction with who you are.* What you could do is always endangered by what you have done. There are millions of individuals who have buried their latent talents, gifts, and abilities in the cemetery of their last accomplishment. They have settled for less than their best. I believe that the enemy of best is good, and the strength of good is the norm. The power of the norm is the curse of our society. It seems like the world is designed to make "the norm" comfortable and "the average" respectable. What a tragedy!

A quick glance at history reveals that the individuals who impacted their generations and affected the world most dramatically were individuals who, because of a circumstance, pressure, or decision, challenged the tide of convention, stretched the boundaries of tradition, and violated the expectations of the norm. *Few great things have ever been done within the confines of the accepted norm.*

In essence, history is always made by individuals who dare to challenge and exceed the accepted norm. Why follow a path when you can make a trail? It is incumbent upon each of us to ask ourselves the following questions: Have we become all we are capable of? Have we extended ourselves to the maximum? Have we done the best we can do? Have we used our gifts, talents, and abilities to their limit?

Just as a seed has a forest within it, so we contain much more than is evident at birth. Everything is designed by God not only to reproduce itself but also to transfer its life and treasure to the next generation. Potential is not fully maximized until it reproduces itself in the following generation.

An old Chinese proverb that states, "*the end of a thing is greater than its beginning*," rings true for our lives. King Solomon concurred with this truth: "*The race is not to the swift or the battle to the strong…*" (Ecclesiastes 9:11b). Every individual is therefore responsible to live to the fullest for the sake of the following generation. King Solomon states it this way: "*A good man leaves an inheritance for his children's children*" (Proverbs 13:22a).

> To live for today is shortsighted; to live for tomorrow is vision.

## A Seedless Life

*Now he who supplies seed to the sower and bread for food will also supply and increase your store of seed and will enlarge the harvest of your righteousness* (2 Corinthians 9:10).

BOOK QUOTE: *Maximizing Your Potential* [Chapter 7]

I will never forget the day I first discovered seedless fruit. One of the pleasures I enjoy within my very busy schedule is accompanying my wife to the food store, which gives us time to plan our family meals and discover new items together.

On one of these occasions, as we approached the produce section, I was intrigued to see a large sign introducing seedless grapes and oranges. At first I rejoiced at the prospect of being able to enjoy grapes for the first time without the inconvenience of having to eject the seeds. (No doubt this newly produced hybrid was developed in response to the market demand for fruit that could be enjoyed without the discomfort of seeds.) So I quickly picked up two pounds of red and white grapes and a bag of oranges, looking forward to eating them.

My impatience to experience the thrill of seedless grapes prompted me to place the bag of grapes beside me in the car so I could enjoy them while I was driving home. What a pleasure, to sink my teeth into fresh, juicy, sweet grapes without having to worry about seeds. It was like a dream come true. Soon after we had arrived home, I sliced into an orange and stood amazed at the fact of a seedless fruit. Again I experienced a new pleasure, sucking the juice from a seedless ripe orange.

Later that day I returned to the kitchen to enjoy the rest of my new discovery and to marvel at this feat of botanical science. Suddenly, in the midst of my pleasure, I was startled by this thought: "If these grapes and oranges have no seeds, how can they reproduce another generation of fruit?" After all, the life and power is in the seed, not the fruit. Immediately I realized that I was enjoying momentary pleasure at the expense of generational reproduction. The fruit was beautiful, ripe, sweet, juicy, and pleasing to eat, but it lacked the potential to transfer its uniqueness to another generation. *In reality the tree is not in the fruit but in the seed.*

> Life and power is in the seed, not the fruit.

## Life and Power Is in the Seed

*For as the soil makes the sprout come up and a garden causes seeds to grow, so the Sovereign Lord will make righteousness and praise spring up before all nations* (Isaiah 61:11).

BOOK QUOTE: *Maximizing Your Potential* [Chapter 7]

God created seeds to guarantee the fulfillment of future generations. Every plant, animal, bird, reptile, and insect possesses within itself the ability and potential to reproduce itself and to continue the propagation of its species. Consider then the prospect if every seed decided to germinate, develop into a beautiful tree, and have juicy, sweet, *seedless* fruit. What would be the result? A natural tragedy! Chaos would ensue and ultimately the genocide of mankind would follow as oxygen disappeared from the atmosphere for the lack of trees.

Please note that the seed in this example did fulfill part of its purpose. It germinated, grew, developed, and even bore fruit. Yet the totality of its potential was not fulfilled because it did not extend itself to the maximum potential of releasing seeds. Because the seed failed to reproduce itself, the next generation of trees was robbed of life, consequently affecting the entire human race and all creation. This is the impact when one element in nature withholds its true potential and refuses to maximize itself.

Tragically, there are millions of people who exist in "seedless lives." They are conceived, grow, develop; they dress up, smell good, and look good; and they even pretend to be happy. Yet everything they are dies with them because they fail to pass on everything God gave them. They have no sense of generational responsibility. They have no idea of their duty to the future. No man is born to live or die to himself. When a seed maximizes its potential, it not only feeds the next generation but also guarantees it through the seeds in the fruit.

God gave you the wealth of your potential—your gifts, talents, abilities, energies, creativity, ideas, aspirations, and dreams—for the blessing of others. You bear the responsibility for activating, releasing, and maximizing this potential as a deposit for the next generation.

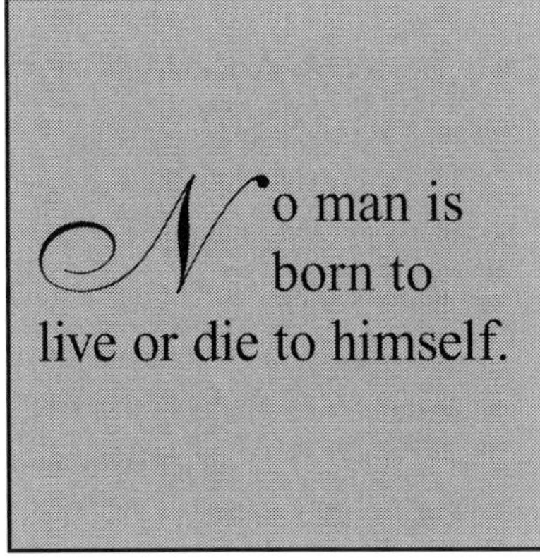

## The School That Was Almost Killed

*The Spirit of God has made me; the breath of the Almighty gives me life* (Job 33:4).

BOOK QUOTE: *Maximizing Your Potential* [Chapter 7]

Several years ago I was invited to speak at a church conference in Gary, Indiana, on the topic of discovering your purpose in life. Before I was introduced, the host invited a gentleman to share briefly on the establishment of an educational institution that had distinguished itself in that community. An unassuming, middle-aged gentleman stepped forward and began to share a story that pierced my soul. He told of how his mother had failed in an attempt to abort him as an unborn child, and he had ended up living in foster homes all over the city for many years. He emphasized how he had dreamed of providing an environment in which young people could grow and learn so that they would not have to suffer what he had experienced. He introduced to the audience the school he had founded and established—a school that had become one of the leading academic institutions for high school students in that city.

Imagine if his mother had been successful. She would have killed a school. Despite his past and his less-than-ideal heritage, this dreamer rose above his circumstances and maximized his potential, which is now benefiting generations to come.

You, and every other individual, possess the responsibility for this awesome treasure buried within, because this treasure within you can be fully released only if you are willing to believe and accept God's dream for your life. If you are willing to submit to His will and purpose for your destiny and to cooperate with His specifications, nothing will be impossible for you.

Determine not to be satisfied with anything less than the full accomplishment of your dream. Surrender to the demands that maximize your potential so that none of your assignment is left undone when you leave this planet. The responsibility to use what God has stored within you is yours alone.

Many individuals are aware of their ability and potential, but they have become frustrated and disillusioned by either their past failures or the negative influence of others. They have chosen to limit or withhold the wonderful gift the Creator has invested in them. Therefore, I strongly urge you to rise up from your temporary fears, shake yourself, and step out once again on the road to being and becoming your true self.

> Man is like an onion. His potential is exposed one layer at a time until all he is, is known by all.

## The Prophet Who Almost Quit

*Now finish the work, so that your eager willingness to do it may be matched by your completion of it, according to your means* (2 Corinthians 8:11).

BOOK QUOTE: *Maximizing Your Potential* [Chapter 7]

The prophet Elijah also exemplifies the importance of living to the fullest and refusing to settle for present circumstances. As recorded in the Book of First Kings, Elijah confronted the prophets of Baal and challenged them to a contest to prove that Jehovah is the true God. The test was to build an altar and call on God to send fire from the heavens to consume the sacrifice. After much prayer and dancing by the prophets of Baal, there was no response or results. Then Elijah began to call on the Lord God, and fire fell and consumed the sacrifice. Afterward, he commanded the people to seize the prophets of Baal, and all were destroyed. When Queen Jezebel, a worshiper of Baal, heard this news, she sent a message to Elijah, threatening his life.

> *Elijah was afraid and ran for his life. When he came to Beersheba in Judah, he left his servant there, while he himself went a day's journey into the desert. He came to a broom tree, sat down under it and prayed that he might die. "I have had enough, Lord," he said. "Take my life; I am no better than my ancestors"* (1 Kings 19:3-4).

After all his great accomplishments and achievements, this distinguished prophet had a death wish with suicidal tendencies. God was not persuaded. He intervened and showed Elijah that he had much more to accomplish before his full potential and purpose would be maximized. Then God instructed Elijah to anoint the next kings over Aram and Israel, and more significantly, to anoint Elisha to succeed him as prophet.

Just suppose Elijah had died when he wanted to quit. His successor, Elisha, who performed twice as many miracles as Elijah, would not have discovered his purpose and fulfilled his potential. It is imperative, therefore, that we never settle for the average of our circumstances because there are thousands of "Elishas" waiting on our obedience to fulfill their lives.

> There are thousands of "Elishas" waiting on our obedience to fulfill their lives.

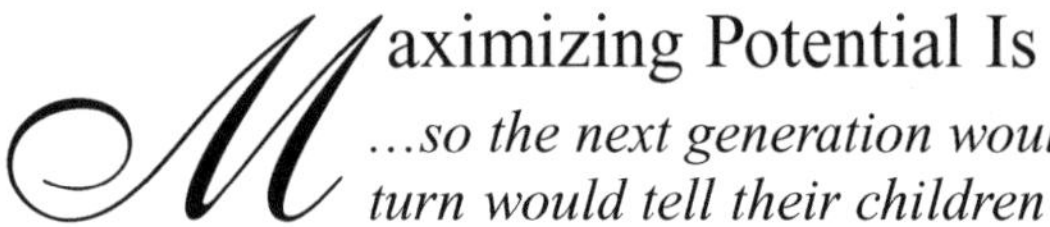

## Maximizing Potential Is Dying Empty

*...so the next generation would know them, even the children yet to be born, and they in turn would tell their children* (Psalm 78:6).

BOOK QUOTE: *Maximizing Your Potential* [Chapter 7]

The wealthiest place on this planet is not the gold mines, diamond mines, oil wells, or silver mines of the earth, but the cemetery. Why? Because buried in the graveyard are dreams and visions that were never fulfilled, books that were never written, paintings that were never painted, songs that were never sung, and ideas that died as ideas.

I wonder how many thousands, perhaps millions, of people will be poorer because they cannot benefit from the awesome wealth of the treasure of your potential: the books you have neglected to write, the songs you have failed to compose, or the inventions you continue to postpone. Perhaps there are millions who need the ministry or business you have yet to establish. You must maximize your life for the sake of the future. The next generation needs your potential.

Think of the many inventions, books, songs, works of art, and other great accomplishments others in past generations have left for you and for me to enjoy. Just as their treasure has become our blessing, so our potential should become the blessing of the next generation. The apostle Paul in his letter to his young friend Timothy describes his life as a drink offering that was poured out for others.

> *For I am already being poured out like a drink offering, and the time has come for my departure. I have fought the good fight, I have finished the race, I have kept the faith* (2 Timothy 4:6-7).

What a sense of destiny, purpose, and accomplishment is contained in these words. There is no hint of regret or remorse, only confidence and personal satisfaction.

Millions of the world's population, both now and in generations passed, have poured out some of their potential, accomplished some of their dreams, and achieved some of their goals. Still, because they have refused to maximize their lives, their cup holds a portion of their purpose, stagnating into depression, regret, and death.

I admonish you, decide today to act on the rest of your sleeping dream. Commit yourself to the goal of dying empty. The implication is evident: "I have completed My assignment, stayed through My course, and finished My task. I have emptied Myself of all My potential. Now it is your turn."

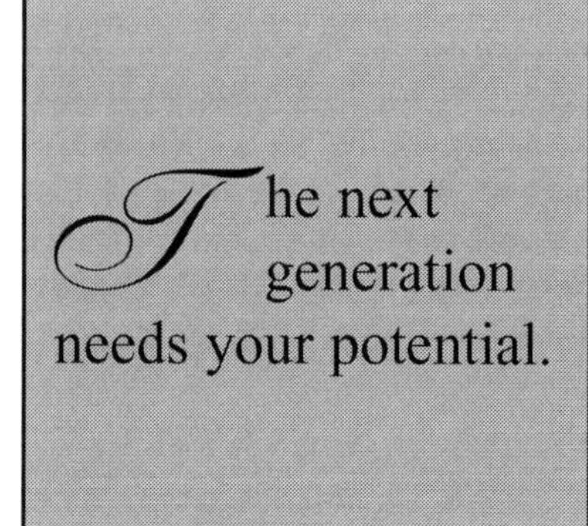

## Don't Be a Generational Thief

*His children will be mighty in the land; the generation of the upright will be blessed* (Psalm 112:2).

BOOK QUOTE: *Maximizing Your Potential* [Chapter 7]

First discover what you were born to be, then do it. Fulfill your own personal purpose for the glory of God. *Your obedience to God's will and purpose for your life is a personal decision, but not a private one.* God has designed the universe in such a way that the purposes of all mankind are interdependent; your purpose affects millions. Maximizing your potential is, therefore, necessary and critical. Your sphere of influence is much greater than your private world.

Suppose Mary had aborted Jesus, or Andrew had failed to introduce Peter to Jesus. What if Abraham had not left the Land of Ur, or Joseph had refused to go to Egypt. Or let's assume that Ananias had not prayed for Saul who became Paul, or that the little boy had refused to give Jesus his lunch. How different the biblical record might read! These examples show that although our obedience is always a personal decision, it is never a private matter.

Don't rob the next generation of your contribution to the destiny of mankind. Maximize yourself for God's glory. Remember, he who plants a tree plans for prosperity. "*The wise man saves for the future, but the foolish man spends whatever he gets*" (see Proverbs 21:20).

Your sphere of influence is much greater than your private world.

## EVIEW the Principles From This Week:

- The life and power to reproduce is in the seed.
- You rob your children when you withhold your potential.
- You must maximize your life for the benefit of the next generation.
- Potential is not fully maximized until it reproduces itself in the next generation.
- Obeying God's will for your life and fulfilling His purpose is a personal decision, but not a private one because your sphere of influence is much greater than your private world.

## Nothing Is Free

*You have been set free from sin and have become slaves to righteousness* (Romans 6:18).

BOOK QUOTE: *Maximizing Your Potential* [Chapter 8]

The cry "We want to be free!" has swept our world in remarkable and frightening ways within the past decade. Particularly in Eastern Europe, the desire for freedom has brought sweeping revolutions, toppling governments and power structures that have repressed and oppressed many peoples. This same yearning for freedom prompts pregnant women to abort their babies, children to take their parents to court, and students to seek greater control over the measures of discipline used in their schools.

Freedom! It sounds so good. Everybody wants freedom. Ethnic groups, social groups, religious groups. Children, youth, adults. All want the right to determine their own lives and to make their decisions without guidance or interference from anyone else.

It should not surprise us, then, that many common phrases express this craving for freedom: Freedom of the press, Freedom of choice, Freedom of religion, Freedom of speech. All reveal the universal longing to be unencumbered by the dictates and the decisions of others.

Is this truly possible? Can we be entirely free? No, I don't think so. Nothing is free. Although advertising tries to convince us that we are getting something for nothing—buy one, get one free—we are still paying for the product the advertiser claims is free. In a similar manner, the cost of sweepstakes and prizes given to entice consumers to buy a particular product or to subscribe to a certain periodical is built into the company's price structure somewhere along the way. We cannot get something for nothing.

This axiom is also true in relationships. We cannot be entirely free to do what we want, when we want, where we want, how we want, and with whom we want. Freedom always has a price because the actions of one person restricts and influences the freedom of another. The woman who aborts her baby takes away the baby's freedom to live, and the student who slaps the teacher who reprimands him takes away the teacher's freedom to keep order in his classroom. Freedom without responsibility cannot be freedom for all who are involved.

> Nothing is free. We cannot get something for nothing.

## The Consequences of Freedom Without Responsibility

*But now that you have been set free from sin and have become slaves to God, the benefit you reap leads to holiness, and the result is eternal life* (Romans 6:22).

BOOK QUOTE: *Maximizing Your Potential* [Chapter 8]

Lawlessness is the freedom to do whatever we want, when we want, with whom we want, with no one telling us to stop. In essence, we defy the standards that govern society to become a law unto ourselves with no sense of responsibility toward anything or anyone.

*Lawlessness always results in slavery, death, and the loss of preexisting freedoms.*

**The Loss of Freedom**

When the serpent convinced Adam and Eve to eat from the one tree, God put them out of the Garden and they lost the freedom to eat from the Garden's other trees. Their desire to be freed from God's restrictions cost them the freedom He had given them to eat from the other trees in the Garden. Thus, *the first penalty of freedom without responsibility is the loss of existing freedoms.*

This proves to be true in all life. The teenager who stays out past his curfew loses his privilege to use the family car. The politician who forgets his campaign promises and breaks faith with the people who put him in office loses his reelection bid and the opportunity to serve his constituents.

**Slavery**

*Slavery is a second consequence of freedom without responsibility.* When the man and the woman disobeyed God and ate from the tree of the knowledge of good and evil, they became slaves to evil. They could no longer see and do what God requires. This loss of the ability to see and do what is right is always a result of choosing to place oneself above the law.

Thus, the mechanic who charges exorbitant rates loses sight of fairness or the worker who takes an extended break assumes the company owes her fail to see the error of their ways. Death inevitably follows.

**Death**

*The third consequence of freedom without responsibility is death.* Notice that God connected the violation of the boundary around the tree of the knowledge of good and evil with death: "*...for when you eat of it you will surely die*" (Genesis 2:16). Disobedience to law always results in death.

The teenager who indulges in late hours will eventually see the death of his parents' trust. Likewise, the politician who neglects to fulfill his promises will suffer the death of his dream for advancement and recognition. Death is the inevitable result of freedom grasped at the expense of obedience to law.

> Death is the inevitable result of freedom grasped at the expense of obedience to law.

## he Nature of Law, Commands, and Demands

*All who sin apart from the law will also perish apart from the law, and all who sin under the law will be judged by the law* (Romans 2:12).

BOOK QUOTE: *Maximizing Your Potential* [Chapter 8]

Merriam Webster's dictionary (10th Collegiate, 1994) defines *law* as "a binding custom or practice of a community: a rule of conduct or action prescribed or formally recognized as binding or enforced by a controlling authority; a rule or order that is advisable or obligatory to observe." It further observes that law "implies imposition by a sovereign authority and the obligation of obedience on the part of all subject to that authority." Thus, a law regulates and governs the behavior of someone or something.

A *command* is an "order given" or an authoritative directive. It "stresses the official exercise of authority" and expresses the will of the authority based upon the established rules and regulations that govern the group. Thus, a *commandment* specifies behavior relative to a law.

A *demand* is "the act of asking with authority." It is based on the recognized authority of the one who asks, and it builds upon a previous command or commandment. Thus, a *demand* assumes that the requester has the right to make the request, and it specifies behavior in a specific instance or circumstance.

Let's use family life to illustrate these principles. As the head of the home, the father may establish the law that the privacy of each individual is ensured. This is a given within the structure of the family. Then he may issue the command that all members of the family should knock on a closed bedroom door and wait for the bidding "come in" before entering that room. This is his mandate or commandment relative to the principle of ensuring the privacy of each individual. Finally, when a daughter in the household is upset because her brother constantly enters her room when she is on the phone, the father may demand that the son knock on his sister's door and wait for her response.

A law regulates and governs the behavior of someone or something.

## Law Provides Direction for Daily Life

*...but I gave them this command: Obey me, and I will be your God and you will be my people. Walk in all the ways I command you, that it may go well with you* (Jeremiah 7:23).

BOOK QUOTE: *Maximizing Your Potential* [Chapter 8]

God has established many laws that influence our lives. Some of these govern the physical world in which we live; others control our relationships within the human family and with God Himself. For example, God has established marriage as the structure in which sexual relationships should be enjoyed and children should be raised. That is His law. "*You shall not commit adultery*" (Exodus 20:14) is one of His commandments built on that law. Hence, when God demands that you should not gratify your physical desires by engaging in intercourse outside the marriage relationship, He is applying to daily life the law He established at creation and the commandment He gave at Mount Sinai. He is specifying how we should behave in a given situation.

*God's demands are always based on His laws and commandments.* He is not capricious, nor is He out to destroy our pleasure. *He knows that we cannot fulfill our potential outside His laws*, so He gives us commandments relative to those laws and He makes demands on us that apply His commandments to our situation. If we resist His demands, we bring upon ourselves the natural consequences of His laws. The law of love is a good example of this principle.

God created us to be loved by Him and to love Him and others in return. Love is an innate quality of His nature and of ours. The commandments "*Love each other as I have loved you*" (John 15:12), and "*Love your enemies and pray for those who persecute you*" (Matthew 5:44b) direct our efforts to understand and apply that law of love to our lives. When we disregard this law, we bear the consequences of loneliness, alienation, and internal turmoil that naturally come to those who fail to love.

We cannot choose whether or not these consequences will come to us, since they are inseparable from the law. Our only choice is whether or not we will love. Thus, we see that God's commandment to love, like all His commandments, is given for our good. Those who obey it are spared the pain that irrevocably assails those who fail to love.

The effects of God's laws cannot be avoided. They are constant and unchangeable, even as He is. Yet, you control the impact of God's laws on your life because the decision to obey or disobey God's commandments and demands is wholly yours. In this manner, *you control your destiny.*

## Read the Fine Print

*This is love for God: to obey His commands. And His commands are not burdensome* (1 John 5:3).

BOOK QUOTE: *Maximizing Your Potential* [Chapter 8]

*Nothing can function at its maximum performance if it violates God's laws or the laws laid down by the manufacturer.* These laws set the boundaries or limitations within which all things must operate. There is no recourse. The preestablished consequences always follow the failure to fulfill the law's obligations.

If something sounds too good to be true, it probably is. Books and television shows may tell us that we are free to sleep around, but they don't caution us about the guilt and the misery that come from such actions. Pro-choice groups may persuade us that we are free to abort our babies, but they do not warn us of the severe depression and never-ending sense of loss that plague many women following an abortion. Cigarette ads may portray healthy, laughing men and women puffing away on the particular brand that tastes best and gives the most satisfying high, but they do not show the hospital rooms, cancer treatment centers, and doctors' offices filled with smokers suffering from lung cancer and emphysema.

Too often we resist obeying rules and living within a given set of laws, stipulations, and regulations because we see them as having a negative rather than a positive impact on our lives. The Scriptures are clear that God's laws are good. They are given for our benefit.

> *If you fully obey the Lord your God and carefully follow all His commands I give you today, the Lord your God will set you high above all the nations on earth. All these blessing will come upon you if you obey the Lord your God* (Deuteronomy 28:1-2).

Every commandment of negative orientation can be restated in a positive manner. "*You shalt not misuse the name of the Lord your God*" (Exodus 20:7a) could be rephrased, "Worship only Me." "*You shall not steal*" (Exodus 20:15) might be reworded, "Leave other people's possessions alone." "*You shall not give false testimony against your neighbor*" (Exodus 20:16) could be, "Tell the truth."

Through *thou shalt nots* God delineates the limits within which you can live a healthy, happy, productive life. They are His means of helping you. He does not intend to unnecessarily harm, restrict, or bind you.

God created you to fulfill your potential, but you must accept the principles and laws that govern it. That's the bottom line.

## isconceptions of Law—Part 1

*We know that the law is good if one uses it properly* (1 Timothy 1:8).

BOOK QUOTE: *Maximizing Your Potential* [Chapter 8]

The limitless ability God has given us to do all we can think, to accomplish all we can imagine, to fulfill every aspiration we entertain cannot survive unless we obey God's laws and live within His limitations. To encourage an accepting attitude toward God's laws and commandments, let us examine some of the misconceptions that surround the concept of law.

**Misconception—Laws Restrict Us**

All parents have heard the complaint, "You just don't want me to have any fun," when they put a restriction upon their children's activities. Whether it is a curfew, a rule about calling home, or a standard that requires the child to avoid being at a friend's home if the friend's parents are not there, the child sees the rules and requirements as the parents' desire to withhold from him the enjoyable things of youth.

Very often we transfer this same attitude into our relationship with God. We see God's thou shalt nots as His means of taking the fun out of life. Then His laws appear to be restrictive instruments that limit our freedom to do what we want, when we want, where we want, with whom we want.

**Misconception—Laws Inhibit Us**

The misconception that law inhibits or restrains us also distorts our understanding of the purpose of law. This perception is readily evident in the attitude of the employee who feels that the obligation to punch a time clock cramps her preferred style of arriving at work five or ten minutes after the designated starting time and making up that time at the end of the day. Or perhaps a young couple believes that an apartment house's rule to rent only to married couples inhibits their freedom to live together. Or, yet again, a club that makes much of its income from a daily happy hour may consider an ordinance that holds establishments responsible for accidents involving their patrons unnecessarily prohibitive.

> Our potential cannot survive unless we obey God's laws and live within His limitations.

# isconceptions of Law—Part 2

*...but showing love to a thousand generations of those who love Me and keep My commandments* (Deuteronomy 5:10).

BOOK QUOTE: *Maximizing Your Potential* [Chapter 8]

**Misconception—Laws Bind Us**

Some laws appear to bind us and we, therefore, find them to be irritating. Traffic laws are good examples of these laws. One day as I rode in the car with my son, I tried to beat a yellow light because I was a little late. As the light changed, my son said, "Daddy, the light is changing." Just as I pressed the accelerator to make the light, he spoke again, "Daddy, you've got to stop," and then "Thou goest too fast, O Dad." Because I had taught him to stop at red lights, I slammed on the brakes and we came to a halt with a terrible screech. The law concerning red lights was particularly binding to me that day.

**Misconception—Laws Rob Us**

The belief that laws prevent us from receiving the best things of life is also a false understanding of the nature of law. This perception often occurs when something we want defies a given law, but we want it anyway. A young Christian girl who wants to marry a nice-looking, well-behaved guy who isn't saved thinks God is unfair when He says not to be yoked with unbelievers (see 2 Cor. 6:14). A young businessman perceives himself to have been robbed when his partner is unwilling to use dishonestly obtained information to make a killing on the stock market. A single mother struggles between giving her tithe to God and spending the money on a much-deserved weekend away from the kids.

All these misconceptions convince us that laws and regulations are encumbrances and burdens that prevent us from enjoying life to the fullest. In truth, laws are provided for our benefit.

> Laws are provided for our benefit.

## REVIEW the Principles From This Week:

- Freedom always has a price. What frees one person may enslave another.
- Laws and commandments benefit us and have a positive impact on our lives.

## The Benefits of Law: Laws Protect

*He who scorns instruction will pay for it, but he who respects a command is rewarded* (Proverbs 13:13).

BOOK QUOTE: *Maximizing Your Potential* [Chapter 8 & Introduction]

It is reported that the newspaper counselor, Ann Landers, receives an average of 10,000 letters each month. Nearly all these letters are from people who are burdened with problems. When Landers was asked if one type of problem is predominant in these letters, she replied that fear is the one problem above all others. People fear losing their health and their loved ones. Many potentially great men and women are afraid of life itself. They never attempt their dreams because they fear failure. Others fail to strive for their aspirations because they fear success and the responsibility and accountability that comes with any measure of success. But we do not need to fear if we obey God's laws.

Laws are given to help us and to make life more enjoyable, how do they accomplish their purpose? What reliable benefits do they offer?

The child who lives with no rules and restrictions is much more likely to get hurt or to end up in trouble than the child who lives within a structure of parental guidance. Because he has no boundaries or guidelines against which he can judge his actions, he may make decisions that jeopardize his safety and well-being. The rule "no playing on the kitchen floor when Mom is making dinner," for example, protects a young child from being scalded. If he is not taught this rule, the child may not even know that he is in danger. Likewise, the restriction "no swimming alone" protects against drowning. In a similar manner, traffic signs such as stop, yield, slow, and detour have all been established not to restrict, but to protect us and others. Laws protect us. They alert us to possible danger.

## The Benefits of Law: Laws Assist

*Great peace have they who love your law, and nothing can make them stumble* (Psalm 119:165).

BOOK QUOTE: *Maximizing Your Potential* [Chapter 8 & Introduction]

One of the greatest tragedies in life is to watch potential die untapped. A greater tragedy is to watch potential live unreleased. How sad to know that the majority of the people on this planet will never discover who they really are, while others will settle for only a portion of their true self. Only a select few will make the quality decision to maximize every fiber of their lives by fully using their gifts, talents, abilities, and capabilities. This we call *maximum living*. Each one of us has the opportunity to pursue maximum living. The question is, Will we choose to exercise that option?

Dreams are visual manifestations of the seeds of destiny planted in the spirit and soul of each human by his Creator. This preoccupation with ideas and imagination in youth is evidence that we are created with the capacity and ability to conceive visions and aspirations that extend beyond our present reality. Perhaps it is this inherent ability to explore the impossible for the possibilities that Jesus Christ, the most maximized man who ever lived, referred to when He stated, "*...unless you change and become like little children, you will never enter the kingdom of Heaven*" (Matthew 18:3).

This simple yet profound command embodies a principle that captures the spirit of maximizing one's self. It implies that the average adult, through the process of growth and development, has lost the free-spirited, open-minded, inquisitive, explorative, daring, believing, and uninhibited nature of a child. It indicates that the ability to dream and explore possibilities diminishes in the course of growth to adulthood. It also communicates the heart and desire of God our Creator that the ability to dream big and dare to attempt the seemingly impossible would be restored in all men and maintained throughout their lifetime.

Laws give us assistance to explore the possibilities. Can you imagine the confusion if everyone addressed their letters however they wished? Some people might put the address of the sender in the upper left corner, but others might put the address of the recipient there. Or one community might have the tradition of putting the stamp on the back of the envelope, while every other community places it on the front. Postal regulations aid the efficient handling of mail so letters go to the sender's intended recipient. Instead of restraining us, laws provide assistance so we can accomplish what we intend.

## The Benefits of Law: Laws Allow For Full Expression

*Let the peace of Christ rule in your hearts, since as members of one body you were called to peace. And be thankful* (Colossians 3:15).

BOOK QUOTE: *Maximizing Your Potential* [Chapter 8]

Laws also allow us to express ourselves completely within the context of community. Consider what would happen if you bought a house in a nice neighborhood to raise your children in a safe, non-violent environment only to have your neighbor open an adults-only bookstore. The traffic on your formerly quiet street now quadruples and your children are exposed to unhealthy materials as people come from the shop leafing through pornographic literature. One night a patron is shot in front of your house by his wife, who is enraged by his attitudes and his actions toward her after he has been looking at his girlie magazines. Suddenly, your nice neighborhood is no longer safe. Civil laws help to control what is and is not permitted within a community so that all may enjoy the environment they desire.

Although these laws may irritate us because they compel us to act in a certain manner, they permit us to enjoy personal preferences within our personal space. Consider, for example, the following situation. A resident in an apartment complex enjoys listening to classical music, but the young man in the next apartment blares his rock music so loud that it rocks his neighbor's walls and drowns out her music.

If you are the young man who prefers loud rock music, the rules of the apartment complex that control noise appear to be restrictive and binding. For the person in the neighboring apartment, however, the regulations permit her to enjoy her own taste in music. *Laws allow each person to enjoy his individual preferences so long as he does not infringe on the freedom of others to do the same.*

Laws allow us to express ourselves completely within the context of community.

## The Benefits of Law: Laws Maximize Potential

*...live by the Spirit, and you will not gratify the desires of the sinful nature. For the sinful nature desires what is contrary to the Spirit, and the Spirit what is contrary to the sinful nature. They are in conflict with each other, so that you do not do what you want. But if you are led by the Spirit, you are not under law* (Galatians 5:16-18).

BOOK QUOTE: *Maximizing Your Potential* [Chapter 8]

Laws help us to do and be our best. The very laws that restrict negative behavior also encourage and uphold positive attitudes and actions. The classroom rule, for example, that makes the entire class responsible for monitoring cheating and gives a failing grade to anyone who copies from another student's paper also encourages excellence because it exerts peer pressure for honesty and guarantees that each person will be graded by his or her own efforts. Thus, the law both sets consequences for negative behavior and rewards those who work hard and do their best.

The Bible clearly shows that laws do not restrict positive thoughts and behavior:

> *The acts of the sinful nature are obvious: sexual immorality, impurity and debauchery; idolatry and witchcraft; hatred, discord, jealousy, fits of rage, selfish ambition, dissensions, factions and envy; drunkenness, orgies, and the like. I warn you...that those who live like this will not inherit the kingdom of God. But the fruit of the Spirit is love, joy, peace, patience, kindness, goodness, faithfulness, gentleness and self-control. Against such things there is no law* (Galatians 5:19-23).

Since the violation of law destroys potential, and obedience to law fulfills potential, law encourages the releasing and the maximizing of potential.

> Law encourages the releasing and the maximizing of potential.

## The Benefits of Law: Law Secure Purpose and Function

*And whatever you do, whether in word or deed, do it all in the name of the Lord Jesus, giving thanks to God the Father through Him* (Colossians 3:17).

BOOK QUOTE: *Maximizing Your Potential* [Chapter 8]

Law allows us to function within God's general design for human life, and the plans and purposes He sets for our individual lives.

> *The blessing of the Lord brings wealth, and He adds no trouble to it* (Proverbs 10:22).

Achieving purpose with God's blessing never brings sorrow. Those, however, who try to fulfill their potential outside His purposes often experience multiplied sorrow. A businessman, for example, who builds his business without God's guidance and direction may attain the same wealth as a man who submitted his dreams and plans to God's will, but his position outside God's plan does not provide the freedom from worry that the other businessman enjoys. Those who must rely only on themselves to protect their gain often become ill from worrying. There is no joy in that kind of wealth.

When the Lord blesses a person with prosperity, He both protects what He has given and He serves as a resource to the recipient. Man needs spiritual resources as surely as he needs physical and material assets.

Potential without law is dangerous. Even as breaker switches cut off electricity when an electrical appliance malfunctions and a free flow of electricity is possible, so God shuts us down when we operate outside His laws. This is His safeguard to keep us from self-destructing.

Potential without law is dangerous.

## Your Potential Needs the Benefit of God's Law

*Everyone who sins breaks the law; in fact, sin is lawlessness* (1 John 3:4).

BOOK QUOTE: *Maximizing Your Potential* [Chapter 8]

Many people throughout history have harmed themselves and others because they tried to fulfill their potential outside God's specifications. Adolf Hitler, for example, was a gifted leader. Using his leadership skills, he came up through the ranks of government until he was legally elected the chancellor of Germany. Once he achieved that position, something went wrong. He violated the rules of leadership.

Power is always given to work through the vehicle of servanthood. When we are in a position of authority, we have the responsibility to serve those under us. Hitler violated that law and made himself a dictator. Instead of using his power to serve and bless the country he ruled, he placed himself above the law and forced people to do his bidding.

Hitler also broke the laws of human dignity and equality because he created and enforced policies that treated all people who were not of Aryan descent, with blond hair and blue eyes, as subhumans and half-humans who were created to serve the perfect race. Many Jews and other non-Aryan peoples were victims of Hitler's beliefs and policies. Eventually he brought death to himself and those who shared his convictions.

Potential is always given to bless, never to harm. If your potential is hurting someone or something, you'd better look carefully at your attitudes and actions. You are probably using your gifts and talents outside their God-given specifications.

Potential is always given to bless, never to harm.

## Potential Dies When Laws are Broken

*As for you, you were dead in your transgressions and sins* (Ephesians 2:1).

BOOK QUOTE: *Maximizing Your Potential* [Chapter 8]

The experience of Hitler and many other people confirms that the violation of the boundaries that delimit potential sets off serious consequences and exposes the violator to potentially threatening circumstances. This is true because violating the specifications set forth by God for the use of potential removes protection, hinders fulfillment, and interrupts performance.

Let's say, for example, that you are a young executive in a local bank. You have worked at the bank for five years, developing a good working knowledge of the banking industry and building a solid reputation for honesty and integrity. Your goal is to become the manager of the main branch.

Your spouse constantly complains that you don't earn enough until one day, in desperation, you take $2,000 from the bank safe and give it to your spouse. Several things happen when you do this. First, you lose the protection of your good reputation. Until now, people have trusted not only your integrity but also the soundness of your decisions. Second, you forfeit the opportunity to rise to the position of branch manager. Third, you interrupt your career because not only the bank you worked for but other employers as well cannot trust you. This one act of disregarding the commandment "*You shall not steal*" (Exodus 20:15) destroys your potential to become a competent, respected banker.

Jesus came to recover the spirit of God's laws so we can recognize them as the blessings they are, and to show us the power that belongs to those who live within their God-given specifications. Only by the power of the Holy Spirit can we live within God's laws of limitation and, thereby, maximize our potential. Laws and limitations established by a manufacturer for a product are always given to protect and maximize the product's potential and performance, not to restrict it.

Flipping a switch is a helpful way to use electricity. Sticking your finger in a socket is not. Even as you cannot live if you ignore the precautions that govern the safe use of electricity, so you cannot experience the full, abundant life Jesus promises if you disregard the specifications that limit the use of your potential. You must abide by God's specifications to enjoy the totality of who you are. His laws and commandments are the security that guarantees you will receive all He planned and purposed for your life.

> A man without God is: potential without purpose, power without conduction, life without living, ability without responsibility.

## EVIEW the Principles From This Week:

- Lawlessness defies the standards that govern society. It shows no responsibility toward anyone or anything.
- Lawlessness results in the loss of existing freedoms, in slavery, and in death.
- Laws set norms or standards and govern or regulate behavior.
- Commandments express the will of an authority relative to a law.
- Demands specify behavior in a specific situation based on previously defined laws and commandments.
- Violating laws and commandments aborts potential and brings inevitable consequences.

## ou Can Recover Your Potential

*You were taught, with regard to your former way of life, to put off your old self, which is being corrupted by its deceitful desires; to be made new in the attitude of your minds; and to put on the new self, created to be like God in true righteousness and holiness* (Ephesians 4:22-24).

BOOK QUOTE: *Maximizing Your Potential* [Chapter 9]

A hush fell over the room as a petite, neatly groomed woman stepped to the podium in the prison room. Her first words startled them. "I am one of you. I lived here for five years. I came here at the age of twenty, leaving behind my husband and my young daughter. Although it has been many years since my release, I still remember the intense loneliness and the consuming despair that filled my first days here. I can also hear in my mind the click of the gate behind me. I doubt those thoughts and feelings will ever leave me."

"I am here today because something very important happened to me here. I met the Lord Jesus Christ, accepted His forgiveness for my past, and entrusted my future to His keeping. My life is very different because of Him. Through His love and mercy, and the support and encouragement of many brothers and sisters in Christ, I have finally forgiven myself for the wrongs that brought me here. Today I am free because He freed me, and I bring to you the opportunity to find this freedom and forgiveness."

"This is true because God created me for a special purpose and placed within me the potential to fulfill all that He planned for my life before I was born. I come to you today as a friend who wants to help you become all that you can be. *No matter what others have said about you, and what you have believed about yourself, you are a competent, gifted person.* I know you may not feel that way, but your feelings are not accurate. You are the beloved daughter of God, created by Him with meticulous care and endowed by Him with everything you need to bless yourself, your family, and, indeed, the entire world. This potential hibernates within you, buried by the actions, attitudes, and lifestyles that brought you here, but it need not remain hidden. *You can recover your potential.*"

Change. The hope for something different. Each of us, at some point in our lives, has been dissatisfied with where we are and who we are. We have been keenly aware that life is not measuring up to our expectations. Some of you may still be there. Others of you, like the former prisoner, have found renewed hope in life. *A life-changing encounter with God through His Son Jesus Christ makes the difference.* The Bible teaches us much about our need for this life-changing encounter and the path we must take if we would experience it.

> It is always better to fail at something than to excel at nothing. Get up and try again.

## Forgiveness

*The Lord is compassionate and gracious, slow to anger and abounding in love. He will not always accuse, nor will He harbor His anger forever; He does not treat us as our sins deserve or repay us according to our iniquities. For as high as the heavens are above the earth, so great is His love for those who fear Him; as far as the east is from the west, so far has He removed our transgressions from us* (Psalm 103:8-12).

BOOK QUOTE: *Maximizing Your Potential* [Chapter 9]

*The journey to recovering your potential begins with forgiveness—God's forgiveness and self-forgiveness.* God's forgiveness is an expression of His love for us. He offers it to all who confess their rebelliousness and accept His gift of new life through His Son, Jesus Christ. Becoming rerooted in God takes care of this first aspect of forgiveness.

Self-forgiveness, however, is often more difficult. God forgives and forgets our sin as soon as we confess it. We, on the other hand, often hold ourselves accountable for our wrongs for a long time. Indeed, many who have accepted Jesus Christ as their Savior still think and act as though their sins are not forgiven. Such behavior short-changes potential because it again places ourselves above God and His word to us. Like Adam and Eve in the garden, we disbelieve what God has said.

Remember, God's promises are true and His power surpasses all other powers. *If God says your sins are forgiven, they are forgiven. You are freed forever from their penalty and their power over you. No one, including satan, has the authority or the right to change or dispute His decision.*

The failure to forgive ourselves places us at risk for future sin. This is true because self-condemnation opens the door for satan and his forces of evil to work on us with doubt and guilt. Guilt prevents us from actively seeking God's power and wisdom because we are ashamed to enter His presence, and doubt enslaves us to feelings of powerlessness and unworthiness. Both deny the power and authority of God in our lives and entice us to rely more on our feelings than the presence of God's Spirit within us. Both destroy potential.

Refuse, then, to allow self-condemnation to steal your potential in Christ. If you have confessed your sin, you are forgiven and God remembers it no more. Forgive yourself and move on. If you would love others and share your potential with them, you must first love and forgive yourself. This is an important step in the journey of recovering your potential.

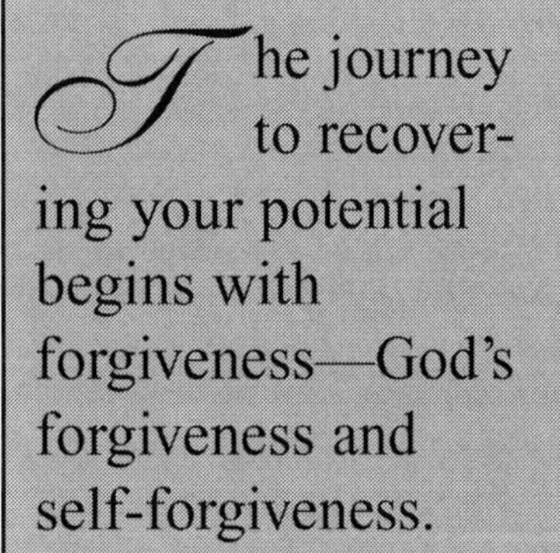

## Your Past and Your Potential

*Create in me a pure heart, O God, and renew a steadfast spirit within me....Restore to me the joy of Your salvation and grant me a willing spirit, to sustain me* (Psalm 51:10,12).

BOOK QUOTE: *Maximizing Your Potential* [Chapter 9]

*A step in recovering potential is the ability to move beyond your past and to use it to inform and improve your future.* All of us have things in our pasts of which we are ashamed. While self-forgiveness takes away the sting of those confessed sins, it does not remove from our minds the memory of those wrongs. We must learn to live with our memories and allow them to be a positive force in our lives.

King David, after his sin with Bathsheba, most certainly was haunted by his wrong (see 2 Samuel 11:1–12:25). Overwhelmed by the enormity of his sin, he could have forfeited his potential to serve God as the king of God's people. Instead, David confessed his sin (see 2 Samuel 12:13 and Psalm 51) and petitioned God. Today David is remembered as a man after God's heart and the greatest king in the history of God's people.

This same restorative power of God can move you beyond the negative opinions, poor judgments, unhealthy relationships, detrimental environments, and adverse circumstances of your past. No sin is too great for God to forgive. No relationship is beyond His restoration. His transforming power can redirect your misguided and harmful actions and enable you to remove yourself from the destructive environments and crippling circumstances that threaten your potential. No memory is too deep for Him to heal. No problem is beyond His blessing and power.

*The key to moving beyond all that haunts you from your past is allowing those memories to empower you instead of destroy you.* For example, if you were addicted to drugs and you know firsthand the destructive forces they unleash, use your experiences to help those who are at risk today of experiencing the same pain you've survived.

*Discouraging, defeating experiences may be part of your past life, but there is no reason why they must continue to discourage and defeat you.* Indeed, they can become stepping stones to the releasing and maximizing of your potential if you are willing to acknowledge your past, to learn from your mistakes, and to allow God's transforming power to turn your loss into gain. With God's help, you are capable of rising above your shortcomings and of redeeming your less-than-perfect decisions. He has not given up on you. He's waiting to see what you will do with the rest of your life. Protect the present and the future from the past by facing the past and moving beyond it. This is an essential element of the journey to recover your potential.

> We must learn to live with our memories and allow them to be a positive force.

## The Greatest Threat—Satisfaction

*I press on toward the goal to win the prize for which God has called me heavenward in Christ Jesus* (Philippians 3:14).

BOOK QUOTE: *Maximizing Your Potential* [Preface]

*The greatest threat to being all you could be is satisfaction with who you are.* What you could do is always endangered by what you have done. There are millions of individuals who have buried their latent talents, gifts, and abilities in the cemetery of their last accomplishment. They have settled for less than their best. I believe that the enemy of best is good, and the strength of good is the norm. The power of the norm is the curse of our society. It seems like the world is designed to make "the norm" comfortable and "the average" respectable. What a tragedy!

A quick glance at history reveals that the individuals who impacted their generations and affected the world most dramatically were individuals who, because of a circumstance, pressure, or decision, challenged the tide of convention, stretched the boundaries of tradition, and violated the expectations of the norm. *Few great things have ever been done within the confines of the accepted norm.*

In essence, history is always made by individuals who dare to challenge and exceed the accepted norm. Why follow a path when you can make a trail? It is incumbent upon each of us to ask ourselves the following questions: Have we become all we are capable of? Have we extended ourselves to the maximum? Have we done the best we can do? Have we used our gifts, talents, and abilities to their limit?

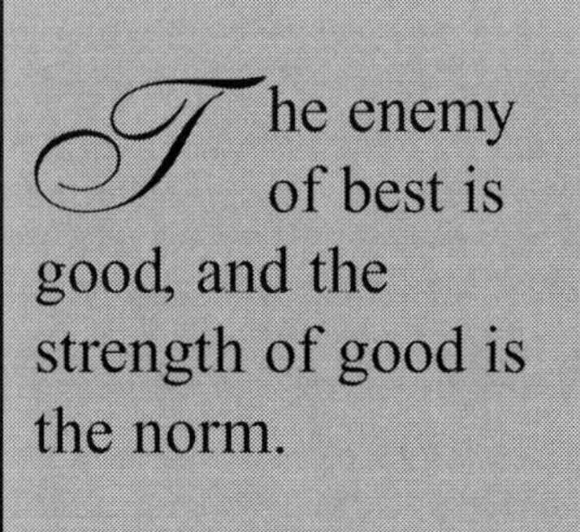

The enemy of best is good, and the strength of good is the norm.

# et Your Joy

*...and the ransomed of the Lord will return. They will enter Zion with singing; everlasting joy will crown their heads. Gladness and joy will overtake them, and sorrow and sighing will flee away* (Isaiah 35:10).

BOOK QUOTE: *Maximizing Your Potential* [Preface]

I learned a lesson that would become a major pillar in my life. I ignored the manufacturer's manual that came with a newly purchased video player/recorder. Because I refused to read and follow the instructions contained therein, I was unable to utilize, maximize, and fully appreciate the full potential of the product. I was settling for less than full capacity. I was a victim of living according to the standards and observations of others. In essence, *the performance of the product was restricted by the limitation my ignorance had placed on its functions.* This limitation of performance can also be extended to those who read the manufacturer's manual but refuse to use the functions inherent in the construction of the product. Therefore, they never experience the full potential of the machine. They only desire to experience the minimum.

In reality, this experience perfectly describes the lives of most of the nearly six billion people on planet Earth. Many live on only four functions: play, stop, pause, and rewind. Day after day they go to jobs they hate, stop to rest in homes they despise, pause long enough to vent their frustration, and then play the games people play pretending to be happy.

What a tragedy! They never experience the joy of the other functions of their lives, such as developing and refining their skills, fulfilling their God-given destiny, capturing their purpose for life, making long-range plans, expanding their knowledge base, increasing their exposure through travel, and exploring the limits of their gifts, talents, and abilities. They have chosen to accept the fate of the millions who have resigned themselves to a normal life, with normal activities, in the company of normal people, striving for normal goals, at a normal pace, with normal motivation, with a normal education, taught by normal teachers, who give normal grades, and live in normal homes, with normal families, leaving a normal heritage, for their normal children, who bury them in a normal grave. What a normal tragedy.

Many live on only four functions: play, stop, pause, and rewind.

## o For It!

*Whatever your hand finds to do, do it with all your might, for in the grave, where you are going, there is neither working nor planning nor knowledge nor wisdom* (Ecclesiastes 9:10).

BOOK QUOTE: *Maximizing Your Potential* [Preface]

I am convinced that our Creator never intended for us to be normal—that is, to get lost in the crowd of "the norm." This is evidenced by the fact that among the 5.8 billion people on this planet, no two individuals are alike; their fingerprints, genetic code, and chromosome combinations are all distinct and unique. In reality, God created all people to be originals, but we continue to become copies of others. Too often we are so preoccupied with trying to fit in, that we never stand out.

You were designed to be distinctive, special, irreplaceable, and unique, so refuse to be "normal"! Go beyond average! Do not strive to be accepted, rather strive to be yourself. Shun the minimum; pursue the maximum. Utilize all your functions—maximize yourself! Use yourself up for the glory of your Creator. *I admonish you: Die empty. Die fulfilled by dying unfilled.*

This book is written for the "normal" person who wishes to exceed the norm. It is for the "ordinary" individual who has determined to be "extra-ordinary." It is for the individual just like you who knows that somewhere deep inside, there is still so much you have not released: so much yet to do, so much left to expose, so much to maximize.

Live life with all your might; give it all you have. Do it until there is nothing left to do because you have become all you were created to be, done all you were designed to do, and given all you were sent to give. Be satisfied with nothing less than your best.

Whatever your hands find to do, do it with all your might unto the Lord.

## Redeeming the Days of Your Life

*Yet to all who received Him, to those who believed in His name, he gave the right to become children of God— children born not of natural descent, nor of human decision or a husband's will, but born of God* (John 1:12-13).

BOOK QUOTE: *Maximizing Your Potential* [Chapter 9]

*A step to recovering our potential is to redeem the time that is left to us.* We cannot undo what is past, but we can make the necessary changes in our lives to permit the wise use of the remainder of our days.

Time is God's gift for accomplishing our purpose and fulfilling our potential. It begins the day we are born and ends when we die. The length of our physical life matches the days required to fulfill our purpose because God planned for the maturing of our lives within the total days He has allotted to us. Therefore, we have sufficient time to maximize our potential. The question is, Will we waste or use wisely the days God has assigned to our lives?

The apostle Paul instructs us to "*see then that* [we] *walk circumspectly, not as fools but as wise, redeeming the time, because the days are evil*" (Ephesians 5:15-16 NKJV). In other words, we must find our purpose and use our potential to accomplish it. Likewise, we need to consciously refuse to allow procrastination, discouragement, and the other enemies of our potential to induce us to waste even one day of our lives. Whenever we use our time to do things that neither release our potential nor help us progress toward the accomplishment of our purpose, we forfeit or delay the opportunity to reach the excellency and completion God intended for our lives.

Just as a seed is full of promise and potential, so your life is abundantly loaded with untapped power and purpose. Likewise, just as a seed needs to be related to the soil and to be fed nutrients to maximize its fullest potential, so you are in need of a personal relationship with the Source and Creator of your life. Only God the Father can restore you to your original purpose and dream, and only He can provide the grace and resources you need to experience true fulfillment. Every product needs to remain related to the manufacturer if it is to maintain its guarantee and warranty.

It is more important to be yourself than to be the best.

## EVIEW the Principles From This Week:

- God created you for a special purpose and gave you the potential to fulfill it.
- You are a competent, gifted person.
- You must experience a life-changing encounter with Jesus Christ if you want to recover your potential.
- The journey to recovering your potential must include:
  1. accepting God's forgiveness,
  2. forgiving yourself,
  3. moving beyond your past,
  4. using your past to inform your future,
  5. redeeming the remaining days of your life.

## The Counter-Development in Your Life

*Fear of man will prove to be a snare* [trap of restriction], *but whoever trusts in the Lord* [in the assessment of his Creator] *is kept safe* (Proverbs 29:25).

BOOK QUOTE: *Maximizing Your Potential* [Introduction]

Most of our social and cultural environment works against our dreams and minimizes the magnitude and scope of the vision in our hearts. We are trained mentally and spiritually to fear our dreams and doubt our destiny. We are discouraged into believing that our passion for greatness is abnormal and our aspirations are suspect. The result of this human "counter-development" process is that the majority of the earth's population lives under the spell and debilitating power of the specter called "fear."

Fear is the source of ninety percent of the lack of progress and personal development in the lives of millions of gifted, talented, and resourceful individuals. Many experts in the field of human behavior have stated that the fear of failure and the fear of success are the two most powerful and most prevalent fears experienced by the human family. The great politician, King Solomon, states this in Proverbs 29:25 (see above).

When we believe the opinions of men and their assessment of our ability, these perceptions and opinions imprison us and eventually become a trap that impedes and limits the maximization of our true potential.

Therefore, the potential that is trapped within many human treasure houses is suffocated, buried, suppressed, and lost to the world. Most people live at minimum performance, willing to do only what is necessary to survive. They live to get by, not to get ahead in life. They maintain the status quo instead of raising the standard in life. They do only what is required and expected.

What a sad and depressing way to live. I challenge you to step away from the crowd of those who maintain, and join the few who are committed to attaining their full potential by endeavoring to maximize their abilities. After all, who else can live your life but you? Who can fully represent you except you? I admonish you to unearth yourself and share your treasure with the world.

> Fear is the source of ninety percent of the lack of progress and personal development.

## Your Only Handicap

*Nathan replied to David, "Whatever you have in mind, do it, for God is with you"* (1 Chronicles 17:2).

BOOK QUOTE: *Maximizing Your Potential* [Introduction]

A few years ago I was invited to the beautiful nation of Brazil to address a leadership conference. During my stay there, my host took me to visit a little town made famous by a sculptor who had lost both hands to the disease of leprosy. As a young man stricken with this horrible disease, he would sit for many hours and watch his father work in his wood carving shop. One day the young man decided to train himself to carve and sculpt wood with his feet and the parts of his arms he had not lost to the leprosy.

The resilient spirit of this young man released his untapped potential, and his work gave evidence that trapped within this cripple was one of the greatest artists the world has ever known. I stood in amazement and disbelief as I viewed some of his magnificent works of wood, installed in the most beautiful churches in that city. We also visited his rendition of the major Old Testament prophets, 12 life-sized carvings that are displayed as one of Brazil's most admired national treasures.

Tears filled my eyes as I was told the story of this great handless sculptor. I could not but think of the millions of people who have both hands, arms, and feet in perfect working condition, but who fail to leave anything to their generation. This sculptor is evidence and testimony that buried within each of us is potential that can be maximized if we are willing to go beyond our fears, to overcome the norms and opinions of society, to hurdle the fabricated barriers of prejudice, and to defy the naysayers. There is no handicap except that of our minds. There is no limit to our potential except that which is self-imposed.

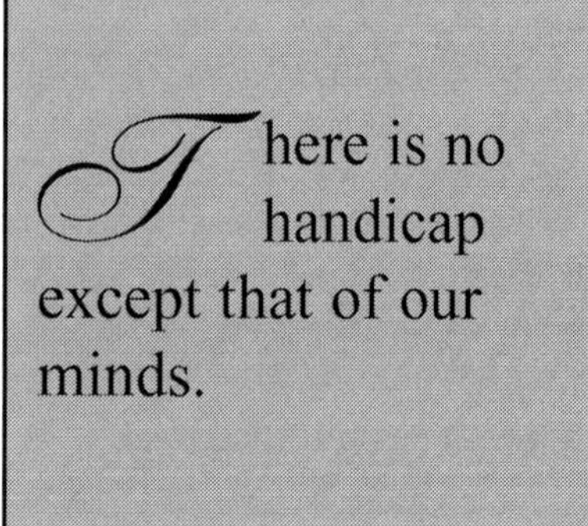

## Question Your Own Limitations

*Jesus looked at them and said, "With man this is impossible, but not with God; all things are possible with God"* (Mark 10:27).

BOOK QUOTE: *Maximizing Your Potential* [Introduction]

Jesus Christ, the specimen of humanity who best demonstrated the unlimited nature of the potential in mankind, said, "*Everything is possible for him who believes*" (Mark 9:23b). What daring spirit this statement ignites. It makes us question our own limitations and disagree with our fears.

It is a known fact that every manufacturer designs his product to fulfill a specific purpose and equips it with the necessary components and ability to function according to that purpose. Therefore, the potential of a product is determined and established by the purpose for which the manufacturer made it. This very same principle is inherent throughout creation. The Master Creator and Designer established His purpose for each item in creation and built into each the ability or potential to perform and fulfill that purpose or assignment. For example, the purpose for seeds is to produce plants; therefore, by design, all seeds possess the ability and potential to produce plants. This ability to reproduce does not, however, guarantee that the seed will produce a plant. This is the tragedy of nature. The destruction of a seed is in essence the termination of a forest.

This principle can be applied to all God's created beings. For example, your life is a result of a purpose in the mind of God that requires your existence. You were created because there is something God wants done that demands your presence on this planet. You were designed and dispatched for destiny. This destiny and purpose is also the key to your ability. You were created with the inherent abilities, talents, gifts, and inclinations to fulfill this purpose. Just as a bird is designed to fly, a fish to swim, and an apple tree to bear fruit, even so you possess the potential to be all you were born to be. Your life has the potential to fulfill your purpose.

## othing Undone

*"My food," said Jesus, "is to do the will of Him who sent Me and to finish His work* (Matthew 4:34).

BOOK QUOTE: *Maximizing Your Potential* [Introduction]

You, and every other individual, possess the responsibility for this awesome treasure buried within, because this treasure within you can be fully released only if you are willing to believe and accept God's dream for your life. If you are willing to submit to His will and purpose for your destiny and to cooperate with His specifications, nothing will be impossible for you.

Determine not to be satisfied with anything less than the full accomplishment of your dream. Surrender to the demands that maximize your potential so that none of your assignment is left undone when you leave this planet. The responsibility to use what God has stored within you is yours alone.

Many individuals are aware of their ability and potential, but they have become frustrated and disillusioned by either their past failures or the negative influence of others. They have chosen to limit or withhold the wonderful gift the Creator has invested in them. Therefore, I strongly urge you to rise up from your temporary fears, shake yourself, and step out once again on the road to being and becoming your true self.

> Man's potential is exposed one layer at a time until all he is, is known by all.

## Look Up and Out

*And do this, understanding the present time. The hour has come for you to wake up from your slumber, because our salvation is nearer now than when we first believed* (Romans 13:11).

BOOK QUOTE: *Maximizing Your Potential* [Chapter 10]

God created everything for a purpose and equipped each created thing with the corresponding potential or ability to fulfill that purpose. All of nature testifies to this great truth, as is evidenced by the fact that seeds always carry within themselves the germ of the trees they were destined to produce. In every bird there is a flock, in every cow a herd, in every fish a school, and in every wolf a pack. Everything is pregnant with the potential to become all it was created to be.

The release and maximization of that potential is dependent, however, on an environment that is conducive to its development and release. For instance, despite the potential of a seed to produce a tree after its kind, and to bring forth fruit in abundance, this great potential can be minimized, restrained, or immobilized by an improper environmental condition. If the seed is placed on a baked clay tile or a stone, or in a polluted substance or toxic elements, its great potential will be restricted and never fully maximized.

This limitation of potential not only robs the seed of the right to fulfill its true potential but it also robs birds of food and of branches for their nests, and deprives people of wood for building houses, of fruit for food, and of fuel for heat and cooking. In essence, this loss of potential due to an improper environment interferes with the entire ecological system. The seed fails to produce a tree, which is prevented from producing oxygen to give life to men, who are then incapable of fulfilling God's will and purpose in the earth. Therefore, any attempt to restrict, abuse, misuse, oppress, or repress the potential of any living thing has a direct effect on the purpose and will of God.

> Until a man can see beyond his own loins, the future is in danger.

## Yet To Be Tapped

*Wisdom is a shelter as money is a shelter, but the advantage of knowledge is this: that wisdom preserves the life of its possessor* (Ecclesiastes 7:12).

BOOK QUOTE: *Maximizing Your Potential* [Chapter 10]

The magnitude and depth of human potential on earth has yet to be tapped. Millions are born, live, and die, never discovering or exposing the awesome potential that resides within them. This tragic state of affairs, which is a global phenomenon, is the result of man's succumbing to life governed by his own devices. The major source of this tragedy is ignorance.

The most powerful enemy of mankind is not sin or satan, but the death-dealing, life-stealing force called ignorance. The Old Testament prophet Hosea recognized ignorance as the primary source of personal, social, and national destruction. When relaying God's explanation for moral and social decay among the nations, he wrote, "*My people are destroyed from lack of knowledge*" (Hosea 4:6a). The implication is that destruction in any area of our lives, whether personally or nationally, is related to a lack of knowledge.

This reality is profoundly true as it relates to the maximization of our potential. The ignorance of mankind concerning the value, worth, and magnitude of human potential causes massive oppression of our wonderful treasure.

Our planet is now home to over 5.8 billion people, all of whom are "created in the image of God" and possess the potential to fulfill the purpose for which they have been born. Over 4 billion of these people live in countries and conditions described as *Third World*. The term *Third World* is not ethnic or racial in orientation, but is more philosophical and conditional in meaning. Technically, it is used to describe any people who have not been allowed to participate in or directly benefit from the industrial revolution, and who therefore have not directly profited from the social, economic, and technological advancement that accompanied this revolution.

The ignorance of man about man is the ultimate cause of all our problems. The key to the knowledge of any product must be the manufacturer because no one knows a product like the one who created it. Therefore, the truth about man cannot be found in the great libraries of our educational institutions or the journals of our scientific investigations. It is found in God's Word.

## The World Needs Your Potential

*"For if you remain silent at this time, relief and deliverance for the Jews will arise from another place, but you and your father's family will perish. And who knows but that you have come to royal position for such a time as this?"* (Esther 4:14).

BOOK QUOTE: *Maximizing Your Potential* [Chapter 10]

God created all men to dominate the earth, not one another. *Therefore, every human possesses the ability and the potential to dominate, rule, govern, and manage the earth.* Each one has within him the spirit of leadership and the aspiration to determine his own destiny. This sacred spirit must be respected, protected, and properly related to God, the Creator, or its power will be turned toward other men to oppress them.

This has been the plight of all Third World people. They have fallen victim to the ignorance of men concerning the equality and purpose for mankind. We have all been created to serve the purposes of God as partners in dominion over creation, for the purpose of manifesting God's nature and Kingdom on earth as it is in Heaven.

Jesus the Christ came into the world for this reason: to restore us back to our Creator/Father God through His atoning work so that we can rediscover our rightful place within His will for His creation—not to create a religion. This great message, called the gospel, has been contaminated by many for their personal motives and has even been used to justify oppression and suppression in many cases. Therefore, it is imperative that we in this generation commit ourselves, our resources, and our energies to destroying the ignorance and error that cloud the truth concerning mankind, God's crown of creation.

You are so valuable and necessary to the destiny of the human race that God chose to come to earth Himself to redeem you to your purpose and true potential. What you were born to do and be caused Jesus Christ to come to give His life for your reconciliation. The world needs your potential.

*Nothing is more tragic than the waste, denial, abuse, and suppression of human potential.* The millions of Third World people in Europe, Asia, Africa, and the Americas, including those who are quietly buried within the walls of the industrial states, must now determine to loose themselves from the mental shackles of the oppressor; to honor the dignity, value, and worth of their brothers; and to provide an environment within which the corporate will and energy of the people may be developed. We must chart a new course based on the principles of the Kingdom of God that will harness the intellectual resources, spiritual virtues, and economic industry of our people and will provide a national incubator that will encourage the maximization of the potential of generations to come.

> The choice is yours. You are responsible to understand, release, and maximize your potential.

## EVIEW the Principles From This Week:

- Everything God created is equipped with the potential or ability to fulfill its God-given purpose.
- You cannot maximize your potential unless you live in an environment that is conducive to its development and release.
- Potential can be minimized, restrained, or immobilized by an improper environment.
- Your potential is lost when you try to live by your own devices.
- Ignorance steals life and deals death.
- You possess the ability to dominate and manage the earth.
- You are valuable and necessary to the destiny of the human race.

Additional copies of this book and other book titles from DESTINY IMAGE are available at your local bookstore.

Call toll-free: 1-800-722-6774.

Send a request for a catalog to:

®

**Destiny Image® Publishers, Inc.**
P.O. Box 310
Shippensburg, PA 17257-0310

*"Speaking to the Purposes of God for This Generation and for the Generations to Come"*

**For a complete list of our titles, visit us at www.destinyimage.com**

Made in United States
Orlando, FL
20 February 2024